Blueprint for Peace

by Richard N. Gardner

STERLING-DOLLAR DIPLOMACY

IN PURSUIT OF WORLD ORDER

Blueprint for Peace

BEING THE PROPOSALS
OF PROMINENT AMERICANS
TO THE WHITE HOUSE CONFERENCE
ON INTERNATIONAL COOPERATION

Edited and with an Introduction by
RICHARD N. GARDNER

McGRAW-HILL BOOK COMPANY

New York · Toronto · London · Sydney

Preface

This book is the work of several hundred dedicated Americans who were drawn together by two simple but important ideas. The first was that the common interests of mankind require intensified efforts of international cooperation. The second was that private citizens can help their Government by formulating and supporting practical proposals on how such cooperation may be achieved.

These Americans presented their proposals at the White House Conference on International Cooperation called by President Johnson and held in Washington from November 29 to December 1, 1965. The proposals were the work of thirty committees reporting on every significant form of international cooperation. Seventeen of the committee reports are presented in the first fifteen chapters of this book. Highlights of the remaining thirteen reports are included in the final chapter. Every recommendation of every committee is included. An appendix gives the names of the members of the thirty committees and of the Government consultants who assisted their work. It should be emphasized that the reports represent the views of private citizens, not official policy, and that not every committee member was in agreement with every part of his committee's report.

Since the reports are carefully negotiated committee efforts, it would not have been appropriate for an editor to make substantive changes. My editorial role has been confined to grouping and ordering the material, and to minor stylistic changes to enhance the consistency and readability of the assembled work. Thus the editor does not necessarily agree with everything contained in this volume, even though he may be in sympathy with much of it. Conversely, his Introduction is a personal statement and does not bear the endorsement either of the private citizens who participated in the White House Conference or of the U.S. Government.

This volume would not exist but for the White House Conference on International Cooperation and the preparations that went into it. The Conference was called by President Lyndon B. Johnson. Its Chairman was Vice President Hubert H. Humphrey. Their

v

role in stimulating this unique dialogue between American citizens and their Government is deeply appreciated.

Grateful acknowledgment is also made to Robert Benjamin who, as Chairman of the Board of the United Nations Association, convened the National Citizens' Commission at the call of the Secretary of State, and to Harlan Cleveland and Joseph J. Sisco, who directed the Government's collaboration with the Citizens' Commission while serving in the post of Assistant Secretary of State for International Organization Affairs. A special word of appreciation is also in order for Raymond D. Nasher, who served as Executive Director of the White House Conference, and for Samuel E. Belk III and Mrs. Jeanne Singer, respectively, who did the heavy staff work in the State Department and the United Nations Association. They and their assistants worked miracles in organizing a Conference of unprecedented size and scope. Preparation of the Conference was greatly facilitated by grants to the United Nations Association by the Johnson Foundation and the Carnegie Endowment for International Peace. The Johnson Foundation was also most generous in making Mel Bloom available to handle press and public relations.

A word is in order, finally, for Norman Cousins, Editor of the *Saturday Review.* His belief in the lasting value of the reports presented to the White House Conference led directly to the publication of this volume.

R. N. G.
New York City
June, 1966

Contents

Contents

I have called this Conference for one reason. I am determined that the United States shall actively engage its best minds and boldest spirits in the quest for a new order of world cooperation.

President Lyndon B. Johnson's message
to the White House
Conference on International
Cooperation, November 29, 1965

Introduction

"The central question," Adlai Stevenson once said, "is whether the wonderfully diverse and gifted assemblage of human beings on this earth really knows how to run a civilization."

It is still very much an open question.

But it is part of the American tradition to believe that all problems are soluble—even the ultimate problem of achieving a just and lasting peace. Our task is not merely to preserve this faith in a time marked by conflict and disillusionment, but to develop some practical proposals that can move us toward our goal.

To seek the best thinking of the American people on how to pursue these tasks, the President of the United States called a White House Conference on International Cooperation from November 29 to December 1, 1965. Nothing quite like it had ever happened before. Some 5,000 people, representing all aspects of American society, gathered in Washington in response to personal invitations. Thirty committees, including leading authorities in each field, presented reports to the Secretary of State containing over four hundred recommendations on subjects ranging from Arms Control to Youth Activities. And two hundred and twenty private organizations presented statements on their activities in the field of international cooperation. The Conference really was, in President Johnson's own words, "a town meeting of the leaders of this nation."

One hundred years ago—fifty years ago—even thirty years ago—a conference of this kind would not have been possible. A generation ago much of the international cooperation on the 1965 agenda did not exist. Modern science, with its awesome powers of creation and destruction, had not yet made cooperation so possible or so imperative. The United States did not participate in sixty intergovernmental institutions and hundreds of international private agencies. And few private citizens and organizations could have been found in the United States with enough interest and experience in international cooperation to conduct a meaningful dialogue with government officials.

How did this unprecedented meeting come about? It started with a resolution of the United Nations designating 1965, the UN's twentieth anniversary, as International Cooperation Year (ICY). Shortly after this resolution was passed, it was decided that ICY should be the occasion, not merely for a celebration, but for a serious effort to evaluate the progress so far achieved in international cooperation and to chart new programs for the future. The idea was first expressed by President Johnson to a group of leading citizens gathered at the White House on October 2, 1964, to witness the signing of the proclamation designating 1965 as International Co-operation Year in the United States:

I want to call a White House Conference to search and explore and canvass and thoroughly discuss every conceivable approach and avenue of cooperation that could lead to peace. That five-letter word is the goal of all of us. It is by far the most important problem we face. It is the assignment of the century for each of you and if we fail in that assignment, everything will come to naught. . . .

You are going to have to be the captains of a movement to lead people to love instead of hate. You are going to have to be the leaders in a movement to guide people in preserving humanity instead of destroying it. You are going to be the leaders in a crusade to help get rid of the ancient enemies of mankind—ignorance, illiteracy, poverty and disease—because we know that these things must go and we also know from our past that if we do not adjust to this change peacefully, we will have to adjust to it otherwise. . . .

I believe that the true realists in the second half of this twentieth century are those who bear the dream of new ways for new cooperation. You will be frowned upon. Some will call you an idealist. Some will call you a crackpot, and some may even call you worse than that. They may say you are soft or hard or don't understand what it is all about in some of these fields, but what greater ambition could you have and what greater satisfaction could come to you than the knowledge that you had entered a partnership with your Government that had pro-vided the leadership in the world that had preserved humanity instead of destroyed it? . . .

To implement this Presidential call to action, Secretary of State Dean Rusk called upon the United Nations Association to take leadership in coordinating private participation in ICY and the White House Conference in which it would culminate. Armed with this mandate, Robert S. Benjamin, Chairman of the Board of UNA, convened a National Citizens' Commission on International Cooper-ation. Its two hundred and thirty members divided into thirty working committees. Other persons were added to the committees for their special competence in the subject matter.

The President created a Cabinet Committee, consisting of representatives from all Federal agencies significantly involved in international affairs, and groups of Government officials were designated to assist the citizen committees. The United States Congress passed a Concurrent Resolution establishing a Congressional delegation for the White House Conference, including distinguished Senators such as Joseph Clark and Frank Church and leading members of the House such as Dante Fascell and Donald Fraser.

The committees of the National Citizens' Commission enjoyed full autonomy. They sought expert advice wherever they could find it around the country. They focused on three main questions:

1. Where do we stand in this particular area of international cooperation?
2. What should be our goals in this area in the years ahead?
3. How can we best achieve those goals?

The results of these labors were the thirty reports laid before the White House Conference and presented in this volume. Inevitably, the reports vary in substantive and literary merit. But taken as a whole, they form the most comprehensive and authoritative collection of studies ever assembled on the ways in which international cooperation can promote the peace and the general welfare of mankind.

Each of these reports was examined at the White House Conference by a panel of private citizens and Government officials. The several thousand participants in the Conference were given an opportunity—not always adequate for the purpose—to ask questions of the panelists and comment on the reports. The Conference passed no resolutions and took no decisions on the various recommendations, but a summary of the proceedings, together with the reports, was received on the President's behalf by the Secretary of State at the closing session.

What did it all add up to? One participant who sought more radical prescriptions for peace dismissed the whole affair as "primarily public relations." Another complained: "I doubt that more than one-third of the participants took what I myself regard as a forward-looking view, and among those I would count no representatives of Government." At the other extreme were those who confirmed the

President's own prediction by dismissing the Conference as the work of "do-gooders" and "crackpots."

Many observers found an ironic contrast between the Conference theme of international cooperation and the manifest lack of international cooperation in so many parts of the world. Hovering over the convocation was the grim reality of the escalating conflict in Vietnam. Was this really the moment for a Conference on International Cooperation? It was tempting to be cynical about the whole thing.

Yet there was another way of looking at the event. It seems incongruous to talk of cooperation in a time of conflict. But it is precisely at such a time that this talk is most necessary to keep a balance in official policy and public mood. It is difficult to organize an effective dialogue between citizens and Government in a period of crisis. But such a dialogue can provide government officials with a better understanding of public attitudes, can force them to consider alternatives, and can give the citizens in turn a better picture of the harsh realities and hard choices facing those who bear official responsibility. It is a salutary exercise to have responsible officials confront their critics and say: "Very well, here is the problem as we see it. What exactly would *you* do about it?"

Perhaps considerations of this kind led one prominent journal to call the White House Conference on International Cooperation "the Conference of the Century . . . the largest, most comprehensive joint planning effort ever undertaken by American citizens and government officials." And perhaps the most important point was made by a foreign diplomat who exclaimed: "The President of the United States actually assembled 5,000 Americans to 'tell him off'! No other head of state has ever done that!"

If the White House Conference has lasting significance, it will mainly result from the impact of the reports of the thirty committees of the National Citizens' Commission. They are presented here for students, scholars, citizens and officials in the United States and around the world who want to continue the search for practical measures of international cooperation. In such a handbook of cooperation, it may be useful to add some further observations, stimulated not only by the Conference but by recent experience in international cooperation—observations about the possibilities and limitations of cooperation in a time of conflict, about areas of cooperation which deserve particular attention, and about how the unique effort at citizen involvement which was the White House Conference might appropriately be followed up.

We may start with a point so obvious that it scarcely bears repeating—except that very few of us have fully grasped its implications. This is that modern science has made international cooperation, not merely a dream or a goal, but a practical necessity.

Science has put into the hands of the leaders of the United States and the Soviet Union single nuclear weapons with more destructive capacity than all the weapons used in all the wars of recorded history. The leaders of both countries have the ability to deliver a substantial number of these weapons on the territory of the other in less than thirty minutes. The inhabitants of their major cities have thus become hostages subject to instant slaughter. In another ten years or so, both of these nations will also be vulnerable to massive destruction from the nuclear stockpile of Communist China. And the day may not be far off when the leaders of other countries will be in a position to try nuclear blackmail on the superpowers.

Thus science has made cooperation a categorical imperative—at least in the sense of mutual forbearance from actions that could trigger the nuclear annihilation of a large portion of humanity. Science has also forced nations to cooperate in order to enjoy its benefits. Without international cooperation, ships and planes would collide in the night; radio and television broadcasts would be jammed; infectious diseases would cross frontiers; international travel, trade and investment would cease; and the unfolding adventure of space exploration would be an idle dream.

Thanks to modern science, man has reached an unprecedented stage of interdependence. The paradoxical result is that even the world's most powerful nations have lost the capacity to promote their security and welfare by acting alone. The only way they can recapture a degree of control over their destiny is through cooperative undertakings with others.

The necessity for cooperation is not merely scientific—it is political as well. The change in our physical environment has been accompanied by changes in attitudes and expectations. Unilateral action considered appropriate a generation ago is no longer considered a real possibility today. Even the great powers seek legitimacy for their actions through association with others. The decision to apply a quarantine to Cuba was made by the United States alone, but President Kennedy was determined to have it ratified by the Organization of American States and fully explained before the United Nations. And the nation's number one foreign policy problem—Vietnam—has been aggravated by the inability of the United States to involve other countries sufficiently with its efforts.

The experience has been similar in the economic field. Bilateral aid has frequently failed to give aid-giving countries the leverage necessary to achieve political or economic results. Recipients of aid are often resentful of "foreign interference"—even of those minimum conditions necessary to insure that aid produces maximum benefit to the people. To an increased extent, therefore, the United States and other countries have been transferring assistance through multilateral agencies, or through multilateral consortia, in order to share responsibility for decisions affecting the vital interests of the recipients.

The deep political and ideological divisions of our time make cooperation more difficult, but they do not make it less necessary or desirable. Many people are puzzled or even enraged by the coexistence of conflict and cooperation. It is a misconception shared by doctrinaires both of the left and of the right that because it is not possible to agree on some things, it is therefore impossible to agree on any.

But in the world community, as in national societies, it is not a matter of all or nothing. Conflict in one area does not preclude cooperation in another. Even between adversary powers there may be measures of cooperation that serve the interest of both.

We disagree profoundly with the leaders of the Soviet Union on the historic mission of world communism and on the proper relation between man and the state. But we share common interests not only in the avoidance of nuclear war but in the promotion of certain kinds of stability and welfare. To take some obvious examples, the United States and the Soviet Union cooperate in the allocation of radio frequencies through the International Telecommunication Union so that both countries can make effective use of their terrestrial and space-borne communication facilities. Each refrains from interfering with the other's vessels on the high seas—even military vessels such as missile-carrying submarines—and neither seeks to interfere with the other's satellites in outer space. On occasion the two countries work in harmony to resolve local conflicts, such as that between India and Pakistan over Kashmir, lest they draw in larger powers or escalate into nuclear war.

Thus, in the nuclear age, even the relations of adversary powers are subject to a certain amount of cooperation. This cooperation involves mutual restraints and reciprocal concessions in the interest of both sides. The incentive is the expectation of reciprocity; the sanction is the fear of reprisal. One of the tragedies of the war in Vietnam is that it has frozen—quite unnecessarily—so many cooperative ventures that were underway between the United States and the Soviet Union.

Conflict does not preclude cooperation; but neither does cooperation preclude conflict. There is no valid reason why the war in Vietnam should hold up Congressional approval of a Consular Treaty with the Soviet Union or an East–West trade bill. At the same time, our desire to cooperate with Communist countries does not mean that we should abandon the defense of freedom. Where Communist leaders use force to achieve their objectives—whether through aggression from without or subversion from within—the non-Communist nations must take appropriate measures to defend themselves. The cause of cooperation is not served by those who equate it with a policy of surrender.

Cooperation means working together for mutual advantage. The central task of diplomacy in the nuclear age is to enlarge the area in which both sides recognize mutual advantage and act upon it. This task is not accomplished by presenting "peace proposals" with a view to winning debating points and propaganda battles. It is tempting for national leaders to call press conferences and announce new initiatives in order to gain political "credit" at home or abroad; but new initiatives are often killed by premature exposure. The best way to advance proposals for cooperation is usually through quiet diplomacy in which both sides can shape the project to their respective interests and share the public credit when it is finally negotiated. Putting on a "Made in U.S.A." label is seldom the best way to market a diplomatic commodity. Indeed, many U.S. initiatives for cooperation may fare better if put forward by other countries. It is not easy for Americans to be so modest. But in the long run the peaceful "image" we so eagerly seek will depend on the quality of our diplomacy more than on the quality of our public relations.

Does the U.S. Government devote enough attention to the promotion of international cooperation? A huge amount of activity in the Department of State and a score of other Government agencies is devoted to cooperation with foreign countries. Yet no one who has worked in the U.S. Government can fail to be struck by the preoccupation of officials with current emergencies and by their difficulty in finding the opportunity to concentrate on long-term problems. So much time is devoted to stamping out fires that not much is left over for fire prevention.

The U.S. Government is not unique in this respect. It probably devotes more attention to long-term planning and to devising cooperative programs than any other country in the world. It must be admitted, however, that this attention is often fitful, erratic, and superficial. It is not enough to have senior officials in the White House, State Department and other agencies galvanized into action once a year when in search of new "initiatives" for the UN General Assembly. ICY encouraged senior officials to think years ahead about such matters as population growth, space broadcasting, the world's housing gap and the conservation of world resources. Now that ICY is over, we need some way to assure continuing high-level attention in the U.S. Government to long-term problems and to imaginative ways of dealing with them. The State Department's Policy Planning Staff could play a more effective role here. It could be strengthened by bringing in scholars and professional men for one- or two-year appointments and by making a Deputy Assistant Secretary of State in each regional or functional Bureau an *ex officio* member of the Council, with responsibility for substantial participation in the Council's work and translation of that work into policy. This latter device might help give the Council a greater impact on operations than it has had in the past. After all, events are not shaped by "planning papers," no matter how brilliant, but by what is actually done or not done in dealing with day-to-day problems.

It is appropriate to call for more vigorous American leadership in international cooperation. It is worth reminding ourselves, however, that cooperation does not become possible just because it is desirable. A favorite cliché of one State Department official is that "it takes two to tango." Well-intentioned people write the State Department each week demanding to know why the United States does not *do* something to set up a UN conciliation service, to establish an effective UN peacekeeping force, or to achieve a verified ban on nuclear testing. The problem is precisely that the United States has made reasonable proposals to do all of these things—and the proposals have been rejected by the Soviet Union. The public statements of some leaders of peace organizations do not always take adequate account of these facts. Perhaps this results from the way many Americans seek to demonstrate their independence and objectivity by being critical of their own government. Perhaps, too, the government has failed to explain its position convincingly to public opinion at home and abroad.

It is good to be self-critical. The record of the United States is far from perfect. Progress toward world order may require modifications in entrenched American policies. But it would be foolish to suppose that peace will be achieved merely by rectifying *our* errors. "My Country, Right or Wrong" is a poor rallying cry for international cooperation, but "My Country, Always Wrong" is no better.

Another trap to be avoided is the belief that because something is international and is called cooperation it is necessarily good. International cooperation is not a sentimental abstraction. It results from practical proposals that meet the test of mutual advantage. And pragmatism is needed not only with regard to substantive proposals, but with regard to the institutional means of carrying them out. The choice between bilateral, regional or global arrangements must be made according to the requirements of each case. It is true that pragmatic tests will often suggest use of a United Nations instrumentality, but it does not serve the cause of cooperation or of the United Nations to insist that a UN forum must always be used.

We should also beware of the tendency to think that every new proposal requires a new institution to carry it out. The reports presented in this volume are not exactly free of this tendency, since most of them call for at least one new agency or conference at the national or international level. It would be foolish to maintain that no new agencies should ever be created. But it would be equally foolish to ignore the very serious problems already created by the multiplication of agencies. The cost of these institutions is not the main problem —although it is a growing one for the less developed countries. The main problem is that the multiplication of agencies has proceeded to a point where it is beginning to impair the efficiency of the entire system. Responsible officials, particularly from less developed countries, cannot attend all the conferences now taking place and still take care of their urgent responsibilities at home. An increasing number of institutions are dealing with the same or similar subject matter. It is becoming more and more difficult to coordinate the parts of the system and insure that scarce resources are employed for top priority tasks. Perhaps a little "birth control"—or at least some better "family planning"—is needed in the realm of international agencies.

Enthusiasts for international cooperation, like enthusiasts for everything else, must come to grips with the necessity for choice. Of course, each specialized constituency—the people concerned with health, education, cultural exchange or transportation—thinks that more money should be spent on its particular subject. But the world does not have money and personnel and political will to do everything at once. If everything has priority, nothing has priority. A meaningful agenda for international cooperation cannot be drawn up by taking the sum of everything the different "experts" propose.

Perhaps the most serious deficiency of the White House Conference was the lack of any meaningful confrontation of the different proposals for action. It is the presence of this confrontation that usually distinguishes decision-making at senior levels of Government from the advice tendered by specialized citizens' organizations—and often explains the otherwise inexplicable difficulty in the dialogue between them.

What are the areas of cooperation that deserve particular attention? Here, in briefest outline, is an agenda for cooperation, in some respects following, in other respects differing from or going beyond, the proposals set forth in this volume:

1. Curbing the Arms Race

Mankind has found it all too easy to get used to living with the arms race. Five nations now have the capacity to explode nuclear weapons. At least ten more have the technical capability to develop nuclear weapons in the next few years. It is in the common interest of the nuclear powers—and in the long-term interest of all mankind —to prevent the further spread of these weapons. Their proliferation would increase the risk of intentional or accidental use, exacerbate political tensions, and divert resources urgently needed for economic development.

The obstacles to concluding a treaty on non-proliferation are not insoluble. The U.S. draft prohibits giving ownership, possession or control of nuclear weapons to a non-nuclear power. It should be possible to meet legitimate Soviet anxieties about German access to nuclear weapons within the alliance. And it should also be possible to devise adequate security guarantees to non-nuclear powers, perhaps through parallel declarations by nuclear powers confirmed in a UN resolution.

Further efforts should be made to conclude a comprehensive ban on nuclear testing. The art of seismic detection has not yet progressed to the point where underground nuclear explosions can be distinguished from earthquakes without on-site inspection. The Soviet Union does not accept this proposition—and rejects the idea of any on-site inspection. Perhaps a way around the present impasse could be found in an international effort to agree on present possibilities of detection and to develop improved methods.

The report of the Committee on Arms Control and Disarmament recommends that the United States seek agreement with the Soviet Union on a three-year moratorium on new deployment (but not on unverifiable research and development) of anti-ballistic missiles. This recommendation deserves the most serious attention—not only because the cost of an anti-ballistic missile system is measured in terms of billions of dollars and because its effectiveness against the Soviet Union is still in doubt—but because a rush to deploy missile defenses could disrupt the strategic balance, raise questions about the effectiveness of nuclear deterrents, and accelerate the production of offensive weapons. A three-year moratorium would provide time for further study of these problems, and would still leave time for deployment of a system against the Chinese nuclear threat that may arise in the mid-1970's.

These and other measures of arms control should have top priority. But work must also go forward on the long-term goal of general and complete disarmament. Even with some measures of arms control, the maintenance of huge nuclear stockpiles, and the modern methods of delivering them, mean accepting a substantial risk of nuclear war for our generation. Continued attention to the long-term goal is therefore more than good propaganda—it is sound policy. It is also sound policy to encourage the fullest discussion by all governments and their citizens of the transformation in international relations and in institutions for keeping the peace which will be required if general and complete disarmament is ever to be achieved.

Obviously, progress toward general and complete disarmament and toward many measures of arms control requires the cooperation of Communist China. Her involvement in disarmament talks—whether bilaterally, at the existing Eighteen Nation Disarmament Conference, or at a World Disarmament Conference—should be actively encouraged by the United States.

2. Keeping the Peace

International cooperation to strengthen the capacity of the United Nations to make and keep peace is essential for general and complete disarmament. It is also essential to reduce the risks of violence while we live in the shadow of the arms race.

The UN needs an effective stand-by military capacity to deal with peacekeeping emergencies. This can be developed within the present constitutional structure. The UN's difficulties do not result mainly from defects in the Charter machinery, but from the failure of its members to make adequate use of that machinery. Every effort must be made to enable the Security Council to discharge its primary responsibility in the peacekeeping field. But past experience with the Soviet Union and the prospect of Communist China's membership in the Council suggest the need to retain the General Assembly's power to authorize peacekeeping operations—operations in which forces are contributed on a voluntary basis and deployed to the territory of countries with their consent. If certain members will not pay assessments for these operations, other methods of financing will have to be found, such as non-mandatory apportionment, to assure that the rest of the membership undertakes a fair sharing of the cost. And further steps should be taken to augment the UN's military capability through the earmarking and training of national contingents on a broad geographical basis. The United States could augment this capability by using military assistance funds to help less developed countries prepare units for UN service. Together with other countries, we might also make military bases available to the UN both for training and for actual use in peacekeeping emergencies.

Concern with the UN's peacekeeping capacity has recently been accompanied by increasing interest in the problems of peaceful settlement and peaceful change. This is as it should be. More needs to be done to anticipate and resolve situations which could lead to armed conflict. More needs to be done to attack the root causes of conflicts temporarily arrested by the interposition of peacekeeping forces. To be sure, the promotion of peaceful settlement is not mainly a matter of machinery, but of political will. It requires the willingness to accept an adverse judgment, to alter deeply entrenched positions supported by powerful domestic interests. Nevertheless, some improvements in UN institutions could be undertaken to assure the greater availability of qualified persons for the tasks of peaceful settlement, to provide added incentives for governments to resort to peaceful settlement, and to incorporate new approaches to the settlement of disputes whose value has been demonstrated by recent experience. Peaceful settlement could be facilitated by greater use of rapporteurs in cases before the Security Council and General Assembly and by creation of a new UN panel for mediation and fact-finding. Such institutions could assist the UN's political organs by bringing the parties together, clarifying the facts, identifying the issues, and recommending possible solutions.

3. Expanding World Trade

New possibilities—as well as new difficulties—are emerging for the expansion of world trade between non-Communist industrial nations, between these nations and the less developed countries, and between these nations and the Communist world.

The Trade Expansion Act gave United States negotiators new authority to remove trade barriers, but it came when the Common Market was preoccupied with its internal problems; ten years earlier it might have produced dramatic results. Nevertheless, every effort must be made to salvage a meaningful settlement from the Kennedy Round, and to prevent backsliding from liberal trade policies on both sides of the Atlantic. The United States will have to revise some of its non-tariff barriers—such as the American selling price method of valuation on chemical imports—if it is to take effective leadership in trade liberalization. In order to assure reasonable access to foreign markets for our exports of agricultural products, we must be prepared to subject our domestic farm programs to international negotiation. And after the Kennedy Round ends, we should put ourselves in a position to move even more boldly—proposing a treaty for the gradual but complete elimination of tariffs over a period of twenty or twenty-five years.

New approaches are also needed on the trade problems of the less developed countries. Permanent tariff preferences are probably undesirable on political and economic grounds, but tariff cuts resulting from the Kennedy Round and subsequent trade agreements should be put into effect immediately with respect to these countries. The temporary preferences thus created would be phased out automatically as part of the general movement toward freer trade. Even more important, a greater effort should be made to reduce tariffs on processed goods of special interest to the less developed countries, and to moderate quotas and excise taxes on raw materials and foodstuffs which cost these countries hundreds of millions of dollars a year in lost exports. More can also be done through technical assistance and reviews of development plans to help them compete in the world market. And new measures of supplementary finance can help assure the less developed countries that sound development plans will not be jeopardized by unexpected shortfalls in export earnings.

New approaches are also needed in East–West trade relations. The United States has let itself fall behind other free world countries in seizing opportunities for expanded trade with Eastern Europe. The legislation which President Johnson sent to the Congress in the spring of 1966 would at least enable American negotiators to offer most-favored-nation tariff treatment to countries like the Soviet Union, Romania and Czechoslovakia in exchange for concessions of equivalent significance to us. It deserves to be enacted—and followed up with further measures to expand trade on a basis of mutual advantage.

4. Aiding Economic Development

For some two billion of the world's three billion people, conditions of life are not compatible with human dignity. Although dramatic successes have been achieved in a few places, living standards for the less developed countries are not improving very rapidly—and in some countries they are deteriorating. The rate of increase of gross national product in the less developed countries as a whole slipped from 5 per cent in the period 1950–54 to 4 per cent in the period 1960–64. With population growth averaging 2 or 3 per cent or more in most of these countries, per capita income for the group is only rising by about 1 per cent a year. If these trends continue, their average per capita income—now about $120—will grow to about $170 in the year 2000. In the same time span, the present $3,000 per capita income of the United States will grow to some $5,000 or $6,000. By the end of the century, in other words, the less developed countries as a group will have achieved only modest improvements in their living standards, while the gap between their standards of life and ours will have nearly doubled.

These figures pose a challenge to the people of all nations. The less developed countries will have to husband their scarce resources and deal with their internal obstacles to progress. And if they are to avoid economic stagnation and even famine on a large scale, they will need to alter profoundly their agricultural institutions and techniques.

For reasons of politics as well as economics, of self-interest as well as idealism, the developed countries should help. A gigantic effort is required to transfer not only capital but the elements of culture necessary to make capital productive. Unfortunately, the level of financial assistance made available to the developing world has begun to level off, and the burden of debt service increasingly offsets the transfer of new resources. The staff of the International Bank has estimated that the less developed countries could put to productive use an additional three to four billion dollars a year.

No area of international cooperation presents a clearer case for

U.S. leadership. It is true that Congress has been reluctant to increase bilateral assistance, to reduce or eliminate interest rates on development loans, or to provide assurance of continuity through multi-year authorizations or appropriations. But a bold proposal to transfer additional resources through international agencies such as the International Development Association might meet with a better Congressional response. At the very least, American policy should aim at increasing to one billion dollars a year the "soft" lending of the International Development Association and raising to three hundred million dollars a year the pre-investment outlays of the UN Development Program. A U.S. offer to put up 40 per cent of these sums on a matching basis might not meet with an immediate response from other developed countries, but it could demonstrate the U.S. commitment to development and restore forward movement now lacking in multilateral aid efforts.

5. *Organizing World Finance*

The search has begun for ways to reform the international monetary system so as to assure the growth and stability of both developed and less developed countries. For the last eight years, the United States has run substantial deficits in its balance of payments. These deficits have been partly financed by increased foreign dollar holdings, but they have also been paid for by large reductions in our gold stock. The United States cannot go on losing gold indefinitely. Yet elimination of the deficit may leave the world short of the liquidity it needs for the continued expansion of world trade. And measures taken to reduce the deficit may have unfortunate consequences. The deficit has already compelled the United States to restrict exports of private capital and to tie foreign aid to American exports. More and more it is reducing our freedom to undertake the very programs of expanded aid and trade which are in the general interest. And some day it may inhibit measures needed to maintain an adequate rate of expansion at home.

In this field of extraordinary complexity, generalizations are dangerous. It would appear, however, that the world's gold supply is growing too slowly to finance the growing volume of world trade, and that the United States can no longer take the principal responsibility for supplementing it. The nations of the world will therefore have to share responsibility for increasing world liquidity to a greater extent than they have done before—by increasing the credit facilities in the International Monetary Fund, by creating a new form of "owned" reserves, or by some combination of the two. If a new reserve unit is created, the national currencies paid in exchange for it by the developed countries could be used for long-term lending in the less developed world. Although international liquidity and development finance are two separate problems, a solution to them may well be found through new machinery enabling the world to deal with both problems at the same time. The less developed countries and the United States share a common interest in pressing forward with this approach.

6. Curbing Population Growth

After years of neglect, mankind is finally moving to cope with the population explosion. There is a growing realization that significantly higher living standards in the less developed countries will never be achieved if population goes on doubling every twenty or thirty years. There is also increasing awareness that urgent action is required to deal with the problem by methods compatible with a free society. If we do not make voluntary family planning possible in this generation, we may make compulsory family planning inevitable in some countries in future generations.

The U.S. Government is now providing direct support for family planning efforts overseas in the form of technical, financial, and commodity aid. The big question is no longer whether the United States will help but whether the countries concerned will move fast enough to train and deploy the necessary administrators, doctors, and health workers. With very few exceptions, the less developed countries have not yet made family planning services available to the majority of their rural populations.

In an area of such sensitivity and significance for mankind as a whole, there is special need for international cooperation. Birth control must not become a cold war issue involving political ideologies, or a subject of disagreement between racial groups. In the nuclear age, no race or nation achieves power or wealth through unregulated fertility. This message can best be transmitted by multilateral organizations in which responsibility is widely shared. The United Nations, the World Health Organization, the United Nations Children's Fund, the UN Regional Economic Commissions and their demographic centers—all should work together to assist effective national programs of family planning.

7. *Conserving the World's Resources*

In the headlong thrust toward industrialization and urbanization, man risks undermining the very basis of his civilization—the resources of his planet. Both the industrial countries and the countries seeking rapid industrialization need to do a better job of conserving precious minerals, preserving wildlife and natural areas, avoiding air and water pollution, developing additional water resources through desalting sea water, and controlling the toxic consequences of drugs and pesticides. The time has surely come for more effective international cooperation in the central task of preserving the balance of nature.

The report of the Committee on Conservation of Resources offers significant proposals for action. It urges an International Trust for the World Heritage to identify, establish, develop and help manage natural areas and archaeological sites of unique value to the world community. It calls for better regulation of the world's fishing practices to prevent depletion of the marine harvest. It asks cooperative efforts to deal with the contamination of man's environment by pesticides, oil pollution of the high seas, and the disposal of nuclear wastes. It proposes an international authority to exploit metal deposits on the ocean floor which may soon be extractable in large quantities. As the United States moves increasingly to deal with problems of pollution and conservation at home, it is in a natural position to call for wise resource management on a world scale.

8. *Exploring Outer Space*

Within a few short years, an American or Soviet citizen, or both, will have landed on the moon. Both countries have already agreed in a UN declaration of legal principles that the moon and other celestial bodies should be free for exploration by all in conformity with international law and not subject to sovereign claims. The next stage would be a treaty embodying these principles, together with other provisions, including a ban on the use of the moon and other celestial bodies as military bases.

The same rockets which launch men to the moon or into orbit can also carry nuclear warheads across continents. Joint ventures in the launching of astronauts have been considered impractical because the Soviet Union, and perhaps even the United States, would not permit the other side to gain access to military information. But the cooperative use of spacecraft and equipment launched under national auspices bypasses some of these problems. Astronauts launched separately by the two countries can meet in outer space and work on joint projects. We should carefully explore the possibility of lunar or orbital laboratories jointly operated by the two countries in the name of the United Nations and for the benefit of all mankind. At first these laboratories might consist only of equipment; later they might be manned by astronauts of the two countries or of other countries. These joint laboratories could gather information about the solar system and the entire universe. They could turn their observations earthward and gather information about our own planet—providing the whole world not only with scientific information but also with the kind of information gathered by nationally operated reconnaissance satellites. Eventually we might develop a UN inspection service capable of patrolling borders and monitoring arms control agreements.

The attempt to land a man on the moon has been conducted as a competition between the two space powers, with large-scale duplication of effort and expenditure. But both sides are now beginning to think of the post-lunar era of space exploration—missions to Mars, Venus, and other parts of the solar system, and the search for intelligent life beyond. Even if political and security considerations preclude joint projects and the complete integration of the two programs, we should at least explore all possibilities for mutual support and rational division of tasks. Perhaps COSPAR and the Technical Subcommittee of the UN Outer Space Committee could be forums for an exchange of views and cooperative planning in the post-lunar phase, so that all members of the UN can participate more fully in the great space adventure.

Cooperation is already well under way in two uses of space that promise vast benefits for men on earth—meteorology and communications. The United States should continue to lead in the development of the World Weather Watch—the cooperative program for weather forecasting and weather research which is being developed under the auspicies of the World Meteorological Organization. In communications, the Interim Communication Satellite Committee (INTELSAT), composed of the U.S. Communications Satellite Corporation (COMSAT) and some fifty foreign partners, is well on the way toward establishing a global communication satellite system. The INTELSAT arrangements, delegating management of the system to COMSAT, were well suited to the early stage of this enterprise, in which the United States had done most of the research and development. When these arrangements come up for review in 1969, it will be appropriate to consider the possibility of a truly international corporation, with a General Conference, Board of Directors, and international staff.

International cooperation in space communications has so far been concerned with point-to-point communication. But within a decade or so, we and other countries may be able to broadcast directly from satellites to community or home receivers. This new stage of communications technology will open up great possibilities for education and better understanding between peoples. But the radio frequencies necessary for direct broadcasting have not yet been assigned by the International Telecommunication Union—and suggestions have even been made to ban such broadcasting entirely. The United States can help assure its constructive use by promoting international studies of what space broadcasting can do for less developed countries and for world peace; by organizing pilot demonstration projects with UN sponsorship in countries like India; by encouraging national and international aid agencies to finance needed ground facilities; and by reassuring friendly countries that this new technology will not be used to broadcast political or commercial messages to their populations against their will.

9. Expanding the Exchange of Ideas

"Wars," in the words of UNESCO's constitution, "begin in the minds of men." If we would eliminate war, we must promote wider agreement on basic values through the exchange of people and ideas. It is in keeping with both our traditions and our interests to work toward an open world society—including all peoples without exception. Many foreign governments have a vested interest in keeping their people from learning too much about the outside world. But modern technology and culture are breaking down official barriers. The United States can assist in this process by seeking the maximum exchange of teachers and students, newspapers and books, motion pictures and cultural presentations. Perhaps even bolder proposals are needed. For example, the United States could offer Soviet leaders the opportunity to address the American people regularly on television, in return for the same privilege in the Soviet Union. We could propose to give them time on the Voice of America, in return for the same amount of time on Radio Moscow. If we really believe in free exchange of ideas, there are many imaginative ways to prove it.

The United Nations should play a central role in this search for greater understanding. More can be done to encourage private groups around the world dedicated to strengthening the world organization. And more can be done to improve the capacity of the UN's Department of Public Information to bring the story of UN activities, including UN proceedings, to the people of the world. The United States should encourage the use of communication satellites by the UN for this purpose. The capacity of these satellites will soon be so large—and small additions to capacity so inexpensive—that channels should be made available to the UN at special rates or without charge.

10. Protecting Human Rights

The ultimate object of public policy—whether of national governments or of international organizations—must be the welfare of the individual. Yet individual human rights are not receiving adequate attention today. It is appropriate that the United Nations is preparing to celebrate 1968—the twentieth anniversary of the Universal Declaration of Human Rights—as Human Rights Year. What is needed is not just a celebration but better progress by UN members in discharging their Charter obligations to promote the human rights of all their citizens.

The United States has taken important action to promote human rights at home. But it has not gone far enough in making the promotion of human rights a central element in its foreign policy. One step long overdue is the ratification of the human rights treaties now before the Senate—the Conventions on Slavery, Forced Labor, and the Political Rights of Women. If these could be ratified, it would enhance U.S. influence in the development of international standards for the protection of human rights. Ratification of the Genocide Convention, another treaty pending in the Senate, would also be desirable.

The development of substantive standards is important; no less important is the development of effective procedures for their implementation. The UN is now considering a proposal to create a High Commissioner for Human Rights. Such a Commissioner could present a professional and comprehensive report each year on the progress of member governments in implementing the standards laid down in the Universal Declaration of Human Rights. He could lend his good offices in dealing with specific human rights situations. He could assist members to organize domestic institutions for the protection of human rights. The establishment of a High Commissioner before the close of Human Rights Year would be a major accomplishment of international cooperation.

Should the White House Conference on International Cooperation be followed up? If so, how?

The first question, at least in principle, has already been answered in the affirmative. In presenting the reports of the committees and the summary of the Conference proceedings to Secretary of State Rusk on the closing day of the Conference, Robert S. Benjamin declared:

In presenting this report to you, Mr. Secretary, for the President, I do so in full confidence that it is more than a report. It is a map, a design, a charter, a launching pad. It marks not an end but another beginning.

The Secretary of State replied:

We would hope very much that no one of you would consider that this Conference ends today, that you will continue to follow these matters wherever you live and whatever your occupation in order to keep your talents available and your contributions coming forward. . . . We will give these studies the most urgent and careful attention. And I think you shall begin to see promptly some of the footprints of your work in the weeks ahead. . . . So your job is not finished and the work that you have done just cannot end today.

In the spring of 1966, just six months after the Conference, the State Department prepared the following inventory of the status of the more than four hundred recommendations for Government action presented by the committees:*

- 33 recommendations already implemented
- 143 recommendations in the process of implementation
- 24 recommendations scheduled to be implemented
- 209 recommendations under study
- 26 recommendations considered impractical at this time and perhaps at any time

Of course, this "box score" hardly provides an adequate measure of the impact of the reports on Government policy. The Govern-

---

* The recommendations for action by private agencies are set forth, together with the report submitted to the Conference by these agencies, in Ethel C. Phillips, *The Record and the Vision* (Published by Interchange for the United Nations Association, March, 1966).

ment might have done many of these things anyway. Some of the recommendations made by the committees were undoubtedly stimulated by Government officials. Yet even in such cases the committees served a useful function by mobilizing support for ideas within the Government and bringing them to national attention. The expression of public support for controversial proposals that had not yet achieved the status of Government policy may have helped, in some cases, to move the Government forward. To take just one example, the proposal of the Committee on Population that the Government be prepared to spend one hundred million dollars a year in support of family planning programs in less developed countries may have played a part in the decision of the Administration, announced a few weeks later, to earmark substantial foreign aid funds for this purpose.

If the Conference had a stimulating effect on Government policy, that is all to the good. But the momentum needs to be maintained. There are still two hundred and nine recommendations "under study" and twenty-six that are considered "impractical." Some of these recommendations undoubtedly do not deserve to be acted upon. But without further stimulus, some meritorious proposals may not receive the attention that they deserve. "Under study" can all too easily become a bureaucratic euphemism for doing nothing.

An appropriate follow-up to the Conference could have a salutary effect on the private community as well as on the Government. We must find better ways to give interested citizens a sense of participation in the development of foreign policy—to cope with the frustration of thousands of Americans with useful ideas who feel unable to "get through" to Government officials. We must counteract the sense of impotence which many Americans feel in coping with international problems. As Norman Cousins puts it: "It is doubtful whether any pain or punishment in the modern world is greater than the one that comes from the inability of an individual to make vital contact with the ideas and events that directly affect his well-being and even his destiny."

The purpose of following up the Conference, of course, should be more than psychological and symbolic. The ICY program created, or at least strengthened, new and interested constituencies in thirty different fields of activity. Many of the individuals involved gained a new insight and a new sense of commitment as a result of sustained analysis of the subject matter in cooperation with their Government counterparts. This new expertise and enthusiasm should not be dissipated—it should be harnessed as a great potential force for international cooperation.

It would not be difficult to provide adequate machinery for continuing the collaboration begun in International Cooperation Year:

First, the head of each Government agency could see to it that recommendations within his field of responsibility were sympathetically and methodically explored; could give periodic reports to the chairmen of the citizen committees on the steps being taken to implement their recommendations; and could make himself and his staff available at least once a year for discussion not merely of these recommendations but of new ideas.

Second, a small panel of citizens could be appointed with responsibility for stimulating and coordinating the interchange between the citizens' committees and their Government counterparts. The panel could prod citizens' committees and voluntary organizations, help identify priority tasks, and open lines of communication.

It would help to have such a group appointed by the President as his Panel on International Cooperation. The panel could meet periodically with the President and his senior advisers. This would provide the best evidence that both Government and private citizens meant to sustain the work of ICY at the highest possible level.

These two steps would help assure an appropriate follow-up to ICY in the United States. But is this enough? International cooperation cannot be guaranteed by Americans talking to other Americans. A dialogue between American citizens and their Government is valuable, but it is no substitute for a dialogue with the other peoples and governments of the world.

If we really want to implement the bold concept of ICY, then let us propose to the Soviet Union that our best qualified citizens meet with theirs to explore each of the thirty subjects discussed at the White House Conference—or other subjects of their choice. These meetings could be of the same character as the famous "Pugwash" conferences—scientists, scholars, and professional men of both countries would participate in their individual capacities without committing their respective governments.

If a series of meetings of this kind were held, it could not fail to have a salutary effect on Soviet-American relations. It would help identify areas of common interest to both sides and mobilize forces in the Soviet Union and the United States for broader and deeper cooperation.

Our U.S. program has been built around the theme of "international cooperation." The Soviet Union prefers the phrase "peaceful coexistence." Perhaps we could compromise and call our joint venture a program in "peaceful cooperation."

Perhaps, too, these conferences could be broadened to include citizens from other Communist countries. Through such a program we could supplement a policy of containment with a policy of engagement—engagement of all parts of our societies on all relevant subjects in a cooperative quest for peace.

President Kennedy, in his American University speech, conveyed the essential spirit with which we should approach such a new effort of peaceful cooperation. "Peace," he declared, "need not be impracticable, and war need not be inevitable. By defining our goal more clearly, by making it seem more manageable and less remote, we can help all peoples to see it, to draw hope from it, and to move irresistibly toward it."

"Our problems are man-made," President Kennedy said, "therefore they can be solved by man. And man can be as big as he wants."

1. *Curbing the Arms Race*

The control of nuclear armed forces is becoming more difficult with each passing year. A major effort must be made—and made *now*—to halt the drift toward international anarchy. There is a desperate need to re-establish confidence in the capability of the United Nations to ensure the peace.

We believe that the United States, as the most powerful nation in the world, can take the lead in seeking agreements on measures of collective security and of arms limitation and reduction. We believe that the United States should do whatever can usefully and safely be done unilaterally as well as jointly. Toward that end we propose a series of steps which taken together would make a systematic and significant beginning to more far-reaching disarmament.

Where We Stand

Challenges and Opportunities

Twenty years have passed since the founding of the United Nations and the onset of the nuclear age—two decades of struggle in man's efforts to control the instruments of force and reduce the incentives to use them. But as the likelihood of conflict has ebbed and flowed, efforts to achieve limitations on arms have had frighteningly little success.

The initial U.S. attempt to establish a United Nations monopoly over atomic energy foundered. A new superbomb, dwarfing the atomic bomb in its capacity for destruction, was developed and deployed. By 1955, arms control negotiators in East and West had conceded that the strictest international inspection might not detect hidden reserves of fissionable materials with sufficient reliability to permit their controlled elimination. And five years later no one was able to prevent the enormous and still continuing expenditures on massive deployments of intercontinental ballistic missiles (ICBM). These failures can be measured in the trillion dollars that the world has spent for armaments in twenty years, and they can be measured in the capacity of either of two governments to destroy in hours hundreds of millions of persons.

Simultaneously with these failures has come one important success: a widespread acceptance of the axiom that general war is inconceivable as a rational instrument of policy; and a corollary interest in methods of harnessing the mutual concern to prevent it.

Other achievements are smaller. They include:

• a rapid communication link between Washington and Moscow for grave emergencies;

• a treaty preventing all but underground nuclear tests, thus halting the radioactive pollution of the atmosphere by the superpowers;

• a UN resolution reflecting the intention of the major powers not to place weapons of mass destruction in outer space and calling upon others to refrain from doing so;

• a set of simultaneous announcements of intentions to slow down the production of fissionable material.

In addition, the United States has made a major effort to construct elaborate controls and handling procedures for the weapons constructed and to devise and adopt strategies consistent with them.

Finally, the U.S. Government has organized and supported the Arms Control and Disarmament Agency.

But the world's problems continue to multiply, and the drift to international anarchy is perceptibly quickening.

FIRST, the number of nations now possessing nuclear weapons or seriously considering their construction is so large that the reciprocal expectations of mutual restraint, upon which efforts to halt the spread of nuclear weapons are ultimately based, are weakening. A failure to surmount this crisis of confidence and to prevent the spread of nuclear weapons to additional countries promises to be at least as costly as some of the major failures of the last twenty years: in the time and attention of statesmen taken from more positive tasks; in expenditures; in the exacerbation of tense political relationships; and in increased risks of nuclear violence.

SECOND, the spread of nuclear weapons has encouraged one or both of the major nuclear powers to seek protection from less powerful nuclear states in anti-missile systems, systems quite capable of catalyzing a new round of offensive weapons.

THIRD, the unresolved problems of Central Europe stand as festering sores in East–West relations, complicating other problems of arms limitation, increasing misunderstanding and friction, and remaining a source of potential military conflict.

FOURTH, there is the buildup of non-nuclear armaments, especially in the developing areas of the world, where internal instability and endemic political differences have recently erupted in conventional war. Further buildup threatens more violence.

FIFTH, there is the problem of Communist China—her absence from the United Nations, her contempt for it, her incipient atomic capability, and the threat that she poses to her neighbors.

SIXTH, there is the failure, so far, of the United Nations to establish any but the most rudimentary and improvised machinery for peacekeeping. Related to this is the propensity of the great powers to bypass the United Nations in the settlement of disputes.

These six fundamental problems are all related, all urgent, and all inescapable; these are the issues to which we have addressed ourselves and concerning which we believe further efforts must be made. The merit of our suggestions is, of course, open to debate and further analysis. What is incontestable, however, is the need for a renewed commitment on all sides to efforts that will reverse a continuing and dangerous trend of competition in national armaments, and total reliance upon them.

We believe that the United States, as the strongest nation in the world, can afford to make the largest effort. As a group of American citizens, we naturally direct our recommendations to our own Government. However, we by no means believe that U.S. Government actions alone can bring about the results desired. And we recognize and value the considerable efforts that our Government has been and is making.

Guidelines and Assumptions

The issues which we have considered have given us reason to be grimly concerned about the future. Mankind can ill afford another twenty years of failure to deal with the realities of the nuclear age. For this reason especially, we are determined to point to the problems that must and can be dealt with now, in the present—problems that will otherwise quickly become more difficult. This applies especially to the problems of proliferation; what we cannot stop, we shall have very little hope of rolling back. And it applies also to the irrecoverable costs of another round of strategic weapon procurement.

In our concern for present problems, we do not mean to slight much more comprehensive measures of arms reduction and much more significant measures for improvements in collective security that the world must continue to seek. But we are aware that the "modest" steps proposed in this report taken together—and some taken separately—would represent more negotiated progress than has been achieved in two decades, and would greatly facilitate further progress. Thus, if we emphasize negotiable measures requiring minimal inspection of Soviet and U.S. territory, it does not mean that we are any less devoted to seeking the maximum degree of general disarmament that can eventually be achieved. It suggests only that we are anxious to achieve what is eventually desirable by making a start with what is presently possible. In particular, we believe that the world military balance is such that there are many measures that can be taken by U.S.–Soviet agreement, or by parallel action, that will improve our security whether or not other nuclear powers accede to them at once.

Because only the far-sighted and the powerful can conceive or venture the actions necessary to turn down the arms spiral and to shape a more peaceful world, we believe that the United States is obligated to take the lead in proposing measures of collective security and of arms limitation; obligated to using its influence to secure their acceptance; and obligated to make effort to conduct its affairs so as to avoid impeding their progress. This is a responsibility of world leadership. In addition, we believe that America's own most urgent security interests lie ever more clearly within the domain of arms control and that we can no longer seek national security chiefly in arms and alliances alone. A nation's gains in turning down the arms competition, in reducing the likelihood of conflict thoughout the world, and in improving the prospect for a world of "cease-fire and peaceful change" have become first-priority concerns. We shall make progress in resolving them only when we recognize them as such and act accordingly.

We assume that accomplishments in one area of arms control will facilitate work in another and that "package agreements" can be useful. And we believe that progress toward political settlements, in Central Europe for example, will both facilitate and benefit from arms control and disarmament agreements. The notion that progress is impossible in one area, e.g., curbing the spread of nuclear weapons, until agreements have been reached on other problems of arms control, is a notion we reject.

Halting the Spread of Nuclear Weapons

The Problem

The spread of nuclear weapons threatens to bring about a painful, expensive, and dangerous reorganization of international relations. It threatens to add new dimensions to the very fears that encourage it: new concerns in the struggle for Arab–Israeli understanding; new barriers to a permanent easing of Indian–Pakistani tensions; and new setbacks to improved relations between Western and Eastern Europe. It threatens established political relationships between countries and within them; dissension over the hard decisions it entails in governments already torn by dissension; realignments associated with shifting power in non-aligned areas; and, for those in major-power alliances, the premature assertion of an unreal independence based on nuclear status alone. There are, in these problems, the seeds of a hundred crises.

Nuclear weapon systems are expensive—more expensive than they appear to be at first—and many of those who want them most can afford them least. Will nuclear deployment replace economic development in parts of Asia, Latin America, the Near East, and will misery and suffering be prolonged in this way? Will the United States be forced to pay indirectly in economic aid for nuclear weapons that it opposes? Or will its refusal to do so alienate its friends? Alternatively, will it be forced to supply nuclear weapon systems to those who should never have demanded them, in an ignominious effort to avoid either being cheated or being hated?

Nuclear weapons are dangerous. The United States devotes a great deal of effort to controlling the circumstances under which its weapons might be used, and rightly so. But the spread of nuclear weapons will put them in circumstances incomparably more dangerous, not only to others but to ourselves, than one of our own weapons out of control.

The spread of nuclear weapons requires a reorganization of international relations as well. Do we prefer an enforced interdependence or the spurious equality in which countries large and small threaten one another in an anarchy of violence-producing potential? The world must be brought together; nuclear weapons can pull it apart.

Finally, we must count it a most serious cost of proliferation that the best hopes and aspirations of the world may be put off for many years while wisdom and labors are devoted to diminishing dangers and resolving problems that might still prove avoidable by prompt and timely efforts.

These are real dangers and urgent ones. We urge immediate steps to avoid them, and these steps need not and should not be restricted to arms control measures. The desire for nuclear weapons stems not only from security concerns but also from political aspirations. And, in any case, it may be amenable to political methods of solution that are not always closely related to guarantees of security. The full weight of U.S. influence and U.S. capacity for constructive diplomacy should be placed at the disposal of this critical problem at this critical time.

Breaking the East–West Deadlock

The key elements of a non-proliferation agreement are already set forth in the Irish resolution adopted unanimously by the UN General Assembly in 1961 and endorsed repeatedly by the United States: first, that the nuclear states "refrain from relinquishing control of nuclear weapons and from transmitting the information necessary for their manufacture to states not possessing such weapons"; second, that the non-nuclear powers "undertake not to manufacture or otherwise acquire control of such weapons. . . ."

Recent attempts to reaffirm this agreement in a treaty have confronted an apparently basic divergence between the Soviet Union and the United States on the issue of nuclear arrangements of NATO. What the Soviets have viewed as proposals for further diffusion the U.S. has, with equal logic, viewed as safeguards against possible future diffusion. It is clear that the matter is most important; it is equally clear that it cannot be settled in a merely bilateral Soviet–U.S. context. This issue is accordingly examined in Section IV, "Europe and Disarmament."

In any case, however, it would be a most serious error, if as a result of Soviet unwillingness to enter a non-proliferation agreement, the United States and others felt precluded from negotiating or encouraging such agreements as may prove possible. The Soviet Government is very likely to respect them. It is opposed to proliferation; it has long ceased to contribute to Communist China's nuclear program; it has recently supported mandatory safeguards for fissionable material monitored by the International Agency for Atomic Energy (IAEA), and it has repeatedly voiced opposition to the further spread of nuclear weapons.

The Longer Run

But even were every non-nuclear power to declare its present intent not to seek nuclear weapons, there would be the longer-run problems posed by the continuing incentives to do otherwise, incentives that must be eliminated or reduced if nuclear weapons are to remain restricted to the five present nuclear powers.

First and foremost among these incentives are the security problems of the non-nuclear powers. Non-nuclear states must be protected from the threat of such force as would persuade them that nuclear weapons were an easy, a necessary, an urgent counter. This requires that nuclear powers commit themselves to refrain from the use, or threat of use, of nuclear weapons against non-nuclear ones. It requires that nuclear powers must pledge themselves to defend the victims of such aggression with all necessary means. But perhaps most important, it means that nuclear and non-nuclear powers alike must commit themselves to refrain from the use of force across national boundaries and must commit themselves, in as wide a variety of circumstances as possible, to prevent others from doing so. So long as boundaries are or might be changed by force, so long will nuclear weapons appear a potentially useful deterrent to aggression.

We therefore support the formulation and ratification of suitable regional agreements aimed at guaranteeing borders to the satisfaction of those countries most tempted to purchase nuclear weapons for this purpose. In addition, of course, we stress the importance of institutionalizing the peacekeeping arrangements discussed below in Section VII.

We recognize, however, that some of the incentives for nuclear proliferation are political, requiring for their diminution either evidence of major-power willingness to cooperate to keep the peace or, to the extent that nuclear renunciation is a sacrifice, evidence that the major powers are themselves showing a comparable restraint in their effort to halt the "vertical" proliferation of their own arsenals. To this end, we suggest six measures on which immediate agreement should be sought:

1. A comprehensive ban on nuclear testing, adequately verified. New improvements in national detection systems might make it possible to accept a treaty in which inspection followed a challenge based upon a threat of withdrawal; ultimately any quota of inspections is no more dependable than such an arrangement would be. Alternatively, new improvements in seismological instruments might make it possible to close the small gap in views of the two sides on acceptable numbers of on-site inspections whose existence prevented agreement in 1963.

2. As an earnest of their intention to limit and reduce strategic weapons, a pledge by the nuclear powers to commit an agreed fraction, such as one-half of one per cent, of their military expenditures to appropriate UN organs for peacekeeping and economic assistance.

3. A complete halt in the U.S., U.K., and U.S.S.R. of production of fissionable materials for use in nuclear weapons. This proposal has already been made by the United States. Alternatively, more gradual measures acceptable to both sides and essentially symmetrical in their effects could be undertaken.

4. A transfer for non-weapons uses of agreed quantities of weapons-grade U-235 by the U.S., U.K., and U.S.S.R. to the International Atomic Energy Agency (IAEA) for the benefit of developing countries. Safeguards should permit the repossession upon demand of any such material used in an unauthorized manner, e.g., in research which is directed toward the development of nuclear weapons.

5. Elaboration and intensification of IAEA inspection and the subordination of all transfers of fissionable material to IAEA controls.

6. Whether the halt be gradual or complete, an opening of all U.S., U.K., and U.S.S.R. atomic energy plants to IAEA inspection to ensure compliance with the agreement. The U.S. initiative in opening the Rowe, Massachusetts, reactor to IAEA inspection should be broadened, unilaterally if necessary, and it should be matched by the willingness of others engaged in peaceful uses of atomic energy to permit inspection.

In addition, the United States should seek an experimental Alaskan–Siberian zone of nuclear and conventional arms limitations centered around the Bering Strait. We believe that this step would be a sound, significant, and imaginative initiative in the development of arms limitations in other parts of the world. Such a zone would involve comparable areas on each side, and the arrangement could be implemented with bilateral or United Nations inspection and supervision.

More generally, we believe that nuclear-free zones in Latin America, Africa, and in the Near East are among the most feasible arms limitation agreements at this time and among the most hopeful ones for a long-term barrier to nuclear diffusion in those areas. In certain cases, the creation of these zones may make necessary minor modifications in present U.S. security practices, modifications of far less importance to the nation than the securing of a nuclear-free zone. The small problems that these changes will raise should not obscure the larger interest.

Controlling Strategic Weapon Systems

Containing the Arms Race

Just as we stress containing the spread of nuclear weapons, we also place high priority on containing the competition in weapon procurement of the United States and the Soviet Union—not least because success in the latter will be useful in the former. At a minimum, and for their own sake, the major powers must strive to check a competition that will otherwise lead periodically to the expensive procurement, deployment, or redeployment of entirely new weapon systems. It is, after all, the continuing competition to perfect and deploy new armaments that absorbs quantities of time, energy, and resources that no static strategic environment would demand; that exacerbates U.S. and Soviet relations with unreal considerations of strategic advantage or disadvantage; that keeps political leaders in both great powers off-balance and ill-prepared for far-reaching agreements; that fixes the attention of both sides on the most threatening aspects of the opposing posture; and, especially, that provides heightened risks of a violent spasm of procurement—one spurring to new levels the cost, distrust, and the explosive dangers of an unending competition in arms.

We also stress containing the arms race because it is an objective that may well be far easier to realize than reductions of strategic weapons, or, put another way, because an ounce of prevention may be worth a pound of cure. This was, for example, the principle underlying the U.N. resolution calling for a ban on weapons of mass destruction in orbit. Perhaps an even more important instance of the potential application of this principle concerns anti-ballistic missile systems (ABM).

Ballistic-Missile Defense

We urge both the United States and the Soviet Union to agree—explicitly or tacitly—to a moratorium of at least three years on new deployment (but not on the unverifiable research and development) of systems for ballistic-missile defense. While the ostensible purpose of the immediate deployment of ABM defenses (at least in the United States) has now become that of dealing with the limited threat posed by China's potential nuclear forces, a U.S. or a Soviet ABM system would almost certainly induce both superpowers to step up their strategic weapon programs in an effort to ensure their respective "deterrent" capabilities.

The reason for our proposal is simple; we do not believe the time is appropriate for a decision to deploy. First of all, there remains the basic question of the military value of the system. Here many technical questions remain to be answered. Secretary of Defense Robert McNamara, in his 1965 testimony before the House Armed Services Committee, summed up the status of the ballistic-missile defense system as follows:

Although the NIKE X development is progressing satisfactorily, there are many technical problems still to be solved, and I believe it is still premature to make any commitment to production and deployment at this time. Over and above the technical problems there are even greater uncertainties concerning the preferred concept of deployment, the relationship of the NIKE X system to other elements of a balanced Damage Limiting effort, the timing of the attainment of an effective nation-wide fallout shelter system, and the nature and effect of an opponent's possible reaction to our NIKE X deployment. Accordingly, we propose to continue the development of the NIKE X system on an urgent basis, and a total of about $400 million has been provided in the FY 1966 budget for that purpose, including $10 million for some preliminary production engineering.

Beyond the technical and military-economic questions, we believe that the United States had not given the political consequences of the ABM deployment sufficient thought and certainly has not yet explored the ways in which the United States and the U.S.S.R. could avoid unintended effects of the systems on the other's deterrent force. There are many other questions still unanswered and unconsidered. Shall the systems be emplaced in Europe? Will they be sold to allies by ourselves or by the Soviets? Can we and the Soviet Union devise ways by which we acquiesce in reduced, but still enormous, deterrent capabilities? Will our action simply play into the hands of the Communist Chinese effort to disrupt U.S.–Soviet relations in general and arms limitation efforts in particular? Does the Chinese threat really require immediate action on the part of the United

States and the Soviets? And how far are we and the Soviets planning to go in building active defenses? The costs involved in the systems under discussion are measured in tens of billions of dollars; their strategic implications are enormous and long-lasting; and their political impact may be the most startling of all—especially in Europe. The matter deserves the closest and most intense discussion and thought; a three-year moratorium would produce it.

We also believe that the political posture of the Soviet Union is delicately poised at the moment; it is very clearly in the U.S. interest to avoid such actions as might deflect the Soviet Government from a course of improving its relations with the West. Encouraging the start of a new round of expenditures and dangers at this moment therefore seems inopportune. And in three years' time, it may be possible, not only to see more clearly what strategic threat the People's Republic of China will and will not soon present, but also what the response of both the United States and Soviet Union should be.

Freeze on Strategic Delivery Vehicles

In the absence of a moratorium, and assuming that ballistic-missile defenses are built, the United States will have to rethink its suggestion of early 1964 that a freeze on offensive and defensive weapons and their characteristics be considered by the United States and the Soviet Union and discussed with their major allies. This is because an agreement along these lines would not be possible during the construction of ballistic-missile defenses; because it seems technically difficult to design a proposal that would freeze a dynamic contest between deployed ballistic-missile defenses and the weapons designed to surmount them, and because it may be more difficult, though this is somewhat controversial, to reach agreement on a freeze of offensive weapons while the defenses that neutralize them were uncontrolled.

These considerations argue against ballistic-missile defenses, and they argue for redoubled efforts to achieve quickly whatever appropriately balanced freeze can be negotiated. In this regard, we believe that the United States should not restrict itself to the details of the initial formulation but should reaffirm its willingness to consider different kinds of freeze proposals from every quarter. Thus, the United States need not freeze as of any given date but might agree on specified weapon levels. Further, it need not freeze characteristics of weapons if no more than a freeze on numbers of weapons seems negotiable. Nor need the United States focus on restrictive, detailed, and technically complicated freezes. The United States might propose instead a freeze so simple and general that it could be "ratified" by simultaneous coordinated announcements and inspected by continually improving unilateral methods—those same methods upon which the United States would rely in the absence of agreement as well, for that limited part of her preparedness that depends upon knowledge of Soviet actions.

Reduction of Strategic Delivery Systems

Of course, the United States cannot be content with containing the competition or freezing it. At a minimum it should continue to seek coordinated methods, with or without formal agreements, to destroy weapons deemed obsolete and superfluous. Such acts would have primary importance as signals of readiness to cooperate; we have noted earlier how important this signal can be in non-proliferation efforts.

More generally, we consider much deeper cuts in strategic inventories—on the order of a one-third cut—to be worth serious consideration. The United States has already accepted the notion that some comprehensive arms control agreements need not include inspection of operational weapon inventories; the U.S. 1964 freeze suggestion made this point. We believe that verification of destruction would be sufficient for some reduction agreements as well.

We also note that the imbalance between U.S. and U.S.S.R. strategic forces is not so great as is often implied—if targets in Western Europe, as well as in North America, are matched against targets in the U.S.S.R. This increases the feasibility of agreement because disarmament agreements can be based on a Soviet willingness to balance part of American reductions with reductions in their threat against our European allies.

Prohibition against Nuclear Weapons in Space

The announcement by the United States of its intention to carry out experiments for the purpose of learning about the military uses of satellites gave rise to serious misinterpretation and led some observers to the erroneous conclusion that the United States was repudiating its intention, now embodied in a UN resolution, to refrain from placing nuclear weapons in space. To ensure against this possible misunderstanding, the U.S. Government should continue to reaffirm, as Ambassador Goldberg has done, its commitment to the General Assembly resolution against weapons of mass destruction in outer space.

Europe and Disarmament

The Present Situation

Since 1945, the confrontation of the United States and the Soviet Union across the German zonal boundary has been a central political fact affecting the arms race. In the early postwar period, the temporary nature of the German partition, the unsettled conditions in Western Europe, Soviet maintenance of troop levels despite substantial Allied disarmament, Soviet probes in other areas of the world, and the general Soviet posture under Stalin generated widespread fears of a Soviet attack across the boundary. The Berlin Blockade and the Korean War seemed to confirm these fears. A rapid buildup of Western arms followed, and the Warsaw Pact nations replied in kind, probably further stimulated by American talk of "rollback" of the expansion of Communism into Eastern Europe.

Over the last decade and for a variety of reasons, the threat of Soviet attack has been waning. In particular, it has become increasingly obvious to both sides, first, that neither will retreat under pressure from Central European positions taken up after the Allied victory and, second, that resort to violence would be irrationally risky. For example, even the abortive uprisings in East Germany (1953) and Hungary (1956) did not result in Western military action in Eastern Europe; the risk of Western attack, as perceived by the Soviet Union, was thus reduced. For the United States, the Soviet split with China and the growth of Eastern European independence within the Soviet bloc have been among the factors diminishing the supposed risk of Soviet attack. In addition, a general recognition of the possibility of unintended war has been still another factor inhibiting the use or threat of violence. But the confrontation continues, while parallel interests in avoiding war provide an overriding motive on both sides for resolving this central and most dangerous issue: an unsettled and divided Germany.

Looked at in terms of current realities, the German problem shows a tangle of partly conflicting, partly parallel interests as among the United States, the Soviet Union, and Germany. To make progress in solidifying the reduction of tension sufficiently to per-

mit more progress in arms control and disarmament, requires that
the parties concerned see parallel interests as outweighing conflicting ones.

The German people—articulately in the West and silently in the
East—want reunification. The United States has backed them in this
desire; indeed, American spokesmen voiced it before the Germans
felt strong enough or self-confident enough to do so. Now the demand for reunification has become a sufficiently strong factor in
West German public sentiment that its continued support by the
United States is crucial to relations with the Federal Republic.

The United States has sought the integration of West Germany
into Western Europe and a close-knit alliance between Western Europe and the United States. This has been one of the most important
persistent strands in U.S. foreign policy in the postwar period. Its
purposes have been twofold: to promote within Germany a stable,
responsible, Western-oriented, democratic government, living in
harmony with the countries of Western Europe that Germany had
conquered and occupied in World War II; to contribute to the
strength, military and other, of the Western Alliance. As ultimate
goals, to which the Alliance and integration contribute, the United
States wants peace and stability in Europe.

The Soviets have sought security, especially the security of the
new borders and the legitimation of the regimes of the Warsaw Pact
states. In some of these states and in the Soviet Union as well, there
is also a genuine fear of Germany, reflecting both the experiences of
World War II and the belief that the "German problem" might be
the cause of another conflict. In addition, the Soviets have sought
continued hegemony in East Germany, both as an end in itself for
political and economic reasons and as a means of ensuring the security of Eastern Europe. They probably judge—rightly—that East
Germany cannot stand on its own as a viable Communist state in the
face of the superior numbers, strength, prosperity, and freedom of
the Federal Republic.

The great common interest of the United States and the Soviet
Union in Europe is in a settled political situation that would result in
enough reduction of the tension of confrontation to ensure continued peace. Germany remains the great issue of the confrontation,
and the one most likely to become the occasion of conflicts from
which neither can readily retreat. Joint interest in avoiding such
conflicts leads to joint interest in resolving this issue. Since the stability recently experienced may well prove temporary under the

pressure of the conflicting goals described above, the importance of the U.S. interest in avoiding conflict is underlined. If a conflict ever arose, it would probably begin with the devastation of Germany, and the interest in peace is at least as important for the Germans as it is for the Soviet Union and the United States.

The key question, of course, is whether this common interest is important enough to overcome the conflict of interests on all sides. U.S. insistence on close military integration of West Germany within the Alliance, and German reinforcement of that insistence, is inconsistent with the German and American desire for reunification, given the Soviet concerns for security. On the other side, the Soviet desire to legitimate the postwar settlement is in conflict with continued Soviet support of the independence of East Germany, since it is now impossible for the Soviets to expect West Germany and her allies to accept the division of Germany as permanent.

Reconciliation of these conflicts must, logically, include some change in military arrangements in both parts of Germany, in connection with a process that makes continued movement toward reunification possible. In general, such evolution can probably take place only in an atmosphere of increasing détente and increased freedom for the Eastern European states in relation to the Soviet Union. The alternate possibility of bringing about a Soviet retreat from East Germany by maintaining or increasing Western pressures (or seizing the opportunity of an unforeseen crisis to force a sudden retreat) is, as a practical matter, excluded. The evolution of the military balance makes it ever less likely that such a risky course could succeed. Further, it is doubtful that our European allies would really favor any such attempt at forcing a Soviet retreat.

The search for détente and the loosening of the ties of the Pact in the East have implications for the Western Alliance. The military element in Western relations must not be viewed as central, and accordingly should be given less emphasis. Some general loosening of Alliance ties must also be accepted, since alliances inevitably show greater solidarity in periods of threat than in periods of calm. Neither of these changes means the withdrawal of the United States from Europe or the lessening of the security ties between America and Western Europe. Rather, the opposite is true, since the defense of Western Europe remains vital to the security of the United States and the evolution of military technology continues to make effective European self-defense more rather than less difficult and costly.

Next Steps

The most important contribution that arms restrictions can make toward peace in Europe lies in measures that signal and encourage détente and help to perpetuate and solidify whatever degree of relaxation can be achieved.

FIRST, we suggest that the United States take the lead in seeking a non-aggression pact between NATO and the Warsaw Treaty Organization. Within the next three years, the NATO Treaty comes under review by its signatories. It would be highly desirable to reaffirm the mutual commitment of North America and Western Europe to their joint security interests in a context which formalizes the defensive nature of these interests. A non-aggression pact would do no more than recognize explicitly what has already been recognized tacitly, that the situation in Central Europe—including the situation in Berlin—can be changed only by mutual consent, not by force. Nonetheless, formalizing this recognition can be an important step in institutionalizing the détente.

SECOND, we believe that the United States should lead its allies in the search for means to reduce, rather than increase, the buildup of nuclear weapons in and near Central Europe. In this connection, solutions to the nuclear problem of the Alliance should be sought in arrangements that do not result in the creation of new nuclear forces. One possible method which meets this condition is the "Select Committee" that the Secretary of Defense has recently suggested. Properly developed, this would provide for more involvement of our Western European allies, especially Germany, Great Britain, France (if she so desires), and Italy in a genuine dialogue on the detailed business of planning for the Alliance's strategic force. The point of such a Committee is to give practical institutional substance to the proposition that the U.S. nuclear forces *are* the Alliance Strategic Force. In this connection, it is important that the Committee function not only at a high ministerial level but also with reference to the whole executive apparatus, military and civilian, through which governments do their work. Further, this principle of more intimate association at the working levels of actual decision-making in major Allied capitals can usefully be extended to non-nuclear matters as well.

One desirable consequence of this procedure could be a more fruitful involvement of the principal NATO allies in discussions of disarmament and arms control. This is especially important in relation to the problems of Europe and in regard to Germany. Heretofore, NATO consultation on disarmament has usually offered little that is positive. This in turn has reflected its sporadic character; when it springs from an ongoing participation in the central military problems of the Alliance, it can reasonably be expected to be better informed and more constructive.

THIRD, we believe that the United States should seek agreement both with her allies and with the Soviets on measures which could reduce the danger of surprise conventional attack in Europe. These could include the manning of fixed observer posts at selected points in NATO and Warsaw Pact countries and the extension of the Huebner-Malinin agreement covering mobile observers more widely through the NATO-Warsaw areas. Both these measures could best be proposed in the context of a NATO-Warsaw non-aggression pact, thus giving such a pact substance.

FOURTH, we believe that the United States should encourage an examination of the problem of parallel troop reductions in West and East Germany by the United States and the Soviet Union. Reductions are not to be conceived as tantamount to withdrawal, which would change the military balance; but rather, as adjustments equitable for both sides which would preserve the balance at less cost and strain for each. An exploration in these terms would have to begin with the Western allies most concerned, but, if it is to have any effect, it must proceed to exchanges with the Soviet Union.

FINALLY, we believe that the United States should explore, first with Germany and the other Western allies most concerned, the nature of the security arrangements with respect to Eastern Europe that progress toward reunification would demand and permit. To take one possible example, a series of arrangements might be concluded between the Federal Republic and East Germany to cover trade, the movement of persons, and the like, leading ultimately to some kind of confederation, when agreement could be reached as to how steps beyond confederation could be taken and what final security arrangements were appropriate to that stage.

Conventional Arms Races
in the Developing Countries

Intense conventional arms races are taking place in several areas of the world at great costs to the participants, at the risk of the peace and tranquillity of their regions, and at the risk of appalling destruction should war break out. Thus, UAR and Israel have per capita rates of military expenditures among the highest in the world. Between them they spent approximately one billion dollars on armaments in 1963. Pakistan and India, in a situation complicated by the threat from Communist China, had accumulated weapons at an increasing rate until conflict broke out between them. And Africa has not been free of an arms buildup.

The international traffic in arms which makes these buildups possible is extremely complex, ranging from direct government-to-government arms sales to the transfer of superpower arms technology from those who have acquired it to those who have not. To some extent this trade is already regulated in the major exporting countries. With minor exceptions, armaments do not enter the world market without the active consent of the governments concerned, both sellers and purchasers. But there is at present very little international coordination concerning the types of weapons that should be supplied and the types of clients that may receive them.

In general, we believe that serious efforts should be made to control the arms traffic and that these efforts, like those directed at nuclear proliferation, should aim first at measures to regulate the traffic directly, and second at reducing incentives for conventional arms buildups.

Consequently the major arms suppliers should refrain from further introduction of sophisticated weapons such as bombers, tanks, and submarines into underdeveloped areas. The past record of both the United States and the Soviet Union is bad. Efforts should be made to encourage the developing states themselves to explore, presumably on a regional basis, the possibility of agreement not to acquire such weapons. Agreement should be sought through the United Nations to limit the sale and acquisition of conventional arms. This appears to be most feasible in the context of regional agreements as a first step and is discussed below. At the least, the United Nations could revive the practice of the League of Nations of printing an "armaments yearbook" on international arms transfers. Such a document would go some distance toward removing some of the exaggerated fears that may develop in relative secrecy.

In the long run, however, as with nuclear proliferation, peacekeeping arrangements will be necessary to allay the anxieties and dampen the ambitions that motivate purchase of arms on the world market.

Communist China and Arms Limitations

With the explosion of two nuclear devices, China has reminded the world that she intends to develop a formidable nuclear and conventional military capability. In the long run, any system of world security and any extensive nuclear or conventional disarmament will have to include Communist China.

But the long run can be very long. At the present time and for a considerable number of years to come, any agreement that might conceivably be negotiated between the United States and the Soviet Union—even including a very substantial reduction in strategic forces or a nuclear freeze—could, from a strategic point of view, be safely implemented while the Chinese continue their efforts to develop their own nuclear force. Even forces much larger than the present *Soviet* force would not find it possible to destroy the present U.S. retaliatory capability diminished by fractions of one-third or one-half. Nor would the United States lack, under the terms of a reduction agreement, the strategic forces necessary to respond to less comprehensive Chinese threats than an all-out attack. Whatever future bombers, land-based missiles, or submarines were retained for protection against the Soviet Union could be designed to be retargetable to Chinese targets.

The Soviet strategic force and technological change will remain the most serious threats for many years, and U.S. force size is not so finely calculated that it cannot cope, albeit with some modifications, with the relatively minor additional strains placed upon it by China. Peking's nuclear strength, for some years, will be capable only of acting as a catalyst on fears and uncertainties; a catalyst that uses the strategic instabilities and interactions between the United States and the Soviet Union to stimulate responses wholly disproportionate to its threat. Thus, a ballistic-missile defense designed to shoot down Chinese missiles might nevertheless lead the Soviet Union into building more missiles or into a corresponding defensive system that would have the same effect on us. That it is in Communist China's political interest, as presently conceived in Peking, to attempt to wield this catalytic power and to disrupt Soviet–American relations is likely; that the United States should guard against the failures of nerve and perception that permit disruption is an equally obvious corollary.

With respect to proliferation, analogous problems exist. While Communist China's nuclear explosions have made nothing impossible except her own foregoing of nuclear weapons, her continued detonations and missile firings will make the attainment of agreements far more difficult. Again, this is not necessarily for strategic reasons but may also be for political ones; China's actions and the anxiety aroused by her political intentions are equally important.

For these reasons we believe that there are advantages, with respect to limiting both proliferation and the arms race, in bringing Communist China into a dialogue that will dispel whatever fears are illusory and permit the world to grapple, in a concrete way, with those that are not. The United States wants to know whether China plans to spread atomic weapons to other countries; whether she wishes to provoke or restrain her neighbors from producing a nuclear capability comparable to her own; whether she would participate in a constructive or a destructive way in formal disarmament talks; and so on. From the standpoint of arms control as well as from others, this information would be of great value. In the long run, the United States will have to talk to China about arms control, and analogous discussions with the Soviets have proven much more useful than was initially anticipated. Moreover, since discussions would be especially useful if undertaken soon, we see no point in delay.

We believe that efforts should be made to open bilateral talks on arms control with the People's Republic of China, similar to those carried on in Warsaw but devoted to arms control. We favor an exploration of conditions under which the People's Republic of China would qualify for and accept the obligations of the UN Charter, and could join the United Nations. We would support suitable initiatives to achieve these ends. And should a World Disarmament Conference be convened, as recommended by the UN Disarmament Commission to the General Assembly, we would favor the invitation of the People's Republic of China to that conference.

Peacekeeping as an Alternative to Armament

The important problems of peacekeeping, of peaceful settlement of disputes, and of assuring peaceful changes are being treated by two other panels. We look forward to seeing their reports. But these problems take on a special significance for us, because without their solution, much of the arms control for which we have argued would be far more difficult to attain. Without confidence in adequate peacekeeping machinery, nations will continue to arm themselves, and their neighbors will respond in kind. Without confidence in the feasibility of peaceful settlements, nations will prepare to settle their disputes by force. And in the absence of machinery for change that is peaceful, nations will anticipate change that is violent. Limitations on arms demand confidence that peace is possible even as they provide it. This is especially important in the developing areas, where the pace of conventional and nuclear preparations is likely to be critically dependent on confidence.

For these reasons, we want to strengthen a growing expectation that world opinion in general, the United Nations in particular, and the major powers especially, will be ready and willing to prevent armed conflicts and, if they occur, to prevent them from being fought to a military conclusion. Such preventive action will obviously require a broad spectrum of military, political, and other capabilities.

To this end, we make the following proposals:

FIRST, a versatile *United Nations Peace Force* should be created under the control of the Security Council and responsive to the General Assembly. Such a force could be composed initially of two elements: standby units voluntarily earmarked by the member states but controlled and supported by them until requested by the United Nations for deployment in a specific operation; and a small elite force of about one to two thousand men available for immediate deployment as a "fire prevention brigade." Such a force could be deployed or developed on a regional basis, if that were desired.

The United States could play a decisive role in the evolution of a United Nations Peace Force by assisting in the development of the necessary UN military staff; by providing logistic support and, upon request, training programs for designated military contingents; and, above all, by encouraging and assisting other nations to pledge the necessary forces.

We also recommend that the International Law Commission and the UN Legal Counsel's Office undertake comprehensive studies on the applicability of international law to international peacekeeping forces.

SECOND, with or without a United Nations Peace Force, confidence in international mechanisms for providing security would be enhanced by the existence of a functioning UN Peace Observation Corps, preferably recruited and trained by the United Nations and available to the Secretary-General. Its main function would be to focus the eyes of the international organized community on a situation which if ignored could endanger the peace. For the purpose of creating a climate conducive to arms control agreements, this mechanism would provide confidence that, at the very least, the international community would take formal cognizance of disturbances of the peace.

For those who would place confidence in the functioning of international guarantees and of international opinion, it is especially important that the Peace Observation Corps be capable of rapid deployment. To this end, the Secretary-General should be authorized to activate the Corps on the basis of preliminary reports that a disturbance has arisen. Units of the Corps could be stationed throughout the world. So that the circumstances and early stages of an outbreak of violence might be reported at first hand, prior consent for fact-finding on their territories by as many states as possible should be a component of the agreement. The Peace Observation Corps could also be utilized to investigate possible violations of arms control agreements.

THIRD, ways and means of providing continuing financial support for the UN Peace Force and the Peace Observation Corps should be an integral part of the arrangements creating them. We continue to support the prescriptive principle that all UN members should pay their fair share of the cost of peacekeeping operations. But we recognize that an objectively reliable method of financing would be useful in a variety of circumstances under which operations might be authorized despite the unwillingness of all to contribute to their costs. Our earlier recommendation that the nuclear powers voluntarily commit a small fraction of their military expenditures, such as one-half of one per cent, to a UN fund would provide one sound method, utilizing commitments insignificant in comparison to national defense expenditures. One can hardly regard the desire for international security arrangements as a serious one if financial commitments so modest as these are not forthcoming.

FOURTH, we recommend that the United States continue to work toward the establishment of a UN Disarmament Organization. While most of the arms limitations proposed in this report can be verified by national means, some—such as the zonal arrangements in the Bering Strait—should be administered and inspected by the United Nations. The United Nations could acquire valuable experience by its involvement in such operations, thus helping to prepare it for the task of administering more comprehensive arms limitations.

FIFTH, in addition to having confidence in the security afforded by a UN Peace Force and Peace Observation Corps, nations acquiescing in arms limitations or restraints will wish to be assured that effective non-military sanctions can be applied against aggressors. The United Nations should conduct continuing studies of the ways in which collective action of this kind can be effective.

SIXTH, criteria for defining aggression will be necessary to persuade the peaceful that violations of their integrity will not go unrecognized for what they are. This requires the clarification of non-aggression provisions; the United States should take the lead in putting forward a non-aggression treaty embodying the proposals made by President Johnson in January, 1964. This might be formulated as a variety of regional arrangements. And the United States should support agreement on what constitutes illegal threat and use of force along the lines of a protocol drafted by a UN special committee in 1964 as follows:

1. Every state has the duty to refrain in its international relations from the threat or use of force against the territorial integrity or political independence of any state, or in any other manner inconsistent with the purposes of the United Nations.

2. In accordance with the foregoing fundamental principle, and without limiting its generality:

(a) Wars of aggression constitute international crimes against peace.

(b) Every state has the duty to refrain from organizing or encouraging the organization of irregular or volunteer forces or armed bands within its territory or any other territory for incursions into the territory of another state.

(c) Every state has the duty to refrain from instigating, assisting, or organizing civil strife or committing terrorist acts in another state, or from conniving at or acquiescing in organized activities directed toward such ends, when such acts involve a threat or use of force.

(d) Every state has the duty to refrain from the threat or use of force to violate the existing boundaries of another state, or as a means of solving its international disputes, including territorial disputes and problems concerning frontiers between states.

3. Nothing in the foregoing paragraphs affects the provisions of the Charter concerning the lawful use of force.

While the foregoing measures might go some distance toward tranquilizing the fears that would otherwise make themselves evident in weapon procurement, they are not in themselves sufficient in the long run. Not only must they be supplemented eventually by much greater peacekeeping efforts, but they must be complemented by the evolution and strengthening of mechanisms by which problems are resolved without arms—methods of peaceful settlement and change.

U.S. influence could do much to encourage rather than impede such progress. We recommend further study of such possibilities as a World Court of Equity, a Standing Panel of Mediators, and a Board of Arbitration. We believe that the United States should reconsider its hesitation to ratify a number of relevant and long-standing conventions. And we recommend the repeal of the Connally Amendment—we cannot expect others to accept the compulsory jurisdiction of the Court if we ourselves are not willing to strengthen it.

It may well be that these are the kind of measures that will finally prove to be most effective in the control of arms. For we understand that it is in the ultimate growth of world law that arms and the problems which they present will eventually be subdued.

Strengthening the Arms Control and Disarmament Agency

The very creation of the ACDA by the United States in 1961 was a significant and long overdue achievement. But ACDA has not yet achieved an effectiveness commensurate with its responsibilities. In part, this reflects the lack of widespread public understanding of, and support for, its purposes and programs. Therefore, we urge a reconsideration by the Congress of its elimination from the original Arms Control and Disarmament Bill of a public services department.

RECOMMENDATIONS

We make the following recommendations:

I. To halt the growth and spread of nuclear arsenals we recommend the following steps:

1. That the United States seek a non-proliferation treaty that prohibits the transfer by atomic powers of nuclear weapons and manufacturing capabilities and their acquisition or manufacture by non-nuclear powers.

2. That the United States seek to establish the conditions—military, political, and economic—in which both the non-nuclear and nuclear powers will perceive that their security and other interests are best served by preventing any further spread of nuclear weapons through adherence to a non-proliferation treaty.

3. That the United States seek an agreement with the other nuclear powers pledging them (a) not to attack or threaten to attack with nuclear weapons a non-nuclear power; and (b) if a non-nuclear power is thus threatened or attacked, to defend it with all necessary means.

4. That the United States seek acceptance of a series of other measures to halt the buildup and spread of nuclear weapons:

   (a) A comprehensive nuclear test ban treaty adequately verified, perhaps utilizing recent improvements in national detection systems making it possible to rely on challenge inspections or otherwise to bridge the gap in acceptable numbers of on-site inspections that appeared to prevent agreement in 1963;

   (b) A U.S., U.K., U.S.S.R. treaty to cease all production of weapons-grade fissionable material;

   (c) The transfer of agreed quantities of such material to the IAEA for peaceful uses by the developing countries;

   (d) Elaboration and intensification of IAEA inspection and the subordination of all transfers of fissionable material to IAEA controls;

   (e) Opening of all U.S.S.R., U.K., and U.S. atomic energy plants to IAEA inspection.

5. That the United States encourage the development of nuclear-free zones in Latin America, Africa, and the Near East, beginning with a U.S.–Soviet Treaty establishing a zone of nuclear and conventional arms limitation under UN inspection in the Bering Strait and including comparable areas in Alaska and Siberia.

II. To limit and reduce strategic delivery capabilities we recommend that the United States seek agreement with the Soviet Union and, if feasible, with the other nuclear powers on the following sequence:

1. A moratorium of at least three years on the deployment of anti-ballistic missile (ABM) systems;
2. A freeze on the number of strategic delivery vehicles;
3. A reduction in total numbers amounting to one-third of each party's medium- and long-range delivery vehicles, beginning with the destruction of obsolete stocks.

III. To curb conventional arms races among the underdeveloped countries we recommend the following initiatives:

1. That the United States seek to have controls established over the traffic in arms by (a) major-power agreement to refrain from introduction of sophisticated weapons; (b) regional non-acquisition agreements; (c) UN-supervised agreements regarding sale and acquisition; (d) the establishment of a UN monitoring system to record the traffic in arms.
2. That the United States join with other major powers to provide adequate security for the less developed nations and that the United States support the establishment of UN peacekeeping procedures to the same end.

IV. To further reduce tensions in Europe and more toward settlement of the outstanding East-West differences we recommend the following measures:

1. That the United States, working with its allies, seek a non-aggression pact between NATO and the Warsaw Pact Organization.
2. That the United States seek to ensure that measures to improve Western security arrangements do not result in the creation of new nuclear forces, but instead provide for greater involvement of our Western European allies in the planning for use of U.S. strategic forces as well as other military planning and arms control problems.
3. That the United States explore arms control, related security provisions, and other measures which would help lead to German reunification; in this connection, the possibilities for balanced reductions of U.S. and Soviet troops and weapons in Central Europe be examined.

V. That the United States attempt to bring the People's Republic of China into a genuine dialogue on disarmament and other security matters: (a) by seeking bilateral talks on arms control matters of joint concern; (b) by ascertaining the conditions under which Communist China could qualify for and accept the responsibilities of membership in the United Nations; and (c) by supporting efforts to bring Communist China into the Eighteen Nation Disarmament Conference or a World Disarmament Conference, if held.

VI. To make the law of the UN Charter more effective and to strengthen UN peacekeeping machinery we recommend:

1. That the United States support the creation of a UN Peace Force, perhaps composed of two parts: (a) standby forces committed by member nations; and (b) an elite force of one to two thousand men recruited by the the United Nations.

2. That the United States offer to provide training and logistic support for the UN Peace Force and encourage others to do so.

3. That the United States support the development of an effective UN Peace Observation Corps recruited by and available to the Secretary-General.

4. That the United States and other nuclear powers commit a fraction, such as one-half of one per cent, of their annual defense expenditures to support the UN Peace Observation Corps and other peacekeeping activities of the UN.

5. That the United States encourage regional and worldwide non-aggression arrangements embodying the proposals made by President Johnson in January, 1964.

6. That the United States devote further study to mechanisms to facilitate peaceful change, such as a World Court of Equity to deal with political disputes, as well as ways and means of making greater use of the International Court of Justice and regional tribunals to deal with juridical disputes.

7. That the United States repeal the Connally Amendment.

THE COMMITTEE ON ARMS CONTROL
AND DISARMAMENT

2. *Keeping the Peace*

The Peaceful Settlement of Disputes

The ability of mankind to settle its disputes peacefully is neither a Utopian dream nor is it an established reality. It is a skill which man learns slowly in the course of his development and progress toward maturity. Over the long term of history man moves toward the things that pay off for him; and the development of skill in the peaceful settlement of disputes has enormous payoffs. In the absence of this skill, man falls continually into wasteful uses of his resources, into unprofitable and unmanageable conflict which stops his development. The increase of skill in the peaceful settlement of disputes, therefore, is an essential part of the whole developmental process of mankind, by which he learns to expand to his full capacities.

One must, therefore, see disputes themselves as part of that long teaching process by which the world teaches us to be more fully human. There are two sides to this learning process. One is the development of what might be called mature conflict behavior on the part of the parties themselves. This is the sort of thing that we see in the development of "security communities" such as between the United States, Canada, and the British Commonwealth after 1817, or among the Scandinavian countries, and now, it is to be hoped, in the whole Atlantic area. The most fundamental element in the development of mature conflict behavior is the learning of long-sightedness, and the realization that a decision which may result in a temporary benefit at the cost of someone else can easily result in a long-term loss.

Critical difficulties and interruptions in the developmental process can occur when one party is long-sighted and the other short-sighted, for unfortunately long-sightedness in one does not always produce the appropriate response in the other. This points up the need for the second process, which is the development of third-party institutions, the law, the courts, the police, the conciliator, the mediator, the marriage counselor, and the United Nations. These operate mainly by increasing the penalties for short-sightedness, by mustering the forces of society against those who break the social contract.

In the international system one sees a steady rise in the third-party institutions representing the larger community of mankind, as it is embodied today in the United Nations. The United Nations itself, however weak as an institution, nevertheless represents the legitimacy of the future and the hopes of the planet. If it were to die, something new would have to be erected on its grave.

The actual task of learning skills of peaceful settlement is difficult, and there is still a very long way to go. We are convinced, however, that there *is* somewhere to go, and that we must seek the path. For unless man learns the skills of peaceful settlement, it is likely that his tenure on earth will be short.

The Concept of Peaceful Settlement

The procedures for peaceful settlement are included in the language of Article 33 of the United Nations Charter: negotiation, enquiry, mediation, conciliation, arbitration, judicial settlement, resort to regional agencies or arrangements, or other peaceful means chosen by the parties to a dispute.

United Nations members have an obligation "first of all" to attempt one or more of these peaceful methods. Yet there have been instances where a state, seeing a threat to its national security or responding to an armed attack, has resorted to the use of force. We will not go into the implications of Article 51 of the Charter and the use of force in individual or collective self-defense before recourse to the Security Council. This subject deserves detailed analysis, including the concept that any United Nations remedy be exhausted before any resort to force. From the use of force in such cases it clearly does not follow that the obligation of a state to seek a peaceful solution is at an end. Nor in such cases are peaceful settlement procedures to be considered unrealistic alternatives to the use of force in conflict resolution.

It is a misapprehension to see negotiation and force as alternatives. U.S. policy makers have not posed these alternatives. In the case of Korea it was the U.S. position that the use of force for the self-defense of an ally was a prelude to the negotiating process looking toward the control of the controversy in response to an attack. Resort to peaceful settlement procedures is a continuing obligation when force is being used. The posing of the alternative of force or negotiation is a potentially dangerous oversimplification, and absolutes do not exist in international relations.

A sophisticated and realistic assessment of the political realities of

pacific settlement necessarily involves the most careful consideration and use of the intangible but important power of public opinion to be mobilized in support of the control of international controversies. The views of Dean Rusk, when Assistant Secretary of
State for United Nations Affairs, remain as relevant today as at the
time at which he stated them in the context of the Palestine situation
in 1948:

Some have stated that the United Nations is helpless in maintaining peace
because it has no police force and that the result is excessive and fruitless
debate. That conclusion is tempting but a little naive. A realistic assessment of the proper role of force and negotiation in the settlement of
disputes will show that a readily available police force is not necessarily
a magical panacea. Disputes come about in situations where emotions
are high, where public opinion is inflamed, where national prestige has
been engaged, and where the parties have made commitments from
which it is difficult for them to extricate themselves. The role of negotiation and debate is to reduce the fever, to find common points of agreement, to introduce the calming effect of impartial opinion, to mobilize
world opinion against the overreaching and excessive view, to bring the
contestants into direct touch with each other, to allow public opinion in
the disputing countries to subside and to place upon the United Nations
as a group political responsibility for results for which the parties could
not readily accept political responsibility.*

Different Kinds of Disputes

Disputes may be approached by considering who are the parties
in interest. The classic controversies between states may have easily
identifiable parties, but where a state is faced with what has come to
be known as indirect aggression, or what the Soviet Union and the
People's Republic of China call a war of liberation, the identity of
the parties may itself be an issue of fact. Of course, a dispute may
well have more than two easily identifiable parties. It may involve
individual governments or groupings of governments, including alliances, neighboring governments or widely separated ones; friendly,
neutral and hostile governments; ideologically similar or opposed
governments. Also the parties may not all necessarily be governments or alliances, but may include an international organization or
a private person or organization.

Then one may consider the nature or quality of the dispute. It

* "Universal, Regional and Bilateral Patterns of International Organization,"
Department of State Bulletin (April 3, 1950), p. 529.

may be a comparatively small technical controversy such as the dispute between the United Kingdom and France over islets in the English Channel which the parties put before the International Court for decision. It may be a long-term controversy concerning territory for which the prospects of settlement seem remote, but which is in suspense as a result of the parties' acceptance of control measures. The India–Pakistan dispute over Kashmir was in this situation for over fifteen years. A dispute may be one specific of the East-West struggle, such as Berlin, or it may be a controversy involving the rising imperialist policy of the People's Republic of China toward the West.

A more detailed classification would include disputes arising out of the violations of the rights of the nationals of one party by others, disputes arising out of alleged violation of international legal obligations such as arms control arrangements, conventions governing trade relations, the United Nations Charter or conventional international law.

In evaluating the intensity of disputes, the differentiating character is the extent to which the issues have or have not engaged the commitment of the parties, or have or have not become important in their domestic politics, thus rendering adjustment difficult for the executive branches of the government parties. This is a distinguishing characteristic of disputes arising out of major political or ideological causes, which may take one or more of the forms described above.

The degree of intensity of a dispute is likely to affect what the parties will recognize as alternative methods of control or settlement. This involves their respective images of the dispute and of their own roles in relation to it. One or more parties to a controversy may seek a range of peaceful alternatives whereas another party may see its own national interests or aspirations leading it inevitably to the use of force unregulated by international organization, or leading toward keeping the dispute active and unresolved.

The Role of the UN

The present posture of the United Nations, with some states or regimes not members, the recent political crisis over financing, and the long history of the veto of collective security and peaceful settlement resolutions in the Security Council, might suggest concentrating on regional organizations. However, we base our position on the conclusion that United Nations political processes remain worthy of serious consideration and contain present and potential reality.

Since the days of San Francisco in 1945, one can discern several policies for the political organization of the world: spheres of influence for the United States and the U.S.S.R., often suggested by the latter, regional collective security organizations, and the United Nations operating on the basis of some *ad hoc* degree of unity between the United States and the U.S.S.R. Now the situation is further complicated by the rise in power of the People's Republic of China, not now a member of any formal international organization. As one reviews United Nations potentialities, these considerations are all to be borne in mind.

If the United Nations is to develop in the political area of peacekeeping and peaceful settlement on the widest basis, this will involve some degree of tough bargaining with the Soviet Union and the sort of great power unity resulting from such a process. It will also involve points of contact with the People's Republic of China to draw it into a dialogue on conflicts to which it is a party. The United Nations will live if the great powers and small states see it as useful and important to their own national interests and therefore use its procedures. To the extent that the organization reflects world opinion, it will be increasingly difficult for any power great or small to ignore its processes.

The United Nations must have a continuing relation to reality. It must have a growth factor in that its financial needs for administration and for operation must be secure. It has reality for small states, as Dag Hammarskjöld observed more than once, and it has stood for an element of legitimacy in a world of disorder, offering the place and the means for hammering out peaceful change as the alternative to the unregulated use of force and subversion. These considerations enter into any realistic assessment, weighing the current organizational crisis.

It is in the interest of the United States to lend its support to the maintenance of a political role for the United Nations in conflict resolution. At the same time it is recognized that initiatives looking toward conflict resolution by peaceful means may in some instances involve initiatives outside the United Nations. Given the present situation of the United Nations, one must of necessity go behind myth and hope to see what the organization has to offer to member states and others in handling those conflicts of national interest which are inevitable.

In the area of peaceful settlement, the organization has a record and some capabilities that are generally understood. The forum and the meeting place for quiet diplomacy represent realities for the control of conflicts in a world in revolution where ideas as well as subversion by military means are weapons. Nor lightly to be vacated is a meeting place with representatives of the new states of Asia and Africa.

How the United Nations process can be used as something more than propaganda can be seen from the discussion of parliamentary diplomacy and quiet diplomacy by Dean Rusk, Philip C. Jessup and Dag Hammarskjöld in the mid-fifties. Their approach is relevant today in considering United Nations potentialities. Rusk defined parliamentary diplomacy as a type of multilateral negotiation containing at least four factors: (1) a continuing organization with interest and responsibilities; (2) regular public debate exposed to the mass media of communication; (3) rules of procedure; and (4) formal conclusions ordinarily expressed in a resolution. Jessup applied this analysis to a series of political controversies in the United Nations.

About the same time Hammarskjöld suggested that the United Nations should develop to give greater emphasis to itself as an instrument for the negotiation of settlement, rather than as a forum to debate the issues. He pointed out that the Charter does not envisage settlements imposed by force. But the obligation of states to settle their disputes by peaceful means does not mean that the principles of justice and international law are to be discarded. He saw the Charter as emphasizing the obligation of peaceful negotiation in which the full weight of world community under Charter principles is brought to bear on an issue.

Strengthening UN Facilities

In general, the procedures or methods of peaceful settlement have been under study throughout the life of the United Nations, and no radical new ideas or suggestions have evolved. The problem is to provide available alternative peaceful methods, all of which have in common the notion of an impartial third party working with the parties to a controversy to get the facts on the table and, if possible, the parties around the table, and then to work first of all for a deflation and stabilization of the controversy and, if practicable, toward a long-term solution. As part of the negotiating situation there is the constant Charter obligation of United Nations members to exhaust one or more of the alternative methods of peaceful settlement mentioned in Article 33. A flexible approach to methods is preferable to any attempt to define a step-by-step approach to what the parties to a controversy should do.

Article 13, paragraph 1(a), of the United Nations Charter provides that the General Assembly shall initiate studies and make recommendations for the purpose of promoting international cooperation in the political field. In 1948–50 the Interim Committee of the General Assembly undertook studies in the field of pacific settlement which involved the United Nations delegate, as a diplomat, looking beyond current controversy to questions of method. The U.S.S.R. boycotted the Interim Committee and its active life ended when the 1950 Uniting for Peace resolution asserted a broader role for the Assembly. Yet the studies were valuable because they involved diplomatic representatives in the types of questions on which we will make recommendations. The studies analyzed the manner in which United Nations commissions and individual negotiators had operated. Consideration was given to United Nations procedures in relation to those of regional organizations. Out of the analysis the Interim Committee's Peaceful Settlement Sub-Committee proceeded to make recommendations.

A majority of members of the United Nations have joined the organization since these 1950 studies. It would be appropriate and useful for the General Assembly, with this increased membership, to pursue the consideration of peaceful settlement under the mandate of Article 13, paragraph 1(a), in seeking more fruitful United Nations approaches. Such a new approach would provide an opportunity to weigh what has been learned about conflict resolution in the last fifteen years and to plan initiatives for the next fifteen.

An examination of United Nations experience of its first twenty years suggests the following general conclusions:

1. The unique third-party role of the Secretary-General, with his explicit and implied powers under Article 99 of the Charter;

2. The value, in conflict situations in which the emphasis is on achieving a settlement, of the single UN mediator—as against the intergovernmental UN commission;

3. The utility, in situations in which the emphasis is on impartial fact-finding, of the three-member commission;

4. The desirability in many conflict situations of allowing the UN mediator flexibility in the timing of his report to the political organ;

5. The need for more frequent use by UN political organs of the power given in Article 37 to recommend the terms of settlement.

These conclusions indicate a general development of the UN peaceful settlement process toward greater use of the Secretary-General and of other skilled individuals, and of giving these UN representatives more flexibility than in the past in their relations with the appointing organ. The exceptions to these general conclusions probably lie principally in situations in which fact-finding is the primary UN objective. Here fixed timetables are frequently essential, and utilizing three-member commissions can add to the authority and political weight of a report.

Methods for third-party elucidation of facts have at least two purposes. They can provide a surveillance of trouble spots, a sort of distant early warning service; and they can provide reliable background, distinct from self-serving declarations of the parties, on the basis of which the mediatory process can proceed. Otherwise the dispute may be destined to remain in an atmosphere of more general hostility. There have been uses of these methods by the Security Council, the General Assembly and the Secretary-General. In situations of indirect aggression, with which the United Nations may be called to deal with increasing frequency, the evident authority and impartiality of a report are important factors.

Use of a rapporteur—a device developed first by the League of Nations and carried over into UN practice—can relieve a political organ from having to act on the uncorroborated statements of the disputants or their partisans. The organ handling a dispute should have a report as objective as possible covering the essential facts at issue and the position of the disputants. This is an essential first step. We recommend the development and use of this fact-finding device.

In practice, preliminary fact elucidation may involve delicate questions of national sovereignty of member states, as opposed to community interest in involvement of United Nations peaceful adjustment procedures to anticipate an unregulated use of force. As part of a continuing study of United Nations capabilities, procedures of this sort need attention.

United Nations experience also suggests the usefulness of having the political organs, more frequently than in the past, recommend terms of settlement. In certain cases this might mean supporting the recommendations of a special representative or a rapporteur previously appointed. In other situations the political organ might develop its own recommendations, with the assistance of a rapporteur. In either case, such action could have the effect of marshalling international political opinion around a particular form of settlement.

General Assembly action in 1947, recommending a partition of Palestine, while not taken under Article 37, was essentially of this character.

While the great and dangerous struggles of our day do not lend themselves to the processes of judicial settlement, the International Court of Justice has resolved a considerable number of disputes between nations. The lack of sanctions has not prevented compliance with decisions of the Court. Yet the number of disputes submitted to international adjudication is still too small. If more nations could submit to the compulsory jurisdiction of the Court, it is likely that the Court would be used more frequently. One of the indications of a well-ordered community is the judicial settlement of disputes. We recommend that the United States withdraw the self-judging reservation to its own acceptance of the compulsory jurisdiction of the Court as a move toward the wider use of the Court.

International arbitration by special tribunals is not to be overlooked. There are various instances in which states have requested the President of the Court to assist in the selection of a member for an arbitral tribunal. Also the Permanent Court of Arbitration at the Hague, in essence a panel of arbitrators with a secretariat and certain rules of procedure, has provided facilities for such arbitrations between states. Both the President of the Court and the procedures of the Permanent Court of Arbitration have also assisted in the judicial settlement of international commercial transactions, in which one party is a state. These are all important inter-related procedures for the judicial settlement of controversies in the international sector.

It is also appropriate to mention the settlement of disputes between commercial enterprises of different nationalities. The voluntary use of arbitration by the parties to such disputes has been one of the most effective means of their settlement. However, broader use of this procedure has been handicapped by the absence of international agreements making such awards enforceable. There are now thirty-one states parties to a 1958 Convention on the Recognition and Enforcement of Foreign Arbitral Awards. Accession to this Convention by the United States without further delay is likely to add to its effectiveness.

Ensuring the Availability of Skilled Mediators

Through mediation and conciliation the skills and, indeed, the art of a disinterested individual (or body) can be brought to bear in a conflict situation. The mediator or conciliator can lead the parties toward stabilization and perhaps settlement. It is an obvious advantage to have available a group of persons of whose background something is known, who are available as mediators and conciliators. Such persons, usually recruited as need arises, have assisted each United Nations Secretary-General with his heavy negotiation load.

The Interim Committee, in its study of peaceful settlement, recommended the creation of a Panel for Inquiry and Conciliation. That proposal, as adopted by the General Assembly, provided for a list of persons nominated by governments but who might be called to act *in a personal capacity*. The United States has let its own nominations expire. The Panel has only been used on one occasion. Nominations to this Panel by governments have been uneven in quality.

We recommend that the Panel receive added emphasis in the organizational structure of the United Nations. The Panel should be reconstituted with appointments made by the Secretary-General rather than by member states. Appointments to the Panel could be for two or three years, with those appointed indicating in advance an intention, if possible, to be available for missions of mediation or conciliation—at the call of the Secretary-General, the Security Council, or the General Assembly. The Panel could be limited to thirty persons in any one year. Appointments to the Panel should be from those who have already demonstrated their skill in dispute settlement and who, as a result of these and other activities, have been given responsibilities involving public leadership and trust. The presidents of the five preceding General Assemblies should each year be ex-officio members of the Panel. The members of the Panel would meet once each year with the Secretary-General to consider measures for improving the ongoing peaceful settlement activities of the UN.

No single institutional development can fully contain the resources of the United Nations community for pacific settlement. But the reconstituted Panel could provide a resource of experienced personnel and a continuing focus for UN considerations in this field. Its formation, the availability of its members for important assignments, and its annual meeting, would help in keeping the attention of the international community centered on the possibility, and the necessity, of dispute settlement. The arrangements for the annual meeting of the Panel might be made, at the Secretary-General's request, by the UN Institute for Training and Research.

Continuing Study of the Art of Mediation

Mediation is an art which, when combined with certain indefinable elements of trust in the mediator and effective support from the institutional setting, facilitates conflict settlement. But an art can be learned, and experience in pursuing it can usually be transmitted to others. This has proved to be the case in industrial and other disputes within national communities. To a more limited extent it has proved true in international disputes.

There is some evidence, confirmed by those with successful experience in resolving disputes in the national and international communities, that the dispute settlement process does involve a series of steps that can be defined with some precision.

It is clear, however, that additional analysis of the dispute settlement process is needed. It is an area in which the variables are legion, and in which the analysis must constantly be tested against the experience of those who have been most successful in the field. There clearly are no easy answers. The sharing of experience and skills should be accelerated, in a setting in which lessons for the future can be learned.

New Approaches

We recommend a continuing dialogue between the government official and the academic community. In particular, we urge a critical examination of some of the premises involving the functioning of international organization in peaceful settlement. Several implicit assumptions might upon examination be found to deserve reformulation:

• That international cooperation in non-political activities leads to cooperation in political activities;

• That the principle of the self-determination of peoples is a norm of the United Nations Charter and stands for the legitimacy of peaceful change;

• That the history of controversies in the United Nations shows that there have been holding operations and controls, but no peaceful, i.e., long-term settlements, except perhaps in the cases of Indonesia, Greece, and Iran;

• That economic development produces political stability;

• That time and delay in international conflicts are likely to have a cooling-off effect;

• That the absence of the People's Republic of China from

United Nations membership limits the range of controversies the UN may be expected to adjust;

• That the structure and procedures of the United Nations, including the notion of peaceful change, represent largely Western conceptual thinking. This might involve comparative studies of the approach of non-Western cultures to conflict resolution and peaceful change in their national law and administration.

We urge also consideration of the social system and how conflict resolution forms part of the system. One concept of research on conflict in relation to a social system has been developed by Kenneth Boulding, who summarized it as follows:

The problem of stable peace is a problem in social systems, yet we persist in trying to solve it as if it were a problem in physical systems, in weapons, in armament, and in things which are merely the parameters of social systems. We have a prejudice, perhaps, against scientific research into social systems because we feel that we understand them already, that all we need is the wisdom of the politician or the diplomat or the State Department official. Unfortunately, the systems have been changing too rapidly for wisdom, for wisdom is based upon the experience of earlier years, and the system of earlier years on which this wisdom is based has totally passed away.

Some specifics of such research might include:

• Dynamics of communications systems in international relations;
• The psychological aspects of pacific settlement, including public opinion surveys;
• The use of models and simulation techniques to improve the decision-making process.

We do not attempt to make a recommendation here on the most effective method of communication between the decision-maker and the academic community. The general purpose would be to make it possible for the busy Government official to do more than skim academic literature. The experience of the Arms Control and Disarmament Agency and the Department of Defense has led to a degree of continual conceptual thinking, often using the device of the fifty-page or longer study in depth and the three-page summary. Perhaps when the State Department has an investment in the particular study, its officials may be likely to turn to it. Moreover, this sort of collaboration can be expected to provide a reservoir in the academic community of people suitable for special government missions.

Whether the newly created Foreign Affairs Research Council will play such a role depends on the extent to which it will provide a relation of give-and-take with Government decision-makers contributing to a dialogue. Reporting and condensation would not necessarily provide this role. Perhaps the National War College and the Foreign Service Institute might also be parties to such dialogue. Within the United Nations the dialogue could be conducted through the facilities of the new Institute for Training and Research.

RECOMMENDATIONS

We make the following recommendations:

1. That the United States support the position that all states, including those not members of the United Nations, have a responsibility (a) to resort to measures of peaceful settlement before initiating the use of force in disputes in which they are involved and (b) to continue to pursue efforts at peaceful settlement even after embarking upon a justified use of force.
2. That more frequent use be made of commissions whose sole or initial responsibility would be to ascertain the facts and to report them to the political organ.
3. That more frequent use be made in UN organs and committees of rapporteurs who would attempt to achieve a consensus of view and report this to the organ or committee involved.
4. That the United States propose to the General Assembly that it reconstitute its Panel on Inquiry and Conciliation, with appointments made by the Secretary-General of an outstanding group of approximately thirty individuals with extensive experience in mediation and conciliation. The members of the panel would be appointed for two or three year terms and would have indicated their willingness, if possible, to be available to the Secretary-General, to the Security Council, or to the General Assembly for missions of fact-finding, of mediation, and of conciliation. Each year the presidents of the preceding five General Assemblies would be ex-officio members of the Panel. The members of the Panel

would meet once each year with the Secretary-General to consider measures for improving the ongoing peaceful settlement activities of the UN.

5. That greater flexibility be introduced into the UN's mediation process by avoiding a strict timetable for reports by those who have been assigned mediation and conciliation responsibilities.

6. That the political organs, and in particular the Security Council, make more frequent use of that provision of Article 37 of the Charter which permits recommendations for settlement to be made to the parties in dispute.

7. That the United States withdraw its self-judging reservation to its acceptance of the compulsory jurisdiction of the International Court of Justice.

8. That continuing emphasis and study be given to the procedures and conceptual framework of conflict resolution by peaceful means, drawing on the data of historical research, considering the potentialities of the United Nations and the approaches of the social sciences, with a view to providing insights and perspectives to parties involved in international disputes.

9. That in such study there be a continuing dialogue between those in the Department of State with responsibility for policy decisions and those outside, especially in the academic community, engaged in this common undertaking.

THE COMMITTEE ON PEACEFUL
SETTLEMENT OF DISPUTES

Peacekeeping Operations

The primary goal sought by the United States is to strengthen the peacekeeping capacity of the United Nations. The great majority of member states share this objective. It is vitally important to be able to act through the United Nations to control actual or impending violence, while the forces of peaceful settlement are strengthened. We agree with the Secretary-General that the peacekeeping operations of the United Nations, "however improvised and fumbling," must be developed "to deal with the sudden antagonisms and dangers of our world, until we can evolve more permanent institutions."

There is complete agreement by all on the Security Council's primary responsibility for maintaining peace and security. That position could be re-emphasized by an undertaking that all cases threatening the peace should first be considered by the Council; that if raised in the Assembly, that body should promptly refer them to the Council for action. Beyond this, it does not seem either wise or desirable to lay down detailed procedures in any rigid formula.

If the Security Council proves unable to act in a matter that appears seriously to threaten the peace, and if the majority of members are concerned to continue effort through the Organization to bring the threat under control, the General Assembly must remain able to do what it can in the situation. Where a conflict appears less urgently threatening, time may well permit the Assembly to refer it back to the Council for further consideration on the basis of the former's recommendations. But this must result from the Assembly's decision in a particular case, not from curtailment of its authority to recommend to the members directly.

The preponderant majority of members share this view of the Assembly's limited competence in the maintenance of peace, including residual authority to recommend measures when the Council is unable to act for the peaceful adjustment on settlement of disputes or situations likely to lead to a breach of the peace. These complementary roles of Council and Assembly have been the basis for peacekeeping operations by the United Nations since its founding.

Since any significantly greater development of peacekeeping operations through the United Nations clearly depends on greater accord between the Soviet Union and the majority of states on this point, the General Assembly should continue the endeavor to define the complementary relations between the two major organs. Nonetheless, a formal compromise seems unlikely in the near future. Should the Security Council prove unable to act in a serious crisis, whether the case is taken up in the Assembly will probably continue to depend—as it has in the past—more on the extent of the membership's willingness to support a specific international action, than on opposing constitutional arguments. In this connection, it is vital that the United States seek through all available channels a clearer understanding among the permanent members of the Security Council on the authorization and financing of future peacekeeping operations.

Peacekeeping in the Total Pacific Settlement Process

The record of United Nations peacekeeping operations shows that they have been more successful in bringing a halt to violent outbreaks than in leading to final solution of the underlying political conflict that caused the original breakdown of peace, which is the ultimate goal of all such operations.

The explosion between India and Pakistan in 1965, after nineteen years of an unstable cease-fire "observed" by a United Nations Mission, resembles in this respect the breakdown of peace in Egypt in 1956, seven years after the Palestine armistice agreements and the establishment of the Truce Supervision Organization. The more recent operation in Cyprus, which from the start combined political conciliation with a peace-supervising Force, has similarly failed to bring real progress toward settlement. The same limitation applies to civilian peacekeeping missions as well: in Borneo (where a fact-finding group ascertained that the local majority favored federation in Malaysia), Indonesia failed to carry through its undertaking of peaceful settlement on the basis of that finding.

Where such groups or other United Nations "presences" have successfully completed their missions—as in Lebanon and Jordan in 1958, or in West Iran in 1963—it has been because they were reinforced by other diplomatic forces strong enough collectively to bring about political settlement of the underlying dispute.

This is not to be construed as criticism of the peacekeeping operations; it is simply to recognize a limitation inherent in their nature as impartial, third-party elements in the total settlement process. When the parties in conflict, or outside supporters of one or another side, have sought to hamper the functioning of a peacekeeping group or to turn it into a partisan operation—as occurred most notably in the Congo—its purpose is frustrated and its effectiveness diminished. A better understanding of this limitation on *all* pacific settlement actions, and of the need for going beyond the temporarily calming result of instituting a peacekeeping mission, is essential for greater success in attaining the real goal of all peacekeeping operations, which is settlement, not merely pacification.

Preparation for Future Operations

So long as the United Nations is charged with these various kinds of peacekeeping activities, it should obviously have the men, matériel and money necessary to carry them out. This goal is accepted by the great majority of members, but they have been less than prompt in producing the means needed to accomplish the mandates they have set the Organization.

There is no serious problem in finding individuals or small groups for minor peacekeeping missions (either from the Secretariat or seconded by governments), nor in meeting their expenses (either through the budget or by agreement of the parties in conflict). But on every occasion when serious violence has appeared to threaten peace and to require a relatively large peacekeeping operation, and the members have agreed on its establishment, it has been necessary to organize and deploy the group almost from scratch. Especially since the Suez crisis, every such operation has also led to proposals for improving United Nations readiness to handle the next emergency.

The needs are obvious, on the part of both the members and the Organization. The governments should hold ready, under a flexible call-up system, men, equipment, supplies, and facilities of kinds and in quantities likely to be needed by the United Nations for such operations. As the nature of future calls cannot be foretold, the more extensive the types of skills and equipment available, the better. Among more obvious needs will be demands for technically trained observers, military police, engineers, medical and relief services, and so forth. At this stage it would be better to have such personnel available for call-up, rather than to establish some more formalized, standing organ that may not meet the particular need of the next operation.

To plan, organize and conduct peacekeeping operations in accordance with United Nations principles, the Secretary-General should have an adequate staff of military and political advisers at Headquarters, and properly detailed and organized information on the men, material, and logistical support available at any time. Then, on appropriate decision of either the Security Council or the Assembly, the fielding of a peacekeeping operation even on a fairly large scale would not be the *ad hoc* performance it always has been.

Experience has shown the need for such intelligent preparations. Yet it has also demonstrated that in contemporary conditions of world conflict only an emergency situation, when fear of action outside the Organization becomes greater than fear of action through it, produces enough international consensus to support a large peacekeeping operation. Once that period is over, the interest of governments lags if the operation goes well, or differences develop among them over the operation itself (as in the Congo). In either case, national willingness to cooperate in the short run is not followed by equal willingness to make commitments for unspecified future undertakings.

Nonetheless, a small group of middle powers—led by Canada and the Scandinavians—have set admirable precedents, both in earmarking some of their own forces for future international needs, and in cooperating among themselves and with the Secretary-General to improve readiness for future United Nations undertakings. Informal conferences in Oslo and Ottawa have set the example for widening the exchange of experience and the standards of preparatory measures. We believe that wider participation by more countries in these preparatory arrangements is desirable in order to enhance the truly international character of future operations. More could and should be done on a similarly informal basis. The Secretariat and members with peacekeeping experience could prepare documentation and studies on numerous phases of such operations, especially on those which differ most from equivalent national undertakings.

The political characteristics of a peacekeeping operation are such that it is normally conducive to its pacifying aim if the great powers are kept out of the exercise. For this reason, troop contributions by any permanent Security Council member are normally excluded. But the United States has provided essential logistical and financial support to most peacekeeping missions, and has also undertaken to do the same in future. Moreover, authority already exists in the Foreign Assistance Act (P.L. 87-195, Sec. 505) for the U.S. Government to furnish military assistance to enable another country "to participate in collective measures requested by the United Nations" to maintain or restore international peace. We feel that use should be made of this authority to help broaden the participation of members in preparatory arrangements.

Great Britain has announced that it will maintain in readiness certain facilities; and in the peculiar circumstances of Cyprus, British troops form part of the United Nations Force. East-West suspicions are probably still too deep, however, to permit involvement by U.S. troop contingents—even of technical elements only—in any on-scene military operations. We commend the idea of a broader and more specific commitment of the Military Air Transport Service, as proposed by a group of Republican Congressmen, to "permanent call . . . for the transport of men and matériel in any United Nations peacekeeping operations." Other transportation facilities might also be specified, and possibly various types of equipment.

The commitment of national governments to international undertakings in the peace and security field, it must be admitted, is still weak, as demonstrated in the reluctance of governments to pay even for the ones they approve. Also, the commitments that are made for call-up forces and facilities are subject to the willingness of each government on each occasion to fulfill its general undertaking. Both approval of the operation in question, and the absence of any more compelling national need for the earmarked men or resources, are necessary before the call of the UN will be heeded.

Financing Peacekeeping Operations

The long-run goal is to have United Nations operations financed on the basis of the principle of collective financial responsibility and through the budgetary procedures of the Organization. This would be in line with our interpretation of the Charter; but it need not mean that all peacekeeping assessments should be apportioned on a single scale. By the same justification for basing the graduated income tax on a sliding scale, relatively costly peacekeeping activities might be allocated on the basis of a special scale.

To some extent, the same effect has been gained by virtue of the method of regular budget allocations combined with generous voluntary contributions from the United States and other governments that have actively supported the Organization's operations; but ideally it would be more satisfactory to regularize the situation. This would not only require all governments recognized to be in arrears to meet their earlier obligations; it would also require Congress to remove the rigid one-third limitation it has set on the portion of the United Nations budget that the U.S. delegates may commit this country to contribute without further authorization. Acceptance of such a degree of collective responsibility is clearly not yet in sight; but the United States should give every support by its own actions to those other members who regularly and voluntarily accept their share of all peacekeeping costs.

It is politically understandable, although regrettable, that the United States placed itself on record before the Special Peacekeeping Committee as reserving "the option to make exceptions" in supporting United Nations operations "if, in our view, strong and compelling reasons exist for doing so." From the beginning the United

States has given powerful support to the United Nations. Indeed, without that support the Organization would have failed. The "privilege" we ask for is at its expense. Based upon our national record and the strong coincidence of interest of the United States and the United Nations, it may be assumed that we will seldom, if ever, resort to this privilege. But the reservation shook the faith of the faithful and encouraged those seeking easy ways to avoid their responsibilities.

The political views supporting this reservation stem in part from the assumption that the United States is paying "more than its share" of the expenses of the Organization, which in turn are becoming "burdensome." On the first count, it is important to note that more than a dozen countries make a larger contribution in terms of their individual capacity to pay than does the United States. On the second, United Nations costs can in no sense be regarded as burdensome. They are trivial in comparison with defense costs and those incurred in direct military action. For this reason, we do not feel that it would be out of order for the United States to contribute something like $25 million toward meeting the current deficit of the Organization. The time and manner of so doing might be decided in light of actions taken by the Soviet Union and France.

It is not only inefficient, it is unseemly, for the Secretary-General to have to go hat-in-hand to members in order to obtain the necessary financing for actions those members have authorized. Even though most peacekeeping missions may for the time being have to be paid for on a voluntary basis, it would be both fairer and probably more effective if the necessary fund-raising for especially costly operations were made the responsibility of a special committee of members. A large and representative group should be established for this purpose by joint action of the Security Council and General Assembly. It would then be available when needed in support of undertakings authorized by either organ, and could serve in an advisory capacity to the Secretary-General on financial matters.

RECOMMENDATIONS

We make the following recommendations:

1. That the United States continue to support the view that within the United Nations matters relating to threats to the peace should

first be considered by the Security Council—which has primary but not exclusive responsibility for the maintenance of peace—and continue also to support the complementary roles of the Security Council and General Assembly in the authorization and conduct of peacekeeping operations.

2. That the United States encourage greater efforts to improve political coordination and smoother working relationships between the United Nations and regional organizations.

3. That the United States encourage a more widespread acceptance of true third-party attitudes in the peacekeeping functions of the United Nations and greater utilization by members and by the Organization of third parties in mediatory, conciliatory, and all other forms of peacekeeping efforts.

4. That the United States continue to encourage the initiative of other members in making armed forces units available under a flexible call-up system for United Nations operations, and in increasing regular exchanges of information among themselves and with the Organization in order to improve the utilization of such units.

5. That the United States offer, to countries interested in making such preparations to participate in United Nations peacekeeping activities but having inadequate resources of their own, the military and financial assistance already available under its foreign aid legislation for the training or equipment of such units.

6. That the United States extend its initiative in pledging logistical support to the United Nations by making its commitment more specific and by a continuing exchange of information with other members and the Secretariat.

7. That the United States explore, in appropriate consultation with governments in whose countries its overseas bases lie, the possible use of those bases in connection with United Nations peacekeeping operations.

8. That the United States encourage the Secretariat and members with peacekeeping experience to prepare and make available documentation and studies on all aspects of such operations, in par-

ticular for the benefit of governments pledging troop units and other support for future peacekeeping operations.

9. That the United States encourage the Secretary-General to strengthen the fact-gathering capacity of the Organization in relation to its problems in peacekeeping, in particular by strengthening his staff of military advisers.

10. That the United States seek to strengthen the role of the Secretary-General in the management of peacekeeping operations by such means as insisting on greater precision in Security Council and General Assembly resolutions and by encouraging the use of advisory committees to assist him on policy matters.

11. That the United States encourage universal financial support of peacekeeping operations by members and avoid, by its own example, making exceptions in support of particular operations.

12. That the United States encourage the United Nations to charge an appropriate committee with the study of alternative plans for financing peacekeeping, with special emphasis on non-obligatory apportionment of costs by means of a special scale and a peace fund.

13. That the United States propose the establishment by joint action of the Security Council and General Assembly of a widely representative committee of members to raise funds, when necessary, for special peacekeeping purposes.

14. That the United States, when time and circumstances seem favorable, make a contribution on the order of $25 million to assist in restoring the solvency of the Organization.

THE COMMITTEE ON
PEACEKEEPING OPERATIONS

3. Developing International Law

Law is a touchstone and a measure of civilization. Among nations, as among men, devotion to the methods of law and adherence to its commands are indispensable elements in a public order that encourages material progress and promotes essential human values.

Within the nations of the world, the level of adherence to the rule of law which men have achieved—in their private affairs and in government—is an unfailing indication of the stage of advancement their nation has achieved. In the world arena, the history of the development of international law is a chronicle of the struggle to civilize international society and to make it serve the true needs and purposes of mankind.

If the processes by which law is developed and applied are neglected—if adherence to the rule of law is not adequately cultivated—all efforts to achieve progress in international affairs must surely fall short of the mark.

Public attention is constantly focused on the failures and breakdowns of law in the international arena. And it must be recognized that the processes of law remain weakest in the very areas, such as peacekeeping, which are most important to us all. On the other hand, it is clear that international law is a growing force in world affairs, and that, indeed, there has occurred in the last twenty years an explosive growth in transnational law and in the contacts, processes and procedures by which it is made and applied. This growth gives ground for hope that the nations of the world will learn in time to subject all their relations with each other to the moderating and civilizing force of such law. It is our task to determine what immediate steps the United States should take to ensure that it makes the most effective possible contribution to that end.

Progress in all major fields of cooperation requires an enabling framework of law. To avoid duplication, we focus attention here on proposals for advancing the rule of law itself.

We recognize that the cause of international law may be served by cooperation among nations in solving common legal problems of a domestic nature. It is toward the international development of law—and not exclusively of international law—that the following recommendations are directed.

The Connally Amendment

In its declaration accepting the compulsory jurisdiction of the International Court of Justice the United States has reserved therefrom "disputes with regard to matters which are essentially within the domestic jurisdiction of the United States of America *as determined by the United States of America.*" The italicized words constitute the so-called Connally Amendment.

It has been the consistent and avowed policy of the United States that international disputes should be settled by peaceful means. One such means is the resolution of international disputes by the International Court of Justice, the judicial organ of the United Nations. Accordingly the United States accepted the compulsory jurisdiction of the Court. We are of the view, however, that its acceptance is belittled in the eyes of other nations by the Connally Amendment. The Amendment enables the United States, in every international dispute brought before the International Court of Justice to which the United States is a party, to decide unilaterally whether the dispute falls within the terms of its declaration accepting the Court's compulsory jurisdiction.

We believe that the United States in deleting the Connally Amendment would be making an important contribution to international acceptance of the principle that the rule of law should govern the settlement of disputes between nations. A willingness on the part of the United States to permit the International Court of Justice to decide for itself what are essentially matters of domestic jurisdiction would encourage other nations to follow the same course.

It is also believed that this would be in the national interest of the United States. At the present time, under the principle of reciprocity, the Connally Amendment can be used by any other state which is brought before the Court by the United States to oust the Court of jurisdiction. Deletion of the Amendment would permit the United States to use the Court to resolve disputes with those states which have accepted equal obligations regarding the Court's compulsory jurisdiction.

The United States has also reserved from its declaration accepting the Court's compulsory jurisdiction "disputes arising under a multilateral treaty unless (1) all Parties to the treaty affected by the decision are also Parties to the case before the Court, or (2) the United States of America specially agrees to jurisdiction." The United States is a party to numerous multilateral international agreements. It will seldom be the case in such situations that all States will be parties to litigation before the Court involving multilateral treaties. The multilateral treaty reservation therefore operates in its practical effect to preclude the Court from exercising its statutory power to pass upon treaty disputes involving the United States where the treaty is multilateral. The deletion by the United States of this reservation will further demonstrate its faith in the International Court of Justice as a vehicle for the settlement of international legal disputes.

Legal Assistance to New Nations

Effective international cooperation requires that new nations should have an adequate legal system and a strong legal profession. These are vast undertakings and require the services of experts in various fields of law. Many of the new countries understandably do not have the necessary legal expertise.

We believe that the United States can do much in this regard. While private agencies in the United States are active in the field, their activities should be supplemented by the Federal Government. We suggest for consideration the creation of a separately funded Federal program to meet the need. The operation of the program should be the responsibility of one or more qualified private agencies under contract with the Federal agency designated to administer the appropriated funds.

We envisage that each contracting private agency would survey the legal assistance needs of interested foreign countries and seek to meet them in one or more of the following ways:

(a) enable qualified members of the legal profession in this country (including scholars, administrators, and practicing lawyers) to accept invitations to temporary posts at foreign law schools and law centers;

(b) on request, locate and in exceptional cases finance opportunities for advanced or specialized training here for legal personnel from those foreign countries;

(c) receive, evaluate and refer, or in appropriate cases and as necessary, fill requests for legal materials needed in such countries.

Exchange of Government Lawyers

While there have been exchange programs between the United States and other countries involving private lawyers, we are unaware of any exchange program involving government lawyers. We believe that such a program would contribute to international cooperation and uniformity in the legal field and would further the development of international law.

Lawyers engaged in government work and state and Federal judges develop a specialized knowledge and skill in the administration of public law. Many countries have common public law problems the solution of which might well be assisted by first hand observation of how these problems are handled by other countries. We therefore recommend the establishment on an experimental basis of an exchange program of U.S. Government lawyers and judges and their counterparts in other countries. It is contemplated that the participants in the program would function principally as observers. We recognize, of course, that security considerations are a factor in some areas of government work. The program therefore would be confined to areas which do not involve security considerations.

A United Nations Law Reporter System

We believe that a substantial impediment to the development of a broadly based international law is the inaccessibility of many of the legal materials upon which such a development must be founded. This, of course, is not true with respect to matters governed by treaties. On the other hand, many aspects of international law are not covered by treaties. As to these aspects, evidence of the views of various states, as reflected in their respective practices, has not yet been made widely and readily available. The problem is not merely that there are too few translations of basic documents into other languages, but that there are serious deficiencies in the available documentation.

International law outside of the treaty field develops largely through the convergence of practices on the part of states. But those practices must first be stated, explained and publicized. Hitherto, this task has been largely performed by a small number of Western states. The statements of international law best known to the world today still bear their imprimatur. The development of an international law recognized in all quarters to be universal will require vast cooperative efforts on the part of all nations.

The present recommendation is submitted with a view to encouraging such an effort. The United Nations, acting in cooperation with the governments of individual nations, is a suitable instrument for the undertaking. What is required is a systematic compilation and digest of materials which reveal the existing practices of states, supplemented by periodic reports on current developments in the field. We contemplate that each government would be asked to submit evidence of its own practices for inclusion in the periodic and cumulative reports. These materials would be translated into various languages and made available to governments, libraries, and scholars throughout the world. The reporter system of compilations and digest could be developed, maintained on an up-to-date basis and disseminated worldwide by the use of modern technology. Available government and university expertise could aid in this program.

We recognize that particular states may not always be prepared to state their own positions on matters of international law. The proposed United Nations Reporter System would nonetheless provide helpful legal points of view and practices already adopted by many states. By setting forth in systematic form the cumulative legal experience of states willing to contribute, the United Nations Reporter System would encourage the emergence of a universal legal consensus, and would thereby contribute significantly to the development of international law.

The United Nations and the World Bank Arbitration Conventions

The United Nations Arbitration Convention of 1958 and the recent World Bank Convention on the Settlement of Investment Disputes reflect an increasing reliance on the legal device of arbitration for settling disputes. The United States has not signed the UN Arbitration Convention; it has signed the World Bank Convention. We believe that ratification by the United States of both conventions would constitute a progressive step in the development of international law.

The UN Convention would, in essence, require the courts of one state to recognize and enforce arbitral awards made in the territory of another state. Although the Convention is not limited to commercial disputes, it authorizes reservations by a state so as to limit the application of the Convention to awards which it considers to have arisen from commercial matters.

The World Bank Convention would establish an autonomous international institution, to be known as the International Centre for Settlement of Investment Disputes. The Centre would maintain panels of impartial conciliators and arbitrators to settle disputes which both parties—a state and a national of another state—have consented to submit to the Jurisdiction of the Centre. An arbitral tribunal constituted under the provisions of the Convention would be required to apply the law agreed upon by the parties. Every contracting state would be required to recognize the award of such a tribunal as binding and to enforce it as if it were a final decision of a domestic court.

At the present time, the enforceability of international arbitral awards is uncertain, mainly because of discrepancies in the controlling law of various jurisdictions. The basic obligation of each state to recognize international arbitral awards as binding and to enforce them in accordance with its usual rules of procedure, is a major advance in international law which these conventions would effect.

We believe, moreover, that the United States could meet the obligations imposed under both conventions without disrupting Federal-state relationships through the enactment of appropriate implementing of Federal legislation based largely on the commerce clause of the Constitution. Such legislation would give the Federal courts exclusive jurisdiction over the recognition and enforcement of arbitral agreements and awards covered by either convention, and allow a defendant who properly raised the issue in an action brought in a state court to remove the case to a Federal court which would be empowered to stay the state court proceeding.

The Consular Convention with the Soviet Union

From the standpoint of the development of international law, the proposed U.S.–U.S.S.R. Consular Convention, now pending before the Senate for its advice and consent to ratification, is particularly significant for its "notification and access" provision. Each government would be obliged to notify the other within three days of the arrest of any of its citizens and to afford access by officials of his government to the arrested person within four days of arrest.

A developing feature of international law is the right of citizens of one state in the territory of another to have the protection of their governments in the event that they are subjected to arrest. Recognition of this right by the governments of the two most powerful states would represent an important step in the advance of international law and could lead to other advances on the part of each in their relations with the other.

Ratification of the Convention would redound especially to the benefit of the United States. The United States has frequently encountered difficulties in trying to aid American citizens who have been arrested or detained in the Soviet Union. Last year, moreover, 20,000 American tourists went to the Soviet Union, compared with slightly over 1,000 Soviet citizens who came to the United States. The United States therefore has more to gain than lose, practically speaking, from a provision which accords legal protection to citizens of each country while traveling in the other.

It has been urged in some quarters that ratification of the Consular Convention would increase the capacity of the Soviet Union to conduct espionage in the United States. We note that the Secretary of State, in his testimony before the Senate Foreign Relations Committee on July 30, 1965, stated that the Consular Convention would not materially affect the problem of Communist espionage and subversion.

Court for the Adjudication of Lower-Level International Disputes

The absence of a simple, effective and readily accessible court to resolve lower-level international disputes is a significant defect in the present international legal system. Numerous disputes arise which are not considered important enough to be referred to the International Court of Justice. The structure and history of the International Court of Justice show that it was designed to handle only cases of the highest importance. The potential utility of a court to resolve these lower-level disagreements is suggested by the rapid expansion of the relations between states.

Such a court could handle certain disputes which are a cause of friction because they cannot readily be solved through diplomatic channels. A lower-level court would be of value to both legal and political officers of governments. The type of court envisaged would merit the respect of practicing lawyers. It should appeal to political officers because it would provide them with a practical optional means for resolving disputes which is not now available.

A formula for jurisdiction which would permit a realistic treatment of international disputes where informal methods of settlement are considered inadequate might therefore be as follows:

1. In disputes in which a settlement would involve a monetary or property transfer type result, there would exist a presumption that recourse would be had to the tribunal when one party considers that this means of settlement is appropriate, subject to non-concurrence by the other state.

2. In the case of disputes where a non-monetary or non-property transfer result would be involved, recourse could be had to the court if the parties so desired.

The distinction is the slight but significant presumption in the first category. It appears acceptable to introduce the slight pressure of such a presumption without seriously impeding the political judgment which is retained.

The most effective means by which a lower-level court structure could be created is probably by a multilateral treaty, which would set out the organization, jurisdiction and procedure of the court. At the start the number of judges should be small; other judges could be added later if desirable. Extreme care should be taken to assure the highest integrity and professional quality of judges.

A start could be made by the United States and friendly, neighboring states, such as Canada and Mexico. These states could draft a treaty establishing a court which could be easily expanded by adherences of other interested states. The structure and jurisdiction of the court should make it possible later for the court to handle cases not only between friendly neighboring states but also between a state and any other state.

Appeal from decisions of the lower court could be allowed if deemed desirable by the participating states. Various simple means for achieving appellate review can be envisaged. If states stress the importance of prompt settlement of disputes it might be thought sufficient for the court to serve, as does the International Court of Justice, as a court of first and final recourse. As a practical matter a sound court structure could function effectively with or without appeal arrangements.

The question of enforcing the judgments of the proposed court need not present a serious problem. A minimum inducement to compliance would be provided by state acceptance of the multi-lateral treaty creating the court. States would ratify such a treaty only if they felt that to do so was in their self-interest. Failure to abide by a court decision would risk suspension from the system. And even if implementation of a decision were refused, it would not be irreparable, since the state suffering from the grievance could turn to other available dispute-resolving devices. The time factor and the nature of the disputes suggest the desirability of relying on informal pressures to achieve compliance.

The establishment of a lower-level court system would be a first step in the development of a strong overall system. It would not interfere with the functioning of existing institutions but would complement their efforts by filling a gap in the present system. It could start out independent of the UN and International Court of Justice and later become linked with them if that proved to be desirable. The law to be applied by the court, the rules of procedure to be adopted, and other important points could be agreed upon in the treaty creating the court.

RECOMMENDATIONS

We make the following recommendations:

1. That the United States delete the Connally Amendment to its reservation to the declaration accepting the compulsory jurisdiction of the International Court of Justice and reservation regarding disputes involving multilateral treaties.
2. That the United States develop a program for legal assistance to new nations.
3. That the United States develop a program with other countries for exchange of government lawyers.
4. That the United States propose to the United Nations the estab-

lishment under UN auspices of an International Law Reporter System.

5. That the United States ratify the United Nations and the World Bank arbitration conventions.

6. That the United States ratify the Consular Convention with the Soviet Union.

7. That the United States endorse the establishment of a court for the adjudication of lower-level international disputes.

THE COMMITTEE ON
INTERNATIONAL LAW

4. *Protecting Human Rights*

The United States is now in a position to make a much stronger contribution than in the past to the development of international institutions and agreements for the protection of human rights. In the last two years this nation has made tremendous strides in the struggle for human equality and dignity. World attention has focused on our efforts. Our domestic successes have clearly strengthened our international capabilities, but they have also increased our international responsibilities. While building a Great Society at home and eradicating the last vestiges of discrimination in domestic law, the United States must at the same time take leadership in building a greater society of mankind directed to similar goals.

The Present Situation

1. New Situation in the Human Rights Field. In the area of human rights the American people face today many inter-related domestic and international issues. We have removed finally most of the domestic obstacles which have in the past prevented our active participation in international efforts to protect "human rights and fundamental freedoms for all without distinction as to race, sex, language, or religion." (Article 55 of the United Nations Charter.) Our foreign policy has regained freedom of action in the sphere of human rights, as we need no longer stand apart from the intensive work of the United Nations, its Specialized Agencies, and the regional organizations in Europe and America, which are all engaged in a valiant effort to protect all human beings against tyranny and injustice.

It was in this spirit that President Johnson, in his San Francisco speech commemorating the twentieth anniversary of the United Nations, expressed both his personal view and that of a great majority of the American people that "the world must finish once and for all the myth of inequality of races and peoples, with the scandal of discrimination, with the shocking violation of human rights and the cynical violation of political rights." Previously, in his speech at

Howard University he put it even more vividly: "In every corner of every continent men charged with hope contend with ancient ways in the pursuit of justice. They reach for the newest of weapons to realize the oldest of dreams—that each may walk in freedom and pride, stretching his talents, enjoying the fruits of the earth."

2. *Past U.S. Attitudes toward Human Rights.* This new attitude toward international endeavors in the field of human rights is in harmony with the position on the subject taken by the United States in the early years of the United Nations. U.S. statesmen were among the first ones to realize the close connection between peace and prosperity, on the one hand, and fundamental freedoms and human rights, on the other hand. In his prophetic vision, President Roosevelt in 1941 linked together the "Four Freedoms" in the following manner:

"In the future days, which we seek to make secure, we look forward to a world founded upon four essential human freedoms.

"The first is freedom of speech and expression—everywhere in the world.

"The second is freedom of every person to worship God in his way—everywhere in the world.

"The third is freedom from want—which, translated into world terms, means economic understandings which will secure to every nation a healthy peacetime life for its inhabitants—everywhere in the world.

"The fourth is freedom from fear—which, translated into world terms, means a worldwide reduction of armaments to such a point and in such a thorough fashion that no nation will be in a position to commit an act of physical aggression against any neighbor—anywhere in the world."

This same note was struck by President Truman at the closing session of the San Francisco Conference, when he pointed out that the Charter of the United Nations adopted at that Conference was not merely an agreement on diplomatic and military cooperation. It recognized that "the seeds of war are planted by economic rivalry and by social injustice," and provided machinery for correcting economic and social causes for conflict. In particular, he said, the Charter was "dedicated to the achievement and observance of human rights and fundamental freedoms. Unless we can attain those objectives for all men and women everywhere—without regard to race, language or religion—we cannot have permanent peace and security."

Similarly, in a speech before the General Assembly culminating her contribution to the drafting of the Universal Declaration of Human Rights, Mrs. Franklin D. Roosevelt indicated that this Declaration "must be taken as testimony of our common aspiration first voiced in the Charter of the United Nations to lift men everywhere to a higher standard of life and to a greater enjoyment of freedom. Man's desire for peace lies behind this declaration."

In a message to the United Nations Commission on Human Rights in 1953, President Eisenhower pointed out that: "People everywhere are seeking freedom—freedom to live, freedom from arbitrary restraint, freedom to think and speak as they wish, freedom to seek and find the truth. We must press ahead to broaden the areas of freedom. The United States is convinced that freedom is an indispensable condition to the achievement of a stable peace."

Our representative to the United Nations Commission on Human Rights at that time, Mrs. Oswald B. Lord, reminded the Commission that the United States since its inception has been dedicated to the advancement of human rights not only at home but also throughout the world. She added: "We recognize the fundamental and intrinsic importance of human rights; we have learned through bitter experience that systematic and deliberate denials of human rights have a direct relationship to the preservation of world peace. Peace and security cannot be assured in a world in which peoples who are denied their individual rights are pressed to resort to measures of violence against their oppressors. And the governments which violate the fundamental human rights of those whom they control cannot be expected to respect the rights of other members of the international community."

President Kennedy, in his speech at the American University on June 10, 1963, put stress on the fact that "peace and freedom walk together," and peace is, "in the last analysis, basically a matter of human rights." Adlai E. Stevenson, the U.S. representative in the United Nations, speaking to the Commonwealth Club in San Francisco in April, 1964, painted a picture of a new, more hopeful world "in which fundamental issues of human rights, which have been hidden in closets down the long corridor of history, are out in the open and high on the agenda of human affairs."

3. *Other Statements on Human Rights.* Others agree with our statesmen on the inter-relationship between peace and human rights. Dag Hammarskjöld once noted that: "We know that the question of peace and the question of human rights are closely related. With-

out recognition of human rights we shall never have peace, and it is only within the framework of peace that human rights can be fully developed."

In the great Encyclical "Pacem in Terris" by Pope John XXIII, references to human rights and world peace are effectively interwoven. He considered as the fundamental objective of the public authority of the world community "the recognition, respect, safeguarding and promotion of the rights of the human person"; he added that "peace will be but an empty-sounding word unless it is based on . . . an order founded on truth, built according to justice, verified and integrated by charity, and put into practice in freedom."

4. United Nations Basic Statements on Human Rights. It is quite fitting, therefore, that the Universal Declaration of Human Rights starts with the statement that "recognition of the inherent dignity and of the equal and inalienable rights of all members of the human family is the foundation of freedom, justice and peace in the world."

The thought was elaborated in the "Uniting for Peace" Resolution in 1950, in which the General Assembly not only established new machinery for maintaining peace but also pointed out that "enduring peace will not be secured solely by collective security arrangements against breaches of international peace and acts of aggression, but that a genuine and lasting peace depends also upon . . . respect for and observance of human rights and fundamental freedoms for all and on the establishment and maintenance of conditions of economic and social well-being in all countries."

5. Human Rights and Peace and Economic Progress. In summarizing these ideas, one can note, in the first place, the general agreement that peace and human rights can no longer be separated. The Nazis and their Axis allies had to suppress liberties at home before they were able to engage in foreign conquests. Since World War II, only those major powers which did not grant fundamental freedoms to their citizens have engaged in conquests and in the subversion of their neighbors. The Western democracies, on the other hand, confronted with a rising tide of nationalism in Asia and Africa, relinquished their past conquests, recognized the right of self-determination, and granted independence to almost all colonial peoples with a minimum of bloodshed. Even in the democracies, however, human rights often suffer amidst preparations for a total war, and a nuclear war would destroy impartially both the free and the enslaved.

Secondly, even where there is no foreign subversion, freedom can flourish successfully only in conjunction with economic progress. As long as a majority of mankind is underfed, underhoused and underclothed, as long as the gap between the poor and the rich nations is increasing rather than decreasing, many suffering peoples will not place human rights high on their list of priorities. Progress in human rights and economic development must go hand in hand. As President Johnson said on August 29, 1965: "[As] the great Woodrow Wilson said of this country a half a century ago, 'We ask nothing for ourselves that we do not also ask for all humanity.' And we ask peace—peace and the real opportunity to help our neighbors to improve the quality of all of our lives, to enlarge the meaning of liberty for all, and to secure for all the rights and dignities intended for man by his Creator."

6. Present Issues in the Human Rights Field. If peace can be maintained in the world, and if a vigorous effort can be made to improve the economic and social conditions in the developing areas of the world, there still will be special problems to be solved with respect to human rights.

Among the basic issues facing the United States in the field of international protection of human rights today are the following:

a. Should we be satisfied with the Universal Declaration of Human Rights or should we assist in the drafting and putting into effect of additional instruments on human rights?

b. If new instruments on human rights are drafted, should they be comprehensive, combining in one document a large number of rights to be protected, or should they be limited to specific rights of special importance?

c. What should be the method of implementing human rights instruments? Are present institutions and procedures satisfactory or should they be improved and supplemented by new ones?

d. Should we concentrate on long-range educational programs, or should we deal also with current problems, with violations of human rights occurring in various countries?

e. If procedures are developed for dealing with current violations, should the right to complain be limited to governments or should it be extended to non-governmental organizations and individuals?

Some of these issues are more urgent than others; most of them relate to the work of the United Nations; but some occur also in a regional context, in connection with the relations between the

United States and the Atlantic Community and between the United States and Latin America. In the United Nations an important deadline has been imposed by a resolution of the General Assembly designating the year 1968, the twentieth anniversary of the Universal Declaration of Human Rights, as the International Year for Human Rights. The Economic and Social Council of the United Nations was requested by the General Assembly to suggest a list of goals in the field of human rights to be achieved by the United Nations by the end of 1968, and each of the goals thus suggested involves action by the United States as well.

7. *United Nations Goals.* The Economic and Social Council has urged, in the first place, that all member states should ratify by 1968 the principal conventions in the field of human rights which have been concluded under the auspices of the United Nations or of its Specialized Agencies. The seven conventions thus recommended for ratification deal with the following subjects: (a) slavery, slave trade, and institutions and practices similar to slavery; (b) forced labor; (c) discrimination in respect of employment and occupation; (d) equal remuneration for men and women workers for work of equal value (discrimination in salaries); (e) discrimination in education; (f) prevention and punishment of the crime of genocide; and (g) political rights of women.

None of these conventions has been ratified by the United States. The Genocide Convention was sent to the Senate in 1949; the Conventions on Slavery, Forced Labor and the Political Rights of Women were sent to the Senate in 1963; and the three conventions on discrimination have not yet been sent to the Senate at all. The Senate has taken no action on the four conventions pending before it.

It may be noted that the Genocide Convention has been ratified by more than sixty states. The other conventions have also been widely ratified. Three of the seven conventions here discussed were prepared by the International Labor Organization, which since 1919 has approved some 120 conventions. But the United States has ratified only seven labor conventions, compared to more than sixty ratifications by the United Kingdom and eighteen by the Soviet Union.

In submitting three conventions on human rights to the Senate in 1963, President Kennedy pointed out that "the fact that our Constitution already assures us of these rights does not entitle us to stand aloof from documents which project our own heritage on an international scale." He added that the "United States cannot afford to renounce responsibility for support of the very fundamentals which distinguish our concept of government from all forms of tyranny."

It is in the interest of the United States to have the standards embodied in the United Nations conventions on human rights adopted by as many countries around the world as possible. But it cannot exhort others to ratify these conventions, if it is not itself a party to them. A shift in U.S. attitude toward these conventions is likely to influence other nations to do the same. U.S. adherence to them would enable our Government to participate in international measures for their implementation. Should some other country violate the agreed standards, the United States would be entitled to complain in good faith about it to the competent international body only if the United States has itself accepted the obligations.

U.S. ratification of the principal international conventions on human rights would allow the United States to play a more active part in the preparation of future instruments. In the period 1953–1960 the United States lost much of its influence by announcing in advance that it was not going to ratify any conventions or covenants on human rights. This position was changed, however, in 1961, when the United States declared its support for the Convention on Consent to Marriage, Minimum Age of Marriage and Registration of Marriages. Since that time, the United States has taken an active part in the preparation of several declarations and conventions.

8. Additional Instruments in Preparation. The Economic and Social Council has also recommended that several other important instruments on human rights be completed or prepared by 1968. Among them the most comprehensive are the two covenants on human rights, one dealing with more than twenty civil and political rights (similar to those guaranteed by the Constitution of the United States), and the other dealing with some ten basic economic, social and cultural rights (such as the right to work and the right to education). The other proposed conventions and declarations relate to specific problems, such as racial discrimination, religious intolerance, freedom of information, discrimination in the matter of political rights, discrimination in relation to women, and the right of asylum.

The Economic and Social Council has recommended that, upon approval of these instruments by the General Assembly, all the members of the United Nations, including the United States, should implement or, where appropriate, ratify them by 1968. Without adequate advance preparation, the United States may find it difficult to comply with this recommendation of the Economic and Social Council, especially with respect to such an intricate instrument as the Covenant on Civil and Political Rights.

9. Refugees. Since the Evian Conference in 1938 the United States has played an active role in the various international organizations established to assist refugees—the Intergovernmental Committee on Refugees, the United Nations Relief and Rehabilitation Administration (UNRRA), the International Refugee Organization, and the United Nations Relief and Works Agency for Palestine Refugees. It has supported also the useful work of the High Commissioner for Refugees functioning under the auspices of the United Nations. But the United States has not ratified the two principal international conventions in this area, the 1951 Convention relating to the Status of Refugees and the 1954 Convention relating to the Status of Stateless Persons, the first of which has been ratified by more than forty states and the second of which has been ratified by almost twenty states. A declaration on the right of asylum is now being prepared by the United Nations, in order to provide additional protection to refugees.

Though the problem of European refugees is largely resolved, the refugee situation in Africa, Asia and the Middle East is constantly deteriorating. New efforts are needed to take care of the increasing numbers of refugees in those areas.

10. European Institutions for the Protection of Human Rights. Two regional arrangements for the protection of human rights are of special interest to the United States, the more sophisticated European one and the more informal inter-American one. In Europe, fifteen countries have ratified the European Convention on Human Rights prepared by the Council of Europe. In addition, ten European states have accepted the jurisdiction of the European Commission of Human Rights to receive petitions by individuals, and nine have recognized the compulsory jurisdiction of the European Court of Human Rights to render binding judgments in cases brought against a state by another state or by the Commission.

Despite close political, military and economic links to Europe, and a common tradition in the field of human rights, the United States has made no attempt to participate in this highly advanced system of protection of fundamental freedoms or to extend it to the whole Atlantic Community. In particular, no action has been taken by the parties to the North Atlantic Treaty to comply with Article 2 of that Treaty obliging them to strengthen "their free institutions by bringing about a better understanding of the principles upon which these institutions are founded." The best way to reach that understanding would have been to establish common institutions and procedures to safeguard the rights of their citizens.

11. Inter-American Protection of Human Rights. In the Organization of American States, the United States has accepted not only some basic principles for the protection of human rights but also some procedures for their implementation.

The Charter of the Organization of American States, adopted at Bogota in 1948, lists among its fundamental principles the political organization of the American states "on the basis of the effective exercise of representative democracy," proclaims the "fundamental rights of the individual without distinction as to race, nationality, creed or sex," and provides that each American state "shall respect the rights of the individual." The Bogota Conference adopted also a comprehensive "American Declaration of Rights and Duties of Man," defining in a general fashion twenty-seven rights and ten duties. To implement this Declaration, the Santiago Meeting of Consultation of Ministers of Foreign Affairs established in 1959 an Inter-American Commission on Human Rights, "charged with furthering respect for such rights." As requested by that Meeting of Consultation, the Inter-American Council of Jurists prepared a more detailed Draft Convention on Human Rights, which contains also provisions for an Inter-American Court of Human Rights.

The Inter-American Commission on Human Rights has not only made general studies but has also examined cases of violations of human rights in several American states. Despite its limited terms of reference, the Commission was able to devise procedures for studying petitions, conducting hearings and even investigating on the spot (for instance, in the Dominican Republic in 1965). It adopted several highly critical reports, including those on Cuba (in 1962 and 1963), the Dominican Republic (1962), and Haiti (1963). The Commission also prepared a draft of an Inter-American Convention on Freedom of Expression, Information and Investigation. A Special Committee of the Council of the Organization of American States prepared in 1959 a Draft Convention on the Effective Exercise of Representative Democracy, and this subject is now being studied also by the Inter-American Commission on Human Rights. On request of the governments concerned, the Organization of American

States also sent technical missions to observe elections in Costa Rica and the Dominican Republic in 1962, and in Nicaragua and Honduras in 1963.

The Inter-American Conference has on its agenda the broadening of the Inter-American protection of human rights, and it is necessary to clarify the U.S. position with respect to the various proposals to be discussed by that Conference, especially those relating to the Draft Convention on Human Rights and the future powers of the Inter-American Commission on Human Rights.

12. Implementation of the Right of Self-Determination. A basic human right, expressly mentioned in the Charter of the United Nations, is the right of peoples to self-determination. In 1960 the General Assembly adopted unanimously the Declaration on the Granting of Independence to Colonial Countries and Peoples, which not only provides for the exercise of the right of self-determination but also stipulates specificially that all states shall observe faithfully and strictly not only the Declaration on Colonialism but also the Universal Declaration on Human Rights. A year later the General Assembly established a Special Committee to watch over the implementation of the Declaration on Colonialism, and that Committee has been receiving petitions, holding hearings and, wherever possible, investigating the situation on the spot. The Fourth Committee of the General Assembly has also developed in recent years the practice of receiving petitions from non-self-governing territories and granting hearings to petitioners. This new practice constitutes an important departure from the prior policy of the United Nations that no organ of the United Nations should consider human rights petitions.

13. Racial Discrimination. In the field of racial discrimination the General Assembly has discussed several specific cases since its very beginning. It has considered the treatment of Indians in South Africa annually since its first session. In 1946 the General Assembly called on all the governments and responsible authorities "to put an immediate end to religious and so-called racial persecution and discrimination," and after condemning racial segregation (apartheid) in 1950, it started dealing with increasing vigor with the apartheid policy of South Africa. In 1962 the General Assembly called for economic sanctions against South Africa, and the Security Council actually imposed an arms embargo in 1963. After the unanimous adoption in 1963 of the Declaration on the Elimination of All Forms of Racial Discrimination, the General Assembly asked for reports on compliance not only from governments but also from specialized agencies and non-governmental organizations. Such reports were actually received in 1964 from thirty-four non-governmental organizations in consultative relation with the Economic and Social Council and from twelve national non-governmental organizations.

14. Human Rights Petitions. Since its establishment the United Nations has had to develop procedures for dealing with large numbers of communications concerning human rights which it receives from individuals and organizations in all parts of the world. The Commission on Human Rights was denied in 1947 the power to take any action with respect to such communications. A confidential list of communications alleging violations of human rights is presented annually to the Commission and is discussed at a private meeting. The United Nations Secretariat also sends copies of communications relating to a particular state to that state. The identity of the authors is not divulged to the Commission or the state concerned, except where the petitioners authorize such disclosure. Some states, though not bound to do so, nevertheless reply to the communications sent to them, and even notify the United Nations of the action taken to remedy the situation.

The United States should, in accordance with its own traditions, adopt a friendly attitude toward the right of petition. The right to complain to an appropriate international organization should not be limited to states, but should be granted also to international non-governmental organizations in a consultative status, to nationl organizations approved for that purpose by the Economic and Social Council, and to individuals. As was done in the European Convention on Human Rights, and was proposed by the United States in 1951, each state party to a human rights convention or covenant should be given a choice among several implementation clauses granting the right to bring a complaint to one or more of the groups listed above.

15. Implementation of Human Rights Covenants. The Third Committee of the General Assembly, after ten years of discussion, has agreed on the substantive provisions of the Covenants on Human Rights, and is embarking now on the study of the measures needed for implementing these Covenants. In its original drafts of the Covenants, the Commission on Human Rights provided only for a system of periodic reports with respect to the Covenant on Economic and Social and Cultural Rights, but made elaborate proposals on implementation for inclusion in the Covenant on Civil and Political Rights.

It envisaged for that Covenant a Human Rights Committee of nine persons serving not as government representatives but in their personal capacity, and a reference to the International Court of Justice, should the Committee reach no solution. It was suggested that the Committee should have jurisdiction over complaints by one state party to the Covenant against another state party, but should not deal with petitions by individuals or organizations. At one time the United States proposed a separate protocol extending the right to initiate proceedings to individuals, groups and organizations; however, that proposal was later withdrawn.

Various other suggestions have been presented for the enforcement of the Covenant. In particular, Uruguay has made several proposals for the establishment of an "Office of the United Nations High Commissioner (Attorney-General) for Human Rights." Under these proposals, the Attorney-General would have had the following powers: (a) to collect and examine information with regard to all matters relevant to the observance and enforcement of the Covenant; (b) to require states parties to submit periodic reports on the implementation of the provisions of the Covenant in the territories under their jurisdiction; (c) to conduct on-the-spot studies and inquiries on matters relating to the implementation of the Covenant; (d) to initiate consultations with a state party on any case or situation which, in his opinion, may be inconsistent with that state's obligations under the Covenant, and to make to that state such suggestions and recommendations as he may deem appropriate for the effective implementation of the Covenant; (e) to receive and examine complaints of alleged violations of the Covenant, submitted to him by individuals, groups of individuals, national and international non-governmental organizations and intergovernmental organizations; (f) if the complaints fulfill various requirements specified in the proposals, to conduct such preliminary investigation as he may consider appropriate, and to undertake negotiations with the state concerned; and (g) to refer the complaint to the Human Rights Committee, if negotiations fail, and to make submissions concerning it to the Committee, orally or in writing, as he may deem necessary. This proposal was designed to provide, as an alternative to direct petitions by individuals and organizations, a procedure channelling such petitions through an eminent public official representing the interests of the world community.

16. Periodic Reports. Without waiting for the adoption of the Covenants and of measures for their enforcement, the United Nations has developed a variety of procedures for promoting human rights. Since the very beginning of the United Nations, most members of the United Nations have been furnishing the Secretariat of the United Nations with information for the United Nations Yearbook of Human Rights. This information related to constitutional provisions, legislative and executive acts, and judicial decisions having a bearing on human rights. Additional information gathered directly by the Secretariat of the United Nations is also published in the Yearbook. In 1956 the Economic and Social Council, on the basis of a U.S. proposal, invited all members of the United Nations and the specialized agencies to report every three years on the developments and on progress achieved in the field of human rights, and on the measures taken to safeguard human liberty in their metropolitan and non-self-governing territories. The summaries of these reports, prepared by the Secretariat, are at present studied by a Committee on Periodic Reports on Human Rights appointed from among its membership by the Commission on Human Rights.

In 1965 the Economic and Social Council revised completely the procedure relating to periodic reports. Among other changes, it requested the Sub-Commission on Prevention of Discrimination and Protection of Minorities, which unlike the Commission on Human Rights is composed not of government representatives but of experts, to make an initial study of all the periodic reports, together with the comments on those reports received from non-governmental organizations in consultative status, and to submit comments and recommendations for the consideration of the Commission. The Commission of Human Rights was requested to appoint an *ad hoc* committee, composed of persons chosen from among its members (i.e., a committee of government representatives), for the study of the reports in the light of comments of the Sub-Commission (and of the Commission on Status of Women) and to submit to the Commission "comments, conclusions and recommendations of an objective character."

In order to enable the Sub-Commission on Prevention of Discrimination and Protection of Minorities to discharge the new functions and "to assure adequate representation to different regions, legal systems and cultures," the Council increased its membership from fourteen to eighteen. Further changes are contemplated by the Commission on Human Rights, which will consider a joint proposal by Costa Rica, India, Liberia, the Netherlands and the Philippines to change the name of the Sub-Commission to "Permanent Committee of Experts of the Commission on Human Rights," and to enlarge the powers of the new Committee by authorizing it "to undertake studies and submit reports and recommendations concerning any matter in the field of human rights and fundamental freedoms, as may be requested by the Commission on Human Rights and the Economic and Social Council."

Should these proposals be accepted, the United Nations would have at its disposal a committee of experts empowered to deal not only with prevention of discrimination and protection of minorities but also with all other problems relating to human rights. In its comments on the reports, this committee would be able to raise a number of important issues and to exert strong influence on the protection of human rights by the reporting nations. A committee of a similar kind exists in the International Labor Organization and its performance has met with considerable success.

17. United Nations High Commissioner for Human Rights. A suggestion was made by Mr. Jacob Blaustein in his Dag Hammarskjöld Memorial Lecture in 1963 that the General Assembly of the United Nations might appoint an independent personality as a United Nations High Commissioner for Human Rights who could assist the Commission on Human Rights in its review of periodic reports and perform other functions.

At the twentieth session of the General Assembly in 1965, Costa Rica presented an elaboration of this proposal, which provides that a High Commissioner be appointed by the General Assembly who "shall assist in furthering the realization of human rights and shall seek to secure the observance of the Universal Declaration of Human Rights." He would "advise and assist the Commission on Human Rights and other organs of the United Nations on the periodic and other reports, or submissions made by Governments, relating to human rights and such other matters as these bodies may request." At the request of any government, he would "render assistance and services, and shall report on such assistance and services, if it is so agreed with the Government or Governments concerned." Finally, he would make annual report to the General Assembly, and special reports in cases of urgency.

18. Human Rights Studies. Another proposal made by the United States in 1956 led the Economic and Social Council to authorize the Commission on Human Rights to prepare studies of specific rights and groups of rights with a view to making objective and general recommendations. The studies were to stress general developments, progress achieved and measures taken to safeguard human liberty. The first such study considered "the right of everyone to be free from arbitrary arrest, detention and exile," and an

elaborate report was submitted to the Commission by a special committee of four in 1962. A second study is now under way relating to
"the right of arrested persons to communicate with those whom it is
necessary to consult in order to ensure their defense." A series of
studies on discrimination has been authorized also by a separate resolution of the Economic and Social Council; studies have been completed with respect to discrimination in education, discrimination in
the matter of religious rights and practices, discrimination in the
matter of political rights, and "discrimination in respect of the right
of everyone to leave any country, including his own, and to return
to his country"; studies in preparation deal with "discrimination
against persons born out of wedlock," and with "equality in the administration of justice."

19. Human Rights Seminars. Finally, in order to enable governments to exchange their experience in solving or attempting to solve
certain problems concerning human rights, the United Nations has
been conducting regional seminars on various subjects, such as: the
protection of human rights in criminal law and procedure; judicial
and other remedies against illegal exercise or abuse of administrative
authority; the participation of women in public life; the status of
women in family law; the purposes and legitimate limits of penal
sanctions; *amparo, habeas corpus* and other similar remedies, human
rights in the developing countries; and freedom of information. None
of these seminars has yet been held in the United States.

20. Other Methods of Implementation. Additional methods for ensuring observance of human rights have been developed by Specialized Agencies of the United Nations, especially the International
Labor Organization, and the regional organizations in Europe and
the Americas. The United States must consider in the near future
which of these procedures it should support and which of them it
would accept not only for other countries but also for itself. In
some cases it might be enough to allow evolution through resolutions of international organizations, but in other cases, especially
with respect to the two Covenants, acceptance of treaty obligations
might be involved.

Future Goals

We believe that the United States, in order to contribute to a
greater society of mankind based on the rule of law, justice and

equity, should take such action as may be needed to achieve the eight goals listed below:

1. Ratification of the Four Human Rights Conventions Which Are Now Pending before the Senate Foreign Relations Committee. Three conventions were transmitted to the Senate by President Kennedy on July 22, 1963: the United Nations Supplementary Convention on the Abolition of Slavery, the United Nations Convention on the Political Rights of Women, and the ILO Convention on the Abolition of Forced Labor. In his letter to the Senate, President Kennedy set forth the considerations which call for their ratification by the United States. We believe that it is now more important than ever for the United States to reaffirm its international commitment to human rights. U.S. law is in conformity with the provisions of these three conventions, and their ratification would not require any change in our domestic legislation. Consequently, we urge prompt action by the Senate to give its advice and consent to ratification of these three conventions.

Also pending before the Senate is the International Convention on the Prevention and Punishment of the Crime of Genocide, submitted by President Truman on June 16, 1949. We recommend that the Senate revive consideration of this convention with a view to early ratification.

2. Future Ratification of the Three Conventions on Discrimination. In addition to the four conventions mentioned above, the Economic and Social Council of the United Nations has recommended for ratification by 1968 (the International Human Rights Year) three conventions: on discrimination in employment, in education, and in women's salaries. A few years ago it would not have been possible for the United States to ratify these conventions, but recent legislation, particularly enactment of the Civil Rights Act of 1964, has gone a long way toward bringing our practice into conformity with the principles of these conventions. Consequently, we recommend that these conventions be submitted to the Senate with a view to its giving its advice and consent to ratification, after the pending conventions have been acted upon.

3. United States Leadership in the Preparation and Adoption of Future Conventions and Declarations. The United Nations has in the past several years been engaged in the preparation of a Declaration and a Convention on the Elimination of All Forms of Racial Discrimination and a Declaration and a Convention on the Elimination of All Forms of Religious Intolerance. The United States has played a leading role in the formulation of these instruments, and we recommend that it play a similar role in the formulation of other instruments. The fact that a proposed international convention may go beyond U.S. legislation, especially on the Federal level, should not act as a deterrent to U.S. participation in the formulation of such an instrument.

In the past the United States has frequently abstained from ratifying an international convention when it was felt that the subject matter of the convention was not within Federal power. We recommend that studies be made of constitutional methods for applying such international conventions in the United States.

4. United States Support for Proposals Relating to the Establishment of Appropriate United Nations Machinery for the International Protection of Human Rights. The United States should support the adoption of sound implementation procedures for the Covenants and other instruments which increase the probability of compliance by accepting states without jeopardizing broad acceptance by the majority of the United Nations membership. This is an area in which the United States ought to play an active role and prepare to take leadership. We believe that the international guarantees of human rights require an executive capacity on the part of the United Nations which it does not have today.

The proposal for a United Nations High Commissioner for Human Rights, introduced by Costa Rica in the Human Rights Commission and now proposed for consideration by the General Assembly, offers one possible approach for the achievement of such an executive capacity.

Another possible approach would be to develop the present Sub-Commission on the Prevention of Discrimination and the Protection of Minorities into a "Permanent Committee of Experts of the Commission on Human Rights," competent to deal with any matter in the field of human rights, as proposed by five nations at the twenty-first (1965) session of the Commission on Human Rights.

We feel that institutional changes which would facilitate an actual comparison of our accomplishments with those of other nations can only redound to our advantage.

5. U.S. Participation in Regional Efforts to Increase the Protection of Human Rights. The countries of the Western Hemisphere have close historic ties, and it is especially important for the United States not to stand apart from efforts extending the protection of human rights in the Americas. While progress might be feasible without U.S. active participation, only by accepting equal obligations would the United States be able adequately to influence the trend of events toward a democratic and equitable solution.

We also believe that as the United States and Canada share with the European countries a common heritage in the field of human rights, it should be possible for them to join the European countries in their enterprising and successful effort to give international protection to human rights.

6. United States and Refugees. The humanitarian efforts of international organizations assisting refugees have always been supported by the United States. The focus of the problem has now shifted from Europe to Africa, Asia and the Middle East, and the problem appears once again to be increasing. The United States should give consideration to increasing its contributions to these organizations on a selective basis. In addition, the United States should consider ratification of the 1951 Convention on the Status of Refugees and of the 1954 Convention on the Status of Stateless Persons.

7. Participation of Universities and Non-Governmental Organizations in a Worldwide Education, Research and Study Program in Human Rights. With a few notable exceptions, most international and national non-governmental organizations, as well as universities, have shown only limited interest in the international protection of human rights. It is not enough for the Government of the United States to promote an action program in this area, if there is no general participation in it. Various organizations and universities should engage in such preparatory studies of each proposed convention and of the various measures of implementation as may be needed to facilitate their acceptance and effective application. They should also play an active role in the evaluation of the steps taken by governments to promote human rights. To the extent permitted by various international procedures, they should assist international organs in the preparation and implementation of international conventions and covenants on human rights.

8. U.S. Planning for the International Human Rights Year in 1968. The United Nations General Assembly has designated 1968, the twentieth anniversary of the Universal Declaration on Human Rights, as International Human Rights Year. Advance planning for observance of this year should be undertaken now. A representative committee needs to be appointed as soon as possible to carry through a program of activity at the state, local and national level. As an element of that program, it would be desirable for the United

States to act as host to one or more United Nations human rights seminars.

RECOMMENDATIONS

We make the following recommendations:

1. That the United States promptly ratify the four human rights conventions which are now pending before the Senate Foreign Relations Committee.
2. That the United States ratify as soon as practicable the three conventions on discrimination.
3. That the United States exercise leadership in the preparation and adoption of conventions and declarations on human rights.
4. That the United States support proposals for the establishment of appropriate United Nations machinery for the international protection of human rights, such, for example, as the proposal for a United Nations High Commissioner for Human Rights.
5. That the United States broaden its participation in regional efforts to increase the protection of human rights.
6. That the United States consider increasing its assistance to international agencies engaged in helping refugees, and reconsider the question of ratifying the 1951 convention relating to the status of refugees and the 1954 convention relating to the status of stateless persons.
7. That universities and non-governmental organizations take a more active part in a worldwide education, research and study program in human rights.
8. That the United States plan in advance for observance of International Human Rights Year in 1968.

THE COMMITTEE ON
HUMAN RIGHTS

5. *Promoting Cultural Exchange*

International cooperation flows from the comprehension of human diversity and the ability to look across national barriers and to recognize the common kinship and destiny of mankind. But cooperation must be based in something more substantial than mere desire; it must be an organic part of a people's approach to life, of their relationships to others and of their national foreign policies.

There are hundreds of different national groups in the world, each with its own history, each with its own traditions, religion and moral values, each with its own style in speech and art and family life. This diversity, for all its values in the human community, is in itself a source of many problems. Although all have profited from modern travel and communication, in every nation there are those who feel confused and endangered by the intense process of acculturation. New tensions have arisen within nations and between them, often side by side with new and ameliorating forms of cooperation.

We are concerned with the free international movement and dissemination of ideas and art works, the tools that bring these to an audience, and above all, with the people who create the ideas and art works and who arrange for their dissemination and communication over the whole surface of the globe.

There is a need for the United States to develop an Ear of America to go along with the Voice of America. The American attempt to be heard has exceeded the effort to listen. The rest of the world should have the opportunity to display its art and thought to Americans.

Aristotle defined a political community as the group of people within the range of a single man's voice. By that definition, the inhabitants of this planet are rapidly becoming a single community. It is necessary to create a structure and a spirit for communication among the members of this community that are consistent with the preservation of the differences between them—but that will also contain these differences and turn them to the common benefit of humanity. To create such a structure and such a spirit is the problem to which programs in international intellectual and cultural cooperation are addressed.

Such a structure consists in part of laws, treaties, and concrete programs for collaboration and mutual assistance. But it also consists of things that are at once less palpable and more immediate—the encounters of individuals from different cultures face-to-face, the sharing across borders of the achievements that each group enjoys, the focusing of common energies not only on men's common values, but on their common problems and concerns.

The American ideal is a world in which diversity reigns and is cherished, but in which the nations together practice tolerance and goodwill and enjoy peace under law. Such a structure of law, if it is to be fully effective, presupposes the growth among men of habits of cultural empathy and capacities for successful communication. Underneath the formal relations of sovereign states there must emerge habits of mind and types of human discourse that are capable of cutting beneath the differences between men to the things that speak to their common dependence and destiny.

We are well aware of the complexities of cultural and intellectual exchange between nations, and of the extraordinary difficulty of achieving the ideal of human community for which such exchange is an instrument. The pursuit of this ideal requires not only enormous dedication and patience, but a combination of great subtlety, imagination, and cool common sense. For the twentieth century, however, it is a necessary ideal, an unavoidable one. We have no alternative but to pursue it.

This is not a heavy burden when it is adopted as an energizing ideal in the life of an individual or a nation. The ideal of human community has never been so necessary, but it has also never been so possible in practical terms. The rewards for each successive approach to it are immeasurable. Intellectual and cultural exchange is therefore not merely a means to the ideal of human community. Each successful exchange is a human encounter which is a specific realization of this ideal and an immediate reward for believing in it.

Where Action Is Needed

Reverse Flow

There is a great need to increase the flow into the United States of the world's creative talent and the world's cultural products, including coordinated information about them. The United States tends to be an exporter of scholars, artists, publications, motion pictures, television, and industrial know-how—but the rest of the world has the impression that we are reluctant to give adequate hearing to ideas and artists from abroad.

In the field of the printed word, for example, glaring gaps exist in the international cultural-intellectual exchange picture. As might be expected, these center chiefly on emergent nations whose languages and cultures have either remained on the periphery of Western awareness or else have made no impact whatever, either because of language barriers or lack of modern communication facilities.

In the library-museum field, there is great need for joint biblio-graphic projects to be carried out with librarian-archivists in the Afro-Asian countries and the United States, the results of which could range all the way from inventories for the scholar-specialist to reading lists for use in elementary and secondary schools.

However, a substantial pre-condition for the success of such work lies in the fuller development of book publication facilities in the Afro-Asian countries and, above all, a corps of skilled translators who can work with all the so-called exotic languages from Arabic to Urdu, from Ibo to Thai, and come out with a literary product that can be made available to the general public by American book and magazine publishers. The American book publishing community stands ready, with varying combinations of foundation and Govern-ment financial assistance, to tackle the job of making available to the public both the classics and the most vital contemporary literature of the newly developing nations; but it remains at a loss in the Afro-Asian area until such time as a body of skilled translator-editors, working in collaboration with foreign consultants, is available to screen and translate material for possible publication.

To this end, we urgently recommend the establishment of a gov-ernment-cum-university fellowship program that would allow for the training of gifted young writers as translator-editors in the exotic language field.

We are concerned about the daily reporting of the news in the American press and on the air. The views held by the American people about other countries are conditioned more by crisis and dis-aster than by historic achievement. There is no easy corrective for this situation, but at least the problem calls for recognition and countervailing effort where possible, such as an international conference in Washington of newspaper and magazine editors to explore ways and means of more effective coverage in the various areas of international cooperation.

Private Citizen Dialogue

A constructive role has been played—and should continue to be played on an expanded basis—by such international gatherings as those at Pugwash and Dartmouth. For it is at such conferences that important lines of communication have been kept open and the techniques of useful dialogue worked out. If this dialogue in the world today between contrasting ideologies should stop, the consequences could well be measured in terms of danger to civilization itself.

The purpose of International Cooperation Year cannot be served effectively, let alone creatively, in a world tense with unresolved dangers posed by crises in Southeast Asia, Latin America, the Congo, and the Near East. We call attention to the "techniques of the dialogue" and the establishment of some form of *two-way* communication and exchange of ideas, in achieving the peaceful ends that make possible, and in turn are made possible by, international cooperation.

The U.S. Government should give increased attention to the need for establishing channels of dialogue, formal and informal, official and unofficial, that may lead toward eventual resolution of world crises.

The New Technology

We are impressed with the important cooperative reality of our present world social and cultural situation. A world society has been brought into being and an international culture exists—at varying stages of development. This new world cultural environment is that of the film, television, radio, the pictorial magazine, and commonly shared "mass" products now in global use through an accelerated technology.

It is largely through these agencies that the greater symbolic and value communication and diffusion of our world culture is presently carried on. An academic conservatism which suggests that the spread of such "common" culture will deprive us of the picturesque uniqueness of local cultures is only expressive of a lack of faith in the innate variety of human experience and expression which will continue to provide richness and diversity in any "live" situation.

There is evidence that the spread of international culture has reactivated interest and pride in local cultural heritages. More effective use should be made—not less—of the technology which is available.

Role of Government

Our Government can augment its role and increase its assistance without the concomitant domination that frequently accompanies assistance programs. Cultural affairs, and the people who administer them here and overseas, ought to be given stations in the hierarchy of the State Department organizational scheme that will signify recognition of cultural matters as a prime element in establishing the U.S. image abroad, free and independent of political and propaganda considerations. The administration of American cultural programs abroad should operate independently of those Government agency desks whose chief, or readily identifiable, functions are political in nature.

The scholarly and artistic communities must be drawn into international educational and cultural activities at the policy making and planning level. The proper role of Government is that of equipping the private groups and financing—a semi-autonomous foundation has been suggested—so that they can engage in exchange in this field, sending and receiving the best of culture and scholarship without being exposed to charges of political or economic opportunism.

Student Exchange

Shortly after World War II, the American Government and American universities embarked on a new adventure in world citizenship. Thousands of students left our shores for study in foreign lands. Thousands of their counterparts journeyed to this country, to begin work in a hundred fields of scholarly interest.

Many of these students were supported in whole or in part by Federal funds—both dollars and foreign currencies. The program has been expanded each year; beginning as an almost exclusively U.S.-European exchange, it now embraces five continents.

Problems have arisen, as inevitably they must in a program of this magnitude. The experience of some foreign students in the United States has been an unhappy one, for a variety of reasons. Some of our own students and faculty have had difficulties in adjusting to life in remote university centers.

But for the vast majority of students, both American and foreign, the exchange program has opened doors to a new realm of enrichment. These students, now mature men and women at work in their own societies, have broadened and deepened their apprehension of life. Their professional horizons have been infinitely extended.

More important, they have unfitted themselves for a world of chauvinism and mistrust. It will never be possible for these men and women to look upon their colleagues in distant lands as creatures of another species. National differences remain, and will endure; but the lesson of man's common hunger for peace and understanding has been learned. In the decades to come, that lesson, in the minds of the future generations of world leaders, will mightily encourage the works of peace.

We are aware of the existence of well-equipped and well-administered services on both a national and community level in this area; but we are aware also of the urgent need for a proper coordination of all significant information gathered in the international student exchange field, initially through the medium of an International Educational Exchange Conference which should be called by the President of the United States.

Beyond such a conference, there is an important role for Federal legislation. In the area of people-to-people cultural and intellectual exchange, the easing of onerous immigration and international travel regulations—particularly as they pertain to scholars and artists—as well as the expansion of existing Congressionally-authorized international cultural-intellectual exchange programs, stand as matters of paramount importance.

Remove Barriers

The talents and ideas people bring with them in the course of their travels are basic assets in any program of international knowledge and understanding. In an age of immediate communication and rapid access, these assets can be multiplied many times.

The same is true of the creative product. Art objects, books, audio-visual materials, music records, and the technological equipment necessary for their display or communication are essential ingredients of cooperation. Here we enter into the realm of tangible objects, technical facilities, and tools, together with the whole network of law and finance that govern their use and movement across the borders of the world's more than one hundred sovereign states.

In terms of legislation needed to facilitate free movement of educational and audio-visual materials used for educational purposes, as well as of books and related educational matter, we urge in the strongest possible terms that Congress implement without delay the Florence Agreement and that the Senate consent to the ratification of the Beirut Agreement. Likewise, we urge speedy passage of a revised U.S. Copyright Act in a form that will bring U.S. practices in this field into general conformity with prevalent international procedure (i.e., the Berne Convention and Universal Copyright Convention). With respect to the revised Copyright Act now before the Congress, we wholeheartedly support repeal of the so-called "manufacturing clause," which discriminates against American writers seeking initial publication in English abroad in the absence of publishing opportunities here.

International Travel

Travel by people in its many ramifications is a basic expression of international cooperation. There can be little world cooperation in a world in which travel barriers—whether in the form of passport or visa restrictions, currency limitations or special taxes—have the effect of choking off the fullest and freest movement of peoples. Hardly two generations ago, the lifetime travel mileage for a human being might be as little as 30,000 miles; today 3,000,000 miles of lifetime travel is not beyond the reach of some individuals.

Regardless of the purpose—education, business, or pleasure—travel is the great convener of people. It makes possible direct personal contact. It provides immediate experiences and insights that are available in no other way. Its effect on the travelers and those who come in contact with them cannot be duplicated by other means.

Much has been done since the founding of the United Nations twenty years ago to increase ease and freedom of travel in all parts of the world, whether through technological development such as the jet transport plane or through the easing of visa, passport, and immigration requirements. But most of the job still remains, even in the United States.

We are uncomfortably aware of tendencies on the part of the U.S. Government to discourage or even restrict freedom of international travel on the part of its citizens because of serious economic reasons. But the same has also been true of other nations, the combined result being completely inconsistent with the cause of international cooperation—or even national educational development. We recognize that a dollar deficit is a serious problem; the price this nation would pay for discouraging travel of its citizens may be even more seriously against the national interest.

A more positive approach to this matter can and should be taken by our Government—both for the sake of our national standing abroad and for reasons of mutual financial benefit to all concerned. We respectfully hope the President and the Federal Government will take an unequivocal stand before the world in reaffirming the right of free travel as a basic element of American policy.

Positive and specific encouragement and support from Government quarters for *two-way* travel between the United States and all other countries can help build up the volume of overseas tourist traffic to this country to a point where balance of payments in the tourist area may become a less serious factor.

There are many things that the United States can do directly and indirectly to attract more foreign visitors to our shores, including further reciprocal elimination of the visitor visa requirement, continued encouragement for carriers and hotels to establish special low rates for foreign students, promotion through U.S. Travel Service channels of major U.S. music, theater and arts festivals, continued efforts to increase the attractiveness of national parks and other resort areas controlled in whole or in part by the Federal Government, and encouragement through the Department of Commerce for the holding of international conferences, congresses, and conventions in the United States.

American universities and foundations, through their system of study and travel grants, can do much in their own way to further the cause of two-way travel, most particularly in the areas of foreign-language study, library-museum exchange, writing, music, and the fine arts.

Returning finally to the matter of Government encouragement and cooperation in the field of travel, we recommend a substantial increase in funds for the U.S. Travel Service in the Department of Commerce. As a means of bridging the apparent communications gap between the travel industry and Government officialdom, we urge the calling of top-level conferences of leaders in government and the travel industry. The aim of such conferences would not only be to discuss and clarify areas of misunderstanding and disagreement, but more especially to explore in a positive way the means whereby the current revolution in international human mobility can be put to work for the best interests in the United States and for greater understanding and mutual cooperation among the whole of mankind.

Business and Culture

Together with travel, major American business organizations over the past generation have taken on more and more of a supranational character, so that such brand names as "Coca-Cola," "GM," or "RCA" are encountered on showroom windows or factory roofs in some of the most improbable parts of the world. Yet, in the majority of instances, the overseas affiliates that bear these names are controlled and largely operated by local management and personnel.

In those countries where state ownership and control of business enterprise are not *de rigeur*, and where economic development in the most elementary sense of the word remains a problem, there exists among government and business administrators a keen interest in American methods of management and employer-employee relationships. We note with decided interest a proposal to establish business schools in emergent nations as well as to hold periodic multinational conference-seminars of management personnel to exchange ideas and to discuss problems. Among the conference centers in the United States where explorations of this type have been and will continue to be pursued are Arden House and Wingspread. A proposal has been made for the expansion via foundations and business corporations of fellowship grants that would enable overseas students to come to the United States for on-the-spot study of American management methods and business administration.

Cultural Projects

The following projects deserve serious consideration:

1. The U.S. traveler overseas or the overseas traveler in the United States should be able to track down at one central location basic information he can use for work in his special field of interest. In almost all categories of activity, there is a continuing need for updated bibliographies and union catalogues; for directories of personnel which are up-dated on a month-to-month basis and which will indicate the whereabouts of key individuals in any overseas organization; a continually up-dated calendar of conferences, seminars, exhibitions, and festivals, broken down into spheres of interest. The hope is that the international traveler—whether educator, artist, or layman-dilettante—can plan his itinerary and personal contacts to optimum effect. Such information centers could be located

not only in the major U.S. ports of entry and exit, but in the chief cities of Europe, Africa, Asia, and Latin America.

2. Music is only one of the powerful media of cultural exchange transcending language barriers. There are also painting, the graphic arts, sculpture, photography, and the crafts. The past successes of exchange exhibitions arranged with and without Government assistance by such organizations as the National Gallery of Art, the International Council of the Museum of Modern Art, the American Federation of Arts, the American Craftsman's Council, and the World Crafts Council have been such as to warrant an even greater, more ingenious and effective expansion of their programs—in terms both of international exchange exhibitions and of traveling exhibitions whether primarily artistic or educational in nature. It is in this area, especially, that the combination of Government grants to sponsoring organizations, plus personal participation by Government officials in exhibition locales becomes most productive.

3. A number of interesting proposals have been put forth with the aim of lending greater flexibility and mobility to the traveling exhibition—and in this connection we are particularly impressed by the suggestion of an Art Ship, or series thereof, which would travel from port to port throughout the world bearing its own well-hung, well-lighted, temperature-controlled exhibits of art, crafts, and films, as well as its own staff of curators and lecturers.

4. A major consideration in the architectural area is centered on the preservation of historic sites and monuments—if only as a living memory of vital heritage from the past and as a reminder of the senselessness of the wars, neglect, and thoughtless "urban renewal" that has produced their destruction (viz., Warsaw, Peterhof in the U.S.S.R., the wooden church architecture in the Zakopane area of Poland, vast areas of New York City, Stockholm, London). Likewise, there are many areas and aspects of the architecture of the past—such as the Moslem relics of Soviet Central Asia—that have been inadequately documented either pictorially or via the printed word; and in many instances it will take a carefully planned cultural exchange program, involving both scholars and materials, to bring the necessary documentation into being. The United Nations and UNESCO can establish more direct and available channels of communication for individual architects throughout the world. Aid for education in architecture can also be made available to developing countries where college facilities in this area are inadequate.

5. In the realm of the performing arts, we believe more attention

should be given to the exchange of individuals as against groups. But it is also important to stress the institutional aspect of cultural-intellectual exchange in the field of the arts by strongly recommending support for the establishment of an International Institute for Advanced Studies in the Arts. Such an Institute would serve as a working center for exchange, study, and demonstration of ideas involving creative and performing artists from all over the world, as well as exchange of persons, events planning, and data coordination. In this same cultural-institutional area, we also recommend increased budgetary support for, (a) the UNESCO Cultural Program, (b) the U.S. Commission on International Education and Cultural Affairs, and (c) the U.S. Center of the International Theater Institute.

6. We recommend official U.S. Government endorsement and participation—through its most prestigious officials from the President down—in international cultural and intellectual enterprises and projects. In the majority of instances, such participation would be twofold: (a) a system of grants-in-aid or matching fund grants to sponsoring organizations or individuals, and (b) public endorsement by word and by personal presence of suitable high Government officialdom.

Among the enterprises and projects where such Government support should apply in whole or in part are:

(a) U.S. membership in and support of the Rome International Center for the Study of the Preservation and Restoration of Cultural Property—an organization composed presently of thirty-eight member countries.

(b) U.S. support for establishment of an International Interlibrary Loan Center designed to assist in two-way traffic in books, periodicals, and other library materials between the United States and those nations (in Asia and Africa, especially) of whose traditions and arts we have as yet only scanty knowledge.

(c) Support for U.S. participation in the major art, crafts, film, television, and music festivals, congresses, or exhibitions throughout the world. Such support should extend also to official U.S. hosting of similar festivals and congresses in this country whether by way of establishing new events or expanding the dimensions of existing ones.

7. We support with enthusiasm the proposal for a Conference on Racial, Religious, and Ethnic Relations in the Modern World, to be held at Ellis Island with the aim of airing and clarifying points of

difference and ground shared in common, and indicating the possibilities for conflict resolution through developing "strategies of reconciliation."

Artists in Residence

We are deeply interested in a greatly expanded and more effective two-way exchange of persons throughout the cultural-intellectual area. Whether in the fields of library-museum work, the creative arts, or the performing arts, visiting artists and intellectuals, here or abroad, should be allowed sufficient time and leisure in the course of their visits to develop a genuine sense of contact with people both in and outside of official and professional circles; to absorb in some depth and breadth the atmosphere and traditions of their host country; and finally, to enjoy an ample period of time in which to exchange ideas, skills, and materials with their colleagues, mentors, or students, as well as their families and friends.

We favor the adoption of a two-way exchange-of-persons patterned on the concept of the artist of intellectual in residence as it is understood in the American university community. Whether composer, painter, writer, educator, librarian, curator, professor, or performing artist, the visitor to this country or overseas under government international exchange auspices should be able to gain insight into his host country not merely in terms of its major urban centers, but in terms of its smaller communities as well.

In connection with the performing arts, especially the theater, we note that presently existing exchange programs have shown a tendency toward over-concentration on performing *groups*. It is suggested that future emphasis be directed more toward gifted and articulate *individuals* in both the creative and performing fields of the theater arts. It is felt that this would result in a more significant and intense level of contact on a people-to-people basis—thereby going beyond the stage of mere "cultural transfer" and achieving a measure of genuine cultural *exchange*.

Music

In the area of music, much can be done over and above the ceremonial recognition and programming by performing organizations. The National Music Council comprises more than fifty national organizations covering every phase of musical activity. Many of these organizations are engaged in varied forms of international exchange involving composers, performers, musicologists, printed music, phonograph recordings, and the like.

The National Music Council and its member organizations are in a position to include matters relating to international cooperation on convention and meeting agendas. Moreover, many of the organizations have their own well-developed channels of international communication that have been and can continue to be of high value in promoting people-to-people contacts. The U.S. Branch of the International Society for Contemporary Music, the American Musicological Society, the Koussevitzky International Music Fund, the Music Library Association, the American Symphony Orchestra League, and the Amateur Chamber Music Players are just a few representative instances in point. It is of more than passing interest to note that the Amateur Chamber Music Players publishes an international directory of unique value to the viola player or pianist who, finding himself a stranger in an unfamiliar city, seeks solace in the joys of chamber music playing in some congenial living room.

Many musical organizations seeking to carry through international exchange programs in the form of study groups, publication projects, or library documentation are hampered by lack of funds. Their work may not show a spectacular public result comparable to that achieved by one of our major symphony orchestras or a dance group, but they are no less important to the cultural-intellectual world community. The need for combined Government-private foundation support on a continuing basis is urgent in many of these areas of endeavor in the music field.

One culture-cum-commerce product subject to little or no language barrier and which has produced a spectacular two-way international flow for nearly half a century has been the phonograph record. Over the past decade, the record industry has achieved a global coverage with its product. In the field of concert music recording, even a casual glance at the Schwann Long Playing Record Catalog will reveal discs readily available in American shops offering performances by symphony orchestras as far afield as Tokyo, Reykjavik, Sydney, and Moscow.

However, commercial channels of distribution by their very nature tend to allow the freest flow of the product most in demand, while much that may be of unique cultural value but little commercial worth tends to disappear from circulation or remain confined to the country of origin. In this connection, it is worthy of note that more and more countries—often with the help of their cultural ministries—have documented in recorded form both the development of their own national creative music and vast areas of their ethnic folk song. But only a very limited amount of this material is readily available through normal commercial channels; and indeed, the very knowledge of its existence is limited to a small number of discographer-musicologists. It might be possible for our overseas embassies to take initial steps toward achieving a library-university availability for such recorded material, with financing to be handled along much the same lines as the proposed "reverse Franklin" program in the field of books.

Another gap in non-commercial international cooperation is represented by the absence of an authoritative and continually up-dated international catalogue of significant music and documentary recording. The last attempt made in this area was the World Encyclopedia of Recorded Music, produced in England. Ten years have passed since the last supplement of WERM. A few months ago, the authors announced suspension of further work, due to lack of support toward further publication. Surely, this could have been and can still be a task for UNESCO, with the United States playing a constructive role at least to the extent of assisting in obtaining major library and university distribution.

Office of the President

The key to the public observance and follow-up of International Cooperation Year lies in the office of the Presidency. We are pleased that President Johnson not only proclaimed wholehearted U.S. support for and participation in ICY but initiated an organization of U.S. citizens to prepare proposals for discussion at the White House Conference on International Cooperation.

There are other areas and occasions after the White House Conference in which the President may wish to bring the prestige of his office and his personal presence. On the broadcast communications level, we would hope for a Presidential talk to the nation, explaining the nature and purposes of ICY and how the American citizen both as an individual and as a member of one or more organizations can play a meaningful role, particularly if ICY is extended to become the International Cooperation Decade.

We also suggest a Presidential initiative in the establishment of a Presidential Medal of Merit in the Arts, Sciences, and the Humanities, for which foreign and U.S. citizens alike would be eligible— in short, a counterpart to the French Legion of Honor. It is hoped that establishment of such an order might coincide with a major international arts festival in Washington, and would also be the occasion for a major Presidential program pronouncement in the field of the arts and the humanities.

Mass Communications

We recognize the enormous power of the media of mass communication in informing and in shaping attitudes about international cooperation. In this connection, we specifically wish (1) to suggest a conference of the chief editors of foreign and American newspapers and magazines for the purpose of examining and adopting ways through which these editors, through their publications, can further international interests and ideals; (2) to encourage the American broadcasting industry to establish, in collaboration with Canada and Mexico, a North American Broadcasting Union comparable to the organizations of this type existing in Europe, Asia, Africa, and Latin America. Such a union would facilitate negotiations for and exchange of television and radio broadcast materials, whether as films or tape, or as live transmissions via satellite.

Future Goals

Given the cultural resources potentially available in the United States, and given their diversified and appealing features, the key to our work has been the search for new channels of communication and for new ways to broaden and deepen existing ones. Such channels enable the peoples of the world not only to share aesthetic experiences but also to concert action on common interests and concerns. We can and should justify the pride we have in our freedom from intellectual or cultural molds by rising above political restraints.

Our efforts should be those by which barriers are breached, not as an academic exercise, but to permit the peoples of the world to come to grips with the problems that beset, and often separate, them. One such problem is the failure to recognize the universality of fundamental aspirations such as peace, justice, beauty. Each nation should contribute whatever it can to realizing such aspirations—this should be the animating purpose of intellectual and cultural exchange.

The leveling of barriers, however essential in today's world, is a means to an end, not an end in itself. The end we seek is the identification of common interests and truly international cooperation in serving them. Every recommendation for action in this field should be tested against relevance and contribution to achievement of the ideal of a human community.

RECOMMENDATIONS

We make the following recommendations:

Basic Principles

1. That the ICY be extended and expanded to ICD, International Cooperation Decade, in view of the long-term nature of the majority of the projects proposed in the field of cultural and intellectual exchange.
2. That the principle of "reverse flow" should govern all aspects of international activity on the part of the United States in the cultural and intellectual exchange field.
3. That special attention be given to information coordination in this area through the combined media of (a) international conferences, (b) permanent secretariats, and (c) data-processing facilities.
4. That Government assistance to private sector efforts in the cultural and intellectual exchange area be predicated on the maintenance of private sector independence in the administration and operation of projects so aided.

General Recommendations

5. That a semi-autonomous foundation be established to coordinate Government-private sector collaboration abroad and to assist in funding activities throughout the cultural and intellectual exchange field.
6. That there be established an Institute for Advanced Study in the Arts, funded by the proposed foundation, which would assume the chief responsibilities in the areas of (a) exchange of persons, (b) special events, and (c) information coordination as they pertain to the creative and performing arts.

7. That there be increased budgetary support through the proposed foundation for (a) the U.S. Committee on International Education and Public Affairs, (b) the U.S. Center of the International Theater Institute, and (c) the cultural program of UNESCO.

8. That there be established an international "in residence" program embracing intellectuals, creative artists, and performing artists, its aim being to provide contact in depth and breadth between grantees under the program and their host countries.

9. That there be encouragement and facilitation of international "citizen dialogue" on matters of international controversy as yet unresolved at the intergovernmental level, whether such dialogue be conducted on an individual-to-individual basis or on a conference level along the lines of those held at Dartmouth and Pugwash.

10. That the position of the chief educational and cultural affairs officer in the State Department be elevated to an Under Secretaryship; and that the administration of American cultural programs abroad be detached from service agencies whose principal or readily identifiable function is essentially political.

11. That in the fields of the major arts, crafts, film, television, and music there be made an even greater, more ingenious and effective expansion of festivals, congresses and exhibitions.

Publishing and Writing

12. That there be continued and increased Government support for private programs working for increased translation of classic and vital contemporary literature from areas of the world hitherto neglected in terms of our own cultural awareness.

13. That there be established a Government-cum-university fellowship program for the training of translator-editors in the so-called exotic language field.

14. That the United States give special attention to the need for support of the UNESCO program for the strengthening of publication projects among the Afro-Asian nations.

15. That the so-called "manufacturing clause" of the present U.S.

Copyright Act be eliminated, thus giving copyright protection to American citizens and residents who write works in English printed abroad.

16. That the U.S. Congress be requested to implement without further delay the Florence Agreement and that the Senate consent to the ratification of the Beirut Agreement.

Library Exchange

17. That the United States lend its support for establishment of an International Library Loan Center to facilitate two-way exchange of books and periodicals.

18. That the United States lend support to joint international bibliographic projects, especially those involving the Afro-Asian countries and Latin America.

19. That the P.L. 480 program, allowing for the procurement of foreign publications through non-convertible counterpart funds, be expanded and intensified.

20. That the Farmington Plan, covering library acquisition of foreign publications, be further strengthened in its application and implementation.

21. That continued effort be made to encourage the international exchange on a government level of microfilm-reproduced official documents.

22. That the Government increase its support of the U.S. Book Exchange Program for free distribution of exchange materials abroad.

23. That the United States lend its support for establishment of an international clearing house for library cataloguing.

24. That the United States lend its good offices and support for the development and adoption of international standardization in the field of library statistics.

25. That there be established in the United States with Government support a center for international photo-reproduction services that would also assist in the development of similar library services in those parts of the world presently lacking adequate facilities of this type.

World Languages

26. That it be made normal practice for all university students to acquire a second world language, preferably one of the four official languages of the United Nations.

27. That an international program be established to bring university students and teachers of other countries to the United States to teach their native language in high schools and colleges, and to send out Americans to teach English in similar institutions abroad.

28. That a program be established in cooperation with language departments of American universities whereby selected graduate students would be given: (a) a special training course for escort-interpreters, and (b) a year or two abroad to become bilingual, provided they agree to serve a specified period with the Government after completing their grants.

Ethnic Relations

29. That a conference be convened to consider racial, religious, ethnic and linguistic relations in the modern world; that the conferees consider whether a subsequent international meeting of the same nature should be held; and that, in either or both cases, special attention be given to the problems of nations in which more than one language is spoken.

Exchange Students

30. That the President of the United States be requested to call an international conference on educational exchange and that in arranging for such a conference means be provided for a series of international planning meetings to determine the agenda and to develop an adequate conference program. Further, that at such a conference means be explored for the establishment of a permanent international Secretariat for the continuing exchange of information and for the mutual planning of international educational exchange in the future.

31. That support be given to the proposed establishment of a "Volunteers to America" or "Exchange Peace Corps" program under

which the U.S. Peace Corps would bring foreign volunteers to serve in this country.

International Travel

32. That the U.S. Government affirm as basic policy the freedom of international travel.
33. That the U.S. Government take the initiative for the progressive elimination of visa requirements on the part of all nations, beginning with amendment of the Immigration Law to extend visitor visa waiver on a reciprocity basis.
34. That the United States encourage international carriers to establish a schedule of minimum student fares.
35. That the agreed-upon pact for direct New York–Moscow air service be implemented without further delay.
36. That the United States initiate discussion with other countries looking toward the formulation of uniform immigration-travel-work regulations as they pertain to performing artists.
37. That the United States foster diplomatic efforts to break down travel barriers resulting from foreign government-imposed currency restrictions.
38. That there be called in Washington a top-level Government-travel industry conference to exchange information on mutual problems and to propose solutions that will serve at one and the same time the purposes of ICY and the interests of the nation.

Architecture

39. That the United States assist in international programs devoted to the documentation of architecture and historical sites in those areas of the world still inadequately covered in terms of scholarly and general publication.

Painting, Sculpture, Crafts

40. That the United States join and share in the support of the Rome International Center for the Study of Preservation and Restoration of Cultural Property.

41. That U.S. participation, with Government support, in major international arts exhibitions abroad be greatly increased.

42. That an Art Ship, or series thereof, be launched to bring to seaport cities throughout the world its own international exhibits of art, crafts, and films, together with its own staff of curators and lecturers.

43. That the Triennial Carnegie International Exhibition be expanded and sent to other cities beyond its home base at Pittsburgh.

Music

44. That the leaders of the music community be encouraged and supported in the development of special events built around the ICY idea.

45. That the United States go beyond its present support of the performance field of music to include programs in scholarly areas of publication, materials exchanges, information coordination, and sound recording.

46. That the United States collaborate in the exchange of persons and programs in the music area involving gifted amateur performers or hitherto unrecognized professionals of exceptional talent.

Theater and Dance

47. That the Institute for Advanced Study in the Arts (Recommendation No. 6) embrace, as a major activity, on an international exchange and group study basis, the work of creative and performing artists in all of the theater arts: musical, spoken, and choreographic.

48. That qualified collegiate and lower-age troupes from abroad be brought to American schools for appearances, and that means be provided for participation of American troupes in foreign theater festivals and foreign schools; and that, on the community, amateur, and non-school level, provision be made for exchange of information, personnel, and production between European workers' theaters and American little theaters.

Motion Pictures

49. That the United States take a major initiative in the international film festival area through the establishment of a biennial Washington Film Assembly (alternating with the Moscow festival) that would serve as a combined film exhibition, international conference, and workshop-symposium.

Radio and Television

50. That the American broadcasting industry be encouraged to establish, in collaboration with Canada and Mexico, a North American Broadcasting Union, comparable to similar groupings in Europe, Asia, Africa, and Latin America.

Newspapers and Periodicals

51. That the mass circulation media in the newspaper and magazine field be encouraged and stimulated to undertake a more effective coverage of world affairs in their total context rather than in terms of isolated events.
52. That there be called in Washington a conference of the chief editors of foreign and American magazines and newspapers for a discussion of ways and means by which the editors, through their publications, can further international interests and ideals.

Business Corporations

53. That international businessmen's organizations (International Chamber of Commerce, Council for Latin America, etc.) sponsor multinational meetings of businessmen to explore questions of productivity, employee incentives and welfare, and employee training.
54. That business corporations participate more directly with educational institutions in the establishment in developing countries of business schools and the programs and curricula of these schools, emphasizing economic development supported by the private sector rather than national social welfare as a development goal by government.

55. That business corporations, through their own foundations or other philanthropic sources, expand the number of fellowship grants to bring more overseas students to the United States for on-the-spot study of American business organization and management methods.

56. That business corporations take steps, with the assistance of their governments if necessary, to make agreements on a basis of reciprocity which will permit bringing art and similar cultural exhibits across national borders.

57. That business corporations, collaborating with universities and interested individuals, arrange for the establishment of an information center which would be aware of businessmen traveling to the United States and of business leaders traveling from the United States who could participate in educational and cultural programs and meetings in the countries being visited.

Training

58. That international training be furthered among national guidance associations through the International Educational and Vocational Guidance Association.

59. That a program be established for training non-governmental women civic leaders, actual and potential, giving them the opportunity to benefit from the vast U.S. experience in the field of voluntary cooperative effort, especially needed in the newly emerging countries.

Technological Change

60. That we recognize that the world is being made one, not through political or other ideological notions, but by scientific and technological fact; and that encouragement should be given to advance-guard agencies in this area (e.g., a World Academy of Art and Science; the proposed International City of Science).

61. That the architectural departments of all the universities around the world be encouraged to invest the next ten years in the continuing problem of how to make the world's total resources serve

100 per cent of humanity through competent design (e.g., World Students' Design Science Decade 1965–75).

Public Relations

62. That the President of the United States be asked to use the prestige of his unique office through continued endorsement of the ideals and goals of ICY, and through taking the initiative in establishing a Presidential Medal of Merit in the Arts, Sciences, and the Humanities.
63. That the Department of State play a special role in the publicizing of international cooperation through more effective use of prominent figures in the arts in the role of "cultural ambassadors."
64. That all channels of communication, private and governmental, be involved in the effort to call public attention to ICY and its follow-up—the reasons for it, its possibilities, and the part to be played by the private citizen in helping make international cooperation a continuing way of life extending through the next decade.

THE COMMITTEE ON CULTURE
AND INTELLECTUAL EXCHANGE

6. *Containing the Population Explosion*

The unprecedented growth in world population poses unprecedented problems for the future of mankind. The high rates of population growth now occurring in many countries, particularly in the less developed areas of the world, impede economic and social development, threaten political stability, and jeopardize man's search for a lasting peace. Action to reduce these high rates of population growth is now urgently required if we are to preserve and extend human dignity in the United States and around the world.

In the last few years some important first steps have been taken toward an understanding of population problems and toward effective measures to deal with them. But the ratio of talk to action is still distressingly high. Much more needs to be done to enlarge our understanding of population problems, to improve techniques of family planning, and to implement effective programs which reduce the rate of population growth.

The population problem can be dealt with in a manner which is consistent with the values of a free society—provided action is taken on a sufficient scale and is taken *now*. Mankind is already dangerously late in waking up to what President Johnson has well described as "humanity's greatest challenge . . . second only to the search for peace."

The Problem We Face

The facts about the world population explosion are now well known. It took hundreds of thousands of years, from the beginning of life on earth to the beginning of this century, for the population of the world to reach 1.5 billion. In the first two-thirds of this century, this number doubled to the present total of something over 3 billion. In the last one-third of this century, if present trends continue, this figure will more than double to over 7 billion.

This unparalleled increase in man's numbers is causing problems even for highly developed countries. The United States, with a population growth rate of about one and one-half per cent a year, is likely to see its present population of 190 million reach more than 300 million by the year 2000. A report by the National Academy of Sciences has revealed a variety of problems which this growth rate is causing, especially among the poor and uneducated—problems involving maternal health, infant mortality and morbidity, family life, housing, and opportunities for education, employment and a better standard of living. The rapid growth in population is adding to other strains on our society in the form of air and water pollution, the breakdown of mass transportation, overcrowding in urban areas, the depletion of precious natural resources, and the destruction of needed recreation areas and open spaces.

Our search for a Great Society in the United States is complicated by present population trends not only for these reasons but particularly because of the relatively faster increase in that portion of the population which does not share the benefits of the affluent society. Parents in our least fortunate economic group have nearly twice as many children as parents in the most fortunate bracket. The relatively high birth rate in poverty-stricken families is not only an important contributing cause of their poverty—it condemns a significant portion of the American people to living in conditions of economic and cultural deprivation.

The results of population growth are ever more ominous in the less developed countries of the world. The average annual increase of population in these countries is approximately 2.5 per cent—sufficient to double population every twenty-eight years. In many countries the annual growth rate has reached 3 per cent or more. In Latin America, the region of the world where population growth is highest, total population will rise from something over 200 million today to approximately 600 million at the end of the century if present trends continue.

Public discussion of the population problem has focused attention on the relation between the number of people and the supply of food. In the less developed areas as a whole, food production has barely kept pace with population growth—and in Latin America, food production per capita has actually declined. The Food and Agriculture Organization has estimated that world food production will have to increase at least threefold by the end of the century to provide an adequate diet for the world's increased numbers. Such an increase seems impossible without a thoroughgoing transformation in existing agricultural institutions and techniques in the less developed areas.

Thus—as a consequence of present population trends—the threat of starvation in many countries is very real. Yet the reason for reducing present rates of population growth in the less developed countries is not exclusively—nor even primarily—that of avoiding starvation. These countries, whose citizens have an average income of little more than $100 a year, are seeking rapid increases in their living standards. To achieve these increases they must achieve a substantial rate of investment as well as meet their current consumption needs. Yet all many of these countries can do is enlarge total economic product as fast as the additional mouths to feed—so that little or nothing is left over for additions to capital stock.

The United Nations has set as the goal of its Development Decade the achievement by 1970 of an annual growth rate of 5 per cent a year in the national income of less developed countries. At the present time the rate of investment required to reach this objective is not being achieved in many of these countries because resources which might otherwise be available for investment must be used to provide necessities for a rapidly growing population. Moreover, even if the United Nations 5 per cent target should be achieved, present rates of population growth would greatly dilute its impact on individual levels of welfare. For the many developing countries with population growth in the region of 3 per cent a year, achievement of the United Nations target figure would mean increases in individual living standards of only 2 per cent a year—in other words, average annual increases per capita of about $2.

Nor can the menace of population growth be calculated in economic terms alone. For the United States and the world, the measure of progress should not be the growth of aggregate statistics, nor even the growth of per capita living standards, but the degree by which each person is assured the ingredients of a full and satisfactory life. These ingredients include not merely the basic necessities such as food, housing, shelter, health and education, but the satisfaction of political, cultural and spiritual needs that are fundamental to all men.

U.S. Ambassador to the United Nations Arthur J. Goldberg put the matter eloquently in his address to the twentieth UN General Assembly:

The ultimate object of any organized society, domestically or internationally, is man—the individual. The effect upon his lot, his fate, his well-being—that will remain the final measure of our success—and our failure. And if we talk about the competition between states, that is the only worthwhile competition—as to which system, which society, best improves the lot of man and upgrades human dignity.

In our opinion, a society devoted to supporting maximum numbers of people at bare subsistence levels is repugnant to the values of modern civilization. The fact that such a society may be registering impressive increases in gross national product and other supposed indices of progress is largely irrelevant.

We believe the central objective of U.S. policy both at home and abroad should be the improvement of the quality of life for the individual human being. If this is so, then the United States must have a rational population policy. As long as we are concerned with the quality of life, we cannot fail but to be concerned with the quantity of life. For these same reasons, it should be clear that the objective of population policy should not be the restriction of life, but the enrichment of life.

From this broader perspective, it is apparent that in many countries population growth—even when accompanied by modest increases in per capita income—may threaten the basis of the good life and perhaps the very foundations of civilized society. The population increase and migration from the countryside have outstripped the capacity of many of the world's great cities to supply minimum levels of housing, sanitation, education and transportation. Uncontrolled fertility has been accompanied by increasing resort to abortion—both legal and illegal. Moreover, increasing numbers of illegitimate children are growing up without the benefits of family life. These conditions multiply individual frustrations and take their toll on society in the form of delinquency, crime, revolution, and even war.

The evidence available from history and the social sciences suggests that man, given the opportunity, will liberate himself from rates of population growth which threaten such serious consequences for the social order. Experience in the United States and abroad indicates that most men and women will limit the number of their offspring if they have an opportunity to do so.

In our judgment, freedom to limit family size to the number of children wanted is a basic human right. Yet this basic right does not yet exist, or cannot yet be implemented, in many parts of the United States and in many other countries of the world. It has been estimated that nearly two out of every three couples in the world today lack access to family planning information and services.

The central aim of U.S. policy in the field of population should be to correct this state of affairs—to make the information and the means for family planning available to all who wish to have them. Fortunately, there are now methods for the regulation of pregnancy that are acceptable and appropriate in every cultural and income level both in our own country and abroad. Each individual should have the opportunity to limit his family size through free choice among all the means that are available.

A free society must necessarily make free choice rather than co-ercion the basis of its population policy. But time is of the essence. The rate of growth of world population is so great—its consequences are so grave—that this may be the last generation which has the opportunity to cope with the problem on the basis of free choice.

Unfortunately, there are no quick and simple solutions to the many problems associated with rapid population growth. It will take time before appropriate measures for the limitation of births can be made available to all who would make use of them. And even if birth rates decline, future increases in population will result from the population growth of the past as more people pass through the childbearing years. Moreover, the application of modern science and medicine in less developed countries will further reduce the death rate and spur population growth.

Thus the United States must base its policy on the assumption of large and continuous increases in population both at home and abroad. Family planning will not quickly or easily alter the demographic facts of life. Nor can it be a substitute for other measures to preserve and extend human dignity—such as the war on poverty at home and economic assistance to less developed countries abroad.

Nevertheless, the success with which the world applies a policy of voluntary family planning in the next few years can spell the difference between rates of population growth that are compatible with human dignity and those that spell certain misery for an increasing minority in the United States and a growing majority overseas. In the words of Dr. B. R. Sen, Director-General of the Food and Agriculture Organization:

The next 35 years, till the end of the century, will be . . . a most critical period in man's history. Either we take the fullest measures both to raise productivity and to stabilize population growth, or we will face disaster of an unprecedented magnitude. We must be warned that in the present situation lie the seeds of unlimited progress or unlimited disaster, not only for individual nations but for the whole world.

Where We Stand

There are at least three prerequisites to effective action on the world population problem—(1) adequate *information* about the demographic facts, the economic and social implications of those facts, and the means of influencing the demographic facts through changes in individual attitudes toward childbearing; (2) *techniques* of family planning which are acceptable and effective in different economic, social, cultural and religious environments; and (3) the *implementation* of nation-wide *action programs* of family planning.

Significant progress has been made during recent years in each of these key areas:

In the field of *information*, much has been done in the United States and overseas to improve knowledge in all aspects of the population problem—in census taking and vital statistics, in the ability to project future population trends, in the inter-relationship between population trends and economic and social development, in individual attitudes toward childbearing, and in the factors which may cause these attitudes to change.

Private organizations have made a major contribution to progress in this area. The International Planned Parenthood Federation, with member organizations in some thirty-five countries and territories, has played a leading part in encouraging the people of the world to use effective and acceptable means of voluntary family planning. Together with its American affiliate, Planned Parenthood-World Population, Inc., it supports conferences, public information, publications, and research designed to make responsible parenthood a universal reality. The Hugh Moore Fund, the Population Reference Bureau, and other organizations have also heightened public understanding of the population problem. The Population Council and the Ford and Rockefeller Foundations have vastly expanded scientific knowledge through their support of research and analysis in demography and in the economic and social consequences of population growth. Special population centers have been created in leading American universities, including Brown, California, Cornell, Chicago, Georgetown, George Washington, Harvard, Johns Hopkins, Hawaii, Miami, Michigan, North Carolina, Pennsylvania, Princeton, Texas, Washington, and Wisconsin.

This extensive private effort has been supplemented by growing support from governments and international organizations. The Agency for International Development, in collaboration with the U.S. Public Health Service, the Bureau of the Census, and universities, has supported research, training institutes, and conferences on population problems. The governments of other countries, in many cases with encouragement and support from AID, have greatly improved their capacities in such fields as census taking, the gathering of vital statistics, the projection of changes in population size and composition, and the analysis of the consequences of such changes for their overall economic plans as well as for particular sectors such as health and education.

National and bilateral efforts are now strongly supplemented by the work of the United Nations and its family of agencies. A population unit in the UN Secretariat has provided useful studies of national and world population trends. The UN Population Commission has stimulated the gathering of demographic and other information necessary for the implementation of family planning programs. UN regional economic commissions in Latin America, Africa, and Asia and the Far East have devoted increasing attention to population problems, and UN Regional Demographic Research and Training Centers have been established in Santiago, Cairo and Bombay. Under UN sponsorship two World Population Conferences, one in Rome in 1954, the other in Belgrade in 1965, have facilitated significant exchanges between scholars and government officials concerned with the scientific study of population.

Progress has also been impressive in the development of family planning *techniques*. Research in recent years has sought to improve the reliability of the rhythm method for the regulation of pregnancies. Laboratory studies and extensive field trials, including some in the developing countries, have confirmed the effectiveness of birth control pills (progestational steroids) and plastic intra-uterine devices (I.U.C.D.). The I.U.C.D. in particular has stimulated hope for relatively rapid reductions in birth rates in less developed areas because it is cheap, highly effective, and requires only a single act— insertion of the device—to bring long-lasting protection from pregnancy.

Research by government and by many of the private organizations mentioned above, especially the Population Council and the Ford and Rockefeller Foundations, has helped significantly in the development of these and other effective techniques for the regulation of pregnancy. The World Health Organization has also begun a program of research in human reproduction which should help to broaden the narrow geographic base which now exists for work in this field.

Progress has also been made, though much more slowly, in the actual *implementation* of family planning programs. In the United States, an increasing number of state governments are supporting family planning services through local health and welfare programs. The number has risen from twelve in 1960 to twenty-six as of mid-1965. On June 7, 1965, the U.S. Supreme Court declared the restrictive Connecticut birth control law unconstitutional. The Federal Government supports local family planning services through general health grants-in-aid to states under a program administered by the U.S. Public Health Service; through a grant-in-aid program for maternal and child health administered by the Children's Bureau of the Welfare Administration; through the program administered by the Bureau of Family Services of the Welfare Administration; and through community action programs supported by grants from the Office of Economic Opportunity.

An increasing number of less developed countries have instituted nation-wide programs of family planning. Korea, the Republic of China, and Tunisia are well on the way to establishing effective family planning programs. The United Arab Republic, India, and Pakistan are significantly expanding their efforts—although these still reach only a small fraction of the population. Turkey is about to embark on a national effort after repeal of a forty-year-old law against contraception. Pilot projects are under way in Malaysia and Ceylon.

Until very recently, no government in Latin America, with the exception of Chile, had an active program of family planning. Now this situation is beginning to change. Increasing emphasis has been placed on the population problem in meetings of the Alliance for Progress, and the first Pan-American Assembly on Population Problems was held in Colombia in August, 1965. Peru and Venezuela have now established population units within their Ministries of Health, and Colombia has done the same within its Association of Medical Faculties.

President Kennedy committed the United States to the task of making more knowledge about family planning more available to the world. With his encouragement, the United States initiated a policy of providing assistance in the population field to other countries upon request. In his State of the Union Message of January 4,

1965, President Johnson pledged to "seek new ways to use our knowledge to help deal with the explosion in world population and the growing scarcity of world resources." Under his leadership, the Executive Branch is now fully committed to action on the population problem.

Growing concern with the world population problem—and support for U.S. assistance to other countries which seek it in implementing family planning programs—have been voiced by leaders of both political parties. Former President Dwight D. Eisenhower has stated that the United States should tell other nations "how population growth threatens them and what can be done about it." Former Vice President Richard M. Nixon has called on the U.S. Government to take leadership in developing "population control programs which are consistent, to the extent possible, with the religious traditions of the nation involved." Legislation designed to stimulate U.S. action in this field has been introduced in Congress under the leadership of senators such as Ernest Gruening of Alaska and Joseph Clark of Pennsylvania.

The U.S. Government is now making a major effort to help other countries deal with their population problems. The Agency for International Development has extended its assistance beyond the statistical, demographic, and public health fields to the direct support of family planning programs. In accordance with a message dispatched to AID Missions on March 3, 1965, the agency will now respond positively to requests for technical, financial, and commodity assistance in support of family planning programs. This message placed particular emphasis on the following points:

• That each AID Mission should assign one of its officers, as Latin American Missions had already done, to become familiar with the problems of population dynamics and program developments in the country and to keep the Mission Director, Country Team personnel and AID headquarters in Washington appropriately advised;

• That AID does not advocate any particular method of family regulation, and that freedom of choice should be available in any program for which technical assistance is requested;

• That requests for AID assistance in this field, as in others, will be considered only if made or approved by appropriate host government authorities;

• That AID is now prepared to entertain requests for technical, commodity, and local currency assistance in support of family planning programs.

• That AID does not consider requests for contraceptive devices or equipment for manufacture of contraceptives, since experience has made it clear that the cost of these latter items is not a stumbling block in countries that are developing effective programs.

The United States is not the only Government prepared to offer assistance in support of family planning programs overseas. Sweden has been doing so for years, and Great Britain and Japan have recently entered the same field. The Development Assistance Committee (DAC) of the Organization of Economic Cooperation and Development (OECD) has begun to study the implications of population growth for the assistance programs carried on by its member countries. This may well stimulate the expansion of existing assistance programs in the population field and the establishment of new ones.

The rising tide of determination to deal with the population explosion was reflected in the United Nations debate on population in December, 1962, when a large number of countries expressed concern with population trends and a desire to do something about them. This debate concluded with the passage—by sixty-nine votes in favor, twenty-seven abstentions, and not a single negative vote—of a resolution calling for intensified international cooperation in research and study of the population problem.

The pace of United Nations activity increased significantly in 1965. The World Health Assembly for the first time called on its Director-General to provide advisory services in support of family planning programs. The Governing Council of the UN Children's Fund instructed its director to prepare a statement on possible activities in the population field. The Economic and Social Council formally requested the Secretary-General of the United Nations to offer "advisory services and training on action programs in population." The United Nations sent an expert mission to India to advise on that country's family planning program.

These achievements—in the study of population problems, in the development of family planning techniques, and in the actual establishment of family planning programs—are all impressive. But they are not enough. More needs to be done in each of these areas if the world is to cope effectively with the population problem. Having examined what has already been done, we now need to consider the tasks that lie ahead.

Future Goals—and How to Achieve Them

The overriding objective toward which population policy should be directed can be stated simply—it is to defend and enlarge the essential values of modern civilization now threatened by unrestricted population growth, by putting every couple in a position to determine the family size it wants.

It would be contrary to everything our country stands for to implement a population policy by coercion. U.S. policy in this area should be guided by two fundamental principles: dissemination of knowledge and freedom of choice. The fact that at present substantial groups in the United States and overseas do not have access to family planning information and services by virtue of limited educational, economic, or other circumstances, constitutes a particularly objectionable form of *de facto* discrimination. Government action to eliminate such discrimination enlarges human freedom, promotes individual dignity, and more effectively implements the historic purposes of our country.

To accomplish these objectives, the three elements of population policy must be implemented with a new sense of urgency:

We must intensify our efforts to increase *information* on all aspects of the population problem. Private organizations should be encouraged to continue their efforts in this field. The U.S. Government should substantially increase its aid to other governments, on their request, in ascertaining the facts about their population situation and the significance of these facts for economic and social development. AID, in cooperation with the Bureau of the Census, should expand its training of foreign personnel in the collection, processing, publication, and analysis of essential data. United Nations agencies should also be encouraged to enlarge their research and technical assistance in this field. International organizations can be particularly valuable in building a broad consensus on population problems and what should be done about them.

Special attention needs to be given also to the problem of communicating family planning information. Family planning programs can only be effective to the extent that they motivate individuals to utilize available techniques for regulating pregnancy. In many areas of the world where birth rates are high, much more needs to be known about how to adapt educational programs to the needs and values of the people.

More attention needs also to be given to the administration and management of effective population programs. Strong research and evaluation units should be established close to the top administrative structure of official agencies to assure that modern techniques of management planning are being fully applied in implementing population programs.

Work should be greatly expanded in the search to improve existing *techniques* of regulating pregnancy. More effort is needed to increase the reliability of the rhythm method, to enhance the effectiveness of the intra-uterine device, and to discover other methods of family planning. The research programs supported by private agencies, by the United States and other governments, and by the World Health Organization in the field of human reproduction should be enlarged as rapidly as possible in order to stimulate further progress in family planning techniques.

The need for intensified effort is greatest of all in the actual *implementation* of family planning programs. The various U.S. agencies concerned with population problems need more staff and funds to meet their growing responsibilities in this critical field. Moreover, the work of these agencies could be made more effective through high-level coordination.

As foreign governments initiate and expand nation-wide programs of family planning, they will increasingly call upon the United States for assistance. The governments of Pakistan, India, and Turkey, for example, have already indicated a desire for U.S. financial support of programs to train family planning workers in large numbers; for U.S. consultants in all fields bearing on the development of country-wide family planning programs; for funds to supplement professional salaries for family planning workers; and for transportation and mass communication equipment.

U.S. direct support of overseas family planning programs in these and other ways should be greatly expanded. We should remember, however, that family planning programs are dependent in the long run on a nation's network of health and social services. An enlargement of U.S. assistance to help other countries strengthen health and social services would not merely be desirable for its own sake; it would provide the essential foundation for the implementation of population policies.

There is a large measure of speculation involved in placing any dollar figure on the amount of assistance that is here required. We believe, however, that the United States should be prepared to make available over the next three years up to $100 million a year in technical, financial, and commodity aid for direct and indirect support of family planning programs overseas. This aid should be related to the maximum possible extent to activities of regional or United Nations agencies, and maximum effort should be made to enlarge the flow of such assistance from other developed countries.

A White House Conference on Population, held within the next two years, could provide a useful stimulus to further action, both in the United States and abroad. To help make such a Conference as productive as possible, it should be preceded by careful research and planning by a committee of experts appointed by the Secretary of Health, Education and Welfare.

RECOMMENDATIONS

We make the following recommendations:

1. That the U.S. Government encourage schools and universities here and abroad to study population in all its relevant aspects—particularly at the graduate level in relation to such fields as medicine, public health, public administration, theology, economic and other behavioral sciences.

2. That the U.S. Government greatly expand its support, both at home and abroad, of research related to the population problem—particularly research on the inter-relation between population growth and economic development, on new or improved techniques of family planning, on the means of communicating these techniques, and on the administration and management of family planning programs.

3. That the U.S. Government set an international example by co-operating with state and local governments and private organizations to make family planning services and information readily available to those in the United States who wish to have them, with the understanding that there be no coercion and that in tax-supported facilities there be full freedom of choice of methods to be used in regulating pregnancy.

4. That the U.S. Government greatly expand its program of training

U.S. and foreign personnel who can themselves train doctors, auxiliary personnel, communications specialists, administrators, and others needed in the implementation of family planning programs in the United States and around the world.

5. That the U.S. Government be prepared to make available upon request up to $100 million a year over the next three years to help other countries implement programs of family planning and strengthen national health and social services necessary for the support of family planning programs.

6. That U.S. assistance to other countries in all of these areas be related to the maximum possible extent to the work of multilateral agencies, particularly the relevant agencies of the United Nations, including the World Health Organization, the United Nations Children's Fund, and the United Nations Development Program.

7. That private organizations be encouraged to expand their work in all of these areas, particularly in those fields where Government assistance is not readily available, and that public and private sources be encouraged to give more generous support to such organizations.

8. That a White House Conference on Population be held within the next two years to consider domestic and international population trends and the appropriate measures to deal with them.

9. That the Secretary of Health, Education and Welfare appoint a committee to prepare this Conference through careful advance planning and research and to advise the U.S. Government on steps that may be taken before the Conference to deal with domestic and international population problems.

10. That the Department of State, the Agency for International Development, and the Department of Health, Education and Welfare undertake improvements in organization, staff, and budgets necessary to discharge their increased responsibilities pursuant to the above recommendations.

THE COMMITTEE ON POPULATION

7. Conserving the World's Resources

The conservation and development of natural resources provide significant opportunities for international cooperation. These opportunities lie not only in increasing the rate of economic growth in many of the less developed nations of the world, but also in facilitating the orderly and rational development of the resources that are shared by the world community. Opportunities for international cooperation are enhanced because natural resources—land, water, minerals, and air—are familiar to all people and because programs for their development are appealing and understandable.

Intensive cooperative efforts are required to speed up the advance of the developing nations—an advance that depends in large part upon an appropriate and effective use of natural resources. The development of realistic plans, knowledge about priorities for resources investment, about the relationships between resource use and economic growth—these and many other elements call for comprehensive and sophisticated analytical techniques that are just beginning to become available. A World Institute for Resource Analysis, capable of developing these techniques and testing their application, could do much to improve the decisions being made on the use of natural resources in the less developed countries. An International Conservation Quinquennium, applying the knowledge gained during the Hydrological Decade, the Biological Program, and the Geophysical Year, could also demonstrate and advance the use of new techniques.

But techniques and knowledge are not enough. It is also necessary to have highly educated persons to do the planning and make the decisions and to have well-trained resource managers to carry them out. Educational efforts at the top level are already being made, but much greater efforts are necessary for the development of practical training programs for resource managers within the less developed countries—for surveyors and mappers, park and game wardens, soil and water conservation officers, technicians in gathering hydrologic and geologic information, and resource project managers.

Water pollution control is also a matter of vital concern to the developing countries. The diseases carried by water shorten life spans and debilitate the people, greatly lowering their economic productivity. There is an urgent need for improvement in sewage disposal practices and in the distribution of potable water. Aside from the need for cooperation on the problems of resource use in the less developed countries, there is a rapidly growing need for cooperation on the resources that are shared by several nations or by the world community as a whole.

Chief among these are the resources of the oceans—both the fisheries of the high seas and the minerals lying on, or under, the deep sea floor. There is direct face-to-face competition among nations for these resources that are the common property of the world community. Under present international arrangements this competition is frequently accompanied by conflict, inefficiency, and depletion. Some authority, such as a Specialized Agency of the United Nations, should be established to promote the orderly and efficient development of these resources.

Another resource that is universally shared is the atmosphere that envelops the earth, an atmosphere that can carry contaminants to all corners. Increasing amounts of lead, carbon dioxide, and radioactive materials in the atmosphere are the concern of all people, and call for major cooperative efforts in the measurement and analysis of the contaminants, their effects, and their control.

Rivers that flow across or along boundaries between nations have always been a source of difficulty and an opportunity for cooperation. The establishment of international river basin commissions and the use of new approaches and techniques could speed the cooperative development of water and related land resources. The international agency for the Mekong and the Canada–U.S. Treaty for the Columbia, two quite different cases, are examples.

The world community has an interest not only in the resources that produce the raw materials for economic development but also in the resources that are a part of its heritage. Certain natural, scenic, and historic resources are unique and irreplaceable and should be shared by all peoples of the world. Establishment of an international trust could, where necessary, help the host countries to preserve and maintain these resources for the benefit of present and future generations of all mankind—such resources as the Serengeti Plains, Angel Falls, Angkor, the Grand Canyon of the Colorado, or the ruins of Incan cities. More vigorous cooperative efforts to protect certain endangered animal species will probably be necessary if their extinction is to be prevented.

In these and several other ways, the United States should seek the cooperation of other nations in improving the conservation and development of natural resources. In making these recommendations, we realize that there are many other opportunities that have not been addressed. In particular, we realize that major efforts should be made to prevent the economic distress that occurs because of violent changes in the price of certain resource commodities. Also, we want to encourage cooperative efforts to increase international investment in resource development.

An International Marine Resources Agency

Certain natural resources are unique in that no one has exclusive rights to their use or exploitation. Under these conditions, there are no restraints on the number of users that may participate in the resource industry. International resources that are included in this category are the fisheries of the high seas; the minerals on, and under, the deep sea floor; the atmosphere; outer space; and the radio spectrum. Of these, the fisheries and minerals are the most important in the production of raw materials.

International marine resources are the common property of the world community and not under the exclusive jurisdiction of any single nation. The sharing of these resources has frequently led to conflict between nations, and exploitation of the resources has been accompanied by both physical and economic waste.

The international fisheries that are shared by the world community are those that lie outside the limits of exclusive rights that are claimed by the coastal states. These limits generally range from three to twelve miles. There is no universally accepted agreement on a uniform width for exclusive fishing limits. In the case of minerals it is generally accepted that the minerals on and under the floor of the continental shelf belong to the coastal state, but the definition of ownership beyond the edge of the continental shelf is unresolved. A recently ratified international convention states that ownership by the coastal state extends out to a depth of 200 meters "or, beyond that limit, to where the depth of the superjacent waters admits of the exploitation of the natural resources. . . ." Thus, in minerals, as in fisheries, there is no effective agreement on the boundaries that divide the resources of the coastal state from those of the world community.

This lack of definition has frequently been a source of conflicts between nations, conflicts that are likely to increase in severity because the growing demands for marine resources tempt nations to appropriate larger areas of the seas for their exclusive use.

In fisheries, more and more nations are claiming extensions of limits out of twelve miles and some even beyond that. Since some of these claims close off areas that have been fished by other nations for many years, controversy is understandable. Impoundments of vessels and threats by warships are growing in number and are disrupting to international amity.

While similar conflicts have not yet occurred for minerals beyond the continental shelves, the potentialities for conflict are becoming more real. Much of the bottom of the deep sea floor is covered by small nodules that contain high percentages of manganese, nickel, copper, cobalt, and other metals. Current studies indicate that it may prove possible to mine these nodules economically in large quantities within the next few years.

Because these resources are clearly outside national jurisdictions, the possibility of their exploitation raises two problems: the efficient and orderly exploitation of the nodules, and the distribution or sharing of the mining rights. Producers must have exclusive mining rights to areas that are sufficiently large to permit them to operate economically and without fear of congestion or interference. And if rights are to be granted for resources that are the common property of the world community, then decisions on the allocation of these rights or on the methods of acquisition must be made within the framework of international law. A Specialized Agency of the United Nations would be the most appropriate body for administering the distribution of exclusive mining rights.

For international fishery resources, besides the problem of conflict, there is the fact that open access to the resources leads to depletion and to economic waste. For most resources, for which exclusive rights can be established, the sole owner or manager of a resource will invest only as much capital and labor as will maximize the net revenue. In international fisheries, however, this net revenue cannot be appropriated by a single user, but is shared by all who wish to participate in a particular fishery. Thus, as long as there is any "sharable profit" available, additional producers will be attracted into the fishery. And as additional producers enter, the amount of each producer's share will diminish until, eventually, all "sharable profit" is dissipated, and the net revenue of the industry is reduced to zero.

For example, a particular fishery may produce 120 million pounds of fish valued at $12 million annually. Under current conditions, the total costs to the producers will also be about $12 million. But it is likely that the same amount of catch and same value could be taken with two-thirds as much effort, or at a cost of about $8 million. Thus $4 million worth of capital and labor is wasted because of open access to the resources. Actually, the maximum net economic revenue might be obtained by even further reductions in effort. It might be possible to catch 100 million pounds of fish at a value of $10 million by the use of $5 million worth of capital and labor, thereby producing a net revenue of $5 million.

The inability to control access to the resource will lead not only to the application of excessive amounts of capital and labor, but also to the depletion of the resource. Each individual producer will attempt to get as large a share of the product for himself as possible. He cannot voluntarily and unilaterally restrain his own efforts in the interest of conservation because anything that he leaves for tomorrow will be taken by others today. It is this inability to restrain the amount of effort that has led to the depletion of numerous marine biological resources such as the whales of the Antarctic.

There have been many cooperative efforts among nations to prevent physical waste of marine fisheries. Such efforts, however, frequently mean increasing the costs of operation and they do nothing to prevent the waste of economic resources. These economic wastes can only be prevented by the establishment of restraints on the number of producers. The costs of excessive numbers of users on the radio spectrum would be clearly and painfully obvious, if controls had not been established to prevent this excessive competition. The costs in fisheries are less obvious but equally severe.

An additional problem in international fisheries may occur when techniques are developed to increase, by artificial means, the fertility of open areas on the high seas. Under current conditions, investments in such techniques are unlikely because the investor has no exclusive right to the fruits of his investment.

It is clear that the efficient and orderly exploitation of marine resources, including both fishery and mineral resources, calls for international arrangements that are beyond those already in existence. It would be desirable to establish a Specialized Agency of the

United Nations similar to those established for atomic energy, civil aviation, and telecommunications. This agency should have the responsibility for leasing exclusive rights to mine the nodules and other minerals on, and under, the deep sea floor. It should have the ability to promote the development of new techniques to increase the yield of biological materials from the sea. And it should have the ability to guide the use of the seas so as to prevent excessive competition and depletion of the resources.

A World Institute for Resource Analysis

Resource conservation and development in most countries could be strengthened by the application of modern techniques of analysis through which natural resources planning can be integrated with manpower development programs, capital requirements, and national and regional planning generally.

A number of agencies deal with analysis and planning of resource developments in particular countries or for particular resources, but there is no one agency that is responsible for integrated analysis and planning for all resources in whatever regional context is most useful. Particularly needed is a place where methods of analysis for development of inter-related resources can be devised, improved, and applied in demonstration situations.

As an example of the necessity for comprehensive and advanced analysis, during the last two or three years an interdisciplinary team including a number of American resource scientists and analysts has been developing a program to correct waterlogging and soil salinity which characterizes much of the Indus Valley in Pakistan. As analysis of the problem proceeded, its ramifications became more and more obvious. Water storage projects, drainage systems, improved use of irrigation water in agriculture, the manufacture of pumps and the provision of fuels to drive the pumps, not to mention a host of institutional changes, all seemed to be necessary if progress was to be made. Various types of systems analysis were utilized in trying to organize the elements of the problem and work out practical, minimum-cost programs.

A World Institute for Resource Analysis, made up of a central staff of experts drawn from such fields as hydrology, ecology, geology, various branches of engineering, soil sciences, economics, education, law, and sociology, could provide the setting and the impetus for much progress in the analysis of resource development techniques in the various countries and regions of the world where economic growth generally must wait on accelerated programs for agriculture, forestry, water resources, minerals, and the other resources.

In addition to research on analytical methods drawn from the various disciplines, such an institute might develop a technical aid service on which the planning and development agencies in various countries might call for help in analyzing their resources and putting workable programs together. Studies in comparative land and mineral law, as well as laws pertaining to the resources, could be undertaken and a legal consulting and drafting service might be organized. The institute could also be a repository of technical library materials which could be drawn upon through modern methods of data storage and retrieval by development agencies and enterprises all over the world.

The main thrust would be to fashion analytical tools and demonstrate their practical use in planning the development of natural resources. An institute along these lines could be sponsored by the United Nations, or it could be set up through some cooperative arrangement between national academies of science, or some other sponsorship might be found.

Cooperation in the Development of International Rivers

Throughout history, the use of rivers has been a source of conflict. The demands on rivers are many. They are a means of transportation; they are used for flood control and for water storage; for irrigation, hydroelectricity, and other purposes; they are a habitat for fish and they support wildlife; they are used for recreation; and they are used for disposal of waste effluents. Accommodation to these varied demands requires management and cooperation. The alternatives are conflict and inefficiency. When a river is an international boundary, or flows across national borders, the need for cooperation is vital.

It is obvious on the face of it that international streams will not be used with maximum effectiveness unless the countries involved approach the development of the river in a spirit of cooperation. People everywhere can understand this. If upstream users pollute a river, those living downstream are penalized by poor quality water.

If water is dammed and diverted upstream, it cannot be used downstream. Unless downstream people, frequently more numerous and with larger industries, cooperate with upstream users, their industries are likely to suffer. The difficulties are aggravated when a river serves as a boundary, for people of two countries then depend on a common watercourse for their livelihood. No other resource so clearly calls for international approaches to development as do the great international streams.

There are some successful examples of international agreement for river development. The Columbia River shared by Canada and the United States is an example, but here the treaty was agreed upon only after years of debate and difficulty. The same thing was true of the treaty relating to the St. Lawrence River reached several years ago between the same two countries. Navigation agreements on the Rhine River have served a useful purpose but there has been little progress in the resolution of pollution control problems. In other parts of the world, a few successes in international planning and development of river systems are far outnumbered by the instances where international cooperation has not been achieved.

The four countries that share the Lower Mekong—South Vietnam, Laos, Cambodia, and Thailand—during the last several years have continued to cooperate in planning the development of that great river even while war has been raging in the area. This is paradoxical and yet promising. President Johnson's proposal that the United States join with others in a large program for development of the Lower Mekong upon the cessation of hostilities in Southeast Asia is an exciting one. Through all the difficulties in that region the United Nations has continued to play an active and important role in helping the countries move forward in the planning phases for the Mekong development.

The United Nations, as well as individual countries and other organizations concerned with water development, might make a major contribution not only to river development but to peace and cooperation among the nations by announcing a program whereby in each major world region a particular river would be selected for intensive study, planning, and development as an example in international cooperation. The best techniques available anywhere in the world could be applied. Financing of the development might be underwritten by an appropriate international organization, or through the cooperation directly of central banks and perhaps private banks in the various countries. Such tangible, practical, understandable kinds of activities could do much to enhance cooperation among nations. A program of model river basin development could be a significant part of the International Conservation Quinquennium recommended below.

Various river basins come to mind as suitable candidates, including the Paraná shared by four countries in South America, the Mekong, of course, the Brahmaputra or Indus shared principally by India and Pakistan, the Zambesi in southeast Africa or one of the other great international streams in that continent.

U.S. Policy toward Non-governmental International Resource Organizations

Numerous organizations and associations are concerned with the conservation and development of particular resources, either in the world as a whole or in a particular region. Some of these organizations are private and some are mixed private and public. The U.S. Government from time to time finds it necessary to decide whether to support or participate in the affairs of such organizations, and if so in what way. The issue concerns the general policy of this Government with respect to such organizations and their activities.

The conservation and development of natural resources on a world scale is such a vast undertaking that there will always be room for numerous organizations concerned with particular aspects of the general subject. Indeed, it would be a mistake in any way to discourage the free and enthusiastic formation of such groups under private auspices, or under mixed government and private auspices. Such groups frequently approach problems in new and promising ways that are later adopted by official agencies of governments. Understanding of problems and policies in the resource field can be enhanced through the lively and widespread activity of private groups.

Organizations on the scene at the present time represent a wide range of interest. Among them are the World Forestry Congress, the International Union for the Conservation of Nature and Natural Resources, an international organization dealing with irrigation and drainage of land, the Inter-American Association of Sanitary Engineering, a World Power Congress, a number of groups concerned with health and medical problems, with administrative problems in the less developed countries, at least one organization concerned with international effects of radiation, professional organizations with worldwide membership in the various sciences such as biology and geology and also in some of the social sciences, and so on.

In addition to all this there are notable efforts by private business and industrial groups through which certain activities relating to research, exchange of information, resource inventories and surveys, and international conferences are carried on. One such example is to be found in an organization made up of various copper-producing companies whose purpose is to sponsor certain kinds of research and informational activities useful to all the members. This and perhaps other groups like it can be of immense benefit to particular resource industries and hence to economic development generally.

The policy of the U.S. Government toward this wide and variegated range of organizations is poorly defined. There are many areas where U.S. Government participation has done much to further cooperative relationships, as, for example, in the International Hydrologic Decade. There are, however, other areas where the U.S. Government has not taken full advantage of its opportunities to advance international comity on resource matters.

The U.S. Government should consult with representatives of a number of private and quasi-public resource groups on possible improvements in U.S. policy with respect to encouragement and participation in such organizations and their programs. The general shape of this policy should be to offer, to the fullest extent practicable, support to such groups through such means as participation in conferences, preparation of technical materials, lending and exchange of technical personnel, and taking out of memberships where this is desirable.

Specifically, we endorse the active participation of the U.S. Government in the International Biological Program, and we recommend that it take membership in the International Union for the Conservation of Nature and Natural Resources; that it aid, through financing and other means, the cooperative efforts of the Inter-American Association of Sanitary Engineering; and that it encourage more attention to natural resource problems of international organizations devoted to public administration.

An International Conservation Quinquennium

Natural resources conservation and development is of worldwide importance now as never before. A world program, making use of new techniques and knowledge, and demonstrating these through practical and appealing conservation activities, holds much promise for advancing the conservation and development of natural resources throughout the world.

The International Hydrological Decade, the International Geophysical Year, and the International Cooperation Year itself have dramatized the importance of worldwide cooperation in making progress in particular fields. Resources conservation and development is an area where the concentration of world effort offers the opportunity for progress both in the field itself and in perfecting the techniques for international cooperation.

An International Conservation Quinquennium could be a rallying point for all who are concerned with resources conservation and development—scientists, engineers, health officials, devotees of wildlife, those concerned with agricultural, livestock and forest development, organizations for the development of fuel and mineral resources, and many others. An International Conservation Quinquennium could dramatize the unique potentials of conservation as a means to international understanding and cooperation. In addition, the ICQ would provide the focal point for the detailed exploration and development of international conservation proposals such as those recommended here.

A fundamental element of the ICQ might be the application of knowledge gained from the other international cooperation programs. Special efforts should be made to apply the results of research undertaken during the International Geophysical Year, the International Hydrological Decade, and the International Biological Program.

Other elements of ICQ might include internationally planned research activities; programs in various countries to demonstrate the application of new conservation techniques; the holding of international conferences on conservation, parks, vanishing species and other aspects of natural resources; ICQ educational units with appropriate audio-visual materials for various levels of the school systems in all countries; materials for adult education programs in all the major languages; perhaps airborne exhibits using several large cargo planes which would move from country to country, and so on. The more obviously international resources such as those shared by nations—international streams, marine fisheries, migratory wildfowl—as well as those such as agricultural and mineral products that enter into world trade in a major way, offer especially good opportunities. Emphasis would be placed on the responsibility of all individuals and all countries for the natural resources and the natural environment of the world everyone shares.

For carrying out the program of the International Conservation Quinquennium, the United Nations itself is the logical leader and sponsor. Appropriate UN agencies would, of course, be involved. A variety of national, governmental, and private organizations over the world would also be encouraged to take part. The essential ingredients would be leadership and a program, plus financing.

A Quinquennium rather than a year or a decade is desirable for several reasons. One year is not long enough for a program of such scope and particularly for practical demonstrations in agriculture and other renewable resources where growing time is important. A decade on the other hand is too long; there is risk of loss of interest and of activities being carried on at too slow a pace.

Preservation of Vanishing Species

Increasing numbers of species of fauna and flora throughout the world are vanishing, or are gravely in danger of extinction. This is a consequence of industrial, technological, and population growth and of the influence of such growth on the natural environment and its ecosystems. The extinction of species represents an irreplaceable cultural and scientific loss.

About 200 species of animals have disappeared in the last 2000 years, 38 per cent of them in the last fifty years. About 250 more are on the danger list, including the Whooping Crane, Hawaiian Goose, three races of Asian Rhinos, Great Blue Whale, Arabian Oryx.

The rate of extinction of species can only be halted if governments, institutions, and individuals are made aware of the dangers of extinction and are encouraged to take action to safeguard them. Efforts are now under way by the U.S. Fish and Wildlife Service, the Survival Service Commission of the International Union for Conservation of Nature, and the World Wildlife Fund, among others.

The preservation of species is largely a non-controversial subject that can be of interest and concern to people of all nationalities and that can be used to stimulate international cooperation and amity. Attempts should be made to provide, for animals and plants threatened with extinction, an appropriate area of natural habitat in a national park, wildlife refuge, wilderness area or equivalent reserve in order to maintain an adequate breeding population for the benefit of future generations.

Environmental Pollution

The environment, on which man's health and welfare depend, is more and more a matter for world concern both because of the large number of people whose life span is shortened and whose energy is sapped by diseases transmitted through the polluted environment and because of the worldwide transmission of contaminants through the earth's atmosphere and oceans. In addition, there is the disfigurement and ugliness that come from unplanned and careless treatment of the natural environment of land, water, and air.

In some countries or areas the problem is one of establishing or improving facilities for the treatment and disposal of domestic and municipal wastes. In others, the problem is one of identifying and analyzing contaminants that are by-products of industrial and technological developments, determining the effects of these substances, and finding ways to deal with them.

In most low-income countries, the disposal of sanitary wastes is generally inadequate. Growing population and increasing urbanization are making the consequences of this inadequacy more severe. Exposure to disease is almost unavoidable and, with debilitation and short life spans, the productive capacity of the people is a small fraction of what it might be. This gross waste in manpower resources, which is one of the greatest impediments to economic development and growth, requires the immediate provision of inexpensive sewage disposal facilities. More intensive international efforts should be devoted to the development and provision of these facilities in low-income countries. These efforts should include cooperative research, technical training, financing, and education.

In many of the high-income countries, technological advances and industrial growth are accompanied by increasing contamination of the environment. The pollutants include radioactive materials, excessive amounts of carbon dioxide and lead in the atmosphere, oil wastes on the high seas, pesticides, and many others. There are several problems created by such pollutants. Identification and quantitative measurement are frequently very difficult. Effects on man's health may be indirect and are not easy to evaluate. Some of the contaminants are slow to disappear and some can accumulate in organic tissues. They tend to be pervasive and some may even contaminate the whole envelope of the earth's atmosphere. The sources of some of these pollutants are widely distributed, and control may be extremely difficult to establish. These problems call for great research effort, not only in the physical and biological sciences but also in the fields of economics, political science, and international relations.

The United States should take the lead in establishing a worldwide monitoring system that can identify and measure the contaminants of the atmosphere and the ocean. It should provide for intensive research on the biological and physiological effects of contaminants; their distribution in air and ocean currents; the sources of pollution; methods for control; and analysis of costs of controls.

The United States should also foster a program for measurements of certain qualitative aspects of the environment, particularly those relating to trace substances that could be associated with chronic toxic effects. This might be done either as a part of the International Conservation Quinquennium or as a separate effort. The objective would be to obtain simultaneous and commensurable measurements of a variety of environmental variables thought to affect health, and of a variety of associated social and economic variables. Statistical analysis of these data would help to answer many difficult and important questions in this field where deliberate experimentation is usually impossible. The effort should be planned by a group including environmental health specialists, experts in statistical inference, economists, and other social scientists.

A Trust for the World Heritage

Certain scenic, historic, and natural resources are part of man's heritage, and their survival is a matter of major concern to all. Some of these resources, however, are in danger of being damaged or destroyed because of inadequate planning; because of the lack of knowledge of the value of the resources; or because of the costs of management and protection.

Some examples of the unique and irreplaceable resources that are part of the world's heritage would include: the Grand Canyon of the Colorado; the Serengeti Plains; Angel Falls; Mt. Everest; archaeological sites such as Angkor, Petra, or the ruins of Inca, Mayan, and

Aztec cities; historic structures such as the pyramids, the Acropolis, or Stonehenge. Also important but in a somewhat different way are the areas whose main value lies in the spectacular animal species they support—the Indian rhinoceros, mountain gorilla, and the orang-utan, for example. Even though falling within national boundaries, resources such as those listed above are of legitimate international concern and should be maintained for the study and enjoyment of all peoples of the world and for the benefit of the country in which they lie.

Many of these areas are already under the protection of national governments, but some lie within states that may find it difficult to bear the costs of preservation and management. The establishment of preserves in some of the less developed countries may conflict with other economic development opportunities. In such cases, the world as a whole may wish to help defray the costs of protection and wish to contribute, in other ways, to the better management and proper use of such areas as a means toward the economic growth of such countries.

In other cases, the danger stems from a lack of interest and failure to appreciate the significance of the resource. In these cases, both national and international educational efforts would be required.

Several steps are necessary for the preservation and long-term maintenance of these areas as a part of the world heritage. The first lies in the compilation of a basic list of areas and sites that might be of international concern. It should be the right and responsibility of each nation to nominate those areas within its boundaries that might be considered for inclusion in the Trust.

The next step would be to evaluate the basic list and select those few areas and sites that meet the high standards that would be required. It is essential that the criteria for selection be highly refined and that the Trust include only those areas and sites that are absolutely superb, unique, and irreplaceable.

International cooperative efforts should be made to raise the funds and provide technical services to facilitate the establishment and continued maintenance of the areas. Educational programs should also be established throughout the world in order to acquaint all people with the value of their heritage and the necessity for its protection. Tourism should be promoted for the benefit of the host countries and to demonstrate the value of protecting such areas.

Practical Training for Resource Management

Development of basic natural resources is essential to improving the levels of living in all countries, but especially in the poorer, less developed ones. A major barrier in the less developed countries, where two-thirds of all mankind live, is the lack of a sufficient number of trained resource technicians and middle-level managers and conservation officers such as surveyors, mappers, forest and park rangers, soil analysts, stream gaugers, mine foremen, area directors of soil and water conservation programs, and so on.

Few of the developing nations possess an adequate supply of men trained to develop and manage their natural resources. Yet the basic wealth of those nations, without exception, consists of those resources, both renewable and non-renewable. Economic development assistance provided by the more developed nations can produce only short-term benefits when the recipient nations are not in a position to continue and sustain the development thus initiated.

Efficient management of minerals, forests, water, soil, wildlife, rangelands, and fisheries requires professional competence. The proposal for a Trust for the World Heritage would have little chance of success unless trained personnel were available to secure its objectives.

Resource management education should be available at three levels: full professional training at universities for "top grades," technical training on a non-degree basis for "middle grades," and "in-service" training. These should be considered not as separate compartments but as complementary parts of a whole.

University training will be provided in the countries where appropriate curricula are available, and more scholarships should be provided for resource studies. Universities in the developing nations themselves should be encouraged to establish resource-oriented courses and departments. In-service training programs should be provided to give the essential basic requirements to resource workers as well as to provide refresher courses for the higher managerial levels.

But it is in the so-called "middle grades" that there is probably the greatest need for training. Studies at foreign universities are sometimes far removed from, or even irrelevant to, local needs and realities. Moreover, the university route is too slow, too expensive, and too elite-directed to meet the urgent and large-scale needs for practical resource skills.

The answer lies in the worldwide development of non-degree, vocationally oriented resource management programs, providing one or two years of training with heavy emphasis on practical field application. Experimentation with curriculum should be encouraged, and there should be no doctrinaire obsession with conventional academic standards. The criterion for curriculum must always be how well it serves the resource needs of its area. Such schools should be located close to those resources whose management needs they are designed to meet. They should be developed on a regional basis wherever possible. In places where such programs have been started, efforts can be concentrated on improving them.

To accomplish these goals, there should be an immediate international inventory of resource management skills by country and by resource, and a concurrent inventory of training facilities. The needs for facilities and skills can be determined and priorities can be fixed in conjunction with information on probable resource development programs. For the attainment of these goals international funds and technical assistance must be made available on a large scale, together with contributions from the countries in which the training takes place.

The initial survey, which could be undertaken by the International Institute for Educational Planning, could lead to proposals for establishing resource management training programs in the various countries, some covering all resources and some specializing in forestry, soils, wildlife, geological or hydrological surveys, depending on the needs of the particular country or region. Suitable help with curricula, teaching staff, and instructional materials could be offered by international agencies and by institutions in countries which already have had experience. First attention might be given to assuring an adequate number of qualified teachers for the resource management programs.

RECOMMENDATIONS

We recommend that:

1. A Specialized Agency of the United Nations be established for international marine resources, including fishery and mineral re-

sources, for the purposes of preventing conflict, reducing the waste of capital and labor, ensuring orderly and efficient exploitation of mineral resources, and preventing the depletion of fisheries.

2. A World Institute for Resource Analysis be established to fashion and test new techniques for analyzing the problems and potentialities of integrated natural resources development as a means toward economic advancement.

3. The countries of the world, through the United Nations and in conjunction with appropriate organizations and societies, establish international river basin commissions, where they do not already exist, for the purpose of promoting cooperative development.

4. The U.S. Government consult with representatives of a number of private and quasi-public international resource organizations on possible improvements in U.S. policy with respect to encouragement and participation in such organizations and their programs.

5. An International Conservation Quinquennium be undertaken as a means of fostering international cooperation for resources conservation and development.

6. Attempts be made to provide adequate habitat for animal and plant species threatened with extinction.

7. More intensive international efforts be devoted to the development and provision of inexpensive sewage disposal facilities in less developed countries and that the United States take the lead in programs for the identification and measurement of contaminants of the environment on a worldwide basis.

8. There be established a Trust for the World Heritage for the identification, establishment, and management of the world's superb natural and scenic areas and historic sites.

9. A survey be made of the needs for resource technicians and managers in developing countries as a basis for the establishment of programs for resource training.

THE COMMITTEE ON CONSERVATION
AND DEVELOPMENT OF NATURAL RESOURCES

8. Assisting Economic Development

One of the most dramatic and significant undertakings in the history of international cooperation is the current attempt of nearly 100 developing nations to modernize themselves with the assistance of a score of industrial nations. This effort truly is of gargantuan proportions, for it involves making profound economic, social, and political changes in the lives of two-thirds of the world's population.

At the center of this modernization process in most of the developing countries today is an attempt to accelerate economic growth in order to raise their societies out of the depths of poverty and, at the same time, to cope with populations growing at an explosive rate.

The United States has taken the leadership in helping these nations achieve their goals. Not only has the U.S. Government made available some $46 billion for foreign economic aid since the end of the Marshall Plan, but it has worked actively to create new multilateral channels through which free world assistance is now flowing to the developing nations. Moreover, private American enterprise has played a supplementary role, primarily through the direct investment of more than $10 billion in the economies of the developing countries since 1950.

Economic development of these nations, however, requires capital, skills, and cooperation on an unprecedented scale. While the free world, for example, disbursed some $6 billion in assistance to the developing countries in 1964 alone, the additional amounts needed to support adequate growth have been estimated variously at between $3 and $20 billion. This annual gap between the need and the ability to increase production is likely to continue, and may grow wider. How to fill this void, both by mobilizing additional resources and by improving the capacity of the developing nations to invest available resources, is the major problem of international economic development today.

While fully recognizing that there are limits to the resources of donor countries and limits to the pace at which the capacity of recipient countries to absorb can be increased, the question persists: What can the United States, drawing upon the resources of both its public and private sectors, do to make more effective its economic aid to the developing nations?

Financial Assistance

Development Performance and Aid Levels

A crucial element in economic development is the success of an aid-receiving government in pursuing policies which foster financial stability and encourage long-range development. To promote such self-help measures, the United States has sought to build a consensus with the recipient government on the goals of that country's development and on the resources and investment policies required to achieve those goals. Moreover, the United States has attempted to work out the explicit understanding that good performance in undertaking self-help policies will be accompanied by increased aid. Such programming, it is believed, not only creates incentives in countries where aid is now concentrated, but sets an example for other nations, encouraging them to refocus their policies toward economic growth.

A paradox arises, however, from the very success of self-help. The approach requiring the least amount of assistance in the long run is the one which demands a relatively large volume of assistance during the early period when self-help measures are initiated and first become effective. This is because rapid growth at the outset makes possible early reforms and increases in internal savings, which can then sooner fully support further growth. At the same time, effective policies and energetic self-help enlarge the capacity of a developing nation to use external resources wisely.

Since most of the countries in which U.S. aid is concentrated are just entering this critical stage, we see no lessening of the need for foreign aid well into the future as long as economic growth is to be accelerated and made self-sustaining in the underdeveloped world. Moreover, delay is likely to heighten the long-range cost for both donor and recipient countries. Not only is the present level of assistance entirely insufficient for prospective needs, it is already inadequate for current needs.

What should be the future volume of U.S. assistance? The U.S. Government is on record in full support of the United Nations' goal of having each industrialized country make available for development assistance the equivalent of 1 per cent of its Gross National Product. This pledge was to be honored during the 1960's, the "Decade of Development." Yet the record shows that while America's GNP has increased remarkably in recent years, the actual volume of aid has decreased, both as a percentage of the national product and in dollar amount. In order to have reached the 1 per cent goal in 1964, the United States would have had to increase its actual economic contributions to developing countries by approximately one-quarter from all sources, public and private.

In recognition of this pledge, we recommend that as a minimum the United States meet the target of 1 per cent of its Gross National Product for development assistance. This is the same target which the United States has urged upon other donor nations.

The Need for a Multi-Year Foreign Aid Authorization

Economic development is a slow, arduous process in any country. When one visualizes more than 100 countries—some of them only contemplating development today and others at various early stages of growth—proceeding unevenly, often haltingly, toward the goal of self-sustenance, the time dimension of foreign economic assistance is put in proper perspective. Aid will be needed for a long time.

While the United States, in its own interest, will continue to play a major role in international development for many years to come, the legislation on which that role is based should reflect the real world—not a world of wishful thinking. We Americans should be explicit that we are engaged in foreign assistance until the goals of development are reached.

A standing or at least a multi-year foreign aid authorization would express the will of Congress and the American people that foreign assistance is a regular and long-term responsibility of the U.S. Government, and that the United States, as a nation, is determined to meet the challenge of disease, ignorance, and poverty overseas, as well as at home, in the interest of world peace and stability.

A standing or multi-year foreign aid authorization would permit the Executive and Legislative branches to focus on the central problems of foreign assistance, such as aid strategies, performance standards, burden sharing with other donors, ways and means of assistance, and other underlying policy issues. They would not then, as at present, battle over the basic question of whether there should be an aid program or not. Congressional supervision, of course, would continue to be exercised through the annual appropriations process, periodic policy reviews, and specific inquiries into agency operations.

Our observation indicates that the current pattern of annual aid authorizations is highly inefficient for the U.S. Government, besides being unrealistic. Not only do senior AID officials have to make twice as many appearances before Congress as most other Government executives, but an enormous amount of agency resources must be channeled into preparation of the request for authorization. Congress itself is burdened unnecessarily in this process, to the detriment of other legislative programs. The uncertain outcome of the annual debate over the very existence of AID, it should be added, is detrimental to employee morale and certainly hampers recruiting efforts to attract the top-caliber personnel required for technical assistance work. The same uncertainty undoubtedly has a deleterious effect upon development planners in those countries which receive American assistance.

We strongly favor a foreign aid authorization which permits the President to conduct a foreign economic assistance program for at least five years, subject to annual appropriations. The annual volume should reach 1 per cent of U.S. Gross National Product, as suggested previously.

Economic and Military Assistance

Economic and military aid are both important tools of foreign policy; both serve short- and long-range U.S. political objectives. For more than ten years, economic and military assistance have been combined in the same legislation, although identified separately as to form and content. The Department of Defense administers the military program under the foreign policy guidance of the Secretary of State, and there is coordination with other forms of assistance through the Agency of International Development.

The desirability of further separating economic and military aid has been debated within the Executive Branch and is the subject of Congressional interest. The Executive Branch has left the question of separation to the Congress to resolve.

We believe that the combined bill for military and economc aid confuses public understanding of the objective of supporting economic development in the developing countries. Investment in long-term social and economic growth is best portrayed independently of our system of military alliances and our capacity to defend the free world. Moreover, if the two programs were separated, our military assistance programs could be more fully related to U.S. security interests as such.

Some Americans view foreign assistance as a combination of tools for securing broad U.S. Security objectives and believe that military and economic aid should, therefore, be contained in the same legislative program. This argument of complementarity has gained support from a variety of Congressional and public advocates of both kinds of foreign assistance. Some are concerned that separation of the two programs will leave military aid less susceptible to foreign policy guidance from both the Congress and the Department of State.

Net advantages, however, probably will accrue from a separation of the statutory authorization of these two kinds of assistance, although coordination of them by the Secretary of State should continue. We therefore recommend that the Congress separate economic and military assistance in its future consideration of U.S. foreign aid programs.

Multilateral Assistance

Since their beginning U.S. aid programs have been conducted in part on a bilateral, in part on a multilateral, basis. Today they are largely carried out within a multilateral framework. A broad spectrum of channels now exists through which U.S. resources can be directed to developing countries, ranging from the strictly bilateral aid relationship between the United States and a recipient country to the complete transfer of direct control over a U.S. contribution to a multinational organization. In between is a variety of arrangements, set up over the years to meet specific situations and purposes.

The increasing reliance of the United States upon new channels of multilateral assistance reflects recognition of the diversity of needs prevailing among developing countries, as well as a mutuality of purpose among donor and recipient nations and a willingness to work in concert.

There have been several significant developments expressive of this shift.

The U.S. Government continues to be a major supporter of multinational development banks such as the World Bank, its affiliate the International Development Association, and the Inter-American Development Bank. Recently the United States agreed to contribute $750 million over a three-year period to the IDB's Fund for Special Operations. The U.S. Government supports the regional development bank in Africa, and is cooperating in the creation of the Asian Development Bank.

The U.S. Government has favored the merger of interrelated United Nations operations into a new United Nations Development Program, and has offered to continue to increase its pledge beyond $60 million annually on a matching basis.

Increasingly, the U.S. Government uses multilateral coordination devices for bilateral assistance, such as working through the Development Assistance Committee of the Organization for Economic Cooperation and Development, through the international consortia for India, Pakistan, and Turkey, and through consultative groups for Nigeria, Thailand, and Colombia.

International administration of aid has enabled the U.S. Government to give essential assistance in politically delicate situations, such as to the United Nations Civilian Operation program in the Congo (Léopoldville) and to the Indus Basin Development Fund, involving India and Pakistan.

In fiscal year 1966, 85 per cent of U.S. development loans in Asia and Africa were committed through international coordinating arrangements and the entire assistance program for Latin America extended through the Alliance for Progress.

These forms of multilateral assistance activity have not only made the utilization of aid more effective, but have encouraged donor countries to undertake more equitable shares of the overall burden alongside the United States.

However commendable past multilateral activities have been, we believe that multinational organizations such as the World Bank and the regional development banks should expand their assistance activities even further. Specifically, these organizations should reinforce policies of performance evaluation and incentive programming to make assistance levels even more directly dependent upon specific self-help measures carried out by recipient countries.

Adoption of these policies, however, assumes two conditions:

First, multinational organizations would have to shift an appropriate portion of their resources from *project* to *program* assistance, planned within the total economic requirements of recipient countries. Program lending is needed to provide foreign exchange for a wide variety of import needs, such as raw materials, semi-manufactures, and industrial equipment and parts which are crucial but inappropriate or individually too small to be treated as separate "projects." Indeed, a developing country may increasingly need non-project assistance as its major "projects" are established.

Second, performance evaluation and incentive programming may require additional funds for those multinational organizations adopting them. As private citizens we believe that it might be necessary to increase the relative U.S. share of these funds as an inducement to other donors to increase their own contributions.

We favor the multilateral approach to the task of development, be it through multinational institutions, formal coordination mechanisms or consultative arrangements. We urge the United States to enlarge the area of close international cooperation in the most appropriate form to meet specific development needs.

Regional Cooperation

In the long run, economic progress in any country undoubtedly requires specialization and the achievement of economies of scale. And these objectives, in turn, depend upon a sufficiently large and politically stable marketing area that individual business enterprises and basic utilities can expand to their optimum operating efficiency.

We cannot hope that countries of the less developed regions will make the same rapid progress toward regional cooperation and market integration experienced under the Marshall Plan by the countries of Western Europe after World War II. Given their brief experience with political independence, the strength of national feelings, the lack of basic skills, and the inadequacy of economic and social infrastructure, the less developed nations can be expected to work primarily as separate and individual entities for some years.

Over the long run, however, these countries must broaden their economic and political horizons. Many of them are of insufficient size to forsake rationally planned economic relationships with neighbors; indeed, some sixty-five of these nations have populations of fewer than 5 million people with low per capita incomes. Few of them can afford to disavow the advantages of cooperative planning, specialization, and market integration which could flow from regional cooperation.

Although national rivalries and antagonisms impede economic progress in some places today, there are some encouraging signs of cooperation.

In Latin America, the ten-year program adopted by five Central American nations, leading to their eventual economic unification, is a promising development. The Latin American Free Trade Association, consisting of nine nations whose combined gross product is more than 80 per cent of the total for Latin America, has made some progress toward its goal of eliminating barriers to trade among its membership. And, increasingly, the Inter-American Committee of the Alliance for Progress (CIAP) and the Inter-American Development Bank have become effective instruments for sound hemispheric economic collaboration.

In Africa, considerable progress has been made. The Organization of African Unity serves as a forum through which mutual problems can be resolved peacefully. Last year an African Development Bank was established, much sooner than anyone had anticipated. A customs union is already in operation among the Cameroun, the Central African Republic, Chad, and the Congo (Brazzaville), and four countries in West Africa—Guinea, Ivory Coast, Liberia, and Sierra Leone—are discussing establishment of a free trade zone. Other projects currently under consideration are a common market for eleven West African countries, to embrace textiles, chemicals, and metallurgical products initially, and cooperative development of several large river basins, such as for the Chad, Senegal, and Niger rivers.

Even in Asia—where the obstacles to broad regional cooperation are perhaps most intractable—progress is being made. The Indus Basin Development Fund and the coordinated development of the Mekong River Basin have proceeded apace, despite the most formidable political difficulties. And now nearing completion is the Asian Highway, an imaginative, cooperative undertaking. The Asian Development Bank will be established shortly. Cooperation for these and other projects on a broad regional scale has been fostered by the Colombo Plan—a major feature of which is stimulation of cooperative action among its members, notably the provision of assistance by the developing countries to each other. The UN Economic Commission for Asia and the Far East (ECAFE) has also taken an active role in stimulating regional cooperation.

It is a major U.S. Government policy to give vigorous and substantial support to these cooperative efforts, so long as they do not result in increasing barriers to trade with other regions. The American commitment to such regional activity has been demonstrated in other much less publicized projects, many of them sponsored by non-governmental organizations, business firms, and labor unions.

We applaud these efforts and their accomplishments to date, and we single out the President's recent initiative in proposing an expanded Southeast Asia Development Program as an especially laudable act of American leadership.

The U.S. Government should take further steps to stimulate public and private regional cooperation as a means of promoting economic development. It should, for example, encourage the regional joint planning of basic utilities and major industrial investments, of trade and payments liberalization, and of institutions to pool knowledge and other resources.

Food and Population

It is becoming clear that one of the great and urgent problems for the remaining decades of this century will be to meet the demand for food of the rapidly growing populations of the developing countries. The number of people in the world is increasing at such a rapid rate that the increase in population between now and the year 2000 is likely *to equal or exceed* the current population. Indeed, there is evidence that only a major mobilization of cooperative effort—both in vastly increasing agricultural production and in undertaking programs of family planning—will avert mass starvation in some countries.

Foreign assistance policy must be based upon full recognition of the urgency of increasing food production in the developing countries at the very time when the amount of new land suitable for cultivation is rapidly diminishing. Increased food output, therefore, must come primarily from higher acreage yields, rather than from opening new land as in the past.

Rapid and sustained increases in yields such as are now needed generally in the developing countries have been achieved in a number of industrial countries and in a few developing countries as a result of major effort. It has been not only a matter of fertilizer, water, improved seed, technical knowledge, and farm credit, but the successful interaction of a myriad of economic and social factors which provide essential incentive, means and support to farmers. Unless crop prices are and can be expected to remain favorable, unless markets are organized to provide the farmer prompt and full returns of things he wants, the individual farmer is unlikely to put forth the strenuous effort and risk the innovations required to raise productivity. Sound patterns of land tenure, fair tax systems, dynamic and open markets are essential.

While there are many varied demands within developing nations for capital and technical assistance, the United States must give priority to responding to requests for assistance in food production and take all appropriate steps to persuade developing countries of the mutually supporting relationship of agricultural and industrial growth. The relative emphasis given to agriculture by the Agency for International Development, consisting in fiscal year 1964 of only 10 per cent of all capital assistance and 12 per cent of all technical assistance, seems out of proportion to the vast scale of the world's food problem.

Agri-business and the agricultural support industry play a key role in development. The fertilizer and seed producers, the feed industry, market cooperatives, agricultural equipment manufacturers and dealers all have a stake in agricultural development. The United States and recipient country governments and private industry should explore together ways and means of utilizing more effectively the knowledge, experience, talent and capital of the private agricultural support industry to expand agricultural production in developing countries.

We feel profound anxiety over the slow progress being achieved in family planning programs in many of the developing nations. The technical means for effective planning now exist, but many educational, organizational, and logistical problems persist. Hopefully the new AID policy of assisting developing nations, upon request, to establish and expand programs of voluntary family planning will help meet some of these needs.

We recommend that substantially increased technical and capital assistance be made available in appropriate support of efforts by the developing countries to expand food production and meet the rising demand for voluntary family planning.

Technical Assistance

The Problem of Personnel

As the developing countries succeed in making economic headway, their need for many kinds of technical assistance increases. The need for professional advice expands in progressive circles of specialization.

The Agency for International Development has found it difficult to maintain a ready pool of personnel able to furnish the wide variety of special expertise required for development work abroad. While the most prompt way of furnishing expertise is the assignment of one of its own direct-hire technicians, the impracticality of this procedure on a large scale has led AID increasingly to award contracts to universities, labor unions, cooperative leagues, savings and loan associations, and other private organizations, or to make service agreements with other U.S. Government agencies, for the furnishing of development specialists.

Universities and non-governmental organizations are major sources of experts capable of performing first-rate technical assistance work. But the demands upon the universities for teaching and research are increasing and many of them are loath to divert their outstanding faculty members to temporary overseas assignments no matter how meritorious they may believe the work to be. A program should be worked out whereby the Agency for International Development would provide financial support to universities and research organizations to expand their professional staff in anticipation that some staff members would be serving abroad on a rotating basis at all times.

Another source of expertise is found in U.S. Government agencies. AID increasingly has relied upon such personnel to supplement its own specialists. Several agencies have formed what might be called "special international corps," cadres of experts made available to AID and the UN agencies from time to time under service agreements.

In the past, an expert's temporary assignment with AID or the UN agencies abroad has sometimes conflicted with his permanent career in another Federal agency. New partnership arrangements have been made, however, which may ameliorate this problem. Other Federal agencies have become more involved in foreign assistance project and program planning and have been giving greater recognition to their overseas responsibilities. Inter-agency problems persist, however, and their solution is only partly within the capacity of AID or the UN agencies. An Interagency Overseas Development Board should be established to engage Federal agencies more effectively in foreign assistance work and encourage their cooperation with AID and the United Nations agencies by furnishing highly qualified personnel. Such a Board would establish policies for making Government personnel more readily available for foreign assignment and would serve as an instrument for solving inter-agency problems arising from such assignment.

While AID currently is making progress in obtaining suitable overseas personnel from other Federal agencies, its apparatus for recruiting experts from universities, state and local governments, and private organizations leaves much to be desired. Lengthy delays occur in the search for specialists. Rarely are those interested in assignment immediately available. Organizations sometimes respond to personnel requests by supplying their least competent employees. Faced with the danger of becoming cut off from the mainstream of promotion and other opportunities in their home organization, many specialists simply refuse to engage in technical assistance work in which they otherwise have a strong interest.

We believe that the problems associated with the recruitment of appropriate technical assistance personnel are so difficult of solution that a somewhat radical approach is required. The Executive Branch should develop a proposal for the establishment of a Development Reserve Corps to maintain a ready supply of trained and experienced technical assistance personnel available for overseas assignment to AID and the UN agencies. Membership in this Corps would be open to qualified persons, whether employees of government, universities, businesses, or other organizations, who have a strong interest in occasional overseas work. Veterans of AID and international organization assistance programs and returning Peace Corps Volunteers would likely furnish many of the candidates.

Administrative processing, which now delays assignment abroad, could be handled at the time of a member's entry into the Corps. While on inactive duty, the member could undertake language and other training by classroom work or correspondence course. The obligation to accept active duty ought to be more flexible than now prevails in the military reserve, yet the sense of obligation to accept it should be maintained. While on active duty, a member's career status and re-employment rights would be protected. Reservists also should earn compensation and retirement credit for both training and active duty.

Personnel for United Nations Agencies

A special personnel problem exists for the United States in recruiting its citizens for work in the technical assistance programs of the United Nations and its Specialized Agencies abroad, not only because of the special skills required but also because of the relatively low salaries paid. Hence, while the U.S. Government contributes 40 per cent of the program costs, American nationals make up a much smaller percentage of the international staffs. The President recognized the problem in a memorandum of August 15, 1964, and urged Federal agencies to take affirmative steps to recruit Americans for this work.

Two proposals for action, one by the U.S. Government and the other by private organizations, have merit as ways to recruit additional technical personnel for the United Nations agencies.

One approach would be active U.S. participation in the Associate Experts Program of the United Nations, a scheme under which 146 young technical experts from the Netherlands, Germany, Sweden, Belgium, Norway, and France served in developing countries in 1964 at the expense of their own governments. Six international agencies now seek such Associate Experts; the Food and Agriculture Organization has asked the United States for fifty Americans and the International Telecommunication Union has asked for four. Probably some 100 recent university graduates from the United States could be usefully employed in the first year of participation.

While the United States initiated the United Nations resolution under which the Associate Experts Program was established, no funds have been made available for it. If they were, it is likely that some of the Americans accepting temporary Associate Expert appointments would remain with the United Nations agencies for permanent careers. In any event, the scheme would make a real contribution to the work of the agencies and increase the number of professional Americans with field experience in developing countries.

A second approach would be a more significant contribution by private organizations to the assistance programs of the United Nations agencies. The American pharmaceutical industry, for example, could be of great help to the World Health Organization, while American fertilizer and seed producers could bring their knowledge to the FAO. A program of White House Internships in International Organizations should be established whereby private businesses and organizations in the United States would furnish annually a small number of their staff experts and junior executives to serve temporarily with the United Nations and its Specialized Agencies.

We envision a modest program of ten to twenty interns each year, chosen by the President and offered by him to the international agencies, with salaries to be paid by the contributing firms and organizations. A special tax ruling authorizing salary payments to be treated as a business expense would, of course, be advantageous. Many American firms and organizations would welcome this opportunity to make a contribution to international development, both in the expertise imported and in the broader understanding of development problems which interns would bring back to their employers.

Coordination with the Peace Corps

The creation of the Peace Corps in 1961 gave outlet to the widespread impulse on the part of Americans, both young and old, to participate constructively in the development of the poorer regions of the world and in building international understanding. The soundness of the Peace Corps idea, the strength of motivation throughout the United States, and the vigor of its overall direction have produced a brilliant record of accomplishment in the years since its establishment. The United States and many countries abroad have benefited richly from its activities. In its first years the Peace Corps has striven with success to establish a position of separateness from short-run diplomatic considerations, while its volunteers live and work with less privileged people. This has put a new face on official American service overseas that should be carefully preserved.

Now that the Peace Corps is well established, however, there is need to give attention to coordinating its activities with other U.S. Government programs, particularly those of the Agency for International Development. Both agencies are deeply involved in development work and each can give support to the other. For example, AID can assist a country with the construction of schools, provision of equipment, and the training of teachers and administrators, while the Peace Corps can supply some of the teachers. AID can provide fertilizer, research, advisors, and other requirements for modern agriculture, while the Peace Corps can supply workers to bring modern practices to the farms. This kind of cooperation is occasionally being developed through the informal collaboration of field staffs. It should take a much more important place in the work of both agencies. Steps should be taken to coordinate activities of the Peace Corps and the Agency for International Development, both in program planning and in field operations.

The success of the Peace Corps has been followed by vigorous efforts on the part of sixteen other nations to send their own young people for service in developing countries. About 1,500 volunteers from these countries are now in the field. This, in turn, has stimulated the interest of educated youth in the developing countries themselves—few in number, but highly motivated—to offer themselves for service not on foreign shores, but in the remote areas of their own countries. This is a tremendously encouraging advance in mutual help in these countries, penetrating social barriers and promising responsibility for self-development. It has been estimated that there are seventy developing countries, in all parts of the world, where "domestic peace corps" could be founded. Already nine such nations have inaugurated programs of voluntary national service. What is now required is a more intensive focus on this relatively new form of self-help in developing countries.

To this end, the International Secretariat for Volunteer Service (ISVS) is providing valuable technical advice and encouragement. Organized by forty-one governments in 1962, the ISVS is carrying forward programs of information exchange which are steadily expanding the Peace Corps idea throughout the world. We believe that the United States should continue its support of this important new venture in international cooperation.

Private Investment

Private American organizations such as business firms, labor unions, cooperatives, voluntary organizations, foundations, and non-profit enterprises bring a wide variety of advantages to the task of assisting developing nations. Their own special resources, whether capital or skills, are valuable contributions. Many of these organizations can operate with great flexibility and ingenuity. Many have long-standing relationships with private organizations elsewhere in the world.

Equally important is the fact that the voluntary nature of most of these organizations serves as an object lesson to the peoples of the developing countries, demonstrating to them the value and viability of free institutions. Just as private organizations, with their independence of means and relative freedom for responsible decisions, ensure a pluralistic social order in the United States, so they can encourage other peoples to create independent institutions which will promote the values of human dignity, freedom, and social responsibility.

Another advantage of private assistance activities should be stressed. To the extent that private organizations increase the number of American citizens who are directly or indirectly associated with development work—whether as overseas representatives or loyal supporters back home—a greater understanding of the goals and difficulties of international development is engendered throughout the United States.

Already a large number of private American organizations are engaged in development work, some of it supported by the Agency for International Development and some by independent means. Enormous opportunity remains, however, for increasing the active participation of these and of other non-engaged organizations in the challenging effort of assisting the developing nations.

American business organizations have access to many resources which the developing countries desperately need, not the least of which is a large amount of relatively mobile capital for investment. The entrepreneurial, managerial, and certain technical skills needed by developing nations can often be found only in the private sector of the U.S. economy.

Private enterprise, moreover, can help greatly to establish the kind of network of effective, decentralized decision-makers within an economy that ensures a multiplicity of independent initiatives in the task of economic development. Historically, such decentralized decision-making has characterized every society which has managed to achieve rapid economic growth while preserving both human freedom and social stability.

The need of the developing countries for increased inputs of capital, skills, and energy is so great today that public assistance cannot be supplied in adequate amounts. Private investment remains the only source, a source largely untapped even in recent years, in spite of attempts by the developing nations and most multinational assistance organizations to stimulate the investment flow through an array of promotional services, special credits, guarantees, tax inducements, and other devices.

The accumulated U.S. direct investment of over $15 billion, combined with the substantial investment of other industrialized countries, accounts for one-tenth of the total production of all developing countries today (largely concentrated in the extraction of oil and minerals). But much more needs to be done. Net new American private direct investment (other than in oil) in all of Asia, Africa, and the Middle East in 1963 was substantially less than that in shopping centers in only *one* of the dormitory counties near Washington, D.C., in the same year!

Why have only a few hundred U.S. private firms—and correspondingly few firms from other industrialized countries—been playing an active role in development activities abroad?

The answer is clear enough. The primary obligation of the managers of private firms is to be prudent trustees of their stockholders' money. Before making any investment, the managers must make a careful calculation in which potential profits are weighed against risks and difficulties as well as against alternative investment opportunities at home and in other industrialized or developing countries. To date, even with special assistance and inducements, this calculus has dictated against investment in the developing countries by all but a small proportion of the American and European firms which could play a valuable role in economic development. A different pattern of decisions will require major changes in the factors involved in the profit-risk equation.

Many aspects of development influence this situation. Investment in power, education, and road-building, for example, are essential to establish the "infrastructure" which is a pre-condition to successful private investment, just as general stability is a necessary, if not a sufficient, condition for attracting investors.

Foreign investors once gave relatively little consideration to the welfare of local populations in their wage, price, and management policies, but this is no longer true. For one thing, increasing amounts have been going in recent years into manufacturing, local distribution, housing, and other non-extractive activities. Many firms with overseas operations today seek to contribute to the development of the host country by adopting policies of modest profit expectations, of re-investing earnings, of employing local nationals as company executives, and of encouraging local participation in ownership.

The exploitative nature of much early foreign investment has left a residue of hostility in many developing countries, and yet, most of their current development plans are predicated upon substantial inflows of foreign private investment as a significant source of capital and skills. The Alliance for Progress, for example, originally anticipated an annual level of $300 million in new U.S. private investment as a major element in Latin American development. Similarly, India's forthcoming five-year plan reportedly calls for a similar volume of foreign private investment annually from all sources.

However, foreign investment activities, important as they are, can never be expected to cover more than a few major industrial and commercial activities in any developing country. Local enterprises must be relied upon to develop the great number of small and medium-sized businesses which are the bulwark of a modern economy. But even taken together, foreign private investment and domestic private enterprise are making only a small contribution to economic development when judged either by their potential or by the size of the need.

The complex problems of stimulating increased private enterprise activity in developing countries have been intensively studied by many responsible individuals and groups during the past dozen years. After examining earlier studies and proposals, we believe that the heightened need to stimulate foreign private investment today justified serious consideration of somewhat more radical approaches to the problem than other groups have felt able to endorse in the past.

Improving the Investment Climate

The extent of private investment in any developing country will depend, more than anything else, upon the attractiveness of that country's general investment climate. Shaped initially by the country's political and economic ideologies, that climate involves, among many other factors, the legal and administrative rules which circumscribe a private investor and the competence and honesty of local government officials who deal with him.

Much can be done by any developing nation to improve its economic climate, if it has the will to do so. Outside counsel can be of great assistance. We recommend the following actions to improve the investment climate in many developing nations which have substantial needs for capital input:

1. That the Agency for International Development, in cooperation with private businessmen, undertake studies in a selected number of countries of the key factors which determine the investment climate therein; that an action program designed to improve the climate in the countries studied be carried out; and that AID take all possible steps in its program activities to improve such investment climate.

2. A serious and thoughtful statement of the case for the beneficial role of private investment in development should be prepared and widely distributed in developing countries.

Encouraging Local Private Enterprise

While many foreign assistance organizations have undertaken programs designed to encourage the development of local private enterprise, the following steps could improve current activities:

1. The existing complex of development banks, industrial development centers, other local financial institutions in support of private and cooperative enterprises should be substantially assisted to assure that they have the proper direction, staffing, and financing to be effective promoters of local enterprise. The expertise of the United States and other industrialized countries as well as that of other developing countries whose institutions may be relevant should be used.

2. In view of the special need for stronger local banking services in many developing countries, the Agency for International Development should encourage commercial banks to expand their joint venture operations with local commercial banks in developing countries.

3. Multilateral agencies should try to devise workable investment guarantee or insurance programs to protect foreign private investors against political risks.

4. Educational programs designed to develop local managerial and other business skills should be expanded.

5. Private business organizations should increase their efforts to furnish entrepreneurial, managerial, and technical skills to local private enterprise through arrangements such as the International Executive Service Corps.

6. Special programs to identify and support local entrepreneurs in the developing countries should be organized and encouraged.

Mobilizing the Resources of the Financial Community

Before World War II, the investment banking community had long been the major mechanism for mobilizing capital for development purposes, both public and private, in industrialized as well as developing countries. Together with its access to capital, the community possessed unique skills for the formulation of "bankable" projects. For many reasons, however, this traditional role has shifted during the past two decades to multilateral and bilateral government agencies.

Today there are substantial arguments for restoring the private investment banking community to a more influential position in future development financing activities. Private financing is highly flexible in nature. Private bankers, for example, can switch from one payments surplus country to another in search of funds with more flexibility than public authorities can accomplish resource shifts through international negotiations. The many public financial international organizations and arrangements, including the International Monetary Fund and various assistance programs, reduce the risk for private capital venturing into the developing countries by promising a more stable and progressive world economic order.

In view of these considerations, we believe the time has come to re-examine the potential contribution of the world investment banking community, both in its capital and its skills, to development financing. We recommend that:

1. The Agency for International Development experiment with contractual agreements with investment banking organizations to investigate, analyze, and document projects in developing countries which are suitable for private or mixed public-private financing.

2. AID explore the feasibility of making its specific risk guarantees available to American buyers of selected new issues of foreign private enterprises, preferably through underwriters.

3. AID, working closely with the Treasury Department and the investment banking community, explore new devices for using its appropriated funds to obtain a multiplier effect in increasing private capital inputs to developing countries.

Encouraging More Direct Investment

Since direct investment from private sources is an ideal vehicle for the simultaneous input of capital, skills, and energies into developing countries, efforts ought to be made to improve the awareness of investors of specific investment opportunities, to improve the profit-risk ratio affecting such opportunities, and to provide a wider range of private-government risk-sharing arrangements.

We recommend that:

1. United States, multinational, and host country agencies collect and systematize much more accurate information about specific investment opportunities than is now available.

2. The Congress enact a proposal for a tax credit equal to a substantial percentage of the investment by United States investors in productive facilities in developing countries, to be applied against the total United States tax liability of such investors.

3. The feasibility of special arrangements, similar to those of the

domestic Small Business Investment Corporations, should be considered by which international investment corporations could be created for operations in developing countries.

4. The U.S. Government should explore the idea of participating with American operating firms in major industrialization projects, when profit potentials are unknown or doubtful but the project is of great importance, by providing a substantial portion of the capital required in the form of advances, junior to debt, to be repaid only if the operation is successful.

Involving Private Operating Firms without Investment

Some important industrial and commercial projects in the developing countries simply will not attract private direct investment under any conditions. Yet if the justification is great enough, a competent operating firm certainly can provide the best source of technical and managerial skills to develop and operate the project effectively. The technique of the cost-plus-incentive-fee contract, now widely used in the United States for operations in the defense, space and anti-poverty programs, appears to have potential adaptability to those special situations where operating skills are needed but investment prospects are nil. This technique has rarely been used in assistance programs to aid industry and commerce.

We recommend that:

1. AID should be authorized to bring American operating and systems firms into high-priority development projects, where normal private investment is not forthcoming, on a cost-plus-incentive-fee contract basis, possibly with an equity option. Initial equity ownership of such projects normally would be vested in a government corporation or development bank in the developing country involved, but provision should be made to transfer ownership to local and United States private investors at the earliest feasible time. Provision should also be made to train local personnel to replace Americans as rapidly as possible.

2. Other national and multinational aid agencies should be encouraged to provide for similar "chosen instrument" arrangements whenever appropriate.

Enlisting Business Leaders as Advisors to AID

Historically, private businessmen have been the major moving force in the economic development of the United States and other industrialized countries. In contrast, government has been more predominant since World War II in assisting economic development abroad. The role of the business community has been random and sporadic, often consisting of participation by business leaders in temporary advisory, study, or evaluation groups, or of service abroad by individual businessmen within government organizations.

We believe that the time is ripe to arrange for orderly high-level participation of the American business community in our foreign assistance programs. If carefully planned, such an approach could help focus attention upon specific investment opportunities and could stimulate individual firms to join in development efforts abroad.

We recommend that:

1. A permanent International Private Investment Development Board be established consisting of a small number of leading American businessmen who would be given extensive advisory responsibilities within the United States foreign assistance program.

2. Other industrialized countries should be encouraged to establish similar arrangements for responsible business participation in overseas development planning and operations.

As we envision the Board, its members would serve full or part-time and be supported by a small staff. They should have funds for international travel and for contracting with consulting and service organizations when necessary.

Among its advisory responsibilities, the Board would seek to identify development situations where private enterprise could play a special role and try to involve specific U.S. firms in these situations. The Board would investigate high-priority development projects to which private firms had not responded and recommend such government support as believed necessary to insure their participation. In instances when this level of support was approved by the AID Administrator, the Board would act as the agent of AID in arranging for participation of a responsible firm or of a special private consortium.

Other Private Organizations

A potential source of contributions to development exists among the numerous non-business organizations in the United States. Local social clubs and organizations, which abound throughout the country, have the capacity to raise funds for overseas projects, but sometimes need guidance to make their projects appropriate.

One AID-stimulated framework for involving U.S. community and service groups in international cooperation is the Partners of the

Alliance program. The basic concept of the Partnership program is to enlist and encourage private initiative for joint community action in support of relatively small, but meaningful, self-help projects in Latin America. Already the Partners of the Alliance program has been the catalyst for direct private-sector alliances between the people of twenty-six U.S. states and areas in twelve Latin American countries. The idea has evoked the enthusiastic response of many kinds of organizations, from scout troops and community service groups to labor unions, professional associations, and local chambers of commerce.

One result of these Partnerships has been the creation of new areas of United States–Latin American private-sector cooperation in the fields of education, technology, culture, and finance. International conferences are planned to discuss specific community needs and self-help efforts in education, health and sanitation, social welfare, agriculture, and industrial and community development, with a view toward securing the support of local U.S. communities.

We recommend that programs parallel in concept to the Partners of the Alliance be established for the developing countries of Africa and Asia.

Another major and traditional form of private participation in development is through private welfare agencies operating abroad. Those agencies registered with the AID Advisory Committee on Voluntary Foreign Aid alone maintain 600 American citizen representatives overseas at their own expense. They employ about 5,000 local personnel and work closely with volunteer counterparts in the host countries. Their work demonstrates that voluntary service can be effective and strengthens the growth of free institutions in recipient countries.

Although many of these organizations are actively participating in relief programs, including the administration of substantial Food for Peace programs, they have long recognized that relief work— however necessary—is not enough, and have sought to extend their programs into self-help, community development, and training activities that get at the roots of hunger, poverty, and disease. Major health and education programs in many developing countries have long been supported by private U.S. organizations.

AID has expanded its support for these private voluntary agencies. The Agency already pays overseas freight costs on supplies for relief, rehabilitation, and technical assistance programs donated to, or purchased by, American voluntary agencies. Through AID, limited amounts of excess property—jeeps, machine tools for vocational training, and the like—have been made available for voluntary agency programs overseas. However, there is a considerable need for closer coordination of these programs to increase their effectiveness.

We recommend that the Agency for International Development and the voluntary agencies collaborate more closely on program development to maximize the contribution of voluntary programs to development.

Yet another type of private organization is the specialized non-profit technical assistance and contract organization, such as the Asia Foundation, the African-American Institute, the Near East Foundation, and Education and World Affairs. These institutions offer a unique combination of area knowledge, technical competence in specific fields, intimate working relationships with governments and institutions in their professional or geographic areas, and private financial support. AID and other Federal agencies have increasingly contracted for the services of some of these organizations in certain phases of overseas assistance, since such contracts provide a flexible and efficient means of project implementation. From a national perspective these organizations constitute another reservoir of expert personnel and specialized area knowledge.

One problem of these non-profit technical assistance organizations is that they frequently operate without adequate funds. Unlike universities, they do not have endowments, state government support, or privileged access to private foundations. Yet, they must compete in the same labor market with universities and government agencies to obtain and hold their specialized personnel. In many cases their capability has been adversely affected by their financial instability. If such agencies are to develop greater institutional strength and expand personnel reserves for technical assistance work, ways must be found to insure their stability and permanence. A modification of existing AID contracting policies ought to take into account the broader institutional and financial requirements of these non-profit institutions and not just the costs involved in servicing specific projects.

We recommend that AID find appropriate means to support the personnel and institutional capabilities of private specialized non-profit technical assistance organizations.

THE COMMITTEE ON TECHNICAL COOPERATION
AND INVESTMENT

Manpower: A Key Problem

The critical factor for newly independent and modernizing states —as, indeed, for all societies—is the effective development and utilization of their own human resources. They need people who are able to provide health and educational services, organize and run business enterprises, mobilize capital, produce foodstuffs, make use of natural resources, build bridges and roads, create markets, carry on trade. The potentialities of every society for social, economic, and political growth—as well as for responsible participation in an international community—are embedded in its people and largely determined by its capacity to develop and utilize their abilities and talents.

In the newly independent states, the manpower skills and abilities needed range from those of managerial, technological, scientific, and other professional personnel to those of skilled craftsmen, technicians, and semiskilled industrial operatives. Such societies are likely to lack not only experienced competent supervisory and managerial personnel but also industrial workers who can read and write, as well as specialists with the skills requisite for the planning and operation of manpower development programs. Perhaps the skills and talents in shortest supply and most acutely needed are those of managerial, scientific, professional, and technical personnel in the middle-to-highest ranges of skill.

Through private enterprises operating overseas, philanthropic foundations, and departments and agencies of the Federal Government, the United States is attempting to assist other societies in their efforts to develop their manpower resources. The ongoing activities, both governmental and private, designed to provide such assistance are wide-ranging in their objectives and forms and frequently inventive in the cooperative relationships they have established. Taken together, they touch many aspects of the processes involved in the identification of manpower needs and in efforts for human resource development. In many instances, they are contributing to overcoming critical manpower deficiencies which frustrate the goals of newly independent states. Clearly, these ongoing activities deserve applause and support.

The United Nations and its related agencies engage in extensive activities designed to help meet the need for managerial, professional, and technical personnel, as well as other categories of manpower, in the newly developing states. One agency alone, the United Nations Special Fund, is helping to finance 186 centers for advanced education and technical training in 74 countries. In many situations, close collaboration between such activities of the United Nations and the United Nations Special Fund and corresponding activities of the U.S. Government and philanthropic agencies can maximize the constructive effects of the respective contributions.

U.S. private enterprises in foreign countries have trained, and currently are training, local nations for almost all types of jobs required in modern industry. They have demonstrated repeatedly that, with appropriate organization and direction, the nationals of newly emerging states can be rapidly and effectively trained as technicians of many sorts. They have also demonstrated that they can give training of this kind more effectively than local trade or vocational schools. On the average, U.S. companies have required between one-third and one-fifth of the time required by local trade and vocational schools to give comparable vocational training. Finally, they have manifested both capacity and willingness to train local personnel for middle-to-top managerial posts.

In many newly developing states, U.S. philanthropic foundations have provided experts to assist in surveying manpower needs, apprenticeship training and a variety of other aspects of manpower analysis and development. In collaboration with U.S. labor unions, they have also helped to make available experienced labor union personnel to assist in the development of responsible labor union leadership in newly developing states. At various points, philanthropic foundations have collaborated in giving help of this kind with AID, the Department of Labor, and other departments and agencies of the U.S. Government, in an appropriately worked out division of effort between the governmental and the private sector.

Technical assistance designed to enable newly independent states to develop their manpower resources is provided both directly and indirectly by the U.S. Government. Direct assistance is given primarily through AID and the Department of Labor, and indirect assistance through the United Nations, the International Labor Organization, the United Nations Special Fund, and other Specialized

Agencies of the United Nations, and the Organization for Economic Cooperation and Development.

In 1964, with the United States playing a major role in its development, the member states of OECD adopted an agreement setting forth common guidelines for their manpower objectives and policies. The agreement represents a landmark in international cooperation among more fully developed Western economies.

With the United States cooperating actively, OECD and the United Nations Specialized Agencies and its Regional Economic Commissions have contributed significantly to vocational training and many other aspects of manpower development. ILO's great stress upon vocational training is reflected in the fact that of the forty-nine UN Special Fund projects assigned to the ILO so far, thirty-one relate to vocational training. The United States, especially the U.S. Department of Labor, has contributed thirty-five experts in the field of apprenticeship and vocational training to the ILO for its technical assistance activities in the developing countries.

Through AID and the Department of Labor the United States is helping some ten developing states to approach their manpower problems and objectives in a comprehensive manner. This involves providing technical assistance for the gathering and analysis of statistics, the assessment of manpower requirements, the founding and operation of employment services, the design of wage and salary policies, the shaping of formal educational systems, and the creation of on-the-job training mechanisms. To carry out its objectives in the manpower area, AID depends heavily upon the resources of colleges and universities in the United States.

Comprehensive strategies of manpower development are needed in a number of the newly independent states. There is a corresponding need for a new category of professional and executive personnel, who might be called specialists in comprehensive planning for manpower development and utilization.

AID and the Department of Labor have established an International Manpower Institute in Washington to help train manpower planners and technicians from the developing countries. These are invited each year to send middle and high-level staff to the Institute for two months to participate in seminars conducted by international experts. The seminars cover comprehensive manpower planning, statistics, vocational training, and employment service operations. The participants are also given opportunities to work with experts in a range of manpower specialities. The United Nations and its Specialized Agencies have also established managerial and technical training institutes.

In order to assure more effective international cooperation on the part of the United States, the Department of Labor recently created another instrument. This is its International Technical Assistance Cadre (DOLITAC), the purpose of which is to improve the quality of technical assistance provided by the Department by making readily available to developing countries groups of competent manpower technicians. DOLITAC represents an effort to improve on the process of selecting individuals for overseas service by avoiding drawn-out negotiations with various bureaus and the time consumed in persuading individuals, making arrangements for families to move, language training, and the like. With manpower technicians committed and available, the time for preparation can be greatly reduced so that requests for assistance can be responded to promptly. Moreover, while serving at home, such personnel can enhance the effectiveness of assistance programs through their own research and directed study on a variety of problems and subjects.

Much of the assistance which the United States provides to help newly independent states fulfill their manpower needs is focused on formal education, involving primary and secondary schools, vocational and technical institutions, and universities. Much of this educational assistance, in turn, is achieved through the international movement of educational personnel—teachers, students, researchers, and administrators. The U.S. Government and a number of private foundations and other non-profit institutions play a significant part in facilitating the flow of educational personnel between the United States and newly emerging as well as other advanced societies.

In many parts of the world, a new or renewed appreciation of the function of education is manifested in emphasis upon the expansion and qualitative improvement of educational systems and opportunities. Qualified educational personnel is at a premium. For many societies, particularly the newly independent states, access to external resources of educational manpower and institutions is necessary. The relevance and utility of U.S. educational personnel to other nations have been growing. A number of new states have been seeking to borrow and adapt to their needs some of the educational aspirations, experiences, and techniques of the United States.

With the accelerating pace of educational growth and change in other parts of the world, U.S. educational personnel need to learn about educational attitudes and innovations tried out elsewhere. Apart from the possible contribution of U.S. personnel to development in other societies, their efforts at home might benefit from a closer observation of educational currents elsewhere.

While the international movement of educational personnel is now substantial, the supply of U.S. citizens capable and motivated to serve abroad remains uncertain. It consists mainly of teachers and researchers drawn from a variety of sources for relatively short periods of time—from schools; colleges; universities; Federal, state, and local governments; consulting firms; private enterprises; and non-profit organizations.

These efforts to train the manpower needed for world development should be intensified. We recommend the following measures:

On-the-Job Training by Private Enterprise. U.S. private corporations operating in Latin America, Asia or Africa should seek to devise programs of training of local personnel along the following lines:

1. In accordance with understandings reached with the host government or with local private enterprise, they would train personnel not only for their own employment but for the needs of the economy of the host country.

2. Operating either singly or in collaboration with other U.S. companies, or in collaboration with local enterprises, each should undertake to train local personnel in excess of its own anticipated requirements. The number to be so trained should be determined by its own training capabilities and the needs and absorptive capacity of the local economy. As a rough initial target, to be adjusted and refined on the basis of locally determined needs and capacities, it might aim at training perhaps twice as many men as it needs itself.

3. The training should relate to: (i) advanced management, (ii) supervisory and foreman responsibilities, (iii) skills in technical crafts, (iv) clerical and office skills, (v) marketing and distribution skills.

Financing of On-the-Job Training. The U.S. Government—and the private U.S. enterprises involved—should seek to finance such extended on-the-job training in one or more of the following ways:

1. By a contract between a U.S. company or group of companies

and the U.S. Government under which AID, the Department of Labor, or some other appropriate department or agency would underwrite the cost.

2. By a contract between such a company or group of companies and the government of the host country under which the host government would bear the cost of such extended training, perhaps with financial assistance from the U.S. Government.

3. In appropriate cases, as a contribution made by the U.S. company to the host country, perhaps negotiated as a part of an economic development agreement.

4. Through support by American philanthropic foundations, including company-affiliated or company-sponsored foundations.

Comprehensive Programming of Manpower Development. To assist newly developing states to design and carry out comprehensive strategies for manpower development, the U.S. Government, building upon work currently under way through AID and the Department of Labor, might undertake:

1. The systematic training of professional and executive personnel in (i) the analysis of manpower requirements, (ii) the analysis of the relationships among manpower requirements and programs of formal education and on-the-job training, (iii) relationships among the foregoing and wage and salary policies and other job incentives, (iv) development of overall strategies to give effect to such integrated planning, and (v) the arts of imparting such skills to others.

2. A program to make men so trained available to newly developing societies which want them and can use them constructively.

Cooperation by Private Philanthropic Foundations. Private philanthropic foundations can help in the training of manpower planners and in making such trained planners available to newly developing states.

THE COMMITTEE ON MANPOWER

9. *Strengthening International Finance*

Over the past two decades international cooperation in monetary affairs and development finance has become a deeply ingrained operational habit among governments. It is now both broad in scope and intensive in detail. Side by side, and to an increasing degree in concert with such institutional development, the role of private financial and business entities has grown in importance and in contribution. Both of these developments have facilitated the very substantial progress achieved in the postwar world economy. To assure the continuation of the progress that has been made, it is essential to take stock of the present and consider our course for the future in all important segments of international finance.

International Monetary Cooperation

A well-functioning international payments system is essential to the expansion and balanced growth of world trade, output, and employment. The central features of the present system include the dollar as a major trading and reserve currency in fixed relation to gold, the continued role of sterling, private credit facilities for financing trade and payments, and, on the official level, a growing network of international monetary cooperation. In the broad sweep of the past two decades this monetary and payments system has effectively met the demands placed on it. Highly flexible and adaptive, it has facilitated vast gains.

Restrictionism, competitive devaluations and other "beggar my neighbor" policies characteristic of the 1930's have been largely averted. Reconstruction and peacetime growth have been strengthened. In the past decade alone, world trade has doubled. Very substantial increases have taken place in real income and output. While there have been problems, economic gains made in many parts of the free world have been most encouraging.

The foundation for postwar international monetary cooperation was laid in 1944 when forty-four nations met at Bretton Woods. Even in the midst of a great world war the nations assembled there were mindful of the need to find an alternative to the exchange tactics and trade restrictions of the 1930's by which governments, often at the expense of each other, vainly sought to maintain employment and living standards. The alternative was conceived as a comprehensive structure that would institutionalize cooperation in exchange policies as a normal mode of behavior for nations at peace. The result was the International Monetary Fund, brought into being just two decades ago.

The International Monetary Fund

The Fund's objectives were defined as the promotion of international monetary cooperation, exchange rate stability, and the elimination of exchange restrictions. These aims were regarded not as ends in themselves but as means of facilitating the expansion of international trade and helping all Fund members to achieve and maintain high levels of production, employment and income. Rules of conduct were prescribed and resources and technical know-how were mobilized with which the Fund could assist members, when necessary, to follow these rules.

As a medium-term credit institution, the Fund stands ready to provide its members with monetary resources to enable them to overcome temporary payments difficulties through orderly and constructive measures rather than internationally destructive ones. Its transactions take the form of sales of foreign currencies to members in exchange for the member's own currency. Through its policies and operations, and through consultations with its members, the Fund is an effective instrument in international financial and monetary behavior.

The Fund began operations with resources totaling $7.2 billion, consisting of country quotas which determined for each member its contribution, voting strength, and the general limits of its ability to call on the Fund's resources. Quotas were generally required to be paid 25 per cent in gold and the balance in national currency. The drawing rights created in return for the gold payment (technically, the "gold tranche") have come to be recognized as an international monetary reserve asset, since foreign currencies equal to the "gold tranche" can be obtained from the Fund practically without question.

Additional medium-term credits may be obtained of up to 100 per cent of the quota, and in rare exceptions even somewhat beyond this limit. Progressively stricter performance criteria must be satisfied as a country uses increasing amounts of Fund credits. Repayment to the Fund, that is, repurchasing its own currency with gold or convertible currencies, is required within three to five years.

As of November, 1965, Fund quotas stood at about $16 billion. To further strengthen the Fund and with it the world payments system, members are implementing a general 25 per cent increase in quotas. This, along with some special additional increases, will raise the total to about $21 billion, including $5.2 billion for the United States. "Gold tranche" positions or quasi-automatic drawing rights, which now stand at $5.6 billion over all, will be increased to $6.8 billion as a result of this action.

The Fund has been especially active in recent years in both developing and developed countries. Dollars, which the Fund used extensively in providing credits in earlier years, have in recent years come back to it in repayments and with beneficial effect to the United States in financing its own deficit. In the last two years, the United States has itself made relatively small technical drawings from the Fund, and in July, 1965, for the first time made a regular drawing of $300 million. The United Kingdom in substantial operations drew $1 billion in 1964 and $1.4 billion in 1965. In both cases calls were made on the Fund's gold and on the General Arrangements to Borrow to obtain the needed currencies, as the Fund's regular resources in those currencies had become limited.

The Group of Ten

The General Arrangements to Borrow, better known as the GAB or "The Group of Ten," took shape in 1962 for an initial five-year period. It came into being as it became evident that the resources of the Fund in the form of currencies other than dollars and sterling might prove to be insufficient in the event of a threat to the stability of the world monetary system. A significant innovation in the payments system, it consists of the ten principal financial centers within the membership of the Fund (with Switzerland, which is not a member of the Fund, subsequently associated through special arrangements). The ten countries agreed among themselves to lend to the Fund, in case of need, amounts of their own currencies totaling $6 billion. In the course of this financial association the "Group of Ten" has also provided a framework for other cooperative activity. The Finance Ministers and Central Bank Governors comprising the

Ten meet from time to time, and their deputies even now are considering measures for improving the functioning of the international monetary system.

Other Forms of Monetary Cooperation

The return to convertibility in the late 1950's brought with it the problem of dealing with highly volatile movements of capital between financial centers, at times placing a strain on the system. Sudden exchange market pressures need to be met firmly and promptly, lest there be growing waves of disruptive speculation.

To meet such situations, the United States in cooperation with eleven major industrial countries and the Bank for International Settlements established, beginning in 1962, a swap network of short-term facilities totaling over $2.5 billion. Because of their nature and purpose, these swaps are essentially bilateral in construction and operation.

Under these arrangements, the United States is able to acquire currencies needed for exchange market operations through short-term swap operations rather than selling gold to foreign monetary authorities. When the temporary outflow of funds reverses itself, the swap can then be reversed. The market operations, spot and forward, themselves have undergone developments and refinements, so that in a short span of years they have become smooth working techniques.

Another recent addition to international liquidity takes the form of special non-marketable securities denominated in the currency of the creditor which the United States has issued to foreign monetary authorities. These range in maturities of up to two years. Such special securities presently outstanding exceed $1.1 billion and are generally held as reserves by foreign central banks.

In the last few years, new scope and importance have also been attached to more frequent consultations among those directly concerned with policy and operations in the financial centers. A specialized subgroup of the Organization for Economic Cooperation and Development (OECD), Working Party 3, consisting primarily of senior officers of treasuries and central banks, meets frequently to come to grips with problems in the balance-of-payments field and in related monetary operations. These consultations are importantly supplemented by the frequent meetings of central bank representatives under the aegis of the Bank for International Settlements in Basle, Switzerland. And generally within the OECD, forums exist for consultation on the broad range of economic policies and programs being pursued by individual countries which have major international financial consequences.

Cooperation in Development Finance

Just as the Bretton Woods conference in 1944 sought to further monetary cooperation, it also sought to attack the financing problems of reconstruction and development. Long-term financial resources were needed at reasonable rates by the countries destroyed by war, as well as by nations whose economic potentials have not yet been developed. The World Bank was established for these purposes to complement the proposed medium-term International Monetary Fund in the payments field.

The World Bank

The International Bank for Reconstruction and Development (IBRD), established at the end of 1945, has grown to a membership of over 100 countries—each of them required also to be members of the Fund. Its authorized capital has been increased from an original $10 billion to the present $22 billion. Almost 90 per cent of the capital is callable and serves as backing for bonds which the World Bank issues in world capital markets. The Bank has borrowed a total of over $4.5 billion in eight currencies to finance its loan operations. In addition, the Bank has sold $1.8 billion of loans from its portfolio to private investors, and generally has broadened the access of its borrowers to the private capital markets.

In the early postwar years, the Bank made almost a half billion dollars of loans to speed reconstruction in Western Europe. Since then its principal focus has been on lending to the developing countries.

The bulk of the Bank's $8.8 billion total lending has been in such basic fields as electric power and transportation, dams and roads, railroads and ports. More than $1 billion has been lent for industrial development, and over a half billion for agriculture. The Bank has recently begun to move in new directions in its lending for advanced and technical education, water supply projects, and for relending through local agricultural credit institutions. These efforts are bearing fruit.

Affiliates of the World Bank

The Bank has grown from a single institution into an integrated family of institutions. The International Finance Corporation (IFC), established in 1956, concentrates exclusively on financing private enterprise development. Essentially as catalyst for much larger private investment, IFC has a small revolving capital and has made net commitments of over $115 million in a broad variety of private industrial enterprises located in thirty countries. The IFC has recently obtained authority to borrow from the World Bank, and thus has increased substantially its resources available for private enterprise lending.

The International Development Association (IDA), established in 1960, represented a new response to the need for sound credits on easy repayments terms for the poorer countries. Its fifty-year interest-free terms are designed to permit countries facing a serious problem of servicing further external debt on conventional terms to maintain the momentum of their development through external borrowing without aggravating their payments situation. IDA has now committed over $1 billion for development projects on its own especially favorable terms. Its original $1 billion capital has been replenished and consideration of further resource needs will soon be undertaken.

Regional and Other Development Institutions

On the regional level, the Inter-American Development Bank, established in 1959, met a financial need for hemispheric cooperation among the American republics. It has made great strides and has become in a real sense the "Bank of the Alliance"—its principal financial arm. During 1964, the African Development Bank came into being, and an Asian Development Bank is coming into existence.

Effective international cooperation requires effective international coordination of the lending policies, philosophies and practices of donor countries and institutions in the various phases of development finance. This has been recognized for some time by the United States, whose major role both in its own programs and through the multilateral institutions in the development effort is well known. The World Bank has brought capital exporting countries together in major consortia and has started consultative groups on several developing countries. The Development Assistance Committee (DAC) of the OECD, located in Paris and numbering fourteen of the major countries providing development assistance, also provides an important method of consulting on direct assistance efforts. These consultative techniques are generally receiving increasing emphasis.

The Private Sector

Increasingly from the latter period of the Marshall Plan and through the period of steady growth of the developed countries, private banking and investment have fulfilled an essential need for credit and capital resources. In this the U.S. capital markets and direct investment of U.S. capital overseas have played a substantial role. This flow was indispensable to an expanding world economy, particularly at a time when other industrial countries were short of capital. The role played by U.S. private resources and initiatives has been accentuated by having to compensate for lack of adequately developed capital markets abroad. In the developing countries, increasing efforts to channel and attract private resources have been markedly assisted by the example and support of international financial institutions.

Are Present Arrangements Adequate?

International financial and monetary cooperation have become commonplace in the postwar period. While occasional failures or frictions in cooperative efforts tend to command attention, very sizable positive achievements are clearly manifest.

A triple-faceted structure of international cooperation now exists to meet a variety of financial stresses and strains on the system. An efficient network of immediately available foreign exchange swap facilities among the key central banks provides a first line of defense for threats in the major foreign exchange markets. The International Monetary Fund, supplemented by the General Arrangements to Borrow, provides a second line of defense for all its members with medium-term resources. Finally, the international attack on intolerably low levels of well-being in the less developed countries is centered in the World Bank family which provides long-term financing for development.

This three-pronged institutional structure is buttressed and interlocked with a number of consultative techniques. At many levels and in many forums face-to-face discussions among financial officials now provide an important lubricant for the smooth and coordinated functioning of the formal machinery that has been built. These include, for example, *ad hoc* meetings of experts, monthly meetings of Central Bank Governors, periodic meetings of Working Party Three of the OECD, and Annual Meetings of the Governors of the 103-nation IMF and World Bank.

Short-Term Official Credits. In the 1930–31 period it proved impossible to raise $150 million in central bank credits to cope with an imminent threat to the world's monetary system, which soon materialized. This is in sharp contrast with 1964 when $3 billion was quickly mobilized in short-term official credit for the United Kingdom. These have now been funded into medium-term credits through the IMF, providing breathing time for corrective actions. Recent further action to extend lines of credit to the United Kingdom in a less critical environment is also notable.

The defenses of the dollar include a ring of reciprocal swap commitments amounting to about $2½ billion which gave it assured short-term credit facilities in all the major currencies. At the same time, these facilities give support to each of the partners of the United States. These accommodations and related market techniques, now fully tested and confidently employed by monetary authorities, proved their value in meeting shocks to the international payments system during the Cuban crisis and following the assassination of President Kennedy.

An initial buffer against serious threats to stability in the foreign exchange market, tailored to meet the needs of the partners in particular circumstances, the instruments and techniques now in operation not only demonstrate the past adaptability of the system—they have future potential as well.

Medium-Term Credits. The International Monetary Fund, as a central and basic element of monetary cooperation, provides an international pool of gold and currencies that governments have *already* unconditionally committed to it. Moreover, with its regular resources supplemented by the General Arrangements to Borrow, the Fund can call upon up to $6 billion in major currencies.

Today, we have in the Fund a proven mechanism. This, however, does not mean that the monetary machinery provided by the Fund cannot be further perfected or that it can substitute for effective efforts by major countries to manage their international accounts appropriately over the longer pull. There may, for example, be a need to perfect our methods of adding to the growth of international monetary reserves through some supplementary type of reserve creation at some time in the future. Recurring strains on sterling exchange have been the subject of concern. The persistent surplus of Continental Europe, reflected in a near tripling of reserves in the last decade, and the persistent deficit in the U.S. balance of payments with its associated large gold outflow, are widely recognized as circumstances requiring fundamental attention.

Long-Term Development Financing. Unlike an earlier period, we now have in being an international institutional framework designed to assist in the effective transfer of needed resources and techniques from developed to developing countries. Nations are joined together in a common effort to help raise dangerously low living standards in an era where modern science and technology have collapsed distances and the benefits of growing economies and world trade are apparent to all.

Some part of this—hopefully an increasing part—can be provided by private business and the financial community. The role of international cooperation at the government level remains vital, however. At the center is the World Bank family operating on a worldwide basis, providing development financing on conventional and on easy repayment terms, as well as equity and loan capital for private enterprise projects. Attuned to regional needs but working in close cooperation with the worldwide institutions, independent multilateral banks serving the continents of Latin America, Africa, and Asia are in being or in the process of creation.

To be sure, improvements of the existing framework are and will continue to be necessary; some of these are going forward today. The attack on development is, in a real sense, still in the developing stages. The development finance institutions, as they seek to tap the private capital markets for added resources, are confronted also with the task of stimulating the development of some of those very markets they seek to enter. New problems are arising as the burden of repayments of the capital-needy developing countries increase. Are the potential consequences only on the developing countries, or on the fabric of the international credit structure as well? How do the multilateral development finance institutions play their proper role not only in coping with emerging problems, but with the existing ones as well? The problems are by no means all financial, and involve questions of the transfer and utilization of real resources, skills, and technology. In a number of cases solutions must be *ad hoc*, but these and myriad other problems are high on the current agenda.

Thus today's international cooperation in monetary and development finance contrasts sharply with the world of the 1930's. Short-term financial pressures have been eased, orderly economic adjustment supported, and growth and development encouraged. Nevertheless, real problems exist. What is the future of these various approaches toward meeting emergency problems? How can these institutions be further developed, their techniques and operations refined, the economies upon which they depend for ultimate resources further expanded? And how can the role of private enterprise in developing countries be furthered by means consistent with our economic traditions?

The Future

International Monetary Cooperation

The international monetary system, in the future as in the past, must ensure adequate financing to meet the needs both of the private and public sectors in transactions transcending national boundaries. In the private sector it is a matter of ensuring the financing of an expanding international trade and facilitating needed private investment abroad; in the public sector of ensuring the ability of financial authorities to deal effectively with pressures on the system. The continuing growth in the volume of international transactions may increase the amplitude of swings in payments surpluses and deficits which must be financed in an appropriate manner.

The dollar has played a key role in facilitating the international exchange of goods and services. It may be noted that free world exports in 1954 totaled $78 billion—in 1964, $152 billion. The dollar has proven its benefit to the payments system as a monetary instrument which can flow smoothly through the exchange markets, through private hands, and through official channels. The dollar will continue to serve as the world's primary trading currency and, indeed, will continue to play an important role in foreign monetary reserves as well.

Dollars held abroad privately have about doubled over the past decade, a rate closely parallel to the increase in world trade. These now total about $12 billion in private hands, and there is another $15 billion held as official reserves; together they clearly point to the essentiality of sustaining unimpaired confidence in the dollar's value and usefulness, both at home and abroad. They demonstrate the need to achieve equilibrium in the U.S. balance of payments. This equilibrium will be a prime factor in assuring that outstanding liquidity—the means of payment in the international economy—does not shrink as a result of heavy demands on the U.S. gold stock.

There is, and must be, no question of the intent of the United States to maintain unimpaired the value of its currency—to maintain a strong, sound, and stable dollar, and behind it a strong and competitive economy. The United States has substantially improved its competitive position internationally over recent years. It is of fundamental importance that wage-price developments do not jeopardize this relationship. In this regard, the recent substantial shrinkage in our trade surplus provides a reminder of the need to be alert to any adverse trends. U.S. performance in its balance of payments is doubly important, since it will play a major role in establishing the basis for "thawing out" the measures taken over recent years to curtail the outflow of dollars, and thus cut the balance of payments deficits more immediately. Action on the immediate problem was appropriate under the circumstances—but the measures must, in fact as in planning, prove clearly temporary. Extended reliance on measures of restraint can be self-defeating in the longer run. The U.S. capital market can be expected to have an important role to play in the world economy of the future and can promise an element of strength to the balance of payments.

There are sources of strength in our balance of payments that should show through increasingly, and current developments should also aid in attaining a position when temporary measures can be reduced or eliminated. No one can predict the timing with any precision—but the favorable factors include, in addition to a strong trade account, heavier returns on U.S. investments abroad, greater participation by our allies abroad in meeting the needs of the developing nations, the development of capital markets and the fashioning of a broader range of fiscal and monetary tools abroad for achieving better adjustment to payments imbalances. Spending by the U.S. Government must of course continue to be scrutinized closely and every saving must be made that can be made within the carefully defined limits of national policy. The needs of the developing nations must not be set aside, and our contribution—directly and through the international lending agencies whose activities should be closely defined and coordinated—will continue to be important.

We are also aware that just as there is a responsibility on the part of the United States to remove the deficit in its balance of payments, there is also a responsibility on the part of those nations with persistent surpluses, the counterpart of the U.S. deficit, to adjust their payments balance and reduce pressures on the international monetary system. Fiscal tools can usefully play a larger role in many such countries.

We have noted earlier in this study that the current payments system both reflects and requires a measure of international financial cooperation on many levels. The payments system, as now developed and reinforced, includes cooperative actions in foreign exchange markets, provision of bilateral short-term "swap" credits by central banks and expanded medium-term credit facilities at the International Monetary Fund. This system has served the free world well in facilitating a greatly enlarged volume of international trade and in meeting speculative outbursts or other threats to orderly foreign exchange markets. These arrangements, appropriately expanded and reinforced, can also serve well in the future—indeed, they provide the underpinning for further steps that might be taken within the scope of a free enterprise economy to ensure a payments system attuned to developing needs.

We do not see any overall lack of international liquidity at this time or in the immediate future. Nevertheless, although it may seem premature to some, it is essential to gain international agreement on the steps that might appropriately be taken if and when any threat of a lack in international liquidity tends to inhibit the mutually beneficial exchange of goods and services.

As the United States achieves and maintains balance-of-payments equilibrium, the question as to ways to assure a sufficient supply of liquidity will be timely. Clearly, the future supply of gold alone cannot give this assurance. Just as clearly, the United States cannot be expected to incur a deficit simply to meet that need. Current planning therefore is essential to meet potential needs of the future. This underscores the appropriateness of the efforts now being undertaken by the Group of Ten as a first step in response to the announcement by the Secretary of the Treasury of U.S. readiness to participate in an international monetary conference which would be preceded by careful preparation and international consultation for agreement on basic issues.

We cannot now set forth any "plan" for a new "reserve asset" or the precise system that should characterize the future. But some broad lines of approach already in use seem clearly worth continuing—even expanding.

First, we would not wish to exclude an appropriate role in any arrangement for the bilateral instruments and techniques that now serve importantly to safeguard against abrupt and serious threats to stability in the foreign exchange markets and serve at the same time to meet particular needs of the two parties concerned. These techniques, tailored and flexible, are a line of defense that protects, and even expands, liquidity when it is temporarily needed.

Second, to the extent that the problems ahead are viewed as those of assuring that financing is available to deal with short-lived fluctuations in private balances or recurrent swings in national balance-of-payments positions, the solution could lie, at least largely, in the range of improved credit availability. Further reinforcement in the International Monetary Fund's resources could well serve this purpose. There also may be ways of making Fund resources in appropriate amounts and in time an even more valuable reserve asset commanding greater automaticity in its use.

Third, the provision of medium-term credits through the use of foreign currency denominated bonds or other imaginative devices should not be overlooked. They might also play a useful supplementary role for handling flows of funds unrelated to the U.S. balance-of-payments deficit. There might, for example, be an expansion of such securities among other countries to provide bilateral reinforcement to the system, just as there might be, in time, some stretching out of the maturities of these securities.

Fourth, the system might be further reinforced as a result of concerted action to devise supplementary assets to be held in official reserves. Various proposals designed to provide a method for creating a supplementary asset should continue to be studied and evaluated in the light of our national interest as well as international need. The International Monetary Fund should continue to play a leading role in the payments system, and any arrangement should use the framework of this experienced organization based on recognized adherence by member governments. Moreover, the arrangement should be subject to voting and other procedures of an acceptable type.

Fifth, the system should be so constructed that it rests solidly on foundations of economic discipline in each of the participating countries—including appropriate fiscal, monetary, and other economic policies. It should neither facilitate the running of continuous balance of payments deficits by any nation, nor should it require short-sighted abrupt adjustment regardless of the consequences nationally and internationally.

In conclusion, the course of careful and patient exploration to arrive at a consensus with U.S. trading partners in the spirit of mutual cooperation on appropriate future improvement of the international monetary system is sound. Monetary cooperation, so fruitful in the past, must characterize the future if that future is to prove equally or more rewarding.

Future Cooperation in Development Financing

In the years ahead, even more than in the past, international cooperation in economic development financing will rely heavily on the World Bank as a channel for the flow of capital from the developed countries into the developing world. It will be reinforced on the regional level by the Inter-American Development Bank, the recently established African Bank, and the emerging Asian Development Bank. The spectrum of hopes, realities, and responsibilities in carrying out this cooperative effort is broad. Only a few will be touched upon here.

In carrying out their primary function of channeling resources from the have to the have-not nations, the development finance institutions must effectively mobilize resources on the one hand and ensure their careful application on the other. If these institutions are to retain their multilateral character, they cannot be heavily dependent on one or a few countries for resources. An important task of the future will be the broadening of the base of available resources. In terms of capital markets, there is the need for more intensified development of those capital markets and techniques which will maximize the accumulation of savings and direct them into investment abroad where the needs are great. The development finance institutions have a role to play in the strengthening of the markets they seek to enter, just as they have a role to play in strengthening savings. And the development of other capital markets becomes even more urgent at those times when the United States faces balance-of-payments strains. Urgent attention needs to be given to broadening the base of financial support of development institutions. This problem calls for cooperative action to strengthen capital markets generally.

A second major problem is presented by the sharply rising burden of foreign debt service of the developing countries. In some cases the threat of default, with potential heavy cost to lender and borrower alike, is imminent. The problem has many facets. The International Development Association is an outstanding example of creative adaptation to meet this emerging need while contributing to sound development, on a basis in which all the capital exporting countries share in the cost. The question of replenishment of IDA resources is now before the World Bank members. It has already committed the bulk of its $1.5 billion resources. New governmental contributions from all developed nations on a substantial scale will be necessary if it is to go forward with its important work of making sound loans on easy repayment terms. The developed nations should fully support the continuation and strengthening of this experiment in international development cooperation.

In strengthening the fabric of development institutions on the regional level, there may be an even more important role for the Inter-American Development Bank as the financial arm of the Alliance for Progress. In Asia, a strong start has been made toward the early establishment of an Asian Development Bank especially adapted to meet the needs and aspirations of the countries of the region. It is already showing its potential to mobilize resources within the region and to attract funds from a wide number of countries outside of it. Present plans call for a capital structure of $1 billion, of which the United States and Japan would each provide up to $200 million, and other industrial countries, both regional and non-regional, would provide an additional $300 million. Once established, the Asian Development Bank could serve not only as a financing institution but also as a focus for regional cooperation on a broad front.

Apart from these immediate steps to strengthen the institutional arrangements for cooperation in development financing, there is a wide scope for long-range improvement in the coordination of bilateral aid programs and aid policies. The World Bank has pioneered in the process of coordinating aid programs of multiple donors in particular recipient countries through aid consortia and less formal consultative groups. If numerous bilateral aid programs are to provide the maximum contribution to development, if resources are to be applied to the highest priority uses, and if performance in developing countries is to be more effectively elicited, the number of key countries for which such coordination arrangements are available will have to be increased.

The importance of the role of private enterprise in the development process also requires fresh emphasis in the years ahead. An all-out effort of the developing countries to attract private capital is essential. The encouragement of well-conceived partnership arrangements between U.S. and local companies is especially important to the future development of many nations. And the development finance institutions have an important part to play in contributing to a fresh emphasis. Recent actions to enlarge the capacity of the International Finance Corporation is one example of a move in this direction. As another important action, early ratification by the United States and other countries of the World Bank–sponsored Convention on the Settlement of Investment Disputes would contribute importantly to this new impetus for private investment.

Satisfactory progress on all these fronts will by no means automatically solve all the serious financial problems confronting the less developed countries. Much remains to be accomplished, and basic to all is what is done by the developing countries themselves—their will and determination toward integrating their economies with the free world community. We look forward to various approaches to the problem which will assure the full emergence, soundly based, of the developing countries into the mainstream of world trade, the increasing satisfaction of the basic wants of their peoples and, with it all, the development of the full potential in these lands and around the world.

RECOMMENDATIONS

We recommend that:

International Monetary Cooperation

1. International monetary cooperation must characterize the future if that future is to prove rewarding in providing an expanding and balanced growth of world trade, investment, output, and employment.

2. In building on the present system, there must be no doubt about the ability of the dollar to serve as a world trading currency and to play an important role in international monetary reserves. Behind a strong, sound, and stable dollar must be a strong and competitive U.S. economy.

3. There is no over-all lack of international liquidity at the present time. It is essential, however, to gain international agreement on

steps that might be taken if and when a lack of liquidity threatens the mutually beneficial exchange of goods and services.

4. We do not set forth any "plan" for the precise international payments system of the future, but there are some broad lines of approach already in use worth continuing and even expanding:

a. There should be an appropriate role in any new arrangement for the bilateral instruments and techniques that now serve as short-term buffers to threats to the system.

b. The International Monetary Fund should continue to play a leading role in the payments system. Ways should be sought to make its resources, in appropriate amounts and at appropriate times, an even more valuable reserve asset.

c. Medium-term credits through the use of foreign currency denominated bonds, or similar instruments, should continue to have a place in the system. Consideration should be given to an expansion of their use among other countries, and, in time, to some stretching out in their maturities.

d. Various proposals to provide a method for creating a supplementary asset to be held in official reserves should be studied and evaluated in the light of our national interest as well as international need.

e. The payments system of the future should rest on the foundations of effective economic discipline in each of the countries, facilitating neither continuous balance-of-payments deficits nor surpluses nor requiring short-sighted and destructively abrupt adjustments.

Development Finance

1. International cooperation in development finance through the World Bank and the regional banks in Latin America, Africa, and Asia should be an essential ingredient of the future to help assure the full emergence of the developing countries, and with this the further advance of the economies of all nations.

2. In effectively mobilizing resources, the development finance institutions should seek to broaden the base of available resources,

and in this regard cooperative action to strengthen capital markets generally is important.

3. The sharply rising burden of foreign debt service of the developing countries requires concerted attention. As one element in this, all developed nations should fully support the continuation and strengthening of the International Development Association as an affiliate of the World Bank.

4. The World Bank should play an increasing role in coordinating development assistance being furnished by the industrial nations, recognizing that basic to all are the efforts of the developing countries themselves.

5. The importance of the role of private enterprise in the development process requires fresh emphasis in the years ahead. One element in this should be the encouragement of well-conceived partnership arrangements between U.S. and local companies. Early approval of the World Bank-sponsored convention on the settlement of investment disputes would be helpful.

THE COMMITTEE ON FINANCE
AND MONETARY AFFAIRS

Supplementary Comment

The undersigned agree with many statements and recommendations here which describe the past accomplishments and potential future contributions of the various international monetary institutions and financial mechanisms. There are certain key areas, however, where a different outlook might usefully be expressed:

1. We would place greater emphasis on the magnitude of the tasks confronting international financial institutions to marshal capital and skills for the less developed countries in the decade ahead. Indeed, we feel that the net flow of capital resources in the immediate period ahead, and forward financing commitments and arrangements—both bilateral and multilateral—will fall short of amounts

needed to cope with the growing needs and to do justice to the growing absorptive capacities of the less developed countries.

2. We believe there is a much more urgent need than is implied here for developing international monetary arrangements. In our opinion, trends toward reduced flows of capital are restraining healthy, free world economic growth. As a substitute for these constraints, we urge that, as the primary means of achieving true equilibrium in international payments, the full weight of U.S. efforts should be applied to establish further expansion of reciprocal financing devices and continued use of the dollar as an international asset. To do otherwise would have an adverse impact on efforts to achieve greater trade liberalization, the provision of more development assistance, and the stimulation of international competition and private investment. The indispensable role of the United States as a free world banker must be recognized in framing new international financial arrangements.

Kenneth R. Hansen
Emile Despres

10. Expanding World Trade

Trade is older than civilization and has throughout history played a major part in its development. Expansion of trade among the peoples of the world has become in turn an expression of the progress they have made in production and distribution, and of their search for higher standards of living and closer cooperation with one another.

Today the development of trade routes, so much a part of the world's economic history, still goes on. Heroic personal adventures in the quest for silks, spices, and precious stones have been replaced by well-organized efforts to acquire from producers almost anywhere in the world the wide range of goods they are particularly adept at supplying, and to develop broader markets for the wide array of goods which prolific nature and prolific technology have provided in rapidly rising volume. These modern trade routes are vital arteries of economic vitality for all nations, and of the international cooperation upon which the progress and security of all peoples are greatly dependent.

The degree of freedom to buy and sell goods in commerce between nations has consistently lagged behind the progress they have made in increasing the volume and efficiency of their production. On the whole each country is usually glad to allow its citizens to sell wherever in the world they can. Promotion of exports encounters little opposition in the exporting country, but often considerable resistance in the countries to which these efforts are directed. This resistance is expressed through tariffs, import quotas, or other forms of trade barriers, and in pressures to increase their restrictiveness.

These and other deterrents to expansion of international trade are significant obstacles to international cooperation since, as of old, the channels of trade are the principal arteries of communication among the peoples of the world. For most nations, exports are a major source of income or at least a vital factor in their international economic positions. While trade barriers have occasionally bought time for viable types of production to take root, they too often have been used to protect uneconomic production and to blunt the stimuli of change emanating from other parts of the world. The readiness of the United States, together with other economically advanced countries, to lower their trade barriers on a sustained and consistent basis has a crucial bearing on the ability of peoples everywhere to achieve their most cherished objectives and to cooperate in building a better world.

Trade Policy—Past and Present

The policy of two-way trade liberalization—the reduction or elimination of impediments to trade, negotiated on a reciprocal basis with the other industrialized nations of the free world—has contributed greatly over three decades to international cooperation and to economic expansion in the United States and abroad. This policy, pursued under Democratic and Republican Administrations alike since the enactment of the Trade Agreements Act of 1934, has yielded great benefits to our free enterprise economy—to our producers in terms of wider markets and keener competition and to our consumers in terms of the availability of an ampler variety of goods at reasonable prices.

Until 1947, the United States as well as other nations had negotiated trade agreements on a bilateral basis—although since 1922, under the principle of unconditional most-favored-nation treatment which was established as a pillar of American trade policy in that year, concessions made by the United States to any one nation were automatically extended to nearly every other nation.

The General Agreement on Tariffs and Trade

Establishment of the General Agreement on Tariffs and Trade (GATT) made it possible for the first time to conduct trade negotiations on a multilateral basis, thus greatly expediting them. The job of the GATT, headquartered in Geneva, is to clear the channels of world trade of needless obstructions and to keep them clear. A measure of its effectiveness is the almost complete absence from the headlines of the "beggar my neighbor" trade and tariff wars which many nations conducted against one another in the past.

As its name implies, the General Agreement is basically a set of rules (negotiated and agreed to by twenty-three countries in 1947 and in effect since January 1, 1948) for the orderly conduct and expansion of world trade. At present, sixty-six nations subscribe to the

GATT, and thirteen others participate under provisional or other special arrangements. The total of seventy-nine accounts for over 80 per cent of world trade and includes all the major trading nations of the free world and the majority of the developing nations.

One basic principle of the GATT is that of non-discrimination. Each participating country agrees that, subject to certain strictly limited exceptions, any tariff concession or trade advantage granted to any one nation shall be extended on an unconditional most-favored-nation basis to all other GATT countries. This serves to safeguard American exporters against actions by other countries which would result in discrimination against U.S. exports. It gives the exporters of other GATT countries the same assurance. Thus, nations are rarely put in the position of having to resort to retaliatory measures, which in the past were often the first step toward a full-scale trade war.

A second basic principle of the GATT is that, with certain strictly limited exceptions, such protection as may be afforded by each GATT nation to its producers shall be by tariffs rather than by quantitative restrictions. Through the years, tariff negotiations under GATT sponsorship have brought about a substantial lowering of the tariffs of the major trading countries. The general prohibition against quantitative restrictions provides assurance that the benefits of tariff reductions will not be frustrated by the imposition of quotas or embargoes which could severely limit or completely prevent access of efficient foreign producers to the protected market.

There is a strong emphasis upon consultation in the operation of the General Agreement. It serves as a forum in which member nations may meet to discuss disputes arising from potential or actual breaches of the GATT trading rules. If one member nation adopts a policy that would infringe on the trading rights of a particular country or would generally damage the trading interests of all or a number of member countries, any member claiming injury may initiate a consultation. If no satisfactory adjustment is reached after consultation, a formal complaint may be lodged. Then a Panel of Conciliation, made up of experts from countries which have no direct interest in the issue, may examine the complaint and recommend a solution.

GATT is also a forum for international trade conferences at which, on a multilateral basis, the reduction or elimination of tariffs and non-tariff barriers to trade can be negotiated. Five major rounds of negotiations have been held under the auspices of GATT since its establishment, and the sixth round—generally known as the Kennedy Round—is now in progress. It is estimated that, through these negotiations, tariffs have been reduced or stabilized on products accounting for approximately half of world trade.

Other Vehicles of Trade Cooperation

Although the General Agreement on Tariffs and Trade provides the only global forum in which trade agreements are negotiated and enforced, there are various organizations which serve as forums for study and discussion of trade policies and the formulation of recommendations to governments. They include the Organization for Economic Cooperation and Development (OECD), consisting of twenty-two nations—the free-world nations of Europe, the United States, Canada, and Japan; the United Nations Economic and Social Council (ECOSOC) and its four regional commissions—for Europe, Asia, Latin America, and Africa; the International Monetary Fund; the International Bank for Reconstruction and Development; and, most recently, the UN Conference on Trade and Development (UNCTAD).

In recent years, the patterns and prospects of world trade have been greatly affected by two new developments—the emergence of regional trading blocs and the growing interest in the problems faced by developing countries in expanding their exports.

The Implications of Regionalism

The first major multinational trading bloc to emerge was the European Economic Community (EEC) in 1958, followed by the European Free Trade Association (EFTA), the Central American Common Market, and the Latin American Free Trade Association (LAFTA). All these groups are in process of eliminating nearly all tariffs, at least on industrial products, among their members; in the case of the EEC and EFTA, this process is expected to be completed in 1967. In addition, the EEC is moving toward a common external tariff against non-member countries and a common agricultural policy among its members.

The members of these blocs have not extended to outside countries the drastic tariff cuts they have made among themselves. This departure from the unconditional most-favored-nation principle is permitted for free-trade areas and customs unions, under certain specified conditions, by Article XXIV of the GATT. The commitment of these members to establish unimpeded free trade among themselves upon a stipulated timetable is considered by the GATT to be of sufficient service to the goal of removing international trade barriers to compensate for the accompanying increase of discrimination inherent in granting free access to goods produced by members but not to outsiders. One of the assumptions behind this view is that such regional groups would be outward-looking and hence prepared to lower significantly their trade barriers against outside suppliers.

Article XXIV is also cited by the EEC as the basis in GATT for its special customs arrangements with the Associated Overseas Countries (former colonies of EEC members, mainly of France) and to Greece and Turkey. These arrangements vary in their particulars. Some of them seriously compromise the principle of Article XXIV that departures from most-favored-nation treatment are justifiable only among nations committed to the establishment of a regional trading unit in which barriers are eliminated on substantially all trade. Special treatment given the trade of the Associated Overseas Countries may post significant problems for non-member developing countries, whose exports may be placed at a substantial disadvantage.

The wider tariff-free markets which the members of these blocs will enjoy should contribute to their economic growth and prosperity and therefore make them better customers for outside suppliers, including the United States. However, there also may be disadvantages for American exporters. For instance, when the EEC customs union is fully in effect, an American exporter of an industrial product to France will face duty-free competition from producers of that product in the other five member nations of the EEC as well as France. So far, however, the dominant effect of the EEC has been an increase in the demand for imports as a result of relatively high rates of economic growth in member countries. Over the longer run, the balance of advantage or disadvantage for third countries will depend in large part on the external commercial policies of such regional groupings. Large corporations can and do overcome such trade barriers by establishing branch plants within these blocs, but this recourse is not as manageable for American enterprises with smaller resources. The overall implications of such barriers for U.S. policy objectives at home and abroad would tend to be harmful.

American farmers may also face problems with the EEC. The common agricultural policy for certain products, notably poultry, has tended to be protectionist. If, as ultimately implemented, the common agricultural policy continues to be protectionist, some American farm exports which compete with domestic EEC production could be seriously impaired.

Trade Problems of Developing Countries

Another important development in international trade is the unsatisfactory trend in the export earnings of the developing countries in recent years, which explains their interest in expanding their exports in quantity and range and at higher and more stable prices. It is natural—and, indeed, commendable—that they want to reduce their dependence on special external aid. The self-sustaining growth of these countries, as part of the free-world economic system, depends in large part upon whether they are able to achieve the expanding markets which spur development. Moreover, it is in the commercial interest of the United States and other developed countries that they do so, because, to the extent that they succeed, they will grow into great new markets for the products of the industrialized nations; to the extent that they fail, the objectives of our aid programs are being frustrated. Trade and aid policies, therefore, must mesh together and complement one another.

About $30 billion of the $36 billion in foreign exchange which became available to the developing countries last year was earned from exports. Fully 85 per cent of this export income is derived from crude materials (including processed foodstuffs). The demand for many of these products in world markets has failed to grow in proportion to the expansion of world trade generally. This is due to a variety of factors, including sharper competition from synthetics, technological developments leading to economies in the industrial use of raw materials, such as metals, and increased production of some of these products in developed countries. While prices of manufactured products have tended to be stable or have increased, prices of many basic commodities have declined. Since the mid-1950's there has been a deterioration in the terms of trade of developing countries as a whole which has caused concern, though there are differences of opinion as to its extent and significance.

Under these circumstances, it is understandable that the developing countries have sought measures to stabilize and if possible increase the prices they receive for their exports of foodstuffs and crude materials. They have also sought to expand the access to world markets for their traditional exports, as well as to reduce their heavy dependence upon this class of exports by widening their markets for the simple, labor-intensive manufactured products which they already produce or can reasonably hope to produce.

The United States and other governments and international institutions, including the GATT, have taken measures to help the trade of developing countries. For example, the United States has taken part in the negotiation of an international agreement on coffee. Through special committees, GATT has been working on the trade problems of the developing countries for some years with emphasis on the market access problem. An International Trade Center was established in GATT in 1964 to give them technical assistance in expanding their exports. On February 8, 1965, formal agreement was reached on a new chapter to be added to the General Agreement. It consists of three Articles framed to take specific account of the trade interests of the developing countries.

These countries are convinced, however, that more needs to be done. They made this clear at the initial meeting of the UN Trade and Development Conference (UNCTAD) in Geneva in the spring of 1964. Seventy-five developing nations formed a caucus and worked with a high degree of vigor and unity throughout the twelve weeks of the Conference; now expanded to seventy-eight members, the caucus continues in being. UNCTAD has been established as a permanent arm of the United Nations, with its own secretariat; it will meet at least every three years, and in the interim will function through a UN Trade and Development Board.

A key demand of the developing countries, pressed at the first UNCTAD conference and ever since, is for a system of tariff preferences by the developed countries to the less-developed countries, later refined to include special provisions for the "least-developed countries." Obviously, this would be inconsistent with the unconditional most-favored-nation principle, a pillar of American trade policy, and of the GATT. The developing countries maintain that this principle has already been breached by the creation of EEC and EFTA and by the various preferential arrangements which the EEC has negotiated or is negotiating with other countries.

It has not been demonstrated, however, that preferences would really provide effective assistance to the developing countries. Continued progress in reducing and eliminating trade barriers on a most-favored-nation basis, combined with measures to improve the productivity, efficiency, and marketing capabilities of the developing countries, would appear to be a better way of stimulating the export earnings of these countries. Moreover, substantial reductions in trade barriers among developed countries, essential to achievement of the policy objectives listed below, would steadily reduce the significance of any tariff preferences to developing countries.

The Trade Expansion Act of 1962

Key provisions of the U.S. Trade Expansion Act of 1962 were framed to take account of the problems and capitalize on the opportunities offered by the emergence of the new trading blocs and the growing interest of the developing countries in playing a wider role in world trade.

The overall authority which Congress delegated to the President to effect a 50 per cent tariff cut, with a very limited number of required exceptions, was intended to enable the United States to negotiate deep cuts in the EEC and EFTA tariffs, so as to reduce the disadvantages which American and other exporters would otherwise face in these markets. In addition, the President was given authority to negotiate tariffs down to zero on items for which the EEC and the United States together accounted for 80 per cent or more of the free world's exports. At the time the Act was adopted, it was confidently expected that Britain would be successful in her application for EEC membership and that this provision would therefore apply to a wide range of products. The subsequent collapse of the British negotiations with the EEC had a substantial impact on the course of the Kennedy Round of trade negotiations, beginning with the reduction of this provision of the Act to almost complete ineffectiveness.

With respect to the developing countries, another key provision of the Act authorized the President to eliminate duties on certain tropical products in return for comparable action by the EEC. The developing countries should also benefit from deep Kennedy Round cuts in the tariffs on other products, particularly if those which they produce or can hope to produce are kept off the "exceptions lists" of the industrial countries.

East-West Trade

Looking beyond free-world trade, there has been growing interest in "East-West" trade in recent years. Beginning in 1948, in response to the expansionist policies of Soviet Communism, the United States imposed security controls on trade with the Soviet bloc and gained the cooperation of other major trading nations in doing likewise. As a result of the decrease in tensions in recent years, however, the Western European nations have eased their controls, while the United States has not done so to the same degree. East-West trade, although still small (for Western Europe, it amounts to less than 4 per cent of total trade), has been growing at the rate of 10 per cent a year.

Sentiment has been growing in the United States for a fresh look at the East-West trade situation. The United States has accorded most-favored-nation treatment to Poland for a number of years and is supporting its closer association with GATT. On April 29, 1965, a Special Committee on U.S. Trade Relations with East European Countries and the Soviet Union, appointed by the President to study the problem, made its report. It held that there is relatively small potential for trade between the Soviet bloc and the United States. In its view, the question was primarily a political rather than an economic one. It concluded, in substance, that the President should be in a position to remove restrictions on trade with individual Soviet bloc nations, or re-impose them, as required by our relations with the countries concerned. Specifically, it recommended:

1. That the power to withhold or release for trade non-strategic goods or advanced technology should be exercised by the President as an instrument for accomplishing foreign policy objectives.

2. That the President should be given discretionary authority to grant or withdraw most-favored-nation treatment from individual Communist countries when he determines it to be in the national interest.

We attach considerable importance to the need for substantial free-world unity in GATT and OECD as a precondition for free-world agreement on effective, enforceable ground rules on trade with Communist countries, and uniform criteria regarding such things as credit terms to Communist countries and realistic definitions of strategic shipments.

Measures Restricting Trade

To round out the record of the evolution of trade policy among the free-world countries, it should be noted that the rather steady reduction of tariffs over the years has led to counter-pressures to protect certain industries regarded as particularly sensitive to import competition. In U.S. policy, such pressures are reflected in the "escape clause" criteria and "peril point" procedures of the 1950's and early 1960's and the introduction and broadening of the "national security" clause. The same phenomena may be noted abroad, e.g., in the severe quotas European countries have imposed against coal imports. The developing countries have a wide variety of non-tariff barriers, but—since they spend most or all of the foreign exchange they receive—these measures do not affect the total quantity of their imports, but only their composition. A long-term international agreement governing trade in cotton textiles was negotiated in 1962 in response to pressures for restrictions against shipments of cotton textiles from so-called low-wage countries. In the United States, under our Federal system of Government, individual states have taken action to discriminate against certain imports. Consumers' boycotts have been organized, sometimes for economic and sometimes for political reasons, and trade unions—particularly of longshoremen—have refused to handle certain items. Steps by local governments and private groups to restrict trade are also taken in other countries.

Measures restricting trade work against one of the main objectives of expanded world trade, which is to effect an international division of labor under which each country concentrates on those items which it can produce most efficiently and imports others. It makes much more sense, therefore, to facilitate the orderly movement of manpower and resources out of uneconomic lines of production rather than to protect them indefinitely. An effort was made to achieve this kind of "resource mobility" through the "trade adjustment" provisions of the Trade Expansion Act of 1962, but these measures have, so far, not resulted in any affirmative findings leading to special government assistance.

Implications of the Kennedy Round

If sufficient success is achieved in the Kennedy Round of negotiations, complications that have been noted as arising from the emergent movements of economic regionalism and the special needs of the less-developed areas would be minimized.

1. Regarding the issues raised by the trend toward economic regionalism through the formation of common markets and free-trade areas:

(a) Successful bargaining in the Kennedy Round would result, on the whole, in a significant lowering of trade barriers against imports from non-member suppliers, thus ensuring that regional economic accords do not move in the direction of intensified protectionism.

(b) The effects of discrimination remaining after the Kennedy Round, favoring the goods of members over imports from outsiders, would be offset to some extent if there were a general and substantial lowering of trade barriers throughout the world, thus contributing to a worldwide expansion of trade.

2. Regarding the trade needs of the developing countries:

(a) The differential between zero (or very low) tariffs on raw materials, on the one hand, and the considerably higher schedules for their shipment in semi-processed or manufactured form, on the other, would be trimmed or eliminated, thus affording relief on one major ground for complaint.

(b) The developing countries, afforded a far more liberal timetable on tariff reductions than the industrialized areas, could derive full advantage from the freeing-up of world export opportunities without sacrifice to what they believe to be their own development prospects.

(c) If these two conditions were attained, within the framework of a general and substantial lowering of trade barriers, there would be less incentive for less-developed countries to seek preferential status in the markets of the industrialized countries (or in particular industrialized areas) with the implications of dependence that necessarily are involved.

Future Goals—and How to Achieve Them

In defining the trade policy goals on which the free world's sights should be focused and toward which its energies should be directed, we started from the premise that a trade policy that promotes international cooperation and adequately serves our overall national interest would

1. advance the principles of freedom of enterprise;

2. protect the interests of consumers in reasonable prices, high quality, and freedom of choice;

3. advance the interest of industry and agriculture in expanding markets and rising productivity, and the interest of labor in more and better jobs;

4. help to ensure the most efficient utilization of resources;

5. minimize the role of foreign trade barriers as a reason for U.S. investment capital to go abroad;

6. promote the freest possible access of American industry to fuel,

raw materials, semi-manufactured materials, and finished components from the most economic sources, with a view to maximizing the competitiveness of American goods in markets at home and abroad;

7. increase the cohesiveness of the free world and strengthen the role of the Atlantic Community as a vital force in achieving it;

8. increase the developing countries to move to a more self-sustaining position increasingly less dependent on outside government financial aid and more capable of attracting and making effective use of private capital (domestic and foreign);

9. ensure that regional free-trade areas and common markets become building blocks for a stronger, more interdependent world economy rather than manifestations of a new form of nationalism;

10. help to achieve vigorous, sustained, and real economic growth in the United States and successful adjustment of American industry, agriculture, labor, and communities to the many challenges of change.

11. help to "build bridges" to the Communist countries, consistent with overall U.S. security interests.

The trade policy that best satisfies these criteria is one aimed at the sustained lowering of trade barriers of all kinds (with appropriate compensatory benefits from other nations or regional instrumentalities) and the acceleration of this process on the part of the industrialized areas of the world. In these areas, repositories of most of the free world's economic power, rests the major responsibility for world progress in lowering the barriers to trade and raising the sights of economic advancement for all peoples. Although the pattern of economic power in the free world has changed considerably since the early postwar years, the United States retains a leadership role in the field of international trade policy. As the leading national economy, the pace at which it is ready to move exerts a considerable influence on the rest of the world. This is so even with the emergence of the European Economic Community as the world's largest bargaining unit.

The pace required of the United States is, of course, influenced by the necessities of the hour. Today, although much of the water has been squeezed out of the extraordinarily high tariffs enacted by Congress in 1930, significant and in many cases high tariffs remain on many products and there is considerable resistance to reducing them. Yet today's imperatives in international trade policy—particularly the answers that must be found to "nationalistic" tendencies in economic regionalism and to the urgent problems of the developing areas—suggest that significant across-the-board reductions of the trade restrictions of this country and the rest of the free world's highly industrialized economies are necessary. The stakes are the highest they have ever been. So is the need for better understanding both here and throughout the Northern Hemisphere of what must now be sought and of how success can be ensured to the benefit of every nation individually and the world as a whole.

Impressive as our record and that of other industrialized nations has been in achieving a substantial lowering of trade barriers in such a relatively short period of time, what these countries have accomplished has not measured up to the degree of trade liberalization of which they are capable and from which they would benefit greatly. In view of the economic and political dynamics of economic regionalism and the aspirations of the developing nations, the need more closely to intertwine the economies of the free world is not a matter of theory or doctrine, but of considerable practical urgency. Steps to fulfill our national capabilities are essential to U.S. leverage in achieving accelerated and reciprocal trade liberalization on the part of the world's industrialized areas generally.

Specific Proposals

Of highest priority in the pursuit of these goals is a successful Kennedy Round of trade negotiations that would move significantly toward its original objectives. The United States should mobilize all the leverage at its command to this end and be prepared with new initiatives based on a highly successful Kennedy Round and aimed at the earliest possible achievement of the goal toward which we have been moving for more than thirty years.

These negotiations are the world's best present hope for protecting the gains that have been made toward freedom of trade, for maintaining the essential element of momentum in further trade liberalization, and for directing the new forces at work in the world economy toward new frontiers of economic progress. We urge that these negotiations be pressed vigorously forward to a successful conclusion. The success of these negotiations would, in itself, be of great benefit to the United States and to the whole free world. Moreover, it would pave the way for further measures of trade liberalization, whereas failure would make progress in this area very difficult and might even set off a new era of protectionism.

As tariffs are lowered, non-tariff barriers assume greater significance as impediments to trade. It is already becoming apparent in the Kennedy Round negotiations that these will be difficult to reduce or eliminate. At the same time, the President's authority to negotiate concerning non-tariff barriers is more limited than the authority he has in the field of tariffs. Therefore, we recommend an ampler grant of authority to the President to negotiate on non-tariff barriers.

Without awaiting this wider authority, we urge continued efforts through negotiations, on an "ad referendum" basis where new legislation may be necessary, to reduce or eliminate non-tariff barriers to trade in return for adequate compensating benefits. In addition to such efforts with respect to quantitative restrictions, taxes, customs valuation, technical and administrative regulations, discriminatory shipping practices, and discriminatory regulations regarding domestic commerce, we urge the negotiation of international agreements to establish:

1. uniform standards regarding dumping, and

2. uniform criteria regarding the treatment of foreign bids in government procurement, so as to afford all suppliers and contractors, domestic and foreign, reasonable opportunities to compete effectively with one another.

For many primary agricultural products, progress in trade liberalization may require that the trade restricting provisions of domestic support policies, as well as other border protection devices, be brought into the negotiations. We recommend that the United States actively support the inclusion in trade negotiations, on a reciprocal basis, of relevant elements of domestic agricultural policies (including export aids), so that the trade-disruptive or trade-restrictive effects of such policies may be minimized.

In this connection, it should be pointed out that the need to minimize the potentially undesirable effects of agricultural support policies has been recognized in the development of U.S. agricultural programs (which include the maintaining of reserve stocks, the requiring of production adjustment as a condition of price support, and the use of much of current production to feed the hungry of the world in ways that minimize the impact of such shipments on commercial sales). It is recognized, of course, that such a negotiation would have to be conducted on an "ad referendum" basis, since in many cases the framework of price support programs is established in legislation and does not provide negotiating authority.

Simplification and standardization of documentation and other border procedures would materially facilitate the flow of world trade. We therefore urge an intensified effort by all nations to achieve this. We also recommend that the United States become a member of the multination Customs Cooperation Council at Brussels, participating fully in the Council's deliberations, and consider adopting the Brussels nomenclature of tariff classification.

In some of the major trading nations there are local government laws and practices, as well as highly organized private actions, which restrict the imports of the respective countries independently of national policies to achieve freer international commerce. There are many state and local government laws in our own country which discriminate in one way or another against imports. Many more have been proposed. By directly impeding or indirectly discouraging the flow of imported goods into these areas, they burden the citizens of these jurisdictions as consumers and taxpayers. This cost, together with the handicap these restrictions impose on our position in international trade negotiations, exceeds whatever benefits they are intended to provide domestic producers. Since national interests and national policy are affected by such legislation, we recommend (a) that efforts be made to discontinue and deter local laws and practices discriminating against imported goods, and (b) that a suitable Government advisory mechanism be established through which the governors of the various states and the mayors of the various cities may ascertain the national implications of existing and proposed state and local legislation affecting imports.

Of basic importance in this connection, however, is the need for a definitively articulated and consistent freer trade policy on the part of the Federal Government itself. Besides the possible constitutional issues involved in such state and local laws, the imperatives of the national interest cannot reasonably be expected to be convincing unless the national Government itself clearly and consistently asserts its special jurisdiction in this area and proves its dedication to a consistent policy of freer trade. If the actions of local governments or the organization of large-scale private boycotts interfering with trade in a manner inconsistent with Federal policy persist, the responsible exercise of a constitutionally authorized Federal authority will be undermined.

A major new development in world trade in recent years has been the urgent and justified interest of the developing countries in expanding and diversifying their exports, forcefully expressed in the UN Conference on Trade and Development. The United States should vigorously support, in constructive and practical ways consistent with its trade policy objectives, the efforts of the developing countries to expand their role in world trade in step with their development needs and growing economic capability. Tariff preferences by the developed countries to imports from developing countries (either a general extension of such preferences or their selective extension by individual developed countries to particular developing countries) do not satisfy these criteria. They in fact divert attention and policy from alternatives likely to produce more extensive and enduring results for trading nations at all levels of economic development. Neither in their foreign aid programs nor otherwise should the developed countries withhold positive support to the establishment in the developing countries of genuinely viable industries solely because they may compete with their own. One of the attributes of advanced economic status is the ability to find constructive, as against restrictive, answers to the challenges of change.

The developed countries should, in negotiations through GATT, work toward increasingly liberal terms of access to their markets for the products of special interest to the developing countries, including a joint effort mutually to move toward duty-free access of these products on a most-favored-nation basis. Where the importation of such products is controlled by quotas, they should be progressively liberalized and, as soon as possible, terminated.

The developed countries should refrain from seeking new bilateral or multilateral arrangements restricting imports from developing countries. If such measures become necessary in extreme cases where adjustment assistance cannot adequately cushion the effect of increased imports in the markets of developed countries, international arrangements may be appropriate—but only for a limited time and under clearly defined conditions. Such restrictions should be measures of last resort and then only as part of a clearly enunciated adjustment effort. These criteria should also be applied to decisions regarding the future status of such arrangements already in effect.

In their own commercial policies, it would be in the interest of the developing countries to work toward freer access of the world's goods into their domestic markets. To be consistent with such a policy, they would do well to concentrate their development programs on economically sound projects holding reasonable promise of becoming efficient and competitive. Uneconomic investments divert scarce resources from economically sound activities, thus retarding the development of these areas and their ability to participate in programs of international cooperation.

The United States should encourage regional integration among developing countries that would benefit the trade of non-members as well as members. It should also continue to support consideration of a possible GATT amendment to permit developing countries, in accordance with appropriate procedures and sound criteria, to integrate their economies on a broad sectoral basis, that is, sanction the establishment of free trade in selected categories of products by less-developed countries on a regional basis.

While emphasizing the need for soundly based economic diversification in the developing countries, the United States should continue to consider sound proposals for transitional international arrangements in primary commodities produced by the developing countries to help to stabilize the vitally important income of these countries from commodity exports. This should be accompanied, consistent with the provisions of our trade agreements legislation, by the negotiated elimination of import restrictions and other impediments on the consumption of these products in the industrialized countries. The International Monetary Fund should continue to concern itself with the impact of sharp price declines on the balance-of-payments positions of the producing countries and provide suitable assistance where needed. Commodity arrangements should protect the interests of importing as well as exporting countries and should be regarded as temporary measures urgently needed to buy time for the truly constructive answers to the problems of the developing countries to take effect.

It is important to remember that the drastic reduction of trade barriers among the developed countries, a major objective of the Kennedy Round, will in itself benefit the developing countries. The stimulus which trade expansion will give to the economies of the developed countries will result in greater demand by them for the products of the developing countries. Indeed, this benefit to them is likely to be greater than any they could obtain through tariff preferences.

In connection with the growing interest in East-West trade, we endorse in general the recommendations on this subject by the President's Special Committee on U.S. Trade Relations with East European Countries and the Soviet Union. We lay special stress upon the desirability, through the bilateral measures suggested here and through appropriate negotiations under the multilateral auspices of GATT, of establishing ground rules for free-world trade with the Soviet Union and its Eastern European associates and of inducing them to bring their trade practices more into line with normal world trade practices. The President should have flexible authority to grant most-favored-nation treatment and to remove or, if necessary, impose other trade restrictions affecting these countries whenever he regards such steps as necessary to the achievement of our foreign policy objectives.

Impact on the U.S. Economy

The full implementation of a number of the objectives set forth in the above recommendations will require changes and adaptations within the American economy to adjust to the consequences of increased freedom of trade. Import competition is only one of many causes of change in the American economy, such as technological progress, automation, changes in public taste and demand, regional movements of industry, the opening and closing of Government installations, and the like. The full benefits of trade expansion—specialization on an international scale according to the relative economic advantages enjoyed by various countries—cannot be attained without changes and effective adjustments.

We therefore recommend that the problem of economic mobility —of facilitating the continuous redeployment of land, labor and capital resources in our dynamic economy—should be viewed in the widest perspective, with a unified, consistent program to help solve both the urgent problems of economic dislocation and the evolving challenges of change from whatever quarter. A number of programs already in being are designed to treat certain specific aspects of the adjustment effort—e.g., aid to depressed areas under the Public Works and Economic Development Act, the manpower retraining program, the adjustment assistance provisions of the Trade Expansion Act of 1962, and others.

As these programs take full effect, they should substantially increase across-the-board economic mobility. They can, of course, be improved, expanded or supplemented, in accordance with sound criteria of public administration, if experience indicates this to be advisable or advantageous. In this context, adjustment to the import and export implications of freer international trade should be accorded major attention as we accelerate the pace of trade liberalization, encounter the impact of unprecedented import competition, and seek to capitalize on unprecedented export opportunities.

226 Blueprint for Peace

RECOMMENDATIONS

We make the following recommendations:

1. That the United States use all the leverage at its command to ensure a highly successful Kennedy Round of trade negotiations.
2. That international agreements be negotiated to establish uniform standards regarding dumping, as well as uniform criteria for the treatment of foreign bids in government procurement.
3. That negotiations on non-tariff barriers proceed as rapidly as possible and, where new legislation may be necessary, on an "ad referendum" basis.
4. That the trade-disruptive or trade-restrictive effects of domestic support policies in the field of agriculture be subject to international negotiation.
5. That intensified efforts be made to achieve simplification and standardization of documentation and other border procedures which materially affect the flow of world trade.
6. That the United States become a member of the multination Customs Cooperation Council in Brussels and consider adopting the Brussels nomenclature of tariff classification.
7. That efforts be made to discontinue and deter local government laws and practices discriminating against imported goods and to discourage highly organized private actions in opposition to imports from particular countries (in this connection, that a suitable government advisory mechanism be established through which governors and mayors may ascertain the national implications of existing and proposed state and local legislation affecting imports).
8. That the United States support, in ways consistent with its trade policy objectives, the efforts of the developing countries to expand and strengthen their role in world trade.

   (a) That the developed countries offer positive support to establishment in the developing countries of genuinely viable industries, even though such industries may compete with their own.

(b) That the developed countries work toward increasing liberal terms of access to their markets for products of special interest to the developing countries.

(c) That the developed countries refrain from seeking or continuing bilateral or multilateral arrangements restricting imports from the developing countries, except in accordance with criteria emphasizing the urgency, temporary character, and precise purpose of such an arrangement as part of an adjustment program.

(d) That the developing countries work toward decreased reliance on generalized "infant industry" protectionism, and concentrate their development programs on economically sound projects holding reasonable promise of becoming efficient and competitive.

(e) That the United States encourage regional integration among developing countries under GATT rules, and continue to support a proposal in GATT to permit regional integration of developing countries in selected broad categories of products.

(f) That the United States continue to consider sound proposals for transitional international arrangements in primary commodities produced by the developing countries, accompanied by the negotiated elimination of import restrictions and other impediments on the consumption of these products in the industrialized countries.

(g) That the International Monetary Fund continue to concern itself with the impact of sharp price declines on the balance-of-payments positions of the producing countries and provide suitable assistance where needed.

9. That the recommendations on East-West trade by the President's Special Committee on U.S. Trade Relations with East European Countries and the Soviet Union be adopted generally (particularly the desirability of negotiations to establish ground rules for freer trade with the Soviet bloc on terms consistent with free-world trading practices, and the desirability of flexible authority for the President with respect to the establishment or removal of trade restrictions affecting these countries).

10. That the problem of achieving adequate mobility of resources in our domestic economy, an essential component of U.S. initiatives for freer international trade, be viewed in the widest perspective, with a unified, consistent program to help solve both the urgent problems of economic dislocation and the evolving challenges of change from whatever quarter (that, in this context, major attention be given to adjustment to the import and export implications of freer international trade).

THE COMMITTEE ON TRADE

11. Helping the World's Cities

Cities all over the world are in deep trouble. Advanced countries struggle with decaying central districts, slums and blight, painful social problems, and serious traffic congestion. Developing countries face urban conditions which are considerably worse—unbelievable, tragic slums and mushrooming squatter settlements with populations in the hundreds of thousands. Inattention, and frequently sheer inability to meet the many urban problems with limited domestic resources, are creating bubbling cauldrons of social and political unrest. In both advanced and developing countries, choked, unplanned, and still-growing cities present not only deplorable social conditions but also an inefficient economic structure and an unhealthy economic climate—factors which inhibit national development.

Urban growth problems are a matter of major international importance. We believe that appropriate efforts of international cooperation can make strategic and decisive contributions to the solution or alleviation of these problems. The problems and pressures, already great, grow greater by the hour. Early action, its scope related to the size of the problems, is imperative.

The Nature of the Challenge

Urban development is the process of growth and change in the urban portion of society. It encompasses the political dynamics and administration of urban places; their economic activities; their changes in physical size, quality, and form; and their social programs and activities. These four broad elements break down into important practical matters that affect the lives of every urban citizen—among them jobs, decent housing, adequate roads, location of industry and residential areas, property taxes, health and sanitation, and recreation. Since urban communities are living entities, there is considerable interaction and potential conflict among these elements.

The goal of urban development planning—a better life and environment for city dwellers both as producers and consumers—can be

achieved only through the planned coordination of the four elements mentioned above and the cooperation of civic groups with
local, regional and national governments. The problems and complications that face urban communities are significantly influenced by
the rate of urbanization—the process by which urban areas grow
more rapidly than rural areas and by which rural populations relo-
cate in the city.

Our earth is rapidly becoming a planet of urban peoples. Today,
throughout the world, "breakneck urbanization" is a universal experience for both advanced and developing countries. In the eight-
eenth and nineteenth centuries, the pace of urban growth was still
slow enough to permit more or less gradual adaptation to the changing urban scene. Since then, rapid change has become commonplace.
In 1962 a group of UN experts gravely warned that the problems of
urban housing and urban development were fast becoming a "full-
fledged crisis." In the first half of the twentieth century, total world
population increased by 50 per cent, but the urban population in
cities of 20,000 or more increased 240 per cent. This "breakneck"
growth of cities shows no signs of slackening. In the second half of
the twentieth century the luxury of gradual, almost unconscious,
adaptation to urban growth has moved out of reach.

In developing nations, the growth of cities proceeds at a pace
even greater than city growth in the advanced countries. As a result,
more than 50 per cent of the urban population of the world now
resides not in industrially advanced countries, but in developing
countries. In Asia alone, it has been estimated that just in the large
cities—those of 100,000 population or more—there will be a net increase in population between the years 1960–75 of more than one-
quarter of a billion people. At the same time, continued urbanization
of advanced countries is fraught with urgent consequences. In some
of these countries, urban growth through migration from rural areas
has proceeded to the point where both relative and absolute reductions in the size of rural population have resulted. If the predictions
and estimates of some responsible experts materialize, children now
of preschool age, living in many parts of the globe, will live in a
world which on the average will be 80 to 90 per cent urban.

In a review of a recently published book on world urban problems, the *Economist* described "the gap between the gathering world
crisis of urbanism and the almost complete failure of governments
and agencies to come to grips with it." We are deeply concerned
with this "gap." Only perfunctory research is needed to disclose that

almost no nation—advanced or developing—pursues adequate urban development planning.

The consequences of such grossly inadequate urban development planning are serious. Man shapes the city, but the city in turn shapes man and his activities. Failure to plan for urban development leads generally to a haphazard, inefficient urban framework for new as well as existing investment. The logistics of the urban system become increasingly complex, tangled, and inefficient. Structures of steel, concrete, and stone may be placed in the path of logical long-term transportation routes, or be of inadequate measure for future needs, leading to great inefficiencies or exorbitant future costs. Housing is treated as an entity by itself and not simply as one part of the unfolding urban scene. Academic circles allude to urban land reform as a critical need (particularly for developing countries), but urban land prices and land uses continue to frustrate rational urban planning and allocation of land in both developing and advanced nations. Many decisions based on short-term advantages are proving to be very expensive in the long run.

Continued unguided growth of already large urban places can lead to unmanageable, unattractive giant cities, suffering from slums and squalor, poor facilities and community services, strangling traffic, and administrative chaos. In spite of all this, the large city, in the absence of nation-wide urban development planning that could produce alternatives, continues to attract new industries and migrants seeking jobs. But its impersonal character makes the task of assimilation difficult, and the migrant finds it hard to become truly a part of the urban community.

It is imperative that effective programs of international cooperation be designed to cope with or ameliorate this situation. Right now there is virtually no recognition in international cooperation programs of the need for a coordinated, multifaceted approach to urban development. The number of nations which integrate urban development planning with national development plans is also exceedingly small. It is not surprising, therefore, that in international cooperation (bilateral and multilateral) there is no international strategy for guiding and recasting urban growth. Such strategy is sorely needed.

In contrast to the overall strategy—geared to increased productivity and more equal distribution of income—which is accepted and is being somewhat applied to rural areas in developing countries, technical cooperation efforts aimed at urban areas of developing countries are essentially unrelated bits and pieces of urban planning. Urban areas—their growth, form, location, and quality—should be treated as a whole. The strategy should encompass the national urban picture, specific attention to major metropolitan areas, and pertinent urban-national and urban-rural relationships.

Each year in developing countries the annual investment expenditure for urban infrastructure and urban housing ranges generally between 20 to 40 per cent of total capital investment. In advanced countries the figure is even higher. These expenditures must be viewed as a whole and in relation to other urban-oriented investment (e.g., industry) if overall development planning is to be successful.

Viewed from the crucial standpoint of output or production, the primacy of the urban areas is also unquestioned. In the United States, despite a superb, incomparably efficient agricultural sector, more than 70 per cent of the Gross National Product is produced in urban areas. In Latin America, where the urban population is less than one-half of the total, the urban population produces an estimated 80 per cent of GNP. This kind of performance puts the city into economic focus and highlights the importance of retaining urban efficiencies and, more important, of improving these efficiencies and developing new efficiencies.

Without international assistance specifically aimed toward this objective, it is unlikely that there will be appropriate recognition soon of the vital nature of urban development in developing countries. Through international cooperation, improved recognition and programming for urban development can also be achieved in the advanced countries. We are convinced, for the foregoing reasons, that priority must be given to efforts at international cooperation for urban development planning before, in Barbara Ward's words, "the urban Niagara of the next forty years engulfs nations, developing and developed alike, and sweeps them beyond the point at which rational human action is possible." *

Here in the United States we are committed to an effort to achieve the Great Society, and President Johnson has said this will be achieved in cities. In less-developed countries the situation for progress and national improvement is closely analogous. If international cooperation is to aid in the modernization and rationalization of the economies of both developed and developing countries, it

* *The Processes of World Urbanization,* Background Paper No. 1 for the United Nations Symposium on the Planning and Development of New Towns (1965).

must not ignore their choked and inefficient but still rapidly growing urban areas. Economic and social evolution of a nation toward
its potential capability as a modern society, with an efficient urban
environment for economic, political, and social activities, cannot be
achieved without urban development planning and the integration
of such planning within national development planning.

Existing Patterns of Cooperation

Many kinds of assistance can be given to countries through international urban development programs. Technical assistance may aid in
the organization and administration of housing agencies or programs, or it may teach new building techniques, such as brick-
making or brick-laying. Training programs may enable a student to
acquire a master's degree in city planning or may increase the number or the skills of carpenters and masons. Loans or grants may enable a country to establish a savings and loan system or enable a city
to eliminate a slum. These kinds of assistance for developing countries have been sponsored by individual nations (bilateral) and by
international organizations (multilateral). Scarcely any aspect of activity related to urban development, housing, building, physical
planning, and the building materials industry has not at some time
been the subject of a technical assistance project or of a loan or a
grant by either a multilateral or a bilateral agency.

But these assistance projects, loans, and other aid have not been
provided for every country. The resources expended in the housing
and urban development field are scant and inadequate relative to the
magnitude of the needs. No nation has received long-term coordinated assistance calculated to create "take-off" conditions, i.e., circumstances wherein domestic capabilities are sufficiently well-estab-
lished and strong to improve housing or urban conditions without
further outside assistance. Assistance is geographically scattered,
generally fragmented, and usually uncoordinated with relation to
other projects or programs. In all too many cases projects, which
are generally limited short-term operations, have not been replaced
by programs, which are broader in scope and are aimed at long-run,
continuing benefits. One good reason for the continued use of
projects instead of programs is that of cost. Programs generally, although not invariably, cost more and/or obligate funds for a longer
period.

United Nations

The most important institution providing international assistance in the urban development field is the United Nations. Within UN headquarters, there are two policy bodies that are close to operations in urban development and housing and represent a fairly high degree of expertise. These are the Economic and Social Council's Committee on Housing, Building and Planning, and the Social Commission. New policy proposals and major action programs stem from these two bodies, particularly the Committee. The work of these bodies generally requires higher-level approval, first by the Economic and Social Council, and second, if need be, by the General Assembly.

The staff and most executive functions in United Nations urban and housing activities are performed by the UN Secretariat. Until 1965, the Housing, Building and Planning Branch of the Bureau of Social Affairs had the great bulk of the Secretariat responsibility. In 1965, the Center for Housing, Building and Planning was created within the UN Secretariat and the staff of the former Housing, Building and Planning Branch was transferred to this new organization. The ECOSOC Committee on Housing, Building and Planning was an important influence in effecting this change, because it saw an urgent need for a broader and more vital urban/housing development activity within the United Nations. As of this writing, however, the organizational change is one of name only—the staff has been augmented only slightly, and organizational relationships remain as before.

Outside UN headquarters but within the UN family are several Specialized Agencies and Regional Economic Commissions which have urban and housing responsibilities of varying degrees of importance. For example, the World Health Organization concerns itself with sanitation and potable water. The International Labor Organization promotes cooperatives and stimulates productivity in housebuilding. The Regional Economic Commissions have the authority to play an important regional role in the urban/housing field. In point of fact, only the Economic Commission for Europe has as yet given this subject area proper emphasis.

It is pertinent to point out here that the trend of activity in the United Nations parallels quite closely that in the United States. Just as the United States has moved from housing programs in a rather limited sense to the broader sphere of urban development programs within which housing is only one (albeit a vital) element, so has the UN moved in the direction of treating the integrated whole. No other alternative appears to offer the same possibilities of efficiency and success.

United Nations programs, whether at headquarters or in the Specialized Agency, consist of providing experts, granting fellowships, conducting demonstration projects, doing studies, and encouraging research. In the very recent past, the Special Fund of the UN has begun to aid research and institutional aspects of technical cooperation and assistance efforts in the urban/housing field. Comparison of the year 1960 with the year 1964 shows an increase in overall UN headquarters cooperation activity as follows:

1. In 1960 the UN program in the field expended $505,480. This involved the use of forty-three experts and the granting of thirty-two fellowships. In 1964 projected expenditure was $1,340,460, involving the use of 139 experts and the granting of forty-nine fellowships. In the five years 1960–64, UN technical assistance expenditures in urban/housing programs were a bare 1 per cent of total UN technical assistance expenditures.

2. In 1960 there were no Special Fund projects in the field of housing, building, and planning. Since 1960 Special Fund projects initiated or approved in this field involve a Special Fund contribution of $3,392,000 and host government counterpart expenditures of $4,845,000. Special Fund loans are primarily "pre-investment" in character, although some funds are used to help pay executive talent to work for governments of developing countries.

To sum up the UN headquarters program in the urban/housing development field: it is small, it has shown but minor increase in magnitude in the last four or five years, and it is still conducted with what is widely recognized as a seriously inadequate staff.

The respected financial giant in the international development field is, of course, the International Bank for Reconstruction and Development. The World Bank and its subsidiary, the International Development Association, have made a few loans for urban projects, principally for water and sanitation improvements. In the main, the World Bank has made it quite clear that it is very reluctant to play an important role in the urban/housing field. Recently it has shown greater awareness of the urban/housing field and has included housing or urban specialists on its country survey teams. In any event, the World Bank's primary role remains that of a lending institution. Any technical assistance aid provided is directly in connection with its loans or contemplated loans.

Organization of American States

By informal agreement between the UN Economic Commission for Latin America, the United Nations Secretariat at headquarters and the Pan American Union, the latter has for years been accorded the initiative and the action responsibility in Latin America for housing and urban matters. For a number of reasons the PAU has not been able to mount a continuing, effective program.

The Inter-American Development Bank in its first four years of existence loaned eighteen Latin American countries about $410 million for seventy-eight different projects in the fields of housing (including establishment of savings and loan institutions), water supply, and sanitation. The IDB loans constitute an important assistance and stimulating device. Nevertheless, it should be noted that they are often project-oriented and not program-oriented. They deal in most cases with components and not the urban whole.

The United States is an important source of capital funds for the IDB. One "window" of the Bank, the Social Progress Trust Fund, was launched by a $394 million U.S. grant. It has since been augmented in 1964 by a further $131 million. The bulk of these funds are going into housing, water, and sanitation projects.

Bilateral Programs: United States

U.S. bilateral assistance programs were begun in the late 1940's. Since its inception, the U.S. program has loomed large in the international assistance and cooperation picture. However, urban/housing programs have generally played a relatively small role in U.S. bilateral cooperation programs. The U.S. Congress has exhibited keen interest in urban/housing programs within U.S. bilateral assistance, and some of the current programs were established through Congressional initiative. In the past two years, the responsible U.S. action agency has moved to strengthen housing and urban development assistance to recipient countries. The new Policy Guidelines on programs in this subject area are encouraging.

The U.S. bilateral assistance and cooperation program is administered by the Agency for International Development. Virtually all policy formulation in bilateral aid is made by AID or by the Department of State. In execution of its programs, AID utilizes manpower and expertise of several sources. First reliance is on AID's own staff, but only very few of AID's staff are assigned to urban and housing activities. Of the 3,300-odd U.S. technicians working overseas for AID in mid-1965, only fourteen were working in the field of housing and urban development.

Additional manpower and services, both in Washington and abroad, are provided for AID by other Government agencies under agreed contractual relationships. In housing and urban development, both the Housing and Home Finance Agency and the Federal Home Loan Bank Board provide assistance. The role of these two agencies under terms of the existing contract for services is relatively passive. Policy, program initiation, program evaluation, and similar key activities are entirely the prerogative of AID. A third significant factor in the U.S. bilateral program is services secured through contractual arrangements negotiated by AID with trade associations, universities, and the like. These are growing in importance generally and in the urban/housing field are becoming quite important in the implementation of programs.

The initiation of the Alliance for Progress to aid our Latin American neighbors has stimulated U.S. urban/housing aid programs there. Special efforts have been launched to mobilize domestic capital for housing purposes by creating housing finance institutions, notably by establishing savings and loan systems. This fills a critical need, for almost without exception institutions for financing housing in Latin American countries have been either inadequate or totally lacking. Considerable effort is also being expended to develop cooperative housing programs in Latin America. Most of this work —establishment of savings and loan and cooperative housing—is being done by contract with trade or service associations.

Until 1964 the annual assistance expenditures of the U.S. Government in the urban/housing field were elusive, since these data had not been kept in distinct accounting categories by the responsible agency. Data on urban/housing program activities for fiscal 1964 show that total technical assistance aid rendered in that period was in the amount of $4.3 million. Total capital assistance, including U.S.-owned foreign currency, amounted to $74 million, of which $57 million was extended to Latin America as part of the Alliance for Progress. In addition, $12.2 million of housing investments in Latin America was guaranteed in the fiscal year 1964 by AID.

Other Bilateral Programs

Several other countries provide important bilateral assistance. The most important of these are the U.S.S.R., France, United Kingdom, Japan, and West Germany. Generally speaking, the U.S.S.R. programs appear to conform to Marxist ideology and practice and concentrate on industry and infrastructure. Some of the French assistance programs in Africa have been directed to rural and urban settlement problems, apparently with some success.

RECOMMENDATIONS

We recommend that:

Urbanization, once a manageable, gradual, and slow-moving force in man's history, has accelerated and has made such impact in the last fifty years that it must be accounted one of the truly great revolutionary forces of the twentieth century. Urbanization has made this the Century of the City. And in terms of man's welfare and well-being, the conclusion must be drawn that this is all to the good. Urbanization poses many perplexing and anxious problems, but it is indeed a net advantage to mankind and an integral and essential element of progress. The task men face is to minimize the problems and to maximize the benefits of urbanization.

Recommendation 1

> The United States should give higher priority and more recognition to urban development programs in its bilateral assistance and should move to secure comparable priority and recognition for urban development programs within the United Nations assistance programs. In particular, the United States should vigorously seek to secure adequate budget and personnel for the newly established United Nations Center for Housing, Building and Planning.

The Agency for International Development, the agency which administers U.S. bilateral assistance, has taken some steps in the direction of placing proper emphasis on urban development programs.

Administrator David E. Bell, in a statement of general policy on urban development, has stressed that AID assistance "should be directed to the building of institutions and capabilities rather than the building of physical structures." AID will make assistance available to developing countries to train personnel who can man the institutions needed to plan for and to achieve orderly urban development. This emphasis on institution building through technical assistance merits the fullest support.

Unfortunately, in all too many cases national governments do not appreciate the need for national planning for urbanization. To encourage developing countries to begin such planning, and to integrate this urban development planning within overall national planning, we recommend that the United States consider the establishment within its bilateral programs of National Planning Grants for the support or creation of necessary planning institutions or to develop necessary urban planning skills in developing nations. In view of the large number of competing program interests in AID and the relatively low priority assigned hitherto to urban development programs, it is felt that a special program of grants administered by the housing and urban experts within AID is advisable, at least until the merits and importance of urban development are more widely recognized.

The United States, moreover, should take a spirited policy initiative in the United Nations so that the United Nations will alter and strengthen its programs appropriately, giving much greater emphasis to the urban component of national development plans. In this connection, we must call attention to the understaffed, underbudgeted, and largely unsupported urban and housing activities within the United Nations. Conclusions or recommendations, by competent United Nations organs supported by expert studies, have led only to pious expressions, paper organization, and ineffectual implementation. It is axiomatic that the efficacy of any policy or program can be no greater than the competence and resources of the institutions or tools created to carry them out. A new United Nations Center for Housing, Building and Planning is in process of establishment. Only if this new instrument is both strong and well supported can an adequate international contribution in the urban field be expected.

Recommendation 2

> The United States should take the initiative within the United
> Nations to inaugurate a concerted international program, sup-
> ported by voluntary contributions of member nations, to attack
> the specific problem of slums and squatter settlements in devel-
> oping countries.

The low-income groups in urban areas of developing countries, a
vast number of squatter and slum families, comprise an army of des-
titute, hopeless, and angry people. The literature on urban problems
gives this group considerable attention. However, effective programs
aimed at improving their lot are rare. In one view, they are a potentially incendiary force in developing countries. On the other hand,
squatters have been described as an important national resource, since
they are for the most part aggressive and searching individuals who
have left either the inner-city slum or the rural hinterlands to look for
something at least a little better. They need assistance and guidance
so that they may obtain improved shelter. The living environment of
these families should be improved by the provision of critical urban
services, such as potable water, waste removal, and educational and
health facilities. Efforts must be made to provide a greater measure
of order and stability for these families and for their communities.

We recommend, therefore, that a concerted international program
to cope with the problems of urban slums and squatter settlements,
supported by a special request for funds from member nations, be inaugurated by the United Nations. The United States should take the
initiative in proposing and supporting this program. The United
States, moreover, should make a significant pledge to a United Nations fund to carry out this program.

We recommend that the program be aimed in major degree at institutional development and elimination of administrative and legal
roadblocks. In particular, we feel that this program for slum dwellers
and squatters should address itself to the inordinately high cost of urban land which is characteristic in so many developing countries and
to the legal issues involved in squatting. The prevalence of the phe-

nomenon of squatting is due in no small measure to the almost complete inability of families to acquire alternative residence or to obtain legal possession of a small plot of urban land.

Recommendation 3

Additional attention and consideration should be focused on the problem of financial resources for carrying out urban development programs. The heartening successes of such undertakings as savings and loan and credit union institutions recently organized in Latin America are an augury of what might be done by even more zealous promotion of these institutions or the introduction of other imaginative and practical instruments or policies.

There is widespread agreement that the financial aspects of urban and housing problems are the most important and critical elements of these complex overall problems. We are convinced that the deep pessimism and negativism frequently associated with the financing problems of urban development and housing are overdrawn. The encouraging results of still quite new savings institutions in Latin America, promoted and established under the Alliance for Progress, suggest that the prospects of mobilization of very important amounts of local capital for housing and like purposes are indeed very favorable. The possibilities of wider introduction of popular savings institutions, of guaranties, insurance, and of strategic international lending should receive greater consideration and, as appropriate, employment.

In this connection, that the United States should take the initiative in the International Bank for Reconstruction and Development to encourage the Bank and its affiliates to consider in greater depth the impact of their loans on urban development as well as their effect on national development. Efforts should be made, for example, to have the World Bank include in development loans funds which would be earmarked for urban development planning (to assess impacts of new or enlarged industry, study possible alternatives in location of future industrial plants, etc.). This proposal is consistent with a position the United States has taken at the United Nations and is logical, since the great bulk of the Bank's loans are put to work in urban areas or are for auxiliary projects which support urban activities.

In recent years the World Bank, through the inclusion of urban and housing experts in its country survey teams, has shown increasing recognition of the existence and importance of an urban component in national development plans. It is important that the Bank's focus and perspective on urban development, as a strategic and weighty element of national development, be sharpened further, and that this be reflected in its lending activities.

Recommendation 4

The United States should establish a World Urban Development Research Laboratory and Institute. This laboratory and institute would be sponsored by the United States, be financed principally by the United States, and be headquartered in the United States. It would function, however, as a world organization, with full international participation, possibly with branches in other regions of the world, and its products would be for all nations.

This new institution would provide a focal point for study, education, and exchange of information and experience. It would attract and provide for foreign students and faculty, visiting foreign experts and practitioners. Results of its studies and research would be published, the more important ones in several languages. It would carry out research of a complex and interdisciplinary nature at one center, but at the same time would promote research in urban problems at various universities throughout the country through grants, more or less in the pattern of the National Institutes of Health. The laboratory might well concern itself, for example, with the new technologies in urban sanitation and water supply, means of quickly and cheaply assembling prefabricated construction components, improved techniques for promoting savings and channeling private funds to investment in urban construction in the less-developed countries, optimum densities in land use under various conditions, stronger means of promoting self-help housing, administration of housing agencies and programs, and interrelations of urban to national development.

The dynamics of urban growth are incredibly important—but also incredibly complex. Being now more than halfway through the Century of the City, we must not tarry longer in mobilizing resources (a) to isolate individual urban problems, identify relationships, assess their probable evolution, and develop solutions; and (b) to ensure much wider adoption of those relatively limited but important approaches and techniques which have been proved effective.

Early and effective action to meet and solve the intricate and serious problems of urban growth is an obligation that we owe to the generations of the future. The happiness, freedom, and contentment of future generations—our sons, daughters, and their children—will depend as never before on the character and efficiency of urban places. In our judgment, the solution or amelioration of the present and coming problems of the city would be one of the most solid blows for world peace and progress that could be struck.

Although this laboratory would make a notable world contribution, it is clearly evident that the United States would benefit substantially from its work. These collateral domestic benefits add to the attractiveness of this international cooperation proposal. At some point in the future, it may be deemed appropriate to transfer the Research Laboratory and Institute to United Nations management under the UN Center for Housing, Building and Planning.

Recommendation 5

> The United States should sponsor a United Nations World Conference on Urban Development to emphasize the importance of urban development and to gain understanding and support from decision makers in the countries concerned.

We recommend that a top-level World Conference for policy makers and principal planners be called by the United Nations. The theme of the World Conference would be "Urban Development: A Major Element of National Development Planning." The planning and conduct of the Conference should be closely patterned after the highly successful Conference on the Application of Science and Technology for the Benefit of the Less Developed Areas held in

1963. Under the general theme, the Conference would include the issues raised in the four previous recommendations—the urban development component in national planning, urban slums and squatting, financial resources, and research in urban development. Many other aspects suggest themselves, e.g., urban administration, transportation, utility and land problems, possible technological breakthroughs, and social development.

The United States should assist in highlighting the importance of the Conference and send a carefully selected delegation of the highest caliber. Observers and participants in the Conference, representing all parts of the globe, should include not only city planners and housing experts, but political and civic leaders, representatives of great institutions of learning, physical scientists, and leaders of industry and labor.

The Conference should be held in 1967 or possibly 1968, so that sufficient time will be allowed for adequate preparation. It would be fitting, and would have great collateral benefit, if the Conference would take place at the inauguration or dedication of the World Urban Development Research Laboratory and Institute.

A Final Word

We were increasingly heartened by evidence that writers and development experts recognize the city as a totality, as a vital political and economic instrument in the progress of mankind, and also by the growing realization that rapid urban growth, multiplying new functions, and rising expectations have put the city into deep trouble. But the hour is late and time is short. The magnitude of the troubles of the city is still not adequately appreciated. The problems are particularly great in developing countries where the resources are few and needs are many. Our proposals are aimed at meeting the more urgent, immediate problems and at mounting the kind of effort and approach that will anticipate and avoid many problems in the future. International cooperation offers great promise for both meeting immediate problems and avoiding others.

Our recommendations deal with world problems in an atmosphere of international cooperation; yet these recommendations dealing with urban problems have very important meaning to U.S. domestic interests and activities. In 1958, a study completed by a private U.S. foundation stated: "The metropolitan problem has been called the major domestic problem of our times. But the nation as a whole has not awakened to its gravity. The piecemeal approach to date is inadequate and self-defeating. Many programs now cancel each other out or have results opposite to those intended." *

Despite significant progress, the situation in 1966, eight years later, is not greatly different. It is clear, therefore, that the United States does not possess all the answers and that it, too, can gain much from international cooperation. In the particular area of urban development, we believe the proposals we have made will not only advance the broad foreign interests of the United States, but will also contribute in very important measure to the enhancement and improvement of vital domestic programs.

THE COMMITTEE ON URBAN DEVELOPMENT

* *The Challenge to America: Its Economic and Social Aspects* (Doubleday & Co., Inc., 1958), p. 44.

12. Exploring Outer Space

The spectacular advances of the last decade in chemistry, metallurgy, and electronics have enabled man to extend his quest for knowledge into the limitless expanse of space. With the moon at our fingertips, we are already reaching for the planets. The great adventure has begun to alter life on earth, but the current stimulus to our scientific and engineering communities, our educational systems, and our industries is only the first manifestation of forces that will affect human society for generations to come. Mankind thrills at the prospect, but with the thrill comes concern that the advance of the nations into space may extend and exacerbate terrestrial rivalries.

The alternative prospect—cooperating in space and thereby establishing patterns that might contribute to a reduction of terrestrial tensions—has strong appeal. Space is essentially international, for an orbiting spacecraft knows no national boundaries, and operations are so expensive that even the most affluent nations may welcome assistance. Though space has implications for national security, it is still relatively uncomplicated and free from the vested interests that make joint action difficult.

We are impressed by what already has been done to cooperate in space. These achievements justify President Kennedy's faith "that space can be explored and mastered without feeding the fires of war, without repeating the mistakes that man has made in extending his writ around this globe of ours." They justify, too, President Johnson's promise that "The race in which we of this generation are determined to be first is the race for peace."

However much has been accomplished, we must address ourselves to new and more ambitious cooperative enterprises. The year prior to ICY witnessed a surge of space activity abroad—the energetic programs of France, the demonstrated competence of Canada and Italy, the entry of the British aircraft industry into spacecraft engineering, the formal establishment of regional space organizations in Europe. These events were harbingers of a broader and deeper technical capability and interest that will be present in Europe, Canada, and Japan five years from now. This increased activity will make possible either new opportunities for cooperation or a repetition of ancient patterns of competition.

The challenge we face in the last half of the 1960's is to keep the hope and promise of cooperation alive. We cannot do it alone, but we must do our part. If we are to realize the technical and political advantages of cooperation, for ourselves and for others, we must continue alert and open to more considerable and advanced cooperative efforts. Otherwise we will offer foreign engineers and scientists no more than is available in their own domestic and regional programs.

If imagination and enlightened self-interest prevail, and we have every confidence they will, the cooperative efforts of the United States will continue to stimulate constructive activities abroad, supplement our own resources of brain and purse, further the common destiny in space, and reduce—in some measure—the political and economic strains that divide us here on earth.

What cooperation has already been achieved in the opening years of the Space Age? In 1965, the International Cooperation Year itself? What cooperation can we pursue and expect for the future? Is there a basic pattern of cooperation which will best serve to bring governments and industry together in international space programs?

Where We Stand

International cooperation in space has grown richly and rapidly in both the governmental and non-governmental sectors. Governmental efforts have produced (1) the cooperative space research projects of the U.S. National Aeronautics and Space Administration (NASA), (2) the cooperative programs of other nations, and (3) the activities of the United Nations and its specialized agencies. Non-governmental activities stem from (4) the international scientific community itself, (5) the global commercial communications satellite system, and (6) the commercial and industrial relationships of private enterprise.

1. NASA

NASA's international programs have involved sixty-nine nations and touched every continent. Agreements already reached for past, present, and future projects provide for:

- U.S. launching of fourteen international satellites,
- accommodation of sixteen foreign experiments on NASA satellites,
- some 200 cooperative sounding rocket launchings in every quarter of the globe,
- ground-based experiments (coordinated with NASA satellite missions) by scientists in more than fifty countries,
- support for the operation of tracking and data acquisition stations in eighteen countries, and
- coordinated satellite launchings and data exchange with the Soviet Union.

All of these activities stem from a mandate laid down in the National Aeronautics and Space Act of 1958, where Congress declared it the national purpose to devote our space activities to peaceful purposes and to execute them in cooperation with other nations and groups of nations.

The international projects which have followed have brought substantial scientific achievement open to all, practical and political benefits, and savings to both sides. Yet each of the participating countries has carried the costs of its own responsibilities in full.

Four of the international satellites under agreement are already in orbit. *Ariel I*, engineered and launched by NASA in April, 1962, carries satellite instrumentation designed, prepared, and funded under the direction of the British National Committee for Space Research. It has provided valuable data on spatial conditions not previously measured in combination. *Ariel II*, a similar satellite, was orbited in March, 1964, and the British are now engaged with NASA in a cooperative project involving a third satellite, this one engineered as well as instrumented by the British. *Alouette*, the Canadian satellite launched by NASA in September, 1962, was designed, funded and engineered by the Canadian Telecommunications Establishment (DRTE). This satellite, the first to sound the ionosphere from above, proved so successful that the Canadian Government then offered to assume full responsibility for a more considerable portion of the established NASA program for ionospheric studies. Accordingly, NASA and DRTE have agreed to the ISIS program (International Satellites for Ionospheric Studies), which provides for NASA to launch four additional Canadian satellites to monitor the ionosphere through the next maximum of the solar cycle. In December, 1964, Italy became the third nation to launch a satellite when an Italian crew used the facilities at Wallops Island, Virginia, and a Scout vehicle to place an Italian-built and instrumented *San Marco* spacecraft in orbit. This was in preparation for the eventual Italian launching of an identical satellite from a towable platform in the Indian Ocean to determine local atmospheric densities in the equatorial upper atmosphere.

Cooperative satellite projects with France and with the new European Space Research Organization are also in progress, and NASA has agreed to a project looking toward the launching of a satellite provided by the Federal Republic of Germany. This brings to ten the number of cooperative satellites in prospect to supplement the four already in orbit.

Apart from complete satellites to be launched by NASA, foreign scientists are invited to propose individual experiments for inclusion on NASA's own satellites. These proposals are reviewed in competition with those submitted by American scientists and, if selected, are funded and prepared by the cooperating countries. Two such experiments have already flown successfully. Fourteen additional ones have been scheduled for later flights, and as many more have been proposed. NASA has recently opened virtually all categories of its spacecraft, including manned spacecraft, to foreign participation on this cooperative basis.

Cooperative sounding rocket projects have special international appeal. To nations wishing to initiate space programs, they offer relatively low-cost opportunities on a smaller but significant scale. To NASA, they offer the use of sites overseas of unique scientific interest and a means of organizing simultaneous launchings in different locations (a practice required for certain scientific objectives). The basic elements in sounding rocket projects are the launching sites, the rockets themselves, the scientific instrumentation they carry aloft, the ground instrumentation to retrieve data from the rockets, and the analysis of the data. The cooperating countries divide responsibility for these elements in ways that suit the requirements of the individual projects. Almost 150 rockets have already been launched in joint NASA projects with fifteen countries, and other launchings are in prospect under current agreements. These projects have brought new knowledge of rare phenomena of the night sky at high latitudes, of the global atmospheric circulation, of geomagnetic phenomena above the equator, of techniques for simultaneous meteorological soundings along an entire meridian, and of events and processes in the near-earth environment.

Joint projects are not, however, limited to satellite and sounding rocket experimentation. Equally important contributions are made through ground-based cooperative projects in which foreign scientists conduct observations or measurements in connection with NASA's orbiting spacecraft. Again, for the most part, these experimenters abroad use their own resources. Ground-based cooperation is paramount in applications of great practical interests—satellite communications and meteorology. The dramatic transoceanic television demonstrations of the Telstar, Relay, and Syncom satellites required special ground terminals costing many millions of dollars both in the United States and abroad. The stations abroad, which now number nine, were constructed by the cooperating countries entirely at their own expense under agreement with NASA. One of their principal values has been the creation of informed interest overseas in a commercial communications satellite system and in frequency allocation questions.

In meteorology, NASA and the U.S. Weather Bureau invited foreign weather services to make conventional observations synchronized with cloud photography by NASA's TIROS satellites. Thus, the TIROS series has afforded forty-two foreign weather services the opportunity to conduct, at their own cost, special observations of local weather conditions and relate them to satellite meteorology. Through this program, the United States has been able to correlate the analysis of weather from cloud pictures taken hundreds of miles above the earth with detailed data on the local weather below.

A joint NASA-Weather Bureau International Meteorological Satellite Workshop in Washington, in November, 1961, which foreign meteorologists attended at their own expense, provided instruction in the use of satellite photographs in operational forecasting. The Weather Bureau has carried this work forward by playing a leading role in the World Meteorological Organization Workshop held in Tokyo in late 1964 and by training foreign meteorologists at the National Weather Satellite Center in programs financed by the trainees' own countries or by fellowships supplied by international organizations.

A new form of cooperation, permitting the direct use of this information, recently became possible with the inclusion of an Automatic Picture Transmission system on TIROS VIII and on the advanced meteorological satellite Nimbus. The camera can provide continuous read-out of cloud-cover photographs. A simple and inexpensive ground station permits the direct and immediate acquisition and printing of cloud-cover photographs taken by the satellite overhead. Thirteen countries have acquired APT sets at their own expense and used them successfully, many reporting direct improvements in forecasting. Present indications are that about twenty countries will be equipped to take advantage of APT transmissions from spacecraft launched in 1966 as part of the TIROS Operational Satellite System. Thus this program is paving the way for the broad-scale international cooperation which will feature the meteorology of the future.

NASA ground-based cooperation also includes projects involving ionospheric and geodetic research which could not be carried out at all without the ground-based participation. The Naval Research Laboratory has conducted similar programs in which foreign ground stations acquire and analyze data from satellites monitoring the sun's activities, particularly X-ray emissions.

To track its satellites and to receive the data they radio back to earth, NASA needs stations around the globe. The establishment of such stations on the territory of other countries requires not only the consent of these countries but also their cooperation in the acquisition of land, the importation of equipment, the movement of personnel, and the use of radio frequencies. Beyond this, the interest of other countries in participating in the technology and adventure of space exploration has prompted them to make available their own technicians to work side by side with ours in many of the stations. At some locations, in England and Canada, the host country of its own volition has assumed responsibility for operating costs. Australia also makes a contribution to the cost of operating stations on its territory. Such stations represent common efforts and centers for the continued growth of understanding and cooperation.

Personnel exchanges and training arrangements have important places in most international efforts. Opportunities have been made for senior scientists from abroad to spend a year or more in NASA centers in research or experimental work. Fellowships at the graduate level are available in American universities for foreign trainees whose travel and subsistence are paid by their own sponsoring agencies. Training directly and specifically required for the execution of cooperative projects is made available at appropriate NASA centers. The requirement for investment on the part of the cooperating country assures careful consideration of the training arrangements, the personnel selected to be sent there, and their future utilization at home.

These wide-ranging joint efforts with Western and neutral, de-

veloped and developing nations, have been extended to space cooperation with the Soviet Union, as a consequence of an exchange
of correspondence between Chairman Khrushchev and President
Kennedy after the successful flight of John Glenn in February,
1962. In his message of congratulations, Mr. Khrushchev repeated
the widespread view that it would be a fine thing if the two nations
could pool their efforts in space. President Kennedy promptly made
specific proposals for such cooperation and suggested that negotiators be designated. The resulting talks between Dr. Hugh L. Dryden and Academician Anatoly A. Blagonravov produced a three-
part bilateral space agreement of June 8, 1962. The first part provides for coordinated launchings by the two countries of experimental meteorological satellites, for the exchange of data thus obtained, and for the exchange of conventional meteorological data,
prior to, and on a secondary basis, during the exchange of satellite
data. The second part provides for the launching by each country
of an earth satellite equipped with absolute magnetometers and the
subsequent exchange of data in order to arrive at a "map" of the
earth's magnetic field. The third part provides for joint communications experiments by means of the U.S. passive satellite *Echo II.*

The communications project is the first to be completed. In February and March, 1964, the facilities of the Jodrell Bank Observatory of the University of Manchester in the United Kingdom were
used to transmit radio signals via *Echo II* to the Zimenki Observatory of the State University of Gorki in the U.S.S.R. These transmissions included radio teletype messages, photograph transmissions
using facsimile equipment, and voice messages. While the technical
benefits from this project should not be overemphasized, it was a
useful exercise in organizing a joint undertaking with the Soviet
Union.

Exchange of magnetic field data obtained by ground-based instruments has begun and will provide a basis for analysis of satellite data.
In the meteorological project, a twenty-four-hour communications
link has been established on a shared-cost basis between Washington
and Moscow to prepare for the exchange of satellite data. Daily two-
way transmissions of data are now taking place over this link under
temporary arrangements until the prime objective, the exchange of
satellite cloud-cover data, can be achieved.

The United States has no desire to establish a bipolarity in space
matters with the Soviet Union. Rather, it wishes to ensure that these

initial cooperative projects are, from the outset, open to other countries and will serve the general interest. Thus, British capabilities were essential to the *Echo II* communications tests. The coordinated mapping by satellite is designed essentially to contribute to the World Magnetic Survey. And other countries will be able to tap into the satellite data exchanges which are expected to materialize between Washington and Moscow.

2. *Other Governments*

International cooperation in space is by no means the exclusive preserve of the United States. Responding to their own needs and encouraged in some measure by the U.S. example, many other governments have joined in a variety of bilateral and regional relationships. To cite but one example of bilateral cooperation, France is known to have undertaken cooperative projects with Argentina, India, the Netherlands, and the Federal Republic of Germany in addition to those with the United States.

Certain regional activities are related directly to NASA's sounding rocket projects. NASA/Norwegian ionospheric studies led to collaborative efforts among all three Scandinavian countries. A small sounding rocket project with Argentina helped engender regional interest, and the Argentine range at Chamical is beginning to serve in a sense as a Latin American training center for the use of sounding rockets in geophysical and meteorological research. Both Argentina and Brazil are now undertaking with NASA joint programs of high-altitude meteorological sounding-rocket studies which will serve as elements in an experimental inter-American meteorological sounding-rocket network.

The most significant development in regional cooperation is the establishment of the European Space Research Organization (ESRO) and the European Launcher Development Organization (ELDO). ESRO, with a budget of some $300 million over an eight-year period, has undertaken a balanced space program featuring sounding rocket experimentation, small first-generation geophysical satellites, stabilized astrophysical satellites, and a larger astronomical satellite—all to be supported by a tracking and data acquisition network and technical and data analysis centers. ELDO, which budgets over $200 million for a five-year booster development effort, has successfully tested the first stage of Europa I, a three-stage launch vehicle designed to put a substantial spacecraft into Earth orbit. The

United States welcomes the appearance of these regional organizations and already has agreed to launch the first two ESRO satellites, which are expected to be ready for flight in 1967.

3. The UN

The United Nations reflects the concern throughout the world that space activity be directed to peaceful purposes. Through its Committee on the Peaceful Uses of Outer Space, the UN has sought to support existing agencies with international functions in space matters, encourage cooperation, and provide a legal framework to govern operations in space.

The UN efforts have resulted in the publication of a biennial collection of reports on national and international space activities, including training opportunities, and in sponsorship of the Thumba Equatorial Rocket Launching Site in India. (Thumba had its origin in a cooperative project between NASA and the Indian Committee on Space Research and with UN endorsement in process, has benefited also from equipment loans by France and the Soviet Union.)

In the legal field, the General Assembly has adopted a set of principles to guide the exploration and use of outer space. Among the more significant are those declaring that outer space and celestial bodies are not subject to national appropriation, that international law and the United Nations Charter apply in outer space, that states bear responsibility for all activity of their nationals in space, that they are liable for damage done by the objects they launch, and that they shall render astronauts all possible assistance in the event of accident, distress, or emergency landing. A legal subcommittee is now attempting to draft international conventions to specify in detail the responsibilities of states in the areas of liability and of assistance to and return of astronauts and spacecraft.

Several of the UN Specialized Agencies play particular and important roles in space. The World Meteorological Organization has made a start in evaluating and planning requirements for a world weather system including satellite systems. In the fall of 1963 an Extraordinary Administrative Radio Conference of the International Telecommunication Union allocated frequencies and established international regulations for the use of radio in space communications and research, including meteorological, communications, and navigation satellites. The convention embodying these arrangements, already ratified by the United States, represents an orderly approach to one of the central problems of the Space Age.

4. *The International Scientific Community*

The scientific community has a long tradition of cooperation embracing correspondence, the exchange of papers, and meetings to discuss common interests. Space science has benefited from this wholesome tradition to an extent only suggested by the fact that 1965 saw at least thirty international conferences devoted to various aspects of space engineering.

The Space Age itself began in the context of a major program of the organized scientific community, the International Geophysical Year (IGY). The organizing body was the International Council of Scientific Unions (ICSU). IGY was so rewarding that ICSU took steps to place its major activities on a permanent basis. For the space segment, ICSU organized the International Committee for Space Research (COSPAR). Today, COSPAR membership numbers thirty national bodies and ten scientific unions; several hundred scientists attend its symposium each year.

COSPAR provides opportunity for scientists to meet in an environment that minimizes political considerations. Through its meetings, symposia, and publications, it facilitates communication. It provides the leading forum for reporting space research results, sponsors World Data Centers for depositing and exchanging experimental data, defines suitable research objectives, and promotes such activities as synoptic sounding rocket investigations. It also provides an appropriate and favorable atmosphere for the development of bilateral and multilateral cooperation of a more operational character.

Another important non-governmental forum, principally for annual symposia emphasizing the engineering aspects of space research, exists in the International Astronautical Federation, which brings together national rocket societies with long-standing interests in promoting space exploration.

5. *Global Commercial Satellite System*

The Communications Satellite Corporation is itself the creature of an effort to bridge differences and achieve cooperation in order to provide a means for reaping the fruits of man's scientific genius. There were varied and conflicting views as to how this nation could best organize itself to develop and use communication satellites for commercial purposes held in the Congress, in the Executive and other branches of the U.S. Government, and within U.S. industry.

The desire and need for establishing and organization were, however, readily recognized as being of higher priority than the different but strongly held philosophies as to which institutional form was preferable. A solution was provided with the enactment into law of the Communications Satellite Act of 1962.

The Satellite Act created the Communications Satellite Corporation (Comsat) and provided for the establishment of this private corporation as the chosen instrument of the United States for the implementation of certain stated policies and objectives. Among the policy objectives which the Congress established were the following:

SEC. 102. (a) The Congress hereby declares that it is the policy of the United States to establish, in conjunction and in cooperation with other countries, as expeditiously as practicable a commercial communications satellite system, as part of an improved global communications network, which will be responsive to public needs and national objectives, which will serve the communication needs of the United States and other countries, and which will contribute to world peace and understanding.

(b) The new and expanded telecommunication services are to be made available as promptly as possible and are to be extended to provide global coverage at the earliest practicable date. In effectuating this program, care and attention will be directed toward providing such services to economically less developed countries and areas as well as those more highly developed, toward efficient and economical use of the electromagnetic frequency spectrum, and toward the reflection of the benefits of this new technology in both quality of services and charges for such services.

The Corporation was formally created in February, 1963, and, after preliminary organization, embarked upon the task of meeting the objectives set forth. High among the list of priorities was the goal of establishing a commercial communications satellite system with full and meaningful international participation.

Preliminary discussions with representatives of foreign governments and communications entities commenced in the latter part of 1963. Early in 1964, representatives of the Communications Satellite Corporation and the U.S. Government, acting in concert, embarked on serious negotiations with a view to concluding arrangements which would provide for the establishment of a global commercial communications satellite system at the earliest practicable date. These negotiations were undertaken initially with representatives of countries whose potential use of communication satellites was of such a magnitude that their participation at the outset appeared to be desirable and would provide a basis for the viability of the system.

The U.S. Government Comsat team did not have any specific instructions concerning the nature of the institutional framework which would bring the system into being. This was left by the Satellite Act to be conceived and developed through negotiations among the partners in this enterprise. The U.S. team did, however, have a clear mandate for international cooperation provided.

It was abundantly clear that the U.S. national policy as reflected in the President's policy declaration of July 24, 1961, and in the United Nations' Resolution 1721 of December 20, 1961, which was formulated and sponsored by the United States, as well as in the policies and objectives of the Satellite Act, called for the establishment of a single global commercial communications satellite system and provided for non-discriminatory access for all nations in order for them to realize the economic, technical, and political benefits of this technology. In economic terms, it was clearly desirable to preclude the establishment of competing systems and therefore to avoid unnecessary and wasteful competition which would affect both lesser and more developed countries. Technical considerations also militated against the establishment of competing systems because of the positive prospects for the efficient operation of a single system, avoidance of unnecessary duplication of facilities and standardization of equipment and the most efficient utilization of a very rare resource—the electromagnetic frequency spectrum. It was hoped that a consensus could ultimately be achieved throughout the world recognizing that it was politically advantageous to establish a single global system in the expectation that destructive political competition between contrasting ideologies would be avoided and that there would be reduction of world tensions. This would permit effective utilization of this technology, including consequential social and economic benefits to all nations.

Early in the course of negotiations, agreement was reached on the concept of a single global system consisting of a space segment—which includes all of the satellites used in the system, and the tracking, control and command facilities required to support the operation of the satellite in orbit—and a number of earth segments comprising stations transmitting and receiving from satellites. This space segment would be jointly owned and financed by the participants in the system and the investment of capital, which would also represent an ownership share, would be in relation to the potential use of the global system by each participant. Arrangements for the construction, ownership, financing and operation of the various earth stations would be left to the discretion of the interested countries. Each country would be free to determine whether a telecommunications entity, public or private, would be authorized to have an earth station, or, where appropriate, to participate in an earth station which would be jointly owned and operated by telecommunications entities of several countries and serve an entire geographic area. This fundamental conceptual distinction between the space segment and the various earth segments is the keystone to a full comprehension of the international arrangements that were ultimately concluded.

Negotiations continued from February of 1964 into the summer and culminated in the conclusion of two inter-related agreements which were opened, in Washington, for signature on August 20, 1964. These agreements established an international partnership or "consortium" for the financing, ownership and operation of the space segment of the system. The first agreement, entitled "Agreement Establishing Interim Arrangements for a Global Commercial Communications Satellite System," is an agreement among governments. The second agreement, called the "Special Agreement," is an agreement which may be signed either by the governments themselves or by telecommunications entities, public or private, designated by the governments signing the first agreement.

The first of these agreements is an agreement among governments establishing certain basic political and economic principles and goals to which all of the countries signing the agreement are committed, as well as the structural framework of the organization. It states the goal of creating a single global commercial communications satellite system at the earliest practicable date, and it expresses the desire that all nations should be permitted to use the system on a nondiscriminatory basis. This Agreement is open for accession by any state which is a member of the International Telecommunications Union. It obligates the partners to cooperate in the establishment of a system which will achieve global coverage in the latter part of 1967. It establishes a governing body, the Interim Communications Satellite Committee, which has overall responsibility for the design, development, establishment and operation of the space segment of the global system. This agreement also provides that the Communications

Satellite Corporation shall be the Manager on behalf of the consortium.

The Special Agreement is consonant with and in furtherance of the principles stated in the first agreement (Interim Agreement) and mainly relates to financial, technical, contractual and administrative matters associated with the establishment and operation of the system.

By the terms of the first agreement (Interim Agreement) the space segment is owned in undivided shares by the signatories to the Special Agreement in proportion to their respective contributions to the costs of the space segment. Determination of investment and ownership quotas was a thorny matter for resolution, but the initial investment quotas were agreed upon as follows: 61 per cent for Comsat; 30.5 per cent for Western European countries; 8.5 per cent divided among Australia, Canada and Japan. The total capital estimated as being required for the establishment of the space segment during the duration of the interim arrangements was set at approximately $200 million. As additional countries have become parties, the quotas of previous signatories have been reduced pro rata to accommodate the quotas of all parties within the total of 100 per cent. Quotas of new parties are set by the Interim Communications Satellite Committee on their application.

When these agreements were first opened for signature on August 20, 1964, they were signed by the United States and twelve other countries. Since that time Comsat has been active in encouraging the participation of other countries and its representatives have or will visit Central and South America, the Far East, the Near East, and Africa for the purpose of explaining the nature of the international agreements, the prospects for participation by particular countries, the development of earth stations and the time frame in which satellites will be available for utilization. As of this writing, these efforts have increased the number of participants in the consortium to forty-six, representing 90 per cent of the world's telecommunications traffic.

The investment quotas for Comsat and the other initial participants were to be reduced pro rata to adjust the quotas of all newly acceding parties. The majority of the countries have quotas of less than 1 per cent. With such a disparity of investment and ownership interests, a basic question which the Agreements had to answer was the composition of the governing committee and the distribution of the voting power among its members. It was decided to limit membership on the Interim Communications Satellite Committee to representatives from each of the partners or groups of partners having an ownership interest and a financial commitment of 1.5 per cent or more. Each member of the Committee has voting power in proportion to the ownership share of the organization or organizations he represents. Although Comsat commands more than a majority of the votes by virtue of its investment quota, which is presently slightly more than 56 per cent, the Agreements specify a number of important subjects on which decisions require the concurrence of a number of parties in addition to the Communications Satellite Corporation, the necessary accumulation of votes being such that countries located in several major geographic regions of the world must be in agreement.

The international arrangements described above represent international cooperation in a meaningful way. They provide an institutional framework in which men can cooperate to develop and exploit scientific inventiveness. In this context it is worthy to underline the following aspects of the Agreements:

• The concept of an international cooperative enterprise, with very widespread membership, for the purpose of sharing the exploitation of a new resource for the economic benefit of all mankind;

• The effort to reduce national rivalries in a new field of economic activity by the concept of a single global system instead of competing national systems;

• A form of organization which recognizes the diversity of national economic systems by permitting participation of either public or private entities on behalf of the signatory countries;

• A form of organization which provides for a wide disparity of investment and ownership reflecting the probable extent of the use of the system by the various participants and which takes this factor into account in the decision-making process; and

• The careful balance of political and economic factors reflected throughout the Agreements.

The Early Bird satellite launched on April 6, 1965, represents the first successful exploitation of outer space for commercial purposes. The demonstration and testing period proved to people on both sides of the Atlantic the feasibility and usefulness of a communications satellite. During this period extensive demonstrations of quality international television transmission became quite familiar. Since June, 1965, when Early Bird was inaugurated into commercial service, daily telephone and telegraph exchanges have taken place between North America and Europe. Early Bird has also provided the first opportunity for international television on a regular commercial basis.

Plans are now well under way toward implementation of the objective stated in the Interim Agreement that basic global coverage be achieved. The Interim Communications Satellite Committee, on behalf of the consortium, has had design studies completed and is in the process of soliciting proposals for a global system satellite. With this program, and plans for meeting other communications requirements, it is anticipated that the global system will begin to be deployed in late 1966. The system will meet a broad variety of communications requirements including voice, telegraphy, broad band data, high-speed data, and television. The services offered by the system will be available on a non-discriminatory basis throughout the globe.

The International Agreements call for appropriate participation by members of the consortium in the design, development and procurement of equipment for the space segment. Pursuant to the international arrangements, Comsat has had foreign technical personnel assigned to work with Comsat in the design and specification of equipment for the space segment. To date, technical experts from England, France, Germany, Japan, the Netherlands, Norway, and Sweden have been nominated and selected by the Interim Committee and Comsat.

6. Commercial and Industrial Relationships

The export of space goods and services by American industries in 1964 approached the $10 million mark. American firms are providing design and engineering services, subsystems, and satellite components to governments and industries abroad requiring assistance as they enter into their early space programs. They have contributed sounding rockets and sounding rocket payloads, communications satellite ground terminals, and, in the large booster field, they have provided fuels and consulting services in the design of subsystems. While the relatively modest figure of $10 million amounts to less than 1 per cent of total annual aerospace exports, it demonstrates a growth which is certain to continue.

Imports into the United States are comparatively small, but it is likely that they will increase in value. Already we have found it desirable to look abroad for diffraction gratings, extensible antennae, power output tubes, optical systems, a radio frequency system, a dynamic balancing facility, and other items. The U.S. Communications Satellite Corporation, as the operating arm of the Global Commercial Communications Satellite System, has already negotiated its first study contracts with foreign agencies and companies. It is only natural that some of these lead to hardware contracts.

With space activity growing throughout the world, and the opportunities for commercial exchanges multiplying, forward-looking countries here and abroad are seeking to broaden the base of their involvement. A significant proportion of the leading American aerospace firms are participating in licensing arrangements or in direct corporate associations with their foreign counterparts.

In the short run, these arrangements will accelerate the growth of space competence abroad. In the long run, they are bound to contribute to a further two-way flow of commerce.

A matrix of international cooperation in space research has evolved in the past few years. The national space programs of Europe are integrated somewhat by cooperative projects. Most of the national space programs are tied in with NASA through memorandums of understanding. The international agencies of ELDO and ESRO share many common bonds.

While the framework of the matrix is provided by governments, the responsibility for execution of programs is shared by industry, and true industrial international cooperation is a requisite to economical and efficient international space research programs.

Cooperative Space Activity during ICY

The pace of international cooperative activity in space is reflected by the events of 1965. The tabulations below record (1) projects implemented during International Cooperation Year and (2) new projects negotiated during the Year.

Projects Implemented During ICY

• Early Bird, first commercial communications satellite, launched on April 6.

• Canadian satellite, *Alouette II*, to monitor ionospheric conditions, scheduled for launching by NASA in November.

• French satellite, FR-1, to measure components of Very Low

Frequency radio emission, scheduled for launching by NASA in December.

• French airglow experiment launched on NASA Orbiting Geophysical Observatory (OGO-C).

• U.K. ion and electron probes scheduled for flight on NASA Direct Measurement Explorer satellite in November.

• Meteorological sounding rockets launched at a rate of one per month during the year from the international range at Thumba, India, and Indian/Pakistani/Australian/U.S. studies supplementing the International Indian Ocean Expedition.

• Seven sounding rockets expected to be launched during twelvemonth period from Sonmiani Beach, Pakistan, in cooperative Pakistani/Indian/Australian/U.S. meteorological studies supplementing the International Indian Ocean Expedition.

• Four sounding rockets launched from Sonmiani Beach, Pakistan, in Pakistani/U.K./NASA studies of upper atmosphere.

• Four sounding rockets launched from range at Coronie, Surinam, in joint Netherlands/NASA investigation of ionospheric winds.

• Six sounding rockets launched from Karikari Peninsula, New Zealand, in joint New Zealand/NASA studies of lower ionosphere during solar eclipse of May 30; an additional launching from Birdling's Flat, New Zealand, scheduled for December.

• Three sounding rockets launched from the range at Andøya, Norway, in Norwegian/Danish/NASA sounding rocket studies; three coordinated launchings scheduled late in the year from Andøya, Wallops Island (Virginia), and White Sands (New Mexico).

• Two sounding rockets launched from Andøya, Norway, in Swedish/Norwegian/NASA studies of auroral phenomena.

• Three sounding rockets launched from Churchill Research Range, Canada, in NASA/French/German/Israeli/Swedish studies of interplanetary dust and noctilucent cloud particles, with additional launchings scheduled later in year.

• Belgian, Italian, Dutch, and Swiss experiments flow on NASA aircraft in vicinity of Marquesas Islands during solar eclipse of May 30.

New Projects Negotiated During ICY

• NASA agreements with Argentine and Brazilian National Commissions for Space Research establishing an inter-American experimental meteorological sounding rocket network (EXAMETNET).

• Agreement between Brazilian National Commission for Space Research and NASA for coordinated sounding rocket investigations of the ionosphere from ranges at Natal, Brazil, and Wallops Island, Virginia.

• U.S./Canadian agreement under which the National Research Council of Canada and NASA will jointly use, operate, and maintain under civilian auspices a sounding rocket facility at Fort Churchill, Canada.

• Agreement with German Federal Ministry for Scientific Research for NASA launching of a German satellite to study earth's radiation belts.

• Agreement between NASA and Indian National Committee for Space Research for sounding rocket investigations in aeronomy, ionospheric physics, and magnetic fields, from the range at Thumba.

• Agreement with Netherlands Committee for Geophysical and Space Research for cosmic ray experiment on NASA Orbiting Geophysical Observatory (OGO-E).

• Agreement by Norwegian Committee for Space Research and NASA for sounding rocket studies of relationship between noctilucent clouds and the composition of the ionosphere.

• Foreign scientists briefed at Houston on opportunities for contributing biomedical experiments to Gemini and Apollo flights.

• Foreign scientists invited to submit proposals for experiments to fly on 1971 Voyager mission to Mars.

Projects for the Future

The rapid growth of space activity abroad is a challenge to American leadership in the field of cooperation. Foreign scientists and engineers will find increasing opportunities in their own national and regional programs for space research of the sort that our cooperative projects have thus far supplied. We must therefore be alert to possibilities for more considerable and advanced cooperative efforts, going beyond the appeal of national programs, if we are to extend the technical and political advantages of cooperation, for others as well as ourselves. To keep gifted minds and capable hands involved in cooperative activity, we must be prepared to enter into joint ventures of unusual technical interest and enterprises uniquely international in character.

What are the possibilities for extending international cooperation in space in the next several years? Obviously, the potential for useful activity is a function of interest, authorization, and funding, *both* here and abroad. An appreciation of the state of the art and the level of funding abroad at once establishes clear limitations to the prospects for joint enterprise. Yet interest and important capability exist overseas and numerous future cooperative projects can be foreseen. Here are some possibilities that deserve attention:

1. New Launching Sites for Satellites. The interest of other countries in establishing new launching sites for satellites on the equator, where maximum advantage can be taken of the earth's rotation and satellites can be placed most efficiently into synchronous orbit, offers opportunities for cooperation in equipping and using these sites. Interest in operations at such locations may be expected to exist not only here in the United States and in countries establishing such sites, but also in such institutions as the European Space Research Organization. It may be, therefore, that a sufficiently wide participating interest can be organized to provide for the establishment of facilities of interest to all at minimum cost to each.

2. Multipurpose Navigation Satellite Systems. Technical studies already completed indicate that multipurpose global navigation satellite systems are feasible. Additional studies are now under way to determine the value of such systems for marine and air navigation, traffic control, distress calls, and assistance in rescue operations. If a positive conclusion is reached as to the contribution which such systems may make, we may look forward confidently to progressive international cooperation in establishing them. As a first step, those countries which could contribute to, or participate in, the conduct of a navigation satellite experiment would do so. Should an experimental project demonstrate the feasibility of an operational system, the nations could extend their joint experimental efforts to provide for the establishment and use of the necessary space and surface facilities for an operational system. In the tradition of navigation aids, the establishment of the space and necessary supporting ground facilities could be carried out as a governmental rather than a commercial enterprise. The provision of equipment for aircraft and ships would more likely be a matter for commercial supply.

3. Experimental Data-gathering Satellite System. Plans already are in being in the United States and elsewhere for testing components of possible future systems using satellites to collect meteorological and other geophysical data. A data-gathering satellite system would collect information from such sensing devices as buoys at sea, meteorological ground stations, and constant-altitude balloons. There are abundant opportunities for international collaboration in developing or deploying these elements of a data-gathering system and ultimately in establishing and employing an operational system. A bilateral arrangement for a first satellite-and-balloon experiment on a significant scale is already in prospect and would afford opportunities for participation by a third nation.

4. Synoptic Sounding Rocket Investigations. The rapid increase in the number of small but sufficient launching sites for probing the atmosphere and ionosphere with sounding rockets offers new opportunities for effective scientific investigations on a cooperative and synoptic basis. Such sites have been established in the Eastern and Western Hemispheres, at high latitudes as well as low, and at strategic points affording access to auroral zones and the geomagnetic equator. Since sounding rockets are limited to obtaining vertical profiles of the atmosphere above the launching site, a broad attack upon the mysteries of the atmosphere and its ionosphere requires coordinated launchings on a broad geographical basis. Such an attack is clearly in view as a consequence of the increasing number and capability of sites. We therefore anticipate coordinated sounding rocket programs of increasing value on an international cooperative basis.

Such programs may be of critical value in probing those high-atmosphere processes which can shed light on the linkage between spatial phenomena and our terrestrial weather. In particular, the skeletal elements of an inter-American meteorological sounding rocket network have been established by NASA agreement with Argentine and Brazilian agencies, on an experimental basis. The participation of additional countries in the hemisphere, extending the net from Canada to Antarctica, is in prospect and promises an important contribution to understanding the global circulation and North-South transfer of energy.

5. Applications of Communications Satellites. It is useful, having indicated the progress to date in international cooperation in communication satellite activities, to contemplate some of the developments and uses in the future. The technology itself requires cooperation and the uses to which it can be put may require similar cooperation.

• Trade and commerce. The nature of international trade and commerce will be significantly affected by the introduction of space communications facilities. Satellites are capable of transmitting data to a number of earth stations simultaneously, instantaneously and accurately. It is possible to foresee use of closed circuit television by major companies doing a worldwide business to link together their offices and affiliates in order to kick off a new sales campaign or to demonstrate a new product or to analyze a new marketing situation in the far corners of the world.

• Information and documents. Using present facsimile techniques it will be possible to transmit business letters and documents to any place on earth in a matter of seconds. Communications satellites will enable documentation and information to be as readily available from Washington to London as from one end of Washington to another.

• Computers. It will become possible to conduct massive computer operations on a global scale, with a computer in one part of the world working through and with a computer in another part of the world. Thus communications satellites can be employed for operations which involve data preparation, correlation, computation and exchange on an intercontinental basis. There are potential applications in finance, in manufacturing, in distribution of goods, in transportation, in billing and in a host of other related areas. Civil engineering is a field of particular interest to the developing countries, dealing as it does with transportation systems, water resources, sanitation, highways, power and conservation projects. A satellite system could be used to link large central computers to civil engineering input/output stations located in remote areas, thus providing access to computer services which would otherwise be beyond the reach of most countries. Such a computer-based system for civil engineering practices, given global application through communications satellites, would provide direct assistance in the development of the basic resources of countries throughout the world.

• Aviation. There seems to be little doubt that satellite communications have potential use in the field of international aviation. It has been said that the greatest need of airlines today is more efficient use of the air space and that this is dependent upon improved efficiency in communications. Early in 1965 the first successful demonstration of two-way communications via satellite between a jet airliner and a ground station located in California took place.

• Television. One of the American broadcasting companies has proposed the development of a satellite system to tie together television broadcasting stations throughout the United States. It would seem that a real potential exists for providing such a service not only on a sound economical basis but also on an international scale. Perhaps the same satellite would be capable of meeting the communications requirements of commercial aviation, commercial television, telephonic and telegraphic transmissions, and a broad variety of other needs.

• Direct broadcasting. The most revolutionary change promised by communications satellites during the next decade may well come about when direct broadcasting from satellites into the home receiver is realized. The satellites which will be employed in the global system will not have this capability, but it is a foreseeable development during the decade of the 1970's. During the early phases of the system, television programs carried by satellite will have to be rebroadcast from stations on the ground to the home receiver. Thus, they pose no radically new problems of national or international control. With the advent of direct broadcasting of television from satellites, a totally new situation will arise which will test the ingenuity and creativity of the architects of international order. It will present in an acute form the conflicting claims of the desire for freedom of information—the freedom to see and hear—on the one hand, and the desire of organized societies to impose some degree of control over the dissemination of spoken and visual material to their own people.

• Medicine. Through the medium of communication satellites, medical education at the graduate level, as well as on a continuing postgraduate basis, could be globally enhanced by transmitting lectures and demonstrations by physicians to audiences any place in the world. There could be tremendous benefits in providing real-time television and an opportunity for real-time global discussion in cases, for example, where there is a special competence, or where there is an epidemic, or in rare or unusual cases that the medical student or practicing physician would ordinarily never see. When available, color television will be quite useful for observing operations and for studying changes in color of a patient. Video tape-recorded material could be stored indefinitely for future use and could be updated as required. Global clinico-pathological conferences would be quite valuable. Fortunately, there is available and in use an accepted code for the international classification of diseases. Educational TV programs can furnish an excellent medium for attracting young people to health careers and for training physicians in medical schools.

President Johnson's legislative program to conquer heart disease, cancer and stroke and related diseases in the United States by means of a regional medical program, as given in House Bill 5140, requires a communications network that will eventually include all physicians and the related scientists. Such a communications system will aid materially in closing the gap between the acquisition of new knowledge in medical centers and research laboratories and its dissemination to the family physician, the specialists, and to the general public. It could be only a short time before this program begins to become a cooperative one on a worldwide basis. By utilization of communications satellites this will extend the high-quality care afforded patients in a relatively small number of medical centers in the world today to others at many thousands of community centers. In years to come, all diseases could be included in such an international program. A new lifesaving surgical technique or a new form of medical therapy could be quickly passed on to doctors around the world. During off-hour transmission times, portable television receiving units could be very helpful on expeditions, such as those to Mount Everest, the polar regions, the desert, or the jungle.

A global medical and life sciences computer network for instantaneous acquisition and exchange of analog and digital data presentation, storage analysis, and retrieval of such data, would foster and accelerate an international study of both normal individuals in different environments as well as patients with various types of illness. X-ray and laboratory studies of particular types of patients could be followed and compared using video tape. Synchronous orbit communication satellites will provide real-time communication with the astronauts in manned satellites at all times and permit ground observers to monitor their condition constantly, when necessary, and to observe the experiments they are carrying out in space, or on the lunar surface.

6. *Mutual Assistance between National and International Tracking and Data Acquisition Networks.* The day when the United States was the only nation to possess a global network for tracking satellites and acquiring data from them is already past. Two new networks are in the process of establishment, one by the government of France, the other by the European Space Research Organization. Cooperative relationships have assured that these networks are entirely compatible with that of the United States. Thus, facilities for mutual assistance have been established, and we may look

forward to international cooperation in tracking and acquiring data from satellites on missions for which such cooperation would be useful and necessary.

7. *Exploration of the Distant Planets.* There stretches before us a continuous spectrum of solar system exploration, reaching beyond even Venus and Mars. The costs of probing the still mysterious and most distant planets will be very great and the technical problems considerable. Yet questions whose answers are needed to advance our knowledge of the earth's environment in space and its own history remain to be resolved through probes to these distant bodies. It is entirely appropriate that such probing be carried out cooperatively by men who can contribute to the enterprise, whatever their nationality may be. It is therefore heartening to see the increasing competence of our neighbors in the space field, for such competence and the support which it wins might be pooled to bring within reach this costly but exciting enterprise. The prospect that substantial contributions to such an effort might be forthcoming from more than one country will clearly bring closer the day when any of us may undertake it. The current balance of effort among the nations suggests that the principal contributions of others might fall in the experiment and spacecraft systems areas while the principal U.S. contributions might fall in the booster and spacecraft support areas.

8. *Remote Sensing.* Toward the end of this decade, a series of manned earth and lunar orbital missions can be foreseen with the objective of exploring systematically the physical characteristics of the earth and moon by means of a variety of remote sensing techniques. Apart from its basic scientific interest, remote sensing may ultimately prove useful in such practical earth applications as monitoring crops, detecting forest fires, observing ice and snow accumulations, mapping ocean currents, and locating mineral deposits. Remote sensing thus has potential for international cooperation on a broad scale.

To prepare for these missions, extensive airborne testing and calibration will be necessary. Initially, cooperating countries might provide test sites and correlative ground data in return for data derived from airborne and space flight operations. In the long run, remote sensing suggests the possibility of cooperation in depth to increase man's knowledge of the earth, his ability to cope with his environment, and his use of national resources.

9. *International Convention to Govern Human Activity on the*

Moon. With multiple manned landings on the moon in prospect within the next several years, the United Nations Committee on the Peaceful Uses of Outer Space could direct its Legal Subcommittee to draft a convention to serve as a guide for nationally-sponsored exploratory expeditions there. The Antarctic Treaty stands as a model providing the essential elements of such a convention: suspension of sovereignty claims, free access by all for scientific purposes, exclusion of military maneuvers and weaponry, and a verification procedure. Such a convention would give substance to the principle, already adopted by the UN General Assembly, that celestial bodies are not subject to national appropriation. It would become, in effect, a code for human activity on the moon.

Opportunity for U.S. Initiative

The United States has a special responsibility to take the initiative in space cooperation because it has the largest and most diversified program and the demonstrated willingness to cooperate. Much of the international cooperation in space today stems from an announcement to the International Committee on Space Research in March, 1959, that the United States, through NASA, stood ready to launch scientific experiments and entire payloads of mutual interest for scientists of other nations. Fresh U.S. initiative may set off a new and expanded round of cooperation.

American initiative can and does take the form of repeated public invitations to other nations to examine our national space program in search of projects, interesting to them as well as to us, that offer opportunity for a literal sharing of responsibilities. We look to the future and a new order and scale of cooperation in the mutual interest.

Continuing initiative confirms our current practice and assures that cooperation will continue on a significant scale in the future. It rededicates the United States, by deeds and not by words alone, to the principle of international cooperation on which American activity in space is based.

THE COMMITTEE ON OUTER SPACE

13.   Using Science and Technology

International cooperation in science is, to scientists, an old story. By its very nature, science is universal, and scientists have always taken for granted that progress in their fields of interest involves free discussion and debate among colleagues throughout the world.

International cooperation in technology is another matter. Discoveries that improve shelter, make transportation more efficient, and in other ways make man's life on earth healthier, happier, and safer, have sometimes spread slowly indeed. Barriers of language, of custom, of technical skills, and of indifference have often impeded the spread of technology.

Today man finds himself in a scientific and technological world. It is a world where scientists, long accustomed to talking to one another across international boundaries, find the occasional restrictions a new and undesirable experience; where, conversely, their technological associates—accustomed to working primarily with things close at hand—are finding new opportunities and new challenges by looking at worldwide problems. There are a vast number of international scientific exchanges, many of which have worked well for long periods of time. In the realm of technological exchange, more remains to be done. Much progress is already apparent.

The list of areas where scientific and, to a degree, technological cooperation already exists is impressive. It includes the activities of countless international organizations, both governmental and nongovernmental—the International Council of Scientific Unions (ICSU) and all its member organizations; the International Federation for Documentation; the International Bureau of Weights and Measures; and many, many more. There are now about 60 intergovernmental scientific organizations, and at least 250 non-governmental scientific organizations. International scientific research programs, which had their origins in the international polar years and found new life with the International Geophysical Year, are now a continuing and accepted part of the world scientific scene. Recent or current ones include the International Years of the Quiet Sun, the International Indian Ocean Expedition and the International Hydrological Decade.

It is worth noting that as this type of international scientific activity has become standard, so also has it become enlarged in scope, to cover, wherever appropriate, technology as well as science. The International Indian Ocean Expedition and the International Hydrological Decade are especially significant examples.

The programs we recommend for the future provide close links between science and technology. Each project that is undertaken will bring back benefits to basic science and to engineering technology, and these will combine to the benefit of man. Earthquakes, for example, are a scientific problem and a human problem, and only by the application of the skills of science to the solution of its part of the problem can the solution to the human problem be found. The world's oceans, too, are a problem in a positive sense—they offer the possibilities of vast resources both of scientific discovery and of food for mankind. It may thus be expected that the exploration of the seas will be undertaken by representatives of every discipline, and every nation, to which knowledge and potential benefit can accrue. The outstandingly successful scientific cooperation in Antarctica holds promise also for the Arctic, where more of the world's population is involved. Other programs in other areas, geographical and intellectual, will be fertile fields for international cooperation in science and technology.

The opportunities for scientific and technological cooperation among nations in the future are thus enormous. Such cooperation can rest on a sound base, for it is already an accepted fact of international life. It has much room to expand, for the needs of mankind—particularly in the developing countries, but also in the more developed areas of the world—are great. It holds the promise of bringing together the intellectual fruits of basic research and the technical arts of development and engineering to produce rapid and positive improvement for all mankind.

Most important of all, international cooperation in science and technology may well provide a pathway to international cooperation in other spheres of human endeavor. This potential has been realized most dramatically, perhaps, in Antarctica. The Antarctic Treaty, signed in 1959 by twelve nations including the United States and the Soviet Union, is unique in that the signatory nations agreed to hold all territorial claims in abeyance for thirty years; military activities are prohibited, the dumping of atomic wastes prohibited, and the Antarctic stations of all treaty nations are open for inspection by any other signatory at any time. This is a remarkable achievement to have been brought about during a cold war. In view of it, mankind may hope that increased cooperation among nations in scientific and technological endeavors may one day lead the way to peace on this earth.

International Programs

Following the highly successful results of the International Geophysical Year (IGY), there are now a number of major international programs underway (or soon to be implemented) that will extend cooperation among the scholars of all nations, particularly in attacking worldwide or regional environmental research problems of the planet Earth. The International Council of Scientific Unions (ICSU) and its associated unions, commissions, and committees have been instrumental in sponsoring these activities, and the National Academy of Sciences/National Research Council has provided the liaison for significant U.S. leadership in the planning and participation of the U.S. scientific community. A few of these programs are discussed briefly below.

International Indian Ocean Expedition (IIOE)

The International Indian Ocean Expedition, conceived at a 1958 meeting of the ICSU Scientific Committee on Oceanic Research (SCOR), has been most actively concerned with the investigation of the relatively unknown Indian Ocean, whose 28 million square miles cover over 14 per cent of the earth's surface. During the past four years twenty-five nations and forty-four ships have been involved in the program, examining the ocean's topography, circulation, and the distribution of plant and animal life. Both scientific and long-range economic benefits are expected from the program.

International planning by scientist-participants has been undertaken through the Scientific Committee on Oceanic Research (SCOR), and intergovernmental planning through UNESCO's Intergovernmental Oceanographic Commission. The Academy serves as U.S. liaison with SCOR, and several Federal agencies are participating in the program. The United States has had fourteen ships and five aircraft engaged in the operations, which will end in 1966 and will be followed by processing of the vast amount of data obtained. Significant new sources of seafood have been found by this expedition.

International Year of the Quiet Sun (IQSY)

The IQSY, an outgrowth of the International Geophysical Year, is a program designed to take advantage of opportunities for studying solar-terrestrial relationships at the minimum of sun-spot cycle. Each of the more than sixty participating countries has planned its own program in consultation with other countries through IQSY National Committees. The Geophysical Research Board of the NAS established the U.S. Committee for IQSY to provide continuing guidance for U.S. efforts during the observational period of 1964–65. The U.S. research program includes meteorology, geomagnetism, aurora, airglow, ionospheric physics, radio astronomy, solar activity, the interplanetary medium, cosmic rays, trapped radiation, and aeronomy. Several governmental agencies are sponsoring or supporting U.S. participation in the IQSY program.

World Magnetic Survey (WMS)

This survey, a continuing project of the IGY, is intended to map the world's magnetic field during the present period of minimum solar activity and is therefore closely allied with the IQSY. Details are sought to serve as a basis for detecting future changes. The survey is also filling in previous information—for example, about certain areas of the oceans. The survey is coordinated internationally by the World Magnetic Survey Board of the International Association of Geomagnetism and Aeronomy, International Union of Geodesy and Geophysics.

International Hydrological Decade (IHD)

UNESCO, which sponsors this program, has budgeted $300,000 for 1965–66 to get it started, and estimates a total of $2 million for the full 1965–75 period. The Decade's chief aims are to establish a worldwide network of stations to measure and track water in the hydrological cycle from rain to the underground water table and back into the atmosphere, and to study expanding water supplies, flood and drought control, developing hydroelectric development and improved navigation. The ICSU Scientific Committee on Water Research (SCWR) is acting as scientific adviser to UNESCO. The Division of Earth Sciences of the NAS has established a U.S. National Committee for the IHD, and the Government will participate. An international program on the broad aspects of water may arise from the deliberations of SCWR and in connection with the Decade.

International Upper Mantle Project (UMP)

Virtually all processes in the earth that affect the crust—earthquakes, mountain building, concentration of minerals, volcanic eruptions—occur in the outermost 600 miles of the earth's radius. The International Union of Geodesy and Geophysics (IUGG) in 1963 recommended establishment of an international Upper Mantle Committee to "encourage and develop international cooperative investigations of the upper mantle, its relationships to and influence upon the development of the earth's crust." Such a committee was later formed and the period from January 1, 1965, to December 31, 1967, was set as one in which "definite accomplishments should be achieved in the main international and interdisciplinary programs emphasized by the Upper Mantle Committee."

International Cooperative Investigations of the Tropical Atlantic (ICITA)

"Equalant" (equatorial Atlantic) has been a project under the Intergovernmental Oceanographic Commission of UNESCO for the intensive investigation of the equatorial circulation system of the Atlantic at different seasons of the year. Its investigational phases are now concluded and most publications are completed, though data analysis continues.

Cooperative Study of the Kuroshio Current

The purpose is to investigate seasonal fluctuations in the Kuroshio system south and southeast of Japan. To be conducted for one year beginning in mid-1965, it is sponsored by the Intergovernmental Oceanographic Commission of UNESCO and draws scientific participation primarily from countries of the Western Pacific.

International Biological Program (IBP)

This program is just getting under way and is discussed below.

Antarctic Research Program

International scientific coordination of this program is provided by the Scientific Committee on Antarctic Research (SCAR) of the International Council of Scientific Unions (ICSU). Research in Antarctica is conducted under terms of the 1959 Antarctic Treaty, signed by the twelve nations which conducted research in the Antarctic during the International Geophysical Year: Argentina,

Australia, Belgium, Chile, France, Japan, New Zealand, Norway, Union of South Africa, Union of Soviet Socialist Republics, United Kingdom, and the United States.

International activities include the translation of Soviet Antarctic reports, cooperation with the International Antarctic Analysis Center in Melbourne, Australia, and a continuing exchange of scientists between the foreign and U.S. Antarctic expeditions. American scientists have engaged in research work at the stations of other nations and a number of foreign scientists are carrying out research in cooperation with U.S. installations and personnel. Conjugate points phenomena are studied at pairs of Antarctic-Canadian stations: McMurdo–Shepherd Bay, South Pole–Frobisher Bay, Byrd–Great Whale River, and Eights–Baie St. Paul.

International Organizations

Many international organizations have facilitated cooperation between scientists and engineers, their institutions, and governmental technical agencies. Some sponsor periodic international congresses. More recently there has been a trend to form interdisciplinary commissions and committees to guide and implement many of the international cooperative programs. Other international organizations have been established to further the technical interests of governmental agencies. In all of these organizations the United States has provided significant leadership and is participating actively.

Some of the activities are as follows:

Non-Governmental Organizations

The National Academy of Sciences/National Research Council is actively engaged through its Office of the Foreign Secretary, Divisions, and Boards in furthering U.S. interests in some thirty international scientific organizations and many international programs, such as those mentioned above. Most of these organizations are under the aegis of ICSU and its affiliated unions. Hundreds of American scientists participate in the activities of these unions, their commissions and committees. Through the auspices of the NAS, U.S. National Committees are linked to the planning and implementation of the activities of International Unions such as those formed for Biochemistry, Biological Sciences, Pure and Applied Biophysics, Pure and Applied Chemistry. Geological Sciences, Geodesy and Geophysics,

Mathematics, Physiological Sciences, Pure and Applied Physics, Astronomy, and Crystallography.

Intergovernmental Organizations and Associations

Agencies of the U.S. Government are also directly associated with many of the activities mentioned above as well as the scientific programs of intergovernmental organizations, commissions, and committees. The professional staffs of U.S. agencies are participating in the work of the UN Specialized Agencies and regional organizations such as the Organization of American States and the Organization for Economic Cooperation and Development (OECD). This latter organization, consisting of the countries of Western Europe, the United States, Canada, and Japan, is providing a valuable forum for the discussion and correlation of national science policies, as well as providing a means for encouraging cooperative research and training. Through the North Atlantic Treaty Organization (NATO), fellowships, advanced training projects, and research activities associate large numbers of U.S. scientists with their colleagues in other NATO countries.

International cooperation in the sciences and technology is strengthened through a variety of specialized bilateral and multilateral conventions and agreements. The Department of Interior through its Bureaus of Commercial Fisheries, Sport Fisheries and Wildlife, Land Management, Mines, and Reclamation is deeply involved in such international associations. Its Office of Saline Water also cooperates on technology in this field with international organizations and through bilateral arrangements. The Geological Survey participates actively in the work of many organizations and commissions concerned with hydrology, topography, and photogrammetry. Cooperative research and training are significant features of these activities.

Similarly, within the Department of Commerce, the Maritime Administration, Bureau of Public Roads, the Patent Office, the National Bureau of Standards, and particularly the Coast and Geodetic Survey are engaged in the work of intergovernmental organizations and specialized agencies. For example, the Coast and Geodetic Survey is concerned with a seismic sea-wave warning service, a worldwide network of seismographs, international cartographic cooperation, and other cooperative efforts in the fields of hydrology and oceanography.

The U.S. participates in intergovernmental science information activities in a variety of ways. Significant U.S. interests include active participation in the science information activities of UNESCO and OECD. Contributions have been made with respect to formulation of program activities and budgets of UNESCO's science information, documentation and library projects and to formulation of a policy for OECD's science information activity. A number of U.S. specialists have contributed considerable time and talent to both of these governmental international organizations in an effort to help strengthen the communication of international scientific information.

International Training and Assistance Activities

Advanced training in the sciences and engineering is an extremely important international activity for which institutions and governmental agencies in the United States provide considerable support. These programs are implemented in a number of ways, such as the exchanges administered by the National Academy of Science under the Fulbright-Hays Act. The NAS is also actively engaged in a number of fellowship programs supported by the National Science Foundation, National Aeronautics and Space Administration, and other governmental agencies leading to the interchange of advanced scholars between institutions in the United States and foreign countries. Other important aspects of Academy-administered activities are the exchange programs between the United States and the U.S.S.R. and, more recently, other East European countries.

Training is a significant function of governmental agencies. For example, the National Bureau of Standards has given technical training to some 800 persons from overseas during the last eight years, largely under sponsorship of the Agency for International Development but also with assistance from international organizations and private foundations. Similarly, NBS staff are active overseas in a number of technical training activities. The Coast and Geodetic Survey also provides specialized training for foreign nationals. In the Department of Interior, the Bureau of Commercial Fisheries, and the Geological Survey are involved in exchange programs and cooperative research and survey projects with other countries.

Another aspect of training activities has been the foreign ferment in educational reform engendered by the massive attack supported by the NSF on the problem of modernizing and upgrading science education offered in American high schools and colleges. These activities involving outstanding American scientists have led to major revisions in course materials as well as large-scale innovative training projects for teachers. Through the efforts of international organizations and the interest of foreign scientists, these American programs have become internationalized and are forming the basis for reform activities throughout the world. There has been considerable interchange of personnel and materials between the United States and some forty countries. AID-supported activities in Latin America, Africa, and the Far East are lending considerable encouragement to related reform activities in which American science education leaders are actively engaged.

The Office of the Foreign Secretary of the NAS is pursuing a number of science assistance programs in developing countries, largely through AID support. The Latin American Science Board is encouraging the creation of a tropical research foundation to attack the serious problem of food shortages. The Pacific Science Board is actively concerned with cooperative activities to advance scientific research and training in the Far East and Pacific regions. Bilateral activities with the government of Taiwan are underway and exploratory discussions with governmental leaders in the Philippines are directed toward scientific cooperation with that nation. It is likely that similar activities will develop in the future through the African Affairs Section and the Middle-East South Asia Science Board.

The Agency for International Development supports a great many efforts to strengthen the sciences and technology in developing countries through American universities and governmental agencies. Increasing attention is being given to the role played by science and technology in foreign assistance by the AID research program, particularly with reference to the creation of new knowledge of the forces and processes of development.

Future Goals

Earthquake Forecasting and Damage Assessment

Earthquakes, unlike most other natural catastrophic phenomena, occur without warning. Fortunately, they are confined to well-defined belts; scientific investigation of their causes, and effects on natural or man-made facilities, can be sharply focused on these restricted areas. Though some estimate can be made on the probability of the level of future seismic activity within these belts, the critical problems of actually predicting an earthquake in time and space and of determining the effects on human lives and resources remain to be solved.

Because disastrous earthquakes occur in many countries, an international cooperative program should be initiated to develop the instrumentation and analytical techniques needed to predict (1) the location and magnitude of future earthquakes and (2) the transitory and permanent effects of such earthquakes on both natural and man-made structures.

An effective international cooperative research program to solve these problems would provide:

1. Broad knowledge of the geologic, geophysical, and hydrologic environment of the earthquake belt, including such information as thickness of and temperature distribution within the crust.

2. Understanding of the tectonic characteristics of the borders of ocean basins, in particular the distribution of major rifts, tectonic features, and the characteristics and stability of the Continental Shelf.

3. Knowledge of the overall seismic characteristics and stress-strain features of the earthquake belts, including such information as frequency, magnitude, and depth of focus of historic earthquakes.

4. Detailed information on the surface manifestations of historic earthquakes in different geologic environments.

5. Engineering knowledge of the response of earth materials in different geologic-hydrologic environments to varying types of earth shock.

6. Capability to continue research on tsunamis as to their causes, means of warning, and their localized effects.

7. Integration of earth sciences information to provide the necessary quantitative data needed by engineers to design earthquake resistant buildings and to plan judicious use of land within earthquake belts.

8. Teams of experts, upon request of a country devastated by an earthquake, to assist in directing and planning the rehabilitation of areas damaged by earthquakes.

The magnitude of such a program requires the combined talents of all earth science disciplines if significant progress is to be made within two decades. Each nation that lies within the earthquake belts should take an active part in the cooperative scientific program. Undoubtedly some aspects of the proposed program would have greater significance to certain nations than to others; because of the differing characteristics of the earthquake belts, certain talents and special capabilities in earthquake prediction will be developed by individual countries. These special talents will undoubtedly be extremely useful to all nations concerned with earthquake hazards. To carry out effectively the exchange of scientific information, a funded program for qualified scientists to study and work with the scientists in foreign countries should be initiated under the supervision of the UN or other international bodies.

Oceanography

Beyond the narrow band of territorial sea, and beyond the Continental Shelf, the ocean and its resources are the common property of all men and all nations. It is the only part of the planet, except bleak Antarctica, where scientists and others can work together in a realm that belongs equally to all. Research on the high seas can benefit all nations, and can be conducted without the restraints imposed by national sovereignty, which handicap the conduct of international cooperative research on land. It is noteworthy that, because of this common ownership, and the consequent necessity for cooperation, it has been possible for the nations to agree on a comprehensive body of international law respecting the uses of the sea and its resources, embodied in the four Conventions adopted at Geneva in 1958.

In addition to the universality of scientific knowledge which is, on the sea as on the land, a stimulus to international cooperation in science, the common ownership of the resources of the sea makes especially attractive their joint exploration, and demands that their utilization be managed internationally on a rational scientific basis. Further, the magnitude of the task of comprehending the ocean, its contents, and its processes, which affect all men, is so vast that no one nation can reasonably undertake the task alone; we simply must work together if we are to obtain the knowledge required to reap the benefits of the sea within a reasonably short time. Such undertakings as a complete mapping of the ocean floor, or broad synoptic studies of a whole ocean, can only be accomplished through the joint efforts of many ships and scientists. Such important projects as the establishment of a network of continuous observations at many points in the World Ocean (as well as on land) to provide a world system for atmosphere and ocean data collection, for forecasting, cannot be carried out except as an international undertaking.

Cooperative efforts in research and development with respect to the ocean can be especially valuable in advancing the underdeveloped nations. The world is getting desperately short of animal proteins, which can be supplied from the sea to ameliorate the increasing nutritional deficiency of a large share of the world's population. The living organisms and other unused resources of the sea can be of large importance in the development of underdeveloped nations, both directly to support their populations and as a basis for export industry. In many cases marine resources can be developed more rapidly and at lower cost than terrestrial resources, both because of their physical nature and location, and because of lack of restraints due to social customs. Finally, in addition to these direct benefits, cooperation in marine sciences is one of the better ways for developing in underdeveloped countries both indigenous scientific competence and general understanding of science, because much of the study of the sea is relatively simple and straightforward, requires a minimum of sophisticated equipment and methodology to be fruitful, and deals with a visible and familiar, although mysterious, part of the real world.

Both on the national and international levels, the multiplicity of governmental agencies involved with the ocean and its resources and the lack of adequate coordinating mechanisms handicap the more effective development of international cooperative scientific activities directed at the ocean and its resources.

Within the U.S. Government there are some twenty different bureaus and agencies concerned with oceanographic research, whose activities are coordinated to some degree through the Interagency Committee on Oceanography (ICO) of the Office of Science and Technology. That this means of coordination is not entirely satisfactory is demonstrated by the numerous proposals now before the Congress for one or another kind of reorganization, and the recent actions of the Executive toward similar ends. Important elements of international activities respecting the ocean and its resources are not coordinated with the planning of the ICO agencies—for example, AID and the section of the State Department concerned with the international fishery commissions.

At the international level, as noted above, important elements of ocean science, which must be properly coordinated if we are to mount effectively some of the needed undertakings, reside in several diverse sections of the United Nations and its Specialized Agencies, which occasionally are more jealous in guarding their jurisdiction than they are zealous in attempting to augment each other's work. Another consequence is that the various regional organizations and commissions, related in one way or another to one or another of the UN Agencies, cannot coordinate their efforts very effectively. These activities require consolidation.

We recommend that the United States give high priority to the following specific activities that can be particularly effective in further advancing beneficial international cooperation in oceanography:

1. Vigorous support of the development of oceanographic competence in selected underdeveloped maritime countries, chosen on the basis of the resources of their adjacent seas and their scientific and technological potential, by:

(a) Building indigenous institutions of excellence in marine sciences, through long-term support of sister-to-sister educational and research programs between U.S. and foreign universities and laboratories.

(b) Supporting cooperative oceanic surveys and research in the seas adjacent to such countries.

(c) Fostering the development of regional research and development organizations for the study and utilization of the resources of the sea.

2. Strong leadership in the international cooperative oceanwide survey program, recommended by the National Academy of Sciences Committee on Oceanography and by the Intergovernmental Oceanographic Commission. The United States might well contemplate undertaking about one-third of the work, and enlisting the participation of other nations for the remainder. This program can be carried out, primarily by government agencies, with guidance and assistance from the academic oceanographic community.

3. In cooperation with other nations, establishment at the earliest possible date of a worldwide system of stations for gathering atmospheric and oceanic data required for forecasting weather and ocean conditions.

4. Continuation of the world exchange of oceanographic data, and search for improvements to existing organizations and methods for data exchange.

5. Strong encouragement to and vigorous participation in cooper-

ative exploration, survey, and research in little-known areas of the World Ocean, such as the South Pacific and South Atlantic.

6. Continued augmented support for cooperative investigations planned by the initiative of scientists and laboratories in the United States dealing directly with their colleagues in other nations.

7. Encouragement of active participation by U.S. scientists and scientific administrators in the work of appropriate international organizations and projects, and development of means whereby such people can be on leave from their posts for several years without financial sacrifice or damage to their professional careers.

8. Strong support for international cooperative research, along the lines outlined in the General Scientific Framework for World Ocean Study, organized through the IOC and the United Nations. There is urgently required a consolidation of the marine activities that are currently the responsibility of numerous different agencies of the UN. To this end, the United States should seek the establishment of a World Oceanographic Organization to consolidate these functions in a single agency. This could also provide a central focus for cooperation with, and among, the numerous regional organizations and commissions concerned with ocean sciences and ocean resources.

9. Development within the United States of better means of coordination of the planning and activity of the many agencies concerned with the international scientific, technological, economic, and political aspects of the ocean and its resources.

10. It is suggested that serious consideration be given to devising a mechanism for transferring to developing nations useful vessels which are to be retired from the U.S. Oceanographic Research Fleet.

Science Education

Modern industrial and agricultural civilization depends directly upon trained manpower: manpower to carry out basic research in the sciences, to develop some of that research for useful purposes, to manufacture goods and materials resulting from that development, and to keep the factories and manufactured products in working order.

This will necessitate an ever-growing population of well-trained scientists and technicians, and this supply, in turn, will depend on a well-integrated and highly developed educational system which has a strong and healthy science component.

In the last decade in the United States, a revolution in the teaching of science has taken place from the elementary level through the graduate level. Many new courses, techniques, teaching devices, and laboratory instruction methods have been devised, tested and widely promulgated. The existence of these has come to the attention of interested teachers in most countries of the world. Many of the newer U.S. materials have been translated into a host of languages. These materials could turn out to be one of America's most useful exports. The United States has much to gain by helping others translate and adopt these materials and develop new courses of their own. In many cases, the U.S. scientific community has learned much about newer teaching methods by cooperation with scientists from other countries, developing as well as developed. In addition to these new materials, the mechanisms of training and retraining teachers in summer, academic year, and in-service institutes have been tried and found most successful.

There are many cooperative international efforts now going forward in the teaching of science; some of these are in UNESCO, the OAS, the OECD, many more of them are bilateral, and many, many more are highly informal.

The United States should offer to cooperate with all nations of the world—particularly the developing nations—in helping them develop new courses, new teaching aids, new training methods, and other educational programs so that they may train adequately and rapidly the army of scientists and technicians which will be necessary for any country that wishes to achieve the status of a modern industrial nation.

The International Exchange of People and Ideas

It is impossible to overestimate the importance of science to all the nations of the world. The importance has become a very practical one: our prosperity and our very health and welfare are affected by the advancement of science and technology.

In recognition of this, governments have been active in coordinating certain aspects of science and technology internationally. Intergovernmental agreements and commissions play a major role in fostering and controlling such activities as communications, shipping, aeronautics, weather prediction, and a host of other services vital and essential to mankind.

On the other hand, it would be a great loss to science if contacts between scientists of different nationalities were limited only to those occasions when they meet one another in an official capacity under governmental auspices. For centuries, one of the most important forces in the advancement of science has been spontaneous, informal contacts between individuals. Science moves forward most rapidly when individual scientists are free to travel and work abroad, taking and bringing, learning and stimulating.

Unfortunately, some of the rules and regulations which have been established for various purposes by national governments have the effect of impeding the international movement of scientists and scholars. Numerous examples of such obstacles can easily be cited.

Therefore, it is recommended that our Government and those of other countries, in their efforts to promote international cooperation, undertake to lessen the obstacles to interchange and thus facilitate one of the most vital and profitable forms of international cooperation—contacts between individuals of different nationalities.

Polar Research

1. *Antarctica.* The 1959 Antarctic Treaty (to which the United States is one of fifteen parties and one of the twelve original signatories) specifies, in Article II, that "Freedom of scientific investigation in Antarctica and cooperation toward that end, as applied during the International Geophysical Year, shall continue, subject to the provisions of the present Antarctic Treaty." Furthermore, because of the size of Antarctica and the difficulties presented by its harsh environment, successful scientific investigation of the area requires international cooperation.

In accordance with Bureau of the Budget directives, the National Science Foundation has been coordinating all U.S. scientific research in Antarctica for many years. In cooperation with other agencies concerned, the Foundation has initiated many projects involving international cooperation. Major current projects are:

a. Continued Belgian-Norwegian participation in the glaciological and geophysical studies on the South Pole–Queen Maud Land Traverse on an annual basis for the duration of the Traverse activities through the austral season 1969–70.

b. Cooperation between U.S. and U.K. geologists in the study of the geology of the South Georgia Islands.

c. Cooperation between the U.S. and Chilean scientists and respective oceanographic vessels on the study of the Humboldt Current.

  d. U.S.–Argentine cooperation in the conduct of an oceanographic survey of the Weddell Sea.

  e. A cooperative program between U.S., New Zealand, and Japanese scientists in the dry valley area of Victoria Land involving the establishment of a temporary station to support studies in geology, glacial geology, limnology, and biology.

  f. Cooperation in the exchange of scientists between the U.S. and Soviet Antarctic Expeditions and a cooperative continuation of the southern conjugate station at Vostok, the northern terminus of which is maintained cooperatively by U.S. and Danish scientists.

  2. *Arctic.* During the last year, the Department of State carried out a preliminary survey of the Arctic research programs of the United States, Canada, Denmark, Finland, Iceland, Norway, and Sweden. It was found that all seven of these nations are working on the same subjects to varying degrees depending upon the extent of their interests. The research includes some twenty-seven scientific disciplines ranging from agriculture and earth sciences to archaeology and sociology.

  In May, 1965, at the invitation of the Department of State, the departments and agencies concerned with Arctic research—the Department of Health, Education and Welfare; the National Science Foundation and the Atomic Energy Commission—named representatives to participate in an Interagency Arctic Working Group. The purpose of the group is to assess the value and feasibility of strengthening international regional cooperation in Arctic research through the joint use of facilities, increased scientific exchanges, and coordination of research planning.

  The working group has met several times and is completing a detailed summary of the total U.S. Arctic program. Their work will be completed when they have made an assessment of foreign Arctic research and then prepared a final report containing recommendations regarding international regional cooperation in Arctic research.

International Hydrological Decade

  The International Hydrological Decade is a concerted attempt on a world scale to take stock of the fresh-water resources of the globe and to organize research on various methods of making more effective use of them. Hydrology is a field which covers the entire history of the cycles of water on the earth.

  The United States, over the next ten years, should be able to make major contributions to these objectives in the primary activities described below. This country is blessed with rich water resources, highly varied in amount and in geographical location, and greatly diversified in agricultural, domestic, industrial, and power uses.

The proposals encompass only those which are fundamental in nature; widely useful to other countries; continental, hemispheric, or global in occurrence; applicable in international regions; and hopefully making use of orbiting satellites or aerial observations over various countries.

1. The United States should have strong participation in the so-called "Virgil Network," consisting of an international system of stations for observation of principal hydrologic and landscape factors. By 1964, fifty-four Vigil Network Stations had been established in the United States. Additional ones are planned and should be developed for years of basic observations and detailed surveys. Hydrologic and physiographic data will be accumulated for international exchange and interpretation.

2. Hydrological bench marks for continuing evaluation of man's impact on his own environment, by his exploitation of nature's resources, should be developed. Such bench marks will aid increasingly in assessing the impact of changes in climatic pattern, land use, and the works of man upon hydrologic behavior. In such an effort, bench marks established in wilderness areas, unaffected as yet by man's activities, will be of great value.

3. Studies of the distribution of snow and ice are important, since these account for about 80 per cent of the water on the land areas of the world. Much has been learned since the International Geophysical Year about two major ice caps, Antarctica and Greenland, but information is still amazingly meager about the amounts, location, and behavior of ephemeral snow cover, ice on and in water, ground ice (permafrost), and mountain glaciers. Snow and ice have a profound effect, as yet insufficiently measured or documented, on global environment.

4. The behavior of sediment has national and international significance. It is surprising that understanding of sediment transport and related phenomena still waits upon intensified worldwide study, considering the beneficent and damaging effects of such transport and deposition in every stream. The rich Mississippi and Nile deltas and the gradual filling of some important reservoirs are but a few examples of these positive and negative results. A long-term program is projected to measure progressive effects of natural and artificial

changes in a selected river basin during periods of development, with particular reference to suspended and bed materials.

5. Specific studies of how much water exists, where it occurs, and how much is actually available for use are needed. Such an inventory in quantitative detail is visualized both for surface waters and, perhaps of even greater importance, for the extractable volume of water underground. The development of intelligible and verifiable water balances in the United States and elsewhere is far in arrears.

6. An improvement of the understanding of the relation between meteorologic and hydrologic parameters is necessary. The data for the establishment of design criteria for the functional requirements of many projects are inadequate. This is true for two controlling phenomena, extraordinary low flows and inordinately high runoff. In the absence of observations of very long duration, predictions as to these phenomena rest on shaky ground. The importance of improving and perfecting predictability is obvious for virtually every single or multipurpose project to be built.

7. The use and understanding of newer methods of remote sensing of hydrological phenomena are essential to the understanding and the predictability of moisture movement and water balances on the earth. Fortunately, promise of increasing success in such efforts lies in the remote sensing with airborne instruments in ordinary aircraft, now in the experimental stage. Much of the movement of atmospheric moisture and the related energy transactions occur in that part of the atmosphere accessible to aircraft. In the course of time, it is probable that orbiting satellites and collateral space instruments may improve prediction efficacy.

8. Measurement of evaporation from large bodies of water and its consequent control have long intrigued workers in this field. The amounts lost are large, and increased experimentation in preventing evaporation is well warranted.

9. Long-range water resource forecasting would be a boon to all mankind. In any such task, the ocean-continent water relation is a paramount consideration, because of the cycle of water movement from ocean to atmosphere to continent and return. This activity will be pursued in consonance with and using the facilities being developed in Item 7. This complex analysis will rest upon detailed appraisals of precipitation, evaporation, runoff, temperature, etc., of land and ocean areas.

10. What has been the effect upon hydrologic processes of man's activities in the increasing artificial heat releases and other artificial

changes on earth? Never before in history has man assumed the role of unprecedented consumer of fossil fuels. Releases of heat, gases, and other wastes to the atmosphere and to all the waters of the earth must be studied to determine how the global water balance of the future might be affected.

11. A rigid identification of the factors which produce accelerated aging of fresh-water lakes is of paramount importance. What are the environmental factors which affect rates of aging, and how may these be economically controlled? In this category, simultaneous worldwide observations of lakes in a variety of environments should shed much light on causes and rates of aging under various climatic and geological conditions.

12. Additional activities will proceed on other phases of hydrological behavior which are not spelled out here. They are to be intensified and perhaps even somewhat re-oriented toward an eventual maximum usefulness to the United States and the other countries of the world.

The International Biological Program

The ultimate welfare of man is intimately bound to the resources available to him on this planet. These resources are not inexhaustible. In the immediate years ahead, the constant advance of civilization, the rapid growth of industry, and the rapidly increasing population of the world will make ever-increasing demands upon biological resources. If the future needs of man are to be met there must be more effective adjustment to his environment. In recognition of the problems facing mankind and the growing concern that biological problems relating to productivity and human welfare should be investigated on an international scale, biologists everywhere have united in a common effort to bring new scientific data to bear upon these questions.

The proposal for an International Biological Program (IBP) was developed by the International Council of Scientific Unions and four of its member unions, and two international unions which are not members of ICSU, after several years of deliberations. In May, 1962, a Planning Committee organized for this purpose outlined an international biological program and proposed as the theme for the IBP "The Biological Basis of Productivity and Human Welfare." The objectives of the plan are, "ensuring world-wide study of (1) organic production of the land, in fresh waters, and in the seas, so that adequate estimates may be made of the potential yield of new as well as existing natural resources, and (2) human adaptability to changing conditions."

The United States, through the National Academy of Sciences-National Research Council, is participating together with 43 other countries, in the IBP. The U.S. National Committee for the International Biological Program (USNC IBP) and its seven subcommittees have prepared a "Preliminary Framework" for the United States share of the International Biological Program. This "framework" comprises not only research, but also symposia and conferences, educational programs, the gathering and publication of existing knowledge, and various kinds of applications, including the conservation of threatened parts of the biological environment. This broad scope offers United States biologists unique opportunities to cooperate with their colleagues from other countries; and especially to foster biological research and training in the less-developed part of the world. Furthermore, the IBP will provide information necessary for an objective estimate of the world's capacity to support life and how to manage his environment more efficiently. It is recommended therefore:

1. That the U.S. Government provide adequate support to enable American scientists to play a leading part in the International Biological Program.

2. That the U.S. Government urge UNESCO, the Food and Agriculture Organization, the World Health Organization, and the International Atomic Energy Agency to increase their assistance and support to the IBP in order that all mankind may benefit from the united effort of the biologists of the world.

3. That appropriate scientific agencies of the Department of Agriculture, the Department of Health, Education and Welfare, the Department of the Interior, and the Smithsonian Institution utilize the opportunities provided by the International Biological Program to advance the scientific understanding which must be attained to solve problems of human and animal nutrition, control of pollution, preservation of natural areas, and the relations between human populations and their biological environment.

4. That the Agency for International Development help scientists of the developing nations to cooperate with U.S. scientists in advancing the biological knowledge in their countries that is needed to solve problems of agriculture, animal husbandry, forestry, fisheries, health and conservation, and that AID work with U.S. sci-

entists involved in the IBP toward this objective. PL 480 funds may be useful for this purpose.

5. That the National Science Foundation, the National Institute of Health, and other scientific granting agencies make adequate budgeting provision to enable U.S. scientists in universities and research institutions to participate fully in the IBP, and that the appropriate Congressional committees be informed of the objectives, plans and needs of the U.S. part of the IBP.

6. That other Government agencies, such as the Department of Defense, the Atomic Energy Commission, and the National Aeronautics and Space Administration take advantage of the opportunities provided by the IBP to advance the scientific understanding needed for their diverse missions, through utilization of their own scientific resources and through support of non-governmental scientists.

7. That Peace Corps volunteers be utilized to further the objectives of the IBP by assisting workers in developing countries.

The Application of Technology to Meet Human Needs

International cooperation in science is excellent and extensive. It ranges from direct personal contact among colleagues throughout the world to participation in international meetings and formal international conferences and organizations.

Such is not the case, however, in the development and application of technology to meet man's needs. Yet, like science, technology is international in character, application, and impact. Moreover, technological resources, as distinguished from natural resources, are increasingly the basis for national prosperity and well-being.

There are many broad human needs, common to all nations, that must be met—for humanitarian as well as practical reasons— humanitarian because all men of good will would like to see the lot of their fellow men improved, and practical because these unmet needs provoke and exacerbate conflict among nations. These needs involve the basic necessities of life—food, shelter, transportation, communication, education, health.

Of the various ways to meet these great human needs, the effective application of modern technology offers the most promise in achieving the quantum jumps in progress that an impatient and desperate world so urgently seeks.

The problem is that the application of technology does not take place automatically or easily, but is an extraordinarily complex and difficult process. Moreover, in many cases political and social progress must take place before the introduction of new technology is feasible. A concerted, cooperative attack on the over-all problem, therefore, is required with a systems approach throughout to ensure a balanced, optimum solution to the *whole* problem.

The problem cannot be solved by private individuals, groups, and resources alone. It requires the active leadership and participation of the various governments of the world. Even in the United States, by far the richest and most technically advanced nation in the world, there are substantial differences in prosperity, technical capability, and general well-being between regions of the country, between industries, and between companies in a given industry. We have launched many government programs to improve the situation —support for education and training, financial and other aid to distressed areas, regional programs for the dissemination of technical information and the application of technology, creating the climate that will encourage innovation and entrepreneurial initiative, and many others.

No nation on earth—rich or poor—has solved all the problems of its people or met all their needs. Each stands to gain by an international cooperative effort to harvest the fruits of modern world technology for the good of all.

To be successful, such an international cooperative effort should follow certain guidelines, among which are:

1. The approach must be interdisciplinary, not only in the technical areas but in others as well. Thus, management specialists, sociologists, economists, political scientists—all must contribute their special skills to the over-all problem.

2. The program must be adapted to the special requirements of each region or environment. Adaptive innovation that tailors technology to specific needs in a given environment is essential. The existing human and natural resources are the base on which technical progress is built.

Efforts to layer a ready-made technology on a society not ready for it is about as useful as Da Vinci designing a flying machine and a submarine centuries before the total technology made either possible.

Technological progress has created a universal demand for the products of new technology. While the demand is universal, however, the ability to innovate and produce new products is limited to a few technically advanced nations. Moreover, the gap between these and the non-technical nations is widening. In the interest of equity and world peace, all nations should be concerned with narrowing the gap, not by slowing the technology of the advanced but by speeding that of the underdeveloped regions, whether these be nations, groups of nations, or even parts of advanced nations.

The major reason why technology does not develop at the same rate in various parts of the world stems from the fact that new technologies develop because of the specific requirements, both technical and economic, of the region. The entrepreneur and innovator dips into the available technology and modifies it to meet the needs of a specific market. Consequently, the international program, to be effective, must be organized on a regional basis, rather than a national one, by areas having common problems and common resources.

3. In underdeveloped areas, provision must be made for at least a minimum social overhead, the prerequisite for industrialization and technical progress. This overhead includes sources of energy adequate to growth, transportation, education, communication—the last two particularly vital for the transmission of skills, techniques, know-how, for learning about new products and thereby creating the demand for them, and the diffusion of technical information. Social overhead also would include such services as weather information, censuses, weights and measures, and the like.

4. The development of human resources in each region is the most crucial objective of the program. Self-sufficiency in this regard not only promotes dignity but is vastly more effective than constant dependence on importing technology from elsewhere.

Creative talent is of more value than the specific invention, for the creative mind will improvise and innovate on the spot where needed. There should be a constant search for people who are able to react to the needs of an environment and innovate improvements.

Management skills are indispensable. An entrepreneurial elite that is *able and willing* to stimulate the introduction of new technology and the innovation of new products and processes is essential.

The *able* part of the requirement can be taken care of by education, on-the-spot training, exchange of technological information, agricultural and industrial extension programs, and the like. One way to speed its growth would be to foster the development of technical societies in underdeveloped areas that parallel and are associated with more advanced counterparts. Another is to sponsor international symposia and technical sessions on engineering research and the technical problems of economic development of less-developed areas. Possible subjects include village power supplies, transportation and communication systems, small-scale industry, and rural electrification.

The *willing* part is another matter. Many medical and other trainees in the United States and other advanced countries, there to be educated so that they can later help their people, decide to stay abroad. This unintended export of technically trained persons from underdeveloped areas to developed ones is a serious problem. Another example—typical in Asia: to satisfy a rural need, rural folk are given training. But once trained they follow the tradition that professionals live in cities. This is another kind of "export"—from the rural areas lacking skills to the already crowded urban areas with a relative surplus of skills.

This leads to a corollary problem—selling the idea of change itself to underdeveloped areas. It is not easy to change age-old habits and customs. Nor is it simply a matter of selling the witchdoctor on modern medicine. It is the subtler problem of disturbing vested interests and adapting technological change to existing cultural patterns, settling for gradual modification instead of dramatic change.

There is a paradox in the role of labor in underdeveloped areas that often baffles the unsophisticated: what is most efficient is not always the most effective. Sometimes improving an existing village hand-weaving operation is better than introducing the theoretically more efficient concentrated production in large textile mills.

To apply technology to meet human needs in the world's less developed countries, a bold, new, open-minded, experimental activity is needed, harnessing the combined talents of many, working in cooperation on the great common problems of man.

In housing, for example, we should experiment with brand-new materials, untried processes and techniques, and radically different designs to determine, without regard to tradition, what is the best shelter for man in a given environment—in hot humid jungles, in the hot dry desert, in the cold north, in rural areas and urban centers.

In education and communication, we should determine what can be done with battery-powered transistorized radios for areas with no electricity, with TV schools for places where there are millions of potential pupils and few schools and teachers, with new techniques of teaching that will expedite and make more effective the learning process.

RECOMMENDATIONS

We make the following recommendations:

1. That a cooperative program be initiated to develop the instrumentation and analytical techniques needed to predict the location and magnitude of future earthquakes, and study the transitory and permanent effects of such earthquakes on both natural and man-made structures.

2. That a long-range and coordinated international research program in oceanography be established for the scientific study of the vast resources of the oceans with a view to their utilization.

3. That a cooperative scientific and technological program be greatly accelerated aimed at widespread dissemination of technology for improving the basic needs of man—such as nutrition, sanitation, health, shelter, and communications—and particularly emphasizing cooperation with developing countries. Important to such cooperation is the utilization of new techniques and teaching methods for the development of scientific and technological manpower.

4. That our Government and those of other countries undertake to remove the obstacles to scientific interchange and facilitate one of the most vital and profitable forms of international cooperation—contacts between individuals of different nationalities.

5. That international cooperation in research be extended in the Arctic Regions of the World.

6. That full support be given to programs such as those proposed under the International Hydrological Decade to establish a worldwide network of stations for measuring and tracking through the hydrological cycle and providing for the study of drought, flood control, improved navigation, and hydroelectric development.

7. That increased efforts be made on an international scale to cope with the mounting flood of scientific information by drastically improving the methods for its translation, storage, and retrieval. International cooperation is indispensable for effective collection, evaluation, and dissemination of critical reference data.

8. That the on-going International Upper Mantle Project, which is considering the relationships between the upper mantle and the earth's crust, continue to receive support.

9. That endorsement and support be given the International Biological Program, a plan for worldwide studies of organic production on land, in fresh waters, and in the seas, including studies of the potential yield of new and existing natural resources and the adaptability of human beings to changing ecological conditions.

THE COMMITTEE ON SCIENCE AND TECHNOLOGY

14. *Harnessing the Peaceful Atom*

The Atomic Age began on December 2, 1942, in a squash court under the stadium of the University of Chicago. On that day, a team led by Enrico Fermi, the Italian-born American physicist, was able to achieve for the first time a self-sustaining chain reaction in a nuclear reactor. This achievement was the culmination of the work of scientists in many countries over a period of almost fifty years to force the atom to release the energy stored within it.

This newly released energy was first applied only for military purposes. Men of good will in the United Nations and other forums sought unsuccessfully from the end of World War II to reach agreement on international control of atomic weapons. In its second decade, atomic energy entered a new phase when President Eisenhower announced the Atoms for Peace Program with his pledge before the General Assembly of the United Nations that the United States would "devote its entire heart and mind to find a way by which the miraculous inventiveness of man shall not be dedicated to his death, but consecrated to his life."

This determination was reflected in the Atomic Energy Act of 1954, which committed the United States to international cooperation for the development of peaceful uses of atomic energy. Other countries rapidly accepted the opportunity, and the International Atomic Energy Agency, European Atomic Energy Community (Euratom), the European Nuclear Energy Agency, and the Inter-American Nuclear Energy Commission were established to develop and promote the peaceful atom. Through international cooperative efforts atomic energy began to provide tools for daily use in industry, agriculture, medicine, and research. Early in its third decade, the peaceful atom is on the verge of achieving economic electrical power from nuclear reactors.

This maturing technology and experience afford new promise of conquering some of the age-old problems of mankind, such as inadequate energy and water resources, and new achievements of far-reaching advantages, ranging from dramatic medical advances and pest control, to massive construction projects. At the same time, it poses hazards, not only because of the danger to health and safety from the uninformed use of atomic energy, but also because nuclear materials, technology, and experience useful for peaceful purposes are also to some degree applicable to military purposes.

The growth of the peaceful uses of atomic energy requires strong international as well as national regulations to protect public health and safety and to protect against the diversion of peaceful programs or materials to military purposes. From the beginning of the Atoms for Peace Program, the United States has insisted on the importance of safeguards against such diversion. This position has received the support of other nations, recently including those of the Soviet bloc, in developing effective International Atomic Energy Agency safeguards. It is of the utmost importance that this cooperation continue, and that the safeguards system continue to be refined and its applicability extended.

Where We Stand

International Atomic Energy Agency (IAEA)

Ninety-three states now belong to the International Atomic Energy Agency, a member of the United Nations family. It was established in 1957 through U.S. initiative. The purpose of the agency is tied to the recognition that atomic energy has implications that transcend national boundaries, that atomic energy needs to be controlled and regulated, and that these controls should range from verification to prevent diversion to military use to the development of standards to protect the general public from the harmful effects of radioactivity. The Agency has also provided a forum for the development of East-West technical contacts and effective discussions. Recent U.S.S.R. support for safeguards applicable to reactors larger than 100 thermal megawatts significantly strengthens the Agency.

The United States supports the IAEA by: providing scientific and technical information; recruiting people to serve the Agency; supporting research projects; providing special nuclear materials and equipment; placing IAEA Fellows in U.S. facilities; reviewing requests to the IAEA for equipment grants; reviewing and commenting on guides and standards proposed by the Agency; and participating in IAEA-sponsored conferences and symposia. Over twenty countries receiving U.S. materials or equipment (either directly or through the IAEA) have agreed to submit these arrangements to IAEA safeguards.

European Atomic Energy Community (Euratom)

The two U.S. Agreements for Cooperation with Euratom authorize the transfer of up to 70,000 Kgs. of contained U-235 and 500 Kgs. of plutonium; 3,623.5 Kgs. of U-235 contained in 96,553.2 Kgs. of total uranium and 11.31 Kgs. of Pu have been sold or leased to Euratom through July 31, 1965.

As a corollary to the AEC-Euratom fast reactor information exchange, the United States agreed to sell Euratom for its fast reactor program about 415 Kgs. of plutonium and the enriched uranium requirements of the program through 1967 (estimated at about 1,700 Kgs. of U-235).

Among the more important formal cooperative undertakings between the United States and Euratom in implementation of the two agreements are:

• *Joint Power Reactor Program*—Three U.S.-type power reactors (involving contracts with U.S. reactor manufacturers) have been or are being built in the Community under this Program (SENN—150 MWe, Boiling Water Reactor in Italy; SENA—266 MWe, Pressurized Water Reactor in France; KRB—237 MWe, Boiling Water Reactor in Germany). The United States will obtain operating experience information and will supply, through sale or toll enrichment, fuel requirements for twenty years.

• *Joint R&D Program*—Each party will spend about $37 million for the period from 1959 through 1969 in its own territory. They will exchange all information and patent rights on this work, which is aimed primarily at the improvement of the performance of the types of reactors under the Joint Reactor Program and at lowering fuel cycle costs.

• *Fast Reactor Information Exchange*—Information will be exchanged on all fast neutron reactor programs for civilian central power station application, including research and development, with which the AEC and Euratom are associated before mid-1974.

European Nuclear Energy Agency (ENEA)

The main objective of the ENEA, the atomic arm of the Organization for Economic Cooperation and Development, is to promote cooperation among the eighteen European member countries in developing nuclear energy for peaceful purposes. The United States and Canada are Associate Members of the ENEA, and Euratom also takes part in its work.

Since 1958, the United States has provided experience and information related to ENEA activities. In some instances, such as the Halden Project (the heavy boiling water reactor in Norway) and the Eurochemic chemical reprocessing plant in Belgium, the United States has also assigned technical personnel. The United States recently agreed to contribute three tons of heavy water to the Halden Project. The United States has participated in the standing committees on reactor physics and neutron data, and has agreed to exchange neutron cross-section data and computer codes. The United States and ENEA have recently co-sponsored two international seminars in the United States, at the Brookhaven and Argonne National Laboratories.

Inter-American Nuclear Energy Commission (IANEC)

IANEC was established by the Council of the Organization of American States in 1959 to facilitate consultation and cooperation among the member governments in matters relating to the peaceful applications of atomic energy. The United States has provided IANEC with technical advice and assistance, and has contributed technically and financially to all five IANEC symposia.

Other International Organizations

The United States cooperates closely with the World Health Organization, the Pan American Health Organization, the Food and Agriculture Organization, the World Meteorological Organization, the International Commission on Radiation Protection, the International Standards Organization, and the Centre Européen pour Recherche Nucléaire (CERN). Equipment has been provided and U.S. personnel have served these organizations in various capacities.

Transfer of Nuclear Materials

The AEC supplies enriched uranium for fueling reactors abroad either under appropriate bilateral Agreements for Cooperation or through the IAEA, with safeguards applicable to the reactor and fuel in either case. Fuel for power is usually sold, but material can be leased with a waiver of use charges for a period of time if technical or economic information of sufficient interest to the AEC is expected. Heavy water, plutonium, U-233, and various transplutonium elements for use in research and development projects are also sold or leased abroad.

Through June, 1965, $84.6 million in revenue has been received for materials valued at $141.7 million that have been transferred. The Commission estimates the total value of materials sold or leased abroad will reach $700 million by 1970 and $8 billion by 1980.

Exchange of Information

Forty major technical information exchanges have been developed. In 1965, for example, agreement was reached with the United Kingdom for extending the exchange on advanced gas-cooled reactor systems. The United States and Canada have had an active exchange on the development of heavy water power reactors since 1960, with the United States spending $1 million a year in this country over a ten-year period in support of the Canadian program. Canada in turn has provided extensive information to the United States on the heavy water reactor concept. The United States and Australia have exchanged information and personnel on high-temperature, gas-cooled reactor technology since 1961.

Beneficial exchanges of visits and information have taken place under the two United States–U.S.S.R. Memoranda for Cooperation on utilization of atomic energy for peaceful purposes. Since 1959, the chairman of the AEC and their Soviet counterparts have exchanged visits, and fourteen scientific delegations have been exchanged in such fields as high-energy physics, controlled thermonuclear reactions, radioactive waste disposal, and power reactors. Furthermore, there have been long-term exchanges of research specialists in high-energy physics. There has also been an extensive exchange of documents.

The largest sources of nuclear information the United States provides abroad are the depository libraries the AEC has distributed to eighty-seven countries and international organizations. They are kept currently supplied with U.S. publications, and the recipients provide the United States with their publications in nuclear science and technology.

Training of Foreign Nationals

Approximately 3,000 people from sixty-seven countries have been trained in nuclear science and technology in the United States since 1955. The Puerto Rico Nuclear Center continues to offer a specialized program for foreign nationals, but the other specialized AEC programs have been replaced by U.S. universities and domestic programs established by many of the foreign atomic energy commissions. Foreign nationals still participate in unclassified research in AEC national laboratories and other facilities.

From 1963–65, 368 nationals of thirty-six countries attended short courses of the Public Health Service dealing with various aspects of radiological health. Foreign students also enrolled in the radiation science courses at universities supported by Public Health Service Training Grants.

To date the Geological Survey has conducted, arranged, or supervised training and specialized programs for about 787 earth scientists and technical personnel from seventy countries. Forty-seven, for fifteen countries, were sponsored by atomic energy organizations or had interests directly related to radioactive materials.

Sister Laboratory Program

This program helps a developing country which has received an AEC research reactor grant to utilize its facilities more effectively. A major research institute in the United States accepts responsibility for advising the country in planning, organizing, and executing a research reactor program, and for providing minor items of equipment not readily available. These "sister" laboratory arrangements are developed on a case-by-case basis subject to the availability of AID funds.

To date, the Brookhaven National Laboratory (BNL) has assisted the Turkish Cekmece Nuclear Research and Training Center and the Argonne National Laboratory has assisted the atomic energy establishments in Korea and the Republic of China. An arrangement was concluded in October, 1965, between the Puerto Rico Nuclear Center and the Colombian Institute of Nuclear Affairs. In prospect are arrangements between BNL and the Democritus Center in Greece and the Oak Ridge National Laboratory and the Thai atomic energy project.

Exhibits and Conferences

The United States supports atomic energy exhibits abroad and participates in international scientific conferences and symposia.

Exhibits have made substantial contributions to the understanding overseas of the peaceful uses of nuclear energy. Major exhibits were mounted at the Geneva Conferences of 1955, 1958, and 1964. The AEC's two traveling exhibits have been shown in Europe, Asia, Africa, and Latin America to over 5.9 million people. A new exhibit especially designed for developing nations was shown in 1965 in El Salvador and Guatemala.

The Conference program includes support for the three Geneva conferences and for a much larger number of smaller specialized symposia. There were twenty-one such symposia in 1964 covering such subjects as radiation preservation of food, marine biology, biophysics, isotopically labeled drugs, human genetics, and reactor technology. In 1965, support will be offered to approximately thirty-five symposia.

Atomic Bomb Casualty Commission

The ABCC is a collaborative Japanese-American enterprise to study the containing nuclear effects on the survivors of Hiroshima and Nagasaki and their descendants. It has the support of the Japanese Ministry of Health and the cooperation of the population of the two cities. The Atomic Energy Commission provided the National Academy of Sciences about $3,225,000 to support the project in fiscal year 1965, which consists of about 900 staff, including approximately forty U.S. nationals. In addition the Public Health Service provides 7–8 medical officers annually, and the Japanese Government provides thirty-five professional and administrative personnel as concrete evidence of its support.

Exchange in Field of Raw Materials

The AEC's Raw Materials personnel advise friendly nations on uranium exploration and development programs, and visit all major foreign developments periodically. These visits are reciprocal. The Geological Survey cooperates with foreign agencies, institutes, and scientists in such matters as the exploration for raw materials, joint scientific and technical studies, and in the training of foreign nationals.

Exchange of Visits and Assignments

There have been hundreds of exchanges of visits between U.S. Government and contractor personnel and foreign nuclear scientists. In addition, U.S. personnel receive long-term assignments to foreign nuclear projects, and foreign personnel receive similar assignments at U.S. facilities. These exchanges are made under special arrangements and represent an outstanding contribution to the development of the peaceful uses of atomic energy and knowledge of radioactivity.

Desalting

The Department of the Interior (Office of Saline Water) and the AEC are studying dual-purpose nuclear power/water desalting plants, while the Departments of State and the Interior, the AEC and other appropriate Government agencies are represented on an Inter-Agency Committee on Foreign Desalting Programs. Over the past two years the United States has participated in five IAEA panel meetings to exchange information on desalting with twenty-five other countries. Some sixty countries were represented at the First International Symposium on Water Disalination held in Washington, October 4–9, 1965. The United States is also carrying out activities in the field of desalting with certain specific countries.

· *Israel:* A team of United States and Israeli experts conducted a preliminary survey of Israel's power and water needs, which indicated that a dual-purpose nuclear plant producing 100–150 million gallons per day and 175–200 MWe may be economically attractive.

· *Soviet Union:* In June, 1964, President Johnson announced a United States–U.S.S.R. cooperative program for the exchange of technical information in the nuclear power-desalting field. After meeting in Washington and Moscow, and reciprocal visits by desalting experts to desalting and reactor facilities, a formal agreement for cooperation in the field of desalting (including nuclear energy) was signed in November, 1964.

· *United Arab Republic:* A United States nuclear power-desalting team visited the UAR in 1964 to investigate the use of dual-purpose power-water plants for specialized agriculture along the Mediterranean Sea coast.

· *Mexico:* Mexico, the United States, and the IAEA executed an agreement on October 7, 1965, to study large nuclear power-desalting plants for California and Arizona and the states of Lower California and Sonora in Mexico.

· *Italy:* A technical team from Italy recently visited U.S. facilities, and there have been preliminary discussions regarding cooperation in the field of desalting, including the use of nuclear energy.

Cooperation on Plowshare

The United States has indicated its willingness to consider international cooperation in its program for the peaceful uses for nuclear explosives (Plowshare). There have been expressions of interest from several countries and exchanges of technical information relevant, in some cases, to specific projects. Australia sent a technical team to the United States for two months to study the scientific, engineering, and safety aspects of Plowshare.

Radiation Applications

The United States has participated in several international projects concerning isotopes applications, especially the radiation preservation of foods. For example, a cooperative program among the United States Army, AEC, and the Atomic Energy of Canada Limited has been arranged to study the radiation pasteurization of freshly killed chickens. Israel has been loaned 7,800 curies of Co-60 for investigating the radiation preservation of citrus products. The United States has assisted the World Health Organization's studies of possible radiation preservation of foods in South America.

High-Energy Physics

High-energy physics is a particularly fruitful field for international collaboration. The scientific interest in this fundamental field is high and the possibility of commercial, industrial, or military application of the research results is remote. In addition, large accelerators are presently available in the United States, in Western Europe, and in the Soviet Union, and the scientific results obtained by the use of these facilities are already made available everywhere.

International collaboration in high-energy physics, including participation of scientists from Soviet bloc nations, has thus been remarkably successful during the past years and good relationships have been established. This collaboration has been principally in the form of: (1) a considerable informal exchange of information on scientific results through the ready availability of scientific journals and preprints; (2) numerous international scientific meetings; (3) exchanges of individuals and research teams, on both short-term and long-term bases; and (4) the exchange of data source materials such as exposed nuclear emulsions.

There have been extensive informal discussions among scientists from the United States, Western Europe, and Soviet laboratories of their respective plans for the design and construction of accelerators. At present there is no formal coordination of plans nor are there any jointly managed accelerator construction projects involving the United States and other countries.

Future Goals

With the Atoms for Peace Program entering its second decade, co-operative programs are generally well established. But there are areas in which cooperation might be expanded, and to which greater emphasis might be given. We must continue to seek new and improved applications of nuclear energy under effective safeguards.

International Safeguards

For more than a decade, the United States has been sharing the benefits of its progress in the peaceful utilization of the atom with other nations through the Atoms for Peace Program. From the beginning, the United States has recognized that the technologies of producing nuclear power for peaceful purposes and of producing fissionable material for weapons purposes are related. For this reason, the Agreements for Cooperation between the United States and other countries or groups of countries have included provisions designed to guard against diversion of materials, equipment, and facilities, including the right of the United States to inspect to assure compliance.

Realizing that the administration of safeguards against diversion should be as general, as uniformly effective, and as clearly unbiased as possible, the United States has encouraged the development and strengthening of the safeguards function of the International Atomic Energy Agency. As the Agency has established sound procedures and the ability to apply them, the United States has amended its Agreements for Cooperation to require the application of IAEA, rather than United States safeguards. Other supplier nations have been encouraged by the United States to do the same. This effort should be continued, with the aim of persuading all supplier nations to require IAEA safeguards as a condition of export.

Concurrently, the United States should seek to strengthen IAEA over the next decade, and to utilize its developing capacity fully. This would involve the efforts not only of the government but also of the nuclear industry and labor, in increasing the support of IAEA, and assisting in the continuous refinement of safeguards to assure their effectiveness while minimizing the interference with the peaceful operations of the facilities to be inspected. The Agency system provides general procedures for applying safeguards to all parts of the reactor fuel cycle; however, specific procedures have not yet been elaborated for fuel element fabrication and spent fuel chemical processing plants. Consideration should be given to early development of these procedures.

Moreover, countries should be encouraged to accept IAEA safeguards voluntarily upon facilities which are entirely domestically developed. The United States made a start about a year ago in voluntarily submitting a large private power reactor, the Yankee Atomic Power Reactor, to IAEA inspection. The United States offer also extended the period of application of Agency safeguards to three other reactors originally submitted in 1962. In June, 1965, the United Kingdom offered to place its Bradwell Nuclear Power Station under IAEA safeguards.

In August, 1965, a number of American industry and government representatives met at the Yankee site in Rowe, Massachusetts, to discuss the role of private industry in safeguards. The results were encouraging: The Yankee experience to date has disclosed no unduly burdensome problems (i.e., interference with operations, increased costs, or disclosure of company confidential information). The industrial representatives present indicated that widespread industrial acceptance of safeguards could be anticipated, but that care should be taken that safeguards not become a burden to the inspected. This meeting represented a significant achievement; the dialogue between government and industry concerning safeguards should be continued, both here and abroad.

The total costs to the IAEA of inspections will increase as more facilities come under IAEA safeguards. These IAEA safeguards give all nations of the world equal assurance, unbiased and credible, of the continuing commitment of atomic energy projects to peaceful purposes. It is recommended that the IAEA bear the cost of all inspections to afford assurance of their independence.

International safeguards for nuclear facilities and materials have been accepted as a cornerstone of U.S. foreign policy. Accordingly, we point out that the effective development of this position necessitates the continuing, consistent, and informed participation by Department of State officials at the highest level.

Finally, the United States should be willing to consider any other proposals to increase the protection against the diversion of nuclear materials to military purposes. However, it is important that full consideration be given to all ramifications of any such proposals, to assure that they would not unnecessarily complicate the problem, rendering the controls more cumbersome and less effective.

Nuclear Power

Intensive international cooperation in the supply of nuclear power plants should be continued, since they appear able to supply a critical need for economical and plentiful power in many parts of the world. The sale of U.S. power reactors abroad not only aids the U.S. balance-of-payments position, but also assures that a safe-guarded reactor is constructed.

The United States has already contributed to the growth of nuclear power overseas through wide dissemination of information on the active U.S. civilian power program and through assurances of the long-term availability from the United States of enriched uranium. AID and the Export-Import Bank have financed foreign nuclear power plants; a limited deferred fuel payment program is available. With the passage of legislation authorizing the private ownership of special nuclear material, the United States offered to sell uranium enrichment services (toll enrichment) after January 1, 1969. The U.S. policy of non-discrimination between foreign and domestic users in the pricing of nuclear materials and services should be continued.

The United States might further encourage the construction of nuclear power reactors to provide needed power in the developing countries through the selective lease or loan of enriched uranium and heavy water.

Large-scale nuclear power plants appear on the verge of achieving economic competitiveness in the United States. Developing nations may find such plants too large for existing utility system capacities and near term growth projections, while nuclear power plants ranging from a few tens of megawatts to perhaps two or three hundred megawatts may offer special advantages in selected regions of the world. The development of improvements for this size plant should continue to be encouraged. Even smaller power outputs from units fueled with radioisotopes may be attractive in specialized applications such as remote weather stations or harbor buoys and in medical applications such as radioisotope powered cardiac pacemakers. Initial demonstrations of such devices have been very encouraging and development of a larger market should result in cost reductions. The IAEA should continue, and perhaps intensify, its efforts to identify situations in which nuclear power might be helpful to developing areas.

Desalting Water

Fresh water is necessary to support life; an adequate supply is basic to the stability and economic viability of a society. Shortages of potable water are reaching critical stages in many parts of the world. Extensive water resources studies are being undertaken by several countries in an effort to meet area water needs. Recent events have underscored the real and present problem of water shortages not only in many foreign countries, but in the United States as well. It must be attacked by vigorous programs—both domestic and international.

One way to meet the needs for fresh water is the desalting of sea and brackish waters. This method is unique because it increases the supply of fresh water as a supplement to that naturally available. Moreover, desalting can draw on another major technological advance of the twentieth century—nuclear power. The conjunction of these two new technologies adds a new dimension to man's quest for adequate water by allowing us to take advantage of the nearly limitless energy resources available from atomic energy and the favorable economics of large-size desalting plants.

A domestic program of evaluation, research and development, and pilot and prototype plant construction has been underway for some time. An expanded domestic program projected to cost $200 million over the next five years has been approved by the President. From this technology, water costs of about 25–30 cents per thousand gallons are expected from dual-purpose nuclear plants with a capacity of several hundred megawatts of electric power and 100 million gallons of water per day capacity. This cost is acceptable in many areas for water required for industrial and municipal use. In the more distant future, very large plants with substantially lower water costs should be feasible.

Through an aggressive and growing program of the Department of the Interior, development of a number of processes applicable to the processing of brackish waters, as well as sea water, is proceeding with encouraging results. These processes will greatly increase the range of application for desalting technology from small plants for isolated communities to large regional plants so that many areas and communities, inland as well as coastal, small as well as heavily populated, may benefit.

As a first step toward the application of this new technology, the United States has been cooperating in technical and economic studies on two projects—one with the Metropolitan Water District of Southern California and the other with Israel. A third study was initiated in October, 1965, between the United States and Mexico under the auspices of the IAEA. This study will consider large nuclear power-desalting plants which could provide electric power and supplemental water for the arid regions of the two countries near the Gulf of California.

We recognize that the construction overseas of nuclear desalting plants could further complicate the nuclear proliferation program. For this reason, we fully and strongly support the policy that any U.S. assistance to a nuclear desalting plant constructed abroad would be conditioned on the acceptance of IAEA safeguards to ensure the peaceful use of the facility and the plutonium produced.

The United States should continue to offer assistance to foreign scientists and technicians in their efforts to understand and solve their national water resources problems. The type of training needs will necessarily vary from country to country. The preparation of a good handbook or textbook would be helpful.

We noted with pleasure President Johnson's announcement of a "Water for Peace" program in October, 1965, at the First International Symposium on Water Desalination. We hope this program may provide a practical solution to many of man's water problems.

High-Energy Physics

International cooperation in the field of high-energy physics is expected to increase in the next five years as a number of unique, new or up-graded facilities are completed and become available in different parts of the world. In particular, the United States could investigate the possibility of additional long-term exchanges with the Soviets wherein U.S. scientists would be allowed to perform research with the Soviet Serpukov 70 Bev Accelerator which is expected to become operational in 1967.

Accelerators of the 200 Bev class are within the capacity of the United States, Western Europe, and the Soviet Union to construct and operate as national projects. A joint accelerator construction and management undertaking in this energy range, in addition to the obvious administrative difficulties, presents scientific disadvantages because the research needs of the numerous scientific groups could not be met effectively by a single international accelerator.

Accelerators of an energy of the order of 600 to 1,000 Bev and higher are expected to be so large and costly to build and to operate that it will be necessary to investigate carefully the possibility and the consequences of an international collaborative effort for such a facility before a final commitment is made to construct and operate an accelerator in this class as a national undertaking.

It is clear that a large accelerator of the 1,000 Bev energy range, constructed and effectively managed jointly by the United States, Western Europe, and the Soviet Union would be a significant achievement in many ways and the feasibility of a joint undertaking of this kind should continue to be investigated. It is recognized, however, that the likelihood of such a project materializing may be remote in view of the many complex technical and non-technical problems which would have to be resolved before such international collaboration could become effective.

An intermediate step, between the informal procedures mentioned earlier and full-scale collaboration among Western Europe, the Soviet Union, and the United States on a major accelerator project, might be to explore the possibility of the U.S. funding and equipping an experimental area at the storage rings of the Centre Européen pour Recherche Nucléaire (CERN), which are now approved as an adjunct to the CERN proton synchrotron. U.S. participation in research with the CERN storage rings would keep American physicists in the forefront of this area, which is particularly important for achieving interaction energies higher than those to be provided by a 1,000 Bev accelerator. Certainly U.S. scientists will, at the least, be highly interested in preparing special experiments for this facility for which instrumentation may be shipped to Europe. In a reciprocal arrangement, perhaps we could offer similar opportunities to CERN at the Stanford Linear Accelerator Center, at the proposed 3 Bev high-energy electron-positron storage ring or, at a later date, at the proposed 200 Bev Accelerator. Arrangements such as these would provide for fuller exploitation of these facilities as well as provide CERN scientists with an excellent opportunity for preparing for research with their proposed higher energy scientific device for Western Europe.

Biological Control of Insect Pests

Sterilization of insects by exposure to radiation with subsequent release of the sterile insects to achieve control of reproduction has proved practical for controlling two types of insects: the screwworm, a serious pest of livestock, and tropical fruit flies, such as the Mediterranean fruit fly, melon fruit fly, and oriental fruit fly. Research is in progress on the possibility of the development of practical ways to aid in the control of the following insects by use of the sterility principle: codling moth, tobacco hornworm, pink bollworm, boll weevil, tsetse fly, cattle warble fly, coffee leaf miner, cereal leaf beetle, and sugar cane borer.

Two general approaches to achieve sterility in insects for release are being investigated. One involves the use of gamma irradiation; the other certain synthetic organic chemicals.

Another line of research underway involves the evaluation of gamma radiation as a means for destroying insect infestations in fruit and vegetable products, to meet quarantine requirements without the possible hazard of toxic insecticide residues.

The joint IAEA/Food and Agriculture Organization program has been concentrated on flies, especially the Mediterranean fruit fly, the olive fly, and, more recently, the tsetse fly. A large-scale project was initiated this year in Central America to demonstrate that the eradication of the Mediterranean fruit fly is scientifically and economically feasible.

We are aware that both in the United States and abroad long, complicated, and costly research is necessary before a field attack on any particular insect can be launched. We believe, however, that in view of the deleterious effects of some insects on man and his environment, research on the biological control of these pests should not only be continued but expanded. Since international action is required for the eradication of some insect pests, the work now underway in this field by the IAEA and FAO should be encouraged.

Food Preservation

The U.S. Government program using radiation for preservation of food is now entering into the development of economic processes after its initial emphasis on research. While this developing technology is not past the pilot plant stage, possible applications of practical value are beginning to appear and to attract financial support. Within a year or two the Army plans to begin procurement of sterilized bacon and shortly thereafter a series of commercial developments should be initiated. Because of the need to obtain clearances by the Food and Drug Administration item by item (or at least by class of item), individual foods will be ready for the market at widely different times.

The IAEA, FAO, World Health Organization, and the Organization for Economic Cooperation and Development have sponsored activities in the field of food preservation by radiation. Also, national programs in various parts of the world, e.g., Venezuela, Austria, Israel, and Japan, have developed a considerable knowledge in this field of activity. Two promising applications include the irradiation of mangoes, one of the world's most common fruits, for control of seed weevil and the irradiation of papayas for shelf-life extension. Another promising product is the banana. Based upon limited data, an extremely low and economical radiation dose will delay the ripening process and double the shelf-life.

In view of the existing international interest and the vitality of national programs, we believe the United States should stand ready to extend the benefits of knowledge already available and being developed for applications to other countries. The United States, for example, could provide support for research and development, equipment, aid in the establishment of pilot plants to demonstrate the feasibility of the process, and encourage and support the standardization of wholesomeness regulations. The work presently underway in the various international organizations should be continued. Greater emphasis should be given to the exchange of information on the economics of food handling, since such data are the basis for the development of any sound food preservation program.

Plowshare Program

The Plowshare Program (AEC's program to develop uses for nuclear explosives) presents both problems and promise. Most interest has been shown to date in nuclear excavation. If complications relating to the Limited Test Ban Treaty can be resolved there are a number of international cooperative projects that might be undertaken in this area. In addition, nuclear explosives might be used in a number of peaceful underground engineering and scientific applications not complicated by Treaty limitations. For example, contained nuclear explosions might be used for copper leaching, mining by block-caving, gas and oil recovery, underground storage, and water resource development. Scientific applications include geophysical studies, neutron physics measurements, and the production of heavy elements.

Pending the solution of the present political and experimental problems in excavation and the actual execution of a practical underground engineering project, it might still be advisable to examine possible cooperative projects with other nations to determine their feasibility. Advantages of such an examination would be to obtain: (1) a clearer assessment in specific cases of the economic feasibility of the various applications, (2) the definition of research problems which would need attention, and (3) the development of wider understanding of this program. This latter advantage might be particularly desirable in Latin America, where the possible use of nuclear excavation is being considered for construction of a sea-level canal.

Health and Safety

Health and safety play a two-fold role in the international development of uses of nuclear energy. Uses in individual countries must be under conditions that gain and hold public confidence, while international commerce is highly dependent upon mutually acceptable standards of health and safety, both in commercial products and in their transport.

The IAEA has, through its publications and convening of panels and symposia, aided in the development of international health and safety standards. The United States has greatly assisted these efforts and should continue to do so. For example, recognizing that radioactive and fissile materials must be safely packaged and handled under standards acceptable to the states through which they move, the IAEA began the development of international regulations for the safe transport of such materials in 1959. Building on regulations adopted by the U. S. Interstate Commerce Commission about 1946, the Agency developed by 1961 procedures for handling and criteria for packaging large quantities of radioactive and fissile materials. Work on criteria for the packaging of irradiated fuels is continuing with active support by U.S. participants. The United States should, of course, support and participate in the panel that is being formed for further review of existing Agency regulations and consideration of suggested amendments.

The IAEA, in cooperation with WHO, International Labor Organization, and the European Nuclear Energy Agency, is initiating a study looking to the development of international standards for the use of radioactive materials in consumer products. We note with pleasure that the first phase of the study will be conducted by a consultant provided by the United States.

Injuries or fatalities may occur from the misuse of radioisotopes. Fortunately, to date such incidents have been relatively rare. In view, however, of the growing uses of radioisotopes in medicine, industry, and agriculture, we believe that the IAEA should be encouraged to explore further means of reducing potential health and safety risks from international commerce in radioisotopes.

The IAEA has carried on an extensive program on technical assistance to states engaged in the development of uses of nuclear energy, ranging from the conduct of small research programs to evaluation of reactor hazards and of procedures for the disposal of radioactive wastes. The United States should continue to participate extensively in these activities.

The mining of uranium is associated with an increased risk of lung cancer in underground miners. While techniques are available for evaluating the conditions creating the risk and some advances have been made in early recognition of the disease, more extensive epidemiological data on miners are required. The United States is one of the first countries to assemble modern epidemiological data on this subject; these data would acquire much greater significance if extended and compared with similar data from other countries.

We understand that all uranium producing countries recognize this problem, but the number of uranium miners in any one country is small. We believe that a carefully planned international study of this problem could advance knowledge of how best to control the hazard much more rapidly than were each country to go its own way, and could serve as a model for the development of international standards for control of other potential dangers in the nuclear energy field.

Assistance in the Event of a Nuclear Accident

Many countries with atomic energy programs are not equipped or might not be prepared to handle an accident involving a serious radiation hazard or damage.

The IAEA has taken the initiative in drafting and attempting to obtain agreement among its member states on general arrangements (administrative, legal, and financial) under which emergency assistance by the IAEA and among the member states can be provided as soon as possible. The Agency has entered into an agreement with the Scandinavian countries which is similar to these general arrangements. The United States has agreed in principle to support a worldwide arrangement and is participating in the Agency's work toward this end.

In the meantime, the United States should stand ready to render any assistance that might be required in the event of an accident. The IAEA has prepared lists of what assistance is available from member states, including the United States, and has circulated this information to all members.

Nuclear Data Standards

With the growing worldwide activity in nuclear science, there is an increasing need for expanded activity in nuclear data standards. While a great deal of nuclear standards work is carried on in the AEC's National Laboratories and the National Bureau of Standards, and at the International Bureau of Weights and Measures at Sèvres, France, there is a definite and growing role to be played by the IAEA in this field.

To date, two committees of experts have been established to foster cooperation in the measurement of nuclear data and information exchange. One of the committees is the European-American Nuclear Data Committee (EANDC), which operates under the auspices of the Organization for European Cooperation and Development; the other is the International Nuclear Data Scientific Working Group (INDSWG), which operates under the auspices of the IAEA. Because of the need for comparison of measurements and absolute measurements, the need for nuclear standards of reference will increase, as will the activities of these data committees.

The IAEA is the natural international agency to carry a major responsibility in the standards field. Because a small but significant role is already being played by the International Bureau in Sèvres, the activities undertaken by the IAEA should be coordinated with that Bureau.

The problems of standarization in the nuclear data program are difficult and numerous. The Agency could specify and develop an area within the standardization program and make the required measurements at its laboratory in Seibersdorf. This, however, would involve a commitment in capital and operating funds which may be too great at the present state of the Agency's development. The IAEA, assisted by its international nuclear data committee, however, should be able to foster such measurements in a number of countries and provide a meeting ground for comparison of measurements and methods.

RECOMMENDATIONS

We make the following recommendations:

International Safeguards

1. That the United States continue to press for the universal adoption of IAEA safeguards and be prepared to place an increasing number of its civil applications involving nuclear reactors and related fuel processing and reprocessing installations under IAEA safeguards as other nations reciprocate.

2. That the U.S. Government increase its efforts to persuade all other suppliers of nuclear assistance (raw materials and equipment) to insist on acceptance of IAEA safeguards as a condition of such assistance.

3. That the IAEA bear the cost of all inspections.

4. That the appropriate agencies of the U.S. Government urge American labor and industry to support the safeguards program strongly, both nationally and internationally. Through the efforts of American industry and labor, a better understanding of safeguards can be achieved at home and abroad.

5. That the U.S. Government, industry, and labor try continually to develop features in the equipment and operational procedures to improve the effectiveness, and ultimately to lessen the costs, of safeguards.

6. That the Department of State give appropriate recognition to international safeguards as an element of foreign policy by assuring participation at the highest level of officials in the implementation of the program.

Nuclear Power

7. That the United States continue to share civil nuclear technology with other nations in the spirit of the Atoms for Peace Program and that these programs of technical cooperation be conducted

in a manner which will encourage and assure that others also share the results of their research and development efforts.

8. That the established policy of offering materials and services under terms which do not discriminate between foreign and domestic users be continued.

9. That increased attention be given to international cooperation toward wider use of radioisotope power sources for special applications such as remote weather stations and harbor buoys and in medical applications such as radioisotope powered cardiac pacemakers.

Desalting Water

10. That the United States press vigorously in acquiring and sharing experience in all areas of water resource technology, including nuclear desalting.

11. That in situations where nuclear energy is utilized, the United States continue to insist that international safeguards be a requirement for the construction of the facility outside the United States.

12. That in view of the importance of acceptance of IAEA safeguards, the United States consider placing under Agency inspection nuclear plants which are used for desalting.

13. That training programs for interested foreign scientists and technicians be designed to equip them to evaluate and solve their own national water resource problems.

High-Energy Physics

14. That the United States press forward with its High-Energy Physics Program because of its scientific importance and because of the need to maintain leadership in this field.

15. That the United States investigate the possibility of additional long-term exchanges in the field of high-energy physics with the Soviet Union through which U.S. scientists would be allowed to perform research with the Soviet Serpukov 70 Bev Accelerator, expected to become operational in 1967.

16. That the United States take the steps necessary to provide for

further cooperation with CERN by appropriate fiscal arrangements to provide for use of new facilities under development at CERN.

Biological Control of Insect Pests

17. That research in the United States on the biological control of insect pests, including the use of radiation, be continued and expanded.
18. That the United States urge the IAEA and the FAO to expand their efforts in the control of economically and medically important insect pests.

Food Preservation

19. That the United States express readiness to assist other countries in establishing cooperative programs in the field of radiation preservation of food by making available equipment and technical advice.
20. That the United States propose that the IAEA and the FAO consider greater exchange of information on the economics of food handling (food spoilage, distribution problems, etc.).

Plowshare

21. That, while it is premature to make a positive recommendation for a specific cooperative project, it is appropriate for the United States to continue research and development and studies of possible Plowshare projects.

Health and Safety

22. A. That the United States encourage the development by the appropriate international organizations of health and safety standards governing the many and varied applications of atomic energy.
B. That in this development U.S. representatives to these international organizations make every effort to ensure that the recommendations of the various organizations are in accord with each other.

23. That the United States actively participate in the IAEA program of periodic review and further development of international transportation regulations.

24. That the United States facilitate its own participation in international commerce by closely following international developments with appropriate amendments to its own transportation regulations.

25. That the United States continue to make available to the IAEA its own services, both in the development of standards and in the evaluation of hazards associated with the siting and operation of proposed reactors.

26. That the United States urge the IAEA to encourage member nations to supplement U.S. epidemiological studies of the biological hazards of exposure to high concentrations of radioactive decay products of radon in uranium mining.

27. That the United States press vigorously the further development of criteria for radiological protection.

Assistance in the Event of a Nuclear Accident

28. That the United States support an IAEA international arrangement on assistance in the event of a nuclear accident involving a serious radiation hazard or damage.

Nuclear Data Standards

29. That the United States propose that the IAEA play an active role in cooperation with the International Bureau of Weights and Measures in coordinating measurements on nuclear data and in providing for the comparison of methods of measurements.

THE COMMITTEE ON THE PEACEFUL
USES OF ATOMIC ENERGY

15. *"Doing Something" about the Weather*

Despite the world's most advanced weather service, our nation each year suffers catastrophic losses of life and property as a result of weather calamities. Hurricanes, tornadoes, hail, floods, drought, and frost exact an annual toll amounting to billions of dollars and hundreds of lives. Other nations of the world also suffer heavy losses of life and property from extreme weather.

The impact of the day-to-day, week-to-week, and month-to-month variabilities of the weather on our normal economic life is much more subtle but no less profound. The weather determines when the farmer should plant, when he should fertilize, when he should spray, and when he should harvest. The weather affects our construction industry. It affects the management of our water resources. It affects air and sea transportation. Flights and voyages are delayed, diverted, and even canceled because of the weather. The needs of our cities and towns for fuel and power are directly related to weather conditions. The weather affects retailing. It affects recreation. Its pervasive influence is felt by all of us in our daily lives. Similarly, the economies of other nations are influenced by the weather. Among the developing nations, the weather exercises a profound influence on agricultural activities that are vital to economic survival.

Because the safety, the well-being, and the economic livelihood of the peoples of the world depend so intimately on the weather, the problems of describing, understanding, predicting, and—perhaps one day—controlling the weather are taking on new dimensions of urgency and importance that are challenging the best minds of our times and generating a fresh desire and willingness to cooperate among the nations of the world. Moreover, the tools and techniques appear to be at hand for an all-out assault on these problems—with the promise not only of success in helping man to live in better harmony with his natural environment, but also of uniting the diverse nations and peoples of the world in a common scientific endeavor that can be exciting and that can yield significant economic and social benefits.

Past Achievements

Notable progress has been made over the past twenty years in transforming meteorology from an art to a science. With respect to the large-scale processes which determine our weather, these advances have proceeded along three distinct but interrelated lines:

Observational. With the perfection of the radiosonde, a device that enables us to probe the temperature, pressure, and the winds of the upper atmosphere, it has been possible to develop an observational network that permits identification of the large-scale features of the atmosphere.

Theoretical. From the insight into the characteristics of the actual atmosphere that was provided by this observing network, it has been possible to extend our scientific understanding of the theory of large-scale air motions and then to construct more comprehensive mathematical models of worldwide weather currents.

Computational. With the development of the high-speed electronic computer, it has been possible to process and analyze the data provided by our upper air network. Equally important, the electronic computer has permitted the theoretician to "experiment" with his mathematical models which simulate and attempt to predict the actual behavior of the atmosphere. In this way he was able to test his hypotheses and refine our scientific understanding of the atmosphere. The computer has opened up new areas of discovery in our search for an understanding of the processes of the weather.

Out of the scientific work in meteorology during the past twenty years has come a growing awareness that the atmosphere is a single physical system—a gaseous envelope encircling the earth—whose behavior is a consequence of the interactions of all of its parts with each other, with the land and water below, and with the solar system beyond. An understanding of the processes of any one part of the atmosphere is directly dependent upon an ability to observe and to understand the entire physical system. The problem is global, not local. Atmospheric disturbances over one area are propagated around the world within a week or two. Weather forecasts for more than three or four days into the future require global observations.

The largest single obstacle that faces us in seeking a scientific understanding of the general circulation of the global atmosphere, and in developing a capability in long-range weather prediction, is the lack of adequate weather data over the entire globe. Currently, we obtain adequate weather data over less than 20 per cent of the earth. The remaining 80 per cent, mostly over the oceans, remains inaccessible except for scattered and inadequate observation stations. Our present computers, our present mathematical procedures for the creation of models of the atmosphere, and our present scientific understanding of the dynamic processes of the atmosphere are still imperfect. But they are sufficiently advanced that if the data needed about the globe's atmosphere can be acquired, an understanding of the general circulation and entirely new capabilities in long-range weather prediction are within reach.

The development of the meteorological satellite now gives us a new and revolutionary tool with which to overcome this obstacle. The meteorological satellite is still in its infancy. We are a long way from realizing its full benefits. But for the first time we have a platform with the potential ability to observe and collect comprehensive data about the atmosphere of the entire globe every day.

The Development of International Cooperation

The atmosphere is global and indivisible. Its movement knows no national boundaries. What happens in the atmosphere over one nation affects the atmosphere in distant parts of the world.

No single nation can observe and collect comprehensive data about the atmosphere everywhere over the globe. The nations of the world must have each other's weather data to help provide early warnings of weather hazards, to further the safety and efficiency of international air and sea transportation, and to promote agriculture, commerce, and industry within their own borders. This need has led to close international cooperation in weather matters.

International cooperation in meteorology had its beginning in the middle of the seventeenth century. In 1654 the Florentine Academy of Science established a network of stations in ten European cities to make and report weather observations. While the network worked under crude conditions, it was the first international network. It lasted until 1667.

Over the next 200 years, there were other attempts to establish and maintain an international network of weather stations. Perhaps the most notable was the network established in 1780 by the Mannheim Meteorological Society. It comprised thirty-nine weather stations stretching from Siberia to Massachusetts and from Greenland to the Mediterranean, and all observations were taken pursuant to uniform instructions and with standardized instruments. The most important contribution of the Society was the publication of twelve uniform volumes of extensive weather data for the years 1781–1792.

The middle of the nineteenth century saw the first modern international cooperative effort in meteorology. In 1853 the Brussels Maritime Congress met, and an agreement was reached among the maritime nations to make regular observations of ocean weather from merchant vessels and to exchange these observations both in peace and war. The success of the Brussels Congress led to the convening of an International Meteorological Conference in 1872 and, a year later, of an International Meteorological Congress. These meetings led to the formation in 1873 of the International Meteorological Organization. Its membership was primarily European (the United States was also a member), and it continued until 1951. It devoted itself to the planning of networks to observe the surface weather and the upper air, to the standardization of meteorological instruments and techniques, and to the planning of special projects such as the International Polar Year Expeditions of 1882–83 and 1932–33.

In 1951 the World Meteorological Organization (WMO) superseded the International Meteorological Organization. WMO is a specialized agency of the United Nations. Its membership is global. Today it comprises 126 nations. WMO provides a forum within which these nations can meet to coordinate their meteorological activities and to plan improvements in their meteorological services. It also provides training assistance in meteorology to the developing countries, prescribes schedules for the observation of weather and for the international dissemination of weather data, and establishes standards for meteorological equipment.

Meanwhile, cooperation among the world's atmospheric scientists has been actively fostered by several non-governmental scientific societies—the International Association of Meteorology and Atmospheric Physics, the International Union of Geodesy and Geophysics, and the International Council of Scientific Unions (ICSU). The last-named served as the coordinating body for the remarkably successful International Geophysical Year, which contributed notably to a better understanding of the atmosphere.

The World Weather Watch

On September 25, 1961, in his address to the United Nations, President Kennedy advanced a program for the peaceful use of outer space. As one part of this program, he stated that the United States "would propose cooperative efforts between all nations in weather prediction and eventually in weather control."

On December 20, 1961, the United Nations, by resolution, called upon the WMO, in consultation with the United Nations Educational, Scientific, and Cultural Organization (UNESCO) and ICSU, to develop measures to improve weather forecasting capabilities, to advance our knowledge of the basic physical forces that affect climate, and to determine the possibility of a large-scale weather modification.

WMO responded with the concept of a World Weather Watch. It would be a cooperative effort among the nations of the world to build a new international system for the complete surveillance of the global atmosphere and for the rapid dissemination of worldwide weather data. The Watch would rest on modern technology—such as the satellite, the electronic computer, and high-speed communications systems—as well as on the traditional technology of meteorology.

On December 14, 1962, by a further resolution, the United Nations recommended that WMO develop the concept of a World Weather Watch in greater detail. It also invited ICSU to develop an expanded program of research in the atmospheric sciences to complement the Watch.

Since then the plan for a World Weather Watch has been under active development by WMO in consultation with its member states and their academies of science. Our own National Academy of Sciences has made a notable contribution to the effort.

The United States has repledged its participation in the work of developing a World Weather Watch. On June 10, 1964, in a commencement address at Holy Cross College, President Johnson stated that "we will move ahead with plans to devise a worldwide weather system—using the satellites and facilities of all industrialized countries. The Space Age has given us unparalleled capacity to predict the course of weather. By working together, on a global basis, we can take new strides toward coping with historic enemies of storm and drought and flood."

On October 23, 1964, the President requested the Secretary of

Commerce to bring the Federal departments and agencies that are concerned with international meteorological programs into closer consultation and coordination. The Interagency Committee for International Meteorological Programs (ICIMP) was formed in response to this request. Through ICIMP the Federal departments and agencies are now formulating detailed plans for the U.S. participation in the World Weather Watch. Scientific advice for the research program has been provided by a special panel of the Committee on Atmospheric Sciences of the National Academy of Sciences.

Future Goals

Modern technology has given us new platforms from which to observe the globe's atmosphere. While the most notable is the meteorological satellite, it is not alone. We also have ocean buoys and horizontal sounding balloons. These platforms are still under development, but they give us the opportunity—for the first time—to collect reasonably complete data concerning the global atmosphere and the interactions between the atmosphere and the underlying ocean and earth surface.

We must now bring these platforms into full development. We must also develop the necessary sensing devices to be placed on these platforms. And we must apply our communications technology to help establish an international system for the timely worldwide dissemination of atmospheric data.

When this new technology is developed, we must collect on a timely basis data that will be responsive to the needs of the scientists seeking an understanding of the general circulation of the global atmosphere and to the needs of the daily operations of the weather services of the nations of the world. While new technology is under development, we must put the data of the global atmosphere that become immediately available, however incomplete, to rapid use in improving the present daily weather services of the nations of the world.

A practical goal is to develop a capability in long-range weather prediction. Recent studies have shown that extensions of daily weather predictions for a period of up to two weeks ahead is a sound scientific possibility. An important prerequisite is a scientific understanding of the general circulation of the atmosphere. We must support and pursue the research program, rich with scientific opportunities, that will give us this understanding.

Further ahead is the scientific exploration of the possibilities and the practical limitations of large-scale weather modification. Fundamental to the study of modifying or diverting hurricanes and altering climate over large areas is an understanding of the physical basis of climate—which implies once again a scientific understanding of the general circulation of the atmosphere.

If these scientific and technological goals can be achieved, the benefits to mankind will be immense.

The ability to provide reliable daily weather predictions for a period of up to two weeks ahead would constitute a very significant achievement of modern science and technology. It would permit agriculture to determine more intelligently when it would be best to plant, fertilize, spray, and harvest crops. It would permit substantial improvement in water management practices. These benefits would be particularly felt by the emerging nations, whose economies are primarily agricultural (and sometimes dependent on only one or two crops) and whose weather services are now poorly developed.

The ability to make reliable long-range weather predictions would bring other important benefits. It would permit more accurate and more timely warnings of severe storms and other weather hazards—and thus help save lives and property. It would permit better weather services to air and marine transportation—and thereby help limit the disruption of transportation schedules and enable flights and voyages to be routed for safety, comfort, and speed of travel. It would assist the planning of outdoor construction and many industrial activities.

The benefits that the peoples of the world would derive if the ability to modify and control weather on a large scale can be developed are even more significant. It we can learn how to dissipate hurricanes and other severe storms, we can prevent the immense destruction of property and the serious loss of life that these storms so frequently cause. If we can provide certain areas of the world with even slight increases in rainfall or small changes in average temperature, we can make a viable agricultural economy possible where it was impossible before.

Finally, unity of purpose and effort in deepening and strengthening our understanding of the global atmosphere—and in developing the applications of that knowledge for the benefit of mankind—

would contribute to improved understanding among nations and peoples.

How to Achieve the Goals

The goals and benefits that have been outlined in the preceding section can be effectively achieved through two programs. One is a World Weather Watch, which has been proposed by the World Meteorological Organization. The other is a research program to achieve a scientific understanding of the general circulation of the global atmosphere.

The World Weather Watch: General

The World Weather Watch will be a system for observing, processing, and disseminating global weather data adequate to meet the needs of atmospheric scientists engaged in general circulation research and to meet the operational needs of the weather services of the nations of the world. It will differ from the present international weather system in two primary respects. It will be truly global, and it will systematically exploit new developments in space technology, in communications, in data processing, and in meteorological instrumentation.

The World Weather Watch will have to provide adequate data to support both general circulation research and operational weather forecasting. There are many similarities in the data requirements of the research and operational communities. Both require observations of the same basic set of parameters—temperature, humidity, and wind velocity from the surface to 100,000 feet—and these observations must be made on a global scale. For general circulation research, however, many key objectives can be achieved with a single set of data covering a period of a few months. The operational services require a continuing flow of data.

To meet the primary needs of general circulation research, it will be essential to establish a global observing experiment comprising a dense network of observing stations and platforms over the entire globe that can gather a complete set of data about the global atmosphere for a period of a few months. To meet the needs of operational weather forecasting, a complete system, including the capability to communicate and process data rapidly, will have to be established. It, too, will cover the entire globe. But while the observing network of this system must be sufficiently dense to meet the needs of the weather services of the nations of the world for global weather data, it will be less dense than the network required by a global observing experiment.

Both a global observing experiment and a complete global observing network for operational weather forecasting are essential. The sequence in which they are instituted will depend on the speed with which we develop new technology and on the cost of its deployment. We should move ahead with improvements in the existing international weather system and with the development of new technology. This work comprises two broad, continuous, and parallel streams of action.

The first stream will be a process of introducing into the existing international weather system proven equipment, techniques, and procedures that are designated to help meet established requirements of the system. The existing international weather system is quite extensive—the result of about a century of gradually expanding international cooperation in weather matters. In the existing system, the nations of the world exchange raw observational data and weather analyses and forecasts covering many parts of the globe. All the nations benefit from this cooperation. The existing system can be improved now with proven technology. This is the purpose of the first stream.

The second stream will be a continuous process of research and development that seeks to add to the total store of proven technology. The second stream will, for example, be concerned with the further development of the meteorological satellite, horizontal sounding balloons, automatic meteorological ocean buoys, the communications satellite, mathematical procedures for the creation of models of the atmosphere, and the high-speed electronic computer. As the second stream makes new technological advances, it will feed them into the first stream and into the global observing experiment.

The World Weather Watch: First Stream

The initial phase of the first stream should seek to achieve three significant improvements in the existing international weather system by 1971.

First, it should seek to improve the ability of the system to observe the global atmosphere and to provide fuller data for weather forecasting. This improvement could rest in part on the Tiros Operational Satellite System and the satellite systems of other nations.

The United States will launch the Tiros Operational Satellite System into orbit in early 1966. With the Tiros we will be able to observe the clouds everywhere in the globe's atmosphere each day on a routine basis. The improvement could also rest on an increase in conventional facilities for observing the atmosphere, notably in the tropics and in the Southern Hemisphere, and on an increase in meteorological observations over the oceans from merchant vessels.

Second, it should seek to extend the benefits of modern computer technology throughout the globe. World Meteorological Centers have now been established in Washington and Moscow, and a third will be established in Melbourne. In addition, there will be a number of Regional Meteorological Centers. Through the computer facilities of these centers, meteorological charts and analyses could be prepared routinely for the entire globe. These charts and analyses would particularly benefit the less-developed nations, who have no computer technology of their own.

Third, it should seek to develop an international communications network for the timely exchange of raw data and for the timely dissemination of weather analyses and forecasts. This network should consist of a communications trunk linking the three World Meteorological Centers and a number of regional communications centers. The specific objectives of the initial phase of the first stream are presently under study by WMO, and final proposals will be considered at the next WMO Congress in 1967.

The World Weather Watch: Second Stream

The second stream will pursue the work of research and development on new technology while the first stream is seeking to improve the existing international weather system. The goal of the second stream should be to bring the new technology to operational status in the early 1970's so that it can then be fed into the first stream.

The second stream is essential if we are to observe, communicate, and process global weather data—for both general circulation research and operational weather forecasting—most effectively and economically. It permits us to develop new technology that can perform the same job as proven technology but at less cost.

Historically, the most costly function of any weather system is its observing function. This will be particularly true for a global system. We have some preliminary estimates of the annual cost to the nations of the world—over and above the costs of their present weather services—of operating a World Weather Watch. With proven technology, it will be about $200 million; with new technology, less than $100 million. If we mix proven and new technology, the cost will be somewhere between. We also have some preliminary cost estimates for a global observing experiment. With proven technology, it will be about $300 million; with new technology, about $100 million. Again, if we mix proven and new technology, the cost will be somewhere between.

These preliminary estimates suggest the significant role that new technology can play in reducing the costs of operating a weather system. As the second stream brings new technological advances into full development, we shall have to determine their cost of performance in determining their final role in the World Weather Watch.

The new technology on which the second stream is focusing is truly exciting. One new observing platform—now in an early stage of development—is the horizontal sounding balloon. It is a relatively small, lightweight, super-pressure balloon that moves at a fairly constant altitude. The balloons will carry sensors that measure the temperature, pressure, and humidity. Their position will be located periodically by instruments on satellites, and this information will permit us to determine the direction and speed of the wind at several levels over otherwise inaccessible places. Another platform—now in an intermediate stage of development—is the ocean buoy. It will provide surface weather and possibly atmospheric sounding data for ocean areas that are now only sparsely covered.

The satellite has many uses. It can observe the atmosphere with its own cameras and sensors. It can collect data by interrogating horizontal sounding balloons, ocean buoys, and remote land stations and can communicate these data to processing centers. It can disseminate weather analyses and forecasts over the world.

The satellite is not yet fully developed for all these uses. The satellite device for locating and interrogating other platforms is now under development. Devices to be placed in a satellite for sensing the vertical distribution of the temperature and humidity of the atmosphere are also under development. They include the spectrometer and the interferometer, now in an intermediate stage of development, and the microwave radiometer and the laser, now in a very early stage of development. We must also develop the equipment and techniques necessary to utilize the communications satellite in the work of the World Weather Watch.

The computer plays an integral role in an international weather system. As we collect new types of data about the global atmosphere with our new observing platforms and our new sensing devices, we must develop new data processing techniques to handle them. And as we increase our scientific understanding of the general circulation of the atmosphere, we must incorporate the new findings into the mathematical models which we have created on our computers for operational weather forecasting.

The General Circulation Research Program

The introduction of both proven and new technology into the international weather system is important. But the most far-reaching improvements in operational weather forecasting will come only with a scientific understanding of the general circulation of the globe's atmosphere. Moreover, this same understanding is necessary if we are to explore seriously the feasibility of large-scale weather modification and control.

It is now only fifteen years since mathematical models of atmospheric conditions were used as a basis for operational forecasting, and only ten years since the formulation of the first model of the atmosphere's general circulation. Since then our models have grown in complexity, and today they incorporate many of the basic physical processes of the atmosphere. These models are the foundation of modern weather forecasting research. They are also the foundation of the models we use in operational forecasting.

Our scientific work to date in weather prediction has made it evident that our ability to increase the accuracy and the time range of our forecasts is limited by our present network for the acquisition of data about the global atmosphere. Our advances in data processing technology and our understanding of the physical processes of the atmosphere have now reached a point that, if adequate data were available, it would be possible to attack directly the problem of long-range forecasting.

The acquisition of data about the global atmosphere is not the only problem, however. We need to be able to deal quantitatively with condensation processes and other forms of heating and cooling better than we do now. There are some unresolved mathematical questions in connection with the control of truncation error, particularly in regions of strong field and topographic gradient. We must learn more about the nature of the interactions between the atmosphere and its underlying earth and ocean surface and the relationship between these small-scale processes and the large-scale motions of the atmosphere. For these interaction studies, we will need to make detailed observations over a number of limited areas of the globe.

Mathematical models of the general circulation of the atmosphere that incorporate all the physical processes that must be taken into account will be exceedingly complex. Their creation will require electronic computers of higher speed and greater capacity than any we now have—as much as a hundred times faster than today's computers. The most complex mathematical model we use in research today requires eighteen hours of calculation on an IBM Stretch Computer to prepare a forecast for a period of twenty-four hours ahead.

The general circulation research program is a complex program and presents many difficult scientific questions. The nature of these questions and the importance of the program make it imperative that we make every effort to attract scientists of creativity and talent to general circulation research and that we provide for the training of young new scientists so that they may enter this field.

Managing and Financing the World Weather Watch

The World Weather Watch will be a global undertaking involving all the nations of the world. At the same time it will be an integrated system, and many of its parts will have to be managed by an international institution. According to present estimates, the establishment and operation of the Watch will cost more than a hundred million dollars each year. It is imperative that the United States, in concert with the other nations of the world, develop international arrangements under which the Watch can best be established and operated as well as a plan for the financing of the Watch.

The World Weather Watch can one day bring vast new social, economic, and political benefits to the peoples of the world. It is incumbent upon the nations of the world that they reach an accord relatively quickly on these matters.

RECOMMENDATIONS

We recommend that the United States commit itself to a new dimension of international cooperation in meteorology, which shall have as its goals:

1. The development of a global weather observing and forecasting system—the World Weather Watch—incorporating advances in instrumentation, space technology, computers, and communications in a manner responsive to the scientific and technological imperative of treating the world atmosphere as a single physical system.
2. A deepened and strengthened understanding of the forces and the influences that determine the course and the changes of worldwide air currents—the general circulation of the atmosphere.
3. The development of the mathematical techniques for forecasting the weather two weeks or more into the future to meet the human and economic needs of our own citizens and the peoples of other nations.
4. The exploration of the scientific possibilities and the practical limitations of modifying the climate over large areas as our knowledge of the physical basis of climate is extended.

To achieve these objectives, we recommend that:

1. The United States participate actively in the planning, design, development, and operation of the World Weather Watch and utilize its vast technological resources in this work.
2. The United States exercise a role of leadership in an international program of research in which specialized observational programs on a worldwide basis proceed hand-in-hand with theoretical studies aimed at understanding the general circulation of the global atmosphere and at converting this understanding into new techniques of long-range weather forecasting.
3. The United States, in concert with other nations, develop the scientific and professional manpower, the institutional arrangements, and the financial support to bring the World Weather Watch and its associated research program into being.

THE COMMITTEE ON METEOROLOGY

16. *Meeting Other Challenges*

Agriculture and Food

International cooperation in food and agriculture should be directed toward no lesser goal than the elimination of hunger in the world. The U.S. Food for Peace program has contributed to the alleviation of hunger and to the promotion of economic development. More than one-fourth of total free world government assistance and nearly all of food aid to the less-developed countries come from the United States.

But food aid alone cannot solve the problem of world hunger. Developing nations look forward to the time when they need no longer be dependent upon assistance but will be able to produce or buy what they need. And the United States would rather sell its products on the commercial market. Even more important from the point of view of the prospective need for food in the years ahead is the fact that, as populations increase and as per capita food demands in the hungry world rise toward minimum nutritional standards, the time is not too far distant when maximum food surpluses from all of the world's food exporting areas would not be able to meet the demand.

Agricultural production in the developing countries themselves must therefore be increased at a rate substantially higher than that which prevails today, and much greater emphasis should be given to international cooperation directed toward that end. While the major effort will have to be made by the developing countries themselves, they will need encouragement and assistance from the developed nations. In the long run the developed nations will themselves reap the benefit of this assistance in the form of increased commercial trade.

We make the following recommendations:

1. That there be greatly increased emphasis on international cooperation directed toward encouraging and assisting the hungry nations to increase their own agricultural production and their ability to process and distribute food. This is not only the major feasible long-run method of meeting future food needs, but it will

337

also contribute substantially to overall economic development and accelerate the rate at which developing countries can achieve economic viability.

2. That food aid be continued and expanded as necessary to help to meet food deficits and to improve nutrition, and that it be directed, wherever possible, to encourage the developing countries to expand and improve their own agriculture. We particularly emphasize the importance of efforts to combat malnutrition of young children in the hungry nations.

3. That the U.S. Government continue its international cooperation with developing nations on a bilateral basis in the fields of agriculture and food; and that it also seek to expand multilateral efforts in these fields and that it encourage participation by private enterprise and voluntary agencies to the maximum extent feasible and appropriate.

4. That there be a major cooperative government and private effort to build public understanding of the importance of international cooperation directed toward solving the problem of hunger in the world.

These recommendations call for a substantial investment of human and physical resources in an effort to reach a goal that we regard as of utmost importance to future progress and peace. We believe that the people of the United States will support that investment and participate enthusiastically in that effort when they understand fully its implications for their own and their children's future.

Aviation

Aviation has served, perhaps more than any other form of transportation and communication, to bring the world community together into common, peaceful programs. In carrying out international activities, the United States is fulfilling its long-standing dedication to the greatest and safest use of aviation for the benefit of the largest possible number of citizens and societies throughout the world.

We make the following recommendations:

1. That the United States develop a dynamic new program to facilitate and encourage the continued growth of international air travel and trade.

Subsections of this recommendation deal specifically with:

a. Facilitation of international air travel and trade
   (1) Preclearance
   (2) Consolidation of inspection procedures
   (3) Simplification of entry/departure documentation requirements
   (4) Visa waivers for visitors
   (5) Modernizing air cargo entry procedures
   (6) Revision of laws relating to airports of entry
b. Elimination of nontariff barriers affecting aviation products
c. Encouraging tourism development
   (1) Expansion of private aircraft tour programs
   (2) Expanded assistance in tourism development
2. That the United States give new emphasis and direction to programs of international cooperation aimed at designing and establishing for the peoples and economies of the world an airways system that will ensure safe, swift, and efficient air commerce and communications between nations.
   Subsections of this recommendation deal with:
   a. systems planning for airways improvements
   b. methods to meet costs of airways systems
   c. common civil/military airways system
   d. utilizing low-cost equipment
   e. utilizing regional international organizations
3. That the United States take the initiative in exploring with other American states a multinational cooperative project to designate, develop, and implement an inter-American skyway connecting the capital cities of the American hemisphere.
4. That the United States undertake to assist other nations in the development or reorientation of their national aviation statutes to provide for comprehensive and effective aircraft accident investigation and accident prevention activities.
5. That the United States reconsider its decision to denounce the Warsaw Convention.
6. That the United States intensify and improve the quality of its international aviation assistance efforts.
   Subsections of this recommendation deal with:
   a. Direction, design, and content of United States assistance programs
   b. Utilizing U.S. personnel skills
   c. Sharing U.S. aviation developmental skills and knowledge

THE COMMITTEE ON AVIATION

Business and Industry

Rapid increases in the extent and complexity of international business activity, coupled with mushrooming changes in industrial technology, are improving the lives of many millions around the world. In turn, the speed with which change is taking place has created many problems, yet unsolved, which impede the economic growth of both the developed and the less-developed countries.

Three problem areas have particular significance because of their importance to the conduct of business internationally and because, although some progress has already been made, greater cooperative efforts are clearly needed to accelerate the pace of improvement. These areas are:

> The Harmonization of Commercial Laws
> The Protection of Industrial Property Rights
> International Engineering Standardization

We should seek ways to facilitate the interchange of goods, technology, and services among nations and to promote the strength of our free enterprise system and the world's economy through better international cooperation—technically, commercially, and legally.

We make the following recommendations:

Harmonization of Commercial Laws

1. That the United States continue and intensify its participation in organizations engaged in unification of law work, and that means be explored for securing the participation of the developing countries in the work of these organizations.
2. That the Departments of State and Commerce review the Uniform Law on International Sale of Goods prepared at The Hague in 1964, identify any changes necessary to meet U.S. business needs, and decide on measures to prevent or limit damage to American traders stemming from possible ratification of the present text by other countries.
3. That the United States ratify the Convention on Service Abroad of Documents, prepared at the 1964 Session of The Hague Conference on Private International Law.
4. That individual lawyers, businessmen and trade and professional groups support and participate in the already-existing programs of the many organizations whose work in the unification of law

field contributes to the harmonization of legal conditions affecting trade and investment.

5. That the United States undertake a program of education and publicity designed to reach our citizens and citizens of all nations, to impress upon them the necessity of achieving an approximation of commercial laws in the interest of promoting international trade and economic development. This can most advantageously be done by the legal and business communities at home and through the commercial officers of the U.S. Foreign Service, with the cooperation of the U.S. Information Agency abroad.

6. That the United States seek to achieve as much uniformity as possible in the tax treaties which it concludes, having regard for the special circumstances of less-developed countries, and to standardize as far as possible the regulations issued thereunder. The Treasury Department is urged to continue its present emphasis on these matters.

7. That the Department of State accelerate its commercial treaty program, endeavor to conclude more such treaties with the less-developed countries, and seek to utilize such treaties as a vehicle for the introduction and implementation of uniform law projects to the extent possible.

8. That the protection afforded unpatented know-how, technical data, and trade secrets be improved and standardized and national requirements governing the licensing of trademarks be simplified, so as to facilitate the flow of technology internationally, free of burdensome governmental regulation. The Departments of Commerce and State should take steps to implement this recommendation through discussions with foreign governments, model laws, and other appropriate measures.

9. That interested Government departments develop a continuing program of coordination of the main efforts already being made to bring about unification of law. Study should be made of the role of U.S. Government agencies in unification work and the possibility reviewed of representation on the Secretary of State's Advisory Committee on International Law of the Department of Commerce with respect to projects affecting business, the Department of Labor with respect to international labor matters, and other agencies as appropriate.

10. That arbitration procedures be unified and modernized in the interest of providing a speedy and inexpensive means of settling business disputes and that ratification of the United Nations Con-

vention on the Recognition and Enforcement of Foreign Arbitral Awards be encouraged. The Department of Commerce should take the lead in instituting the necessary studies and consulting with interested business and professional groups.

11. That the World Bank proposal for a convention on the settlement of investment disputes, including an Arbitration and Conciliation Center, be supported and other means explored for the protection of private investments against arbitrary and unjust treatment.

12. That the area of Federal-state relations be studied with a view to finding a feasible basis on which the United States and other Federal systems of the same type could adhere to international agreements raising a Federal-state problem.

13. That other areas of common agreement be identified so as to facilitate U.S. adherence to international conventions and treaties which promote the international cooperation objectives of this Government, such as the ECS Carnet Convention.

14. That the Department of Commerce step up its program of disseminating information on foreign commercial laws to the American business community, and in addition systematically provide to its commercial officers abroad for circulation to foreign business and legal circles, information on state and Federal developments in the field of business law.

Protection of Industrial Property Rights

1. That the United States re-evaluate, on a continuing basis, its position on and possible participation in the various multilateral agreements in effect or under consideration throughout the world;

2. That the United States solicit the interest and advice of the interested public with regard to our participation in international cooperation in the industrial property rights field;

3. That the United States study the possibility of and, where applicable, promote and arrange informal discussions between countries for:

   a. extending and improving existing and proposed international patent and trademark conventions;

   b. harmonizing and standardizing the domestic laws both in the developed and less-developed countries;

   c. simplifying and improving domestic laws and procedures in the international setting;

   d. encouraging the adoption and maintenance of modern patent and trademark laws and providing workable and effective procedures for protection by all nations taking into account their differing economic bases;

e. developing bilateral and multilateral agreements between industrial property offices designed to facilitate and speed the processing of patent and trademark applications and to eliminate duplicative efforts in the examination of corresponding patent applications filed in more than one country, by the exchange of information, procedures, personnel, etc.;

f. harmonizing and unifying the laws of different countries by international agreements eventually leading to the establishment of both an international patent system and an international trademark system.

4. That the United States cooperate in the study of the feasibility of establishing centralized sources of information concerning patents and trademarks as a service to industrial property offices and to the public.

International Engineering Standardization

1. That those recommendations which apply to international standardization, as set forth in the Report of the Panel on Engineering and Commodity Standards of the Commerce Technical Advisory Board (the LaQue Committee), be considered favorably, particularly as they involve the following major areas:

a. Formation of an officially recognized Standards Institute, responsible for representing the interests of the United States in international standardization.

b. Participation by the U.S. Government, where appropriate, in pointing out the urgency of the problem, recognizing the Institute as a responsible body, and helping assure maximum possible compatibility between international standards and those recognized and used in the United States.

c. Participation by U.S. industry in supporting the activities of the most competent men in international standardization organizations, and in supporting both the Standards Institute and technical societies in their efforts to discharge the responsibilities of the United States in international standardization activities.

2. That a large-scale educational program be undertaken, under the auspices of the above-mentioned Standards Institute, to impress upon members of industry, of the Federal Government, and of trade and standards-making associations the importance of increased activity in the area of international standardization.

3. That a cost-benefit analysis be made immediately, to identify the effects on the economy of this country of participation in international standardization activities.

4. That there be a particular effort made to encourage participation, with assistance from the Federal Government, in standardization activities now starting to evolve in areas such as Latin America, the Far East, and Africa.

THE COMMITTEE ON BUSINESS AND INDUSTRY

Communication

Existing communications systems and technology appear to be adequate for almost any demands which the peoples of the world make upon them. The future technical development of facilities is only a matter of time; and with the long history of International Telecommunication Union cooperation, it can be expected that that organization will be able to accommodate the multilateral use of new technical developments. Continued and expanded participation in the ITU and technical assistance programs is generally recommended.

But advances in telecommunications technology and continued cooperation in helping the developing countries meet their domestic technical needs and in maintaining an efficient international telecommunications system are insufficient.

Whatever telecommunications systems exist or are developed must be used to meet the critical need throughout the world for information, particularly medical, technical, and educational information, which is indispensable to social progress in all areas, especially in the less-developed areas of the world. At the same time, there are sources of information and collections of data capable of satisfying most of the needs for information.

These facts suggest that the present need and opportunity are for a marshalling of information, technology, and communications resources at a source where those who need and seek information may communicate with those who have or can secure the information, and thus permit existing data to be communicated to the nations and individuals that need and can use them. The establishment of an institution or agency to perform this function and systematically to communicate information to those who need it in such fields as medicine, agriculture, and meteorology could have tremendous impact on the peaceful and healthful development of peoples and nations throughout the world.

Accordingly, it is recommended that the United States propose and support the establishment by the United Nations of an agency to act as a world source of knowledge and reference for the collection, communication, and dissemination of all types of information useful for peaceful purposes through the world. It is recommended that this agency should be called the Voice of Peace.

It is at present economically unfeasible to add communications in many places where they are needed. Therefore, part of any successful plan for the dissemination of knowledge is an arrangement to provide communications service at a price even an underprivileged group can afford, plus aid in providing facilities such as communication channels, and radio and television equipment where these are needed.

One of the problems of establishing adequate communications systems is capital. Most developing countries will need assistance in this respect. However, since we are not proposing elaborate networks for these countries but at most some microwave channels, the amount of capital required is not prohibitive, and it is likely that skeleton networks will be started in most places in a matter of a few years in any event. Established aid programs will probably have to provide a large part of the needed funds. Where radios and television sets will be needed in many communities, small factories for assembling these can also be established at a modest cost, and these can serve also as a training ground for technicians and as a source of jobs for trainees once they have been adequately educated.

The Voice of Peace might constitute a training center for volunteers from cooperating countries by offering an opportunity to secure a greater knowledge of their respective fields. It would also create an additional area of international cooperation through the association of participants from many countries and a greater awareness of the needs and opportunities in various areas either participating in or using the facilities of the Voice of Peace.

The Voice of Peace would have immediate value to the peoples of the world and would continue to increase in value, since the facilities to transmit knowledge are now substantial and growing rapidly. One can see the Voice of Peace using satellite voice communications, facsimile, television, and other forms of communication. It is foreseeable that through the years the need will develop for communications to more remote areas. There is the possibility, or probability, of the extension of existing commercial facilities to such areas and of the development of more direct means of communicating information to such areas by various kinds of retransmission, including the possibility of direct satellite broadcasting.

As part of the United States contribution to the Voice of Peace proposal this country could offer to support the Voice of Peace by the creation of schools to train operators of the memory centers, programmers, and other essential personnel. The American Peace Corps could provide volunteers to these schools in order to permit the Peace Corps itself to support the Voice of Peace by providing persons trained in the use of input and output devices for duty throughout the world.

As described here the Voice of Peace is merely a broad initial concept. Once such an undertaking has been initiated and put into context there would undoubtedly develop many areas of international cooperation related to the Voice of Peace, and it is believed that the Voice of Peace would quickly gain almost universal acceptance among the nations of the world. The Voice of Peace would not only be a great contribution to peace and progress throughout the world but would also dramatize the idea of international cooperation for peaceful purposes among all nations. The United States could indicate its desire for international cooperation and could contribute substantially toward peaceful international cooperation by proposing and offering full support to the Voice of Peace as an agency of the United Nations.

THE COMMITTEE ON COMMUNICATION

Disaster Relief

Years ago, news of a disaster reached the United States so slowly that relief measures often were undertaken long after the emergency had passed. Today, advances in travel and communications have greatly accelerated the speed with which help is dispatched. While it took months to organize assistance to Japan following the great earthquake of 1923, U.S. aid was on the scene in Yugoslavia only hours after the Skopje earthquake of 1963.

The U.S. Government since 1812 has provided different kinds of assistance to other lands. Such aid from the United States was somewhat diffuse until 1946, however, when the President established the Advisory Committee on Voluntary Foreign Aid to tie together governmental and private programs in the field. The Advisory Committee is now attached to the Agency for International Development of the State Department.

As the need for a coordinating body with responsibility for direction of U.S. efforts in foreign disaster relief became more apparent, this authority was delegated in 1961 by the Secretary of State to the Administrator of AID, who was charged with funding and operational coordination of emergency disaster relief operations under the Foreign Assistance Act of 1961 as amended, and the Agricultural Trade Development and Assistance Act of 1954 (Public Law 480). Subsequent establishment of the Office of Disaster Relief Coordinator in the AID Office of Material Resources and issuance of the AID Foreign Disaster Emergency Relief Manual in 1964 made it possible to coordinate U.S. Government efforts much more effectively.

U.S. voluntary agencies with active programs in other countries have long participated in disaster relief. They, too, have worked toward a coordinated program. The American Red Cross (a voluntary agency in concept), because of congressional action charging it with certain disaster responsibilities, has a unique position in relation to its role in foreign disasters—it coordinates with both AID and the 104-nation League of Red Cross Societies. Through such coordination, AID is kept informed of actions undertaken by both the American Red Cross and other national Red Cross units.

Thus three principal elements in the United States, the Government, the voluntary agencies, and the Red Cross, have emerged as coordinated channels of U.S. assistance in foreign disasters. The American people, however, have provided the real capability through their continued support of all three, with an increased awareness of the role of the United States in foreign disaster relief and a demonstrated willingness to contribute their money, their time, their talent, and their hearts.

Increased technological capability to assist, however, has not kept pace with the ever-growing threat of population growth, urbanization, industrialization, and other developments which have placed more and more people in the path of catastrophes. Disasters strike all too often in areas that once were sparsely populated. The disaster problem is increasing, instead of lessening.

U.S. participation in international disaster relief has been a true expression of the compassion of the American people for people in distress throughout the world. In 1964 alone, this compassion was translated into deed by the distribution of $22.5 million in assistance to people in forty-one nations who suffered from hunger, disease, and homelessness as the result of some sixty-two catastrophic occurrences or epidemics. This has been made possible by public support of Federal and voluntary agency programs.

Although it has been possible to achieve coordination of efforts to provide assistance to disaster victims in foreign countries, coordination alone is not enough. There is continuing need to improve our response in getting relief supplies to the suffering. Complete, advance intelligence is needed on the characteristics of disaster-prone countries. U.S. Missions abroad need to develop specific disaster plans for mobilization of U.S. relief and its distribution, and such plans must be in keeping with operational plans of the nations involved. Where no such plans exist, the U.S. Mission, and voluntary agencies and U.S. private industry abroad, need to provide in concert with the United Nations appropriate support for efforts to develop indigenous pre-emergency plans, rescue and relief teams, and recovery and rehabilitation programs.

Knowledge and breakthroughs in science, communications, and technology within the United States need to be applied to the solution of international disaster problems. U.S. Government, voluntary agencies, and private industry need rapid intelligence from the disaster scene in order to provide prompt and efficient assistance. And within the United States, actions need to be taken to improve the type of equipment and supplies that are available, to study the feasibility of stockpiling in or near disaster-prone countries, and to work out intricate problems of transportation from supply sources to the country where a disaster has occurred, and from the point of landing to the disaster area.

We make the following recommendations:

1. That pre-disaster planning by U.S. Government missions overseas be directed by the Ambassador. who can deal most effectively with appropriate officials of the government of the country in which the Mission is located.
2. That each U.S. Government Mission develop a pre-disaster plan based on the disaster potential of the country in which it is located and incorporating disaster relief capabilities of the U.S. Government, voluntary agencies, and other U.S. resources in the country.

3. That the United Nations continue its effort in international disaster relief in mobilizing scientific and technical skills and equipment and promoting pre-disaster planning on a national and regional level.

4. That each U.S. Government Mission support appropriate efforts by the United Nations, the League of Red Cross Societies, and the national government to develop indigenous disaster preparedness plans and organizations.

5. That the Office of the Disaster Relief Coordinator develop a repository of information containing U.S. Government, voluntary agency, Red Cross, private industry, and scientific and technical knowledge on disasters. It should also include information on material resources, equipment, communications systems, and new technology that could be utilized in connection with foreign disasters. There should be listed the names and current locations of specialists who could be called upon to assist in appraising disaster-caused needs and recommending both immediate and recovery action.

6. That the U.S. Government and American voluntary agencies stockpile certain basic supplies for which there is recurring demand in disaster situations and that they also consider stockpiling food commodities under Public Law 480, Food for Peace.

7. That the United Nations be urged to provide emergency communications equipment to underdeveloped nations in disaster-prone areas and that consideration be given to assisting such UN action by providing some equipment with AID funds.

8. That the transportation industry be called upon to develop a plan within the United States for swift, coordinated movement of disaster supplies to shipping ports and international airports for transshipment overseas.

9. That U.S. private industry working with U.S. Government agencies use its scientific and technical capabilities to develop compact, lightweight, universally acceptable units, such as shelters, temporary housing, field hospitals, etc., and durable lightweight, weather-resistant packaging and shipping containers for disaster relief supplies.

10. That U.S. Missions accumulate and make available to the Office of the Disaster Coordinator, AID, specific, up-to-date information on local and foreign transportation capabilities which could be utilized in support of U.S. efforts to aid a stricken population.

11. That the Disaster Coordinator, AID, and the U.S. Government

Missions establish a system for rapid clearance of landing and over-flight rights and free entry involved with movement of disaster relief supplies into a disaster area.

12. That endorsement and support be given to any worldwide efforts contributing to the conformity of identification and use of international non-proprietary names for drugs and medicines frequently used in disaster situations and that the World Health Organization of the UN be urged to continue this project.

13. That all pharmaceutical manufacturers spell out dates of manufacture, shipment, or expiration on drugs that are likely to deteriorate in order to eliminate misunderstandings arising from varying numerical date systems.

14. That disaster rehabilitation assistance beyond that given during the emergency and short-run recovery period be multilateral and coordinated through the United Nations. (The UN could act as a clearinghouse for accepting such rehabilitation relief requests and channeling them to those nations which indicate a capability for providing the requested aid.)

15. That through all news media the U.S. public be informed of specific needs created by foreign disasters, the aims of the United States in disaster relief actions and the need for public support of the actions of both the U.S. Government and American voluntary agencies.

16. Recognizing that some types of disasters cannot yet be prevented, predicted, or controlled, the United States and the UN should develop the means for continuously sharing with all interested nations relevant information concerning scientific and technical developments that will alleviate or minimize destructive consequences of disasters.

THE COMMITTEE ON DISASTER RELIEF

Education and Training

President Johnson in his Smithsonian speech on the goals of our participation in educational cooperation with other countries, September 16, 1965, pledged that the United States would play its full role in a new and noble adventure:

First, to assist the education effort of the developing nations and the developing regions.

Second, to help our schools and universities increase their knowledge of the world and the people who inhabit it.

Third, to advance the exchange of students and teachers who travel and work outside their native lands.

Fourth, to increase the free flow of books and ideas and art, of works of science and imagination.

And, fifth, to assemble meetings of men and women from every discipline and every culture to ponder the common problems of mankind.

Our first recommendation is encouragement of American educators to accept assignment abroad. Too few Americans are employed by international organizations active in education. Many Americans encounter serious difficulties in accepting positions overseas.

Measures are urgently needed to assure that (a) American employers make educators available for overseas assignments unless domestic needs are clearly overriding, (b) the individual does not suffer financially or professionally, and (c) service abroad is considered by employers and associates as enhancing the individual's value in related fields of activity at home. Foreign assignments for educators require encouragement also because the experience may enrich their teaching and stimulate the international flow of ideas.

Our second recommendation—White House sponsorship of an international conference on education—would provide an occasion to bring educators from abroad to the United States at a most opportune time. The conference could also bring together a number of organizations that have proposed holding international conferences on specialized questions. The theme of the conference might be the innovating role of education in promoting economic development and world peace.

Our third recommendation—assistance to education in developing countries—calls for a still greater effort by the U.S. Government and by private agencies through bilateral and multilateral channels. It stresses the need to be specific about ways and means to reduce illiteracy and to build or to improve educational systems. The recommendation also calls attention to the importance of adapting aid to the requirements of the particular community.

Federal programs for assisting educational development abroad require longer-term fund commitments. Education rarely produces significant results in a single fiscal year, and for this reason substantial economies result from better programming. We also favor further assistance to science education abroad to stimulate international scientific cooperation and to publicize American achievements.

Our fourth recommendation—augmented opportunities for American educators to teach and study abroad—emphasizes an exchange idea set forth by the President. There is a growing recognition that all teachers need a special appreciation of the educational achievements, problems, and cultures of other societies. Direct experience is a most effective way to gain such understanding. It would also enhance the instruction given by teacher-training institutions in the international field. The student Year Abroad and other direct-experience programs should be strengthened and related more closely to college curricula.

We also would encourage foreign universities to organize their own Study-Abroad programs in the United States. We recognize the desirability of bringing more qualified foreign teachers and professors into American classrooms. An Exchange Peace Corps could perhaps prove useful.

Our fifth recommendation—making Americans more knowledgeable about the world—is predicated on the principle expressed by President Johnson "that the conduct of our foreign policy will advance no faster than the curriculum of our classrooms." We urge augmenting the experimentation under way to enrich curricula at all academic levels for better understanding of other peoples and so that our citizens may participate wisely in the formulation of American foreign policy. There is need to share through additional clearinghouse services curricular and other materials that have been developed recently.

An informed interest in international affairs, supported by up-to-date editions of textbooks, visual aids, and other educational materials describing international developments, U.S. foreign policy, and the contribution of other societies to the modern world, is needed on school and college campuses. We recommend better coordinated and integrated information on the American role, private and public, in international education in order to gain a broad view, detect gaps, and allocate new resources.

We make the following recommendations:

1. That the administrative officers and governing bodies of schools and colleges, with appropriate assistance from the Federal Government and other agencies, adopt policies which will encourage American teachers to accept short-term assignments abroad and

with international organizations, having in mind that in the long run this will greatly enhance American education.

2. That the Government, in connection with the closing of International Cooperation Year, initiate discussions looking toward an international conference on innovations in education.

3. That public and private assistance to raise the educational level of developing countries be materially increased at once, and that the programs be developed in consultation with educational groups in the United States and in developing countries.

4. That the support be provided so that studying and teaching abroad can become a normal part of the professional career of American educators at all levels.

5. That public and private agencies, local, state, and national, at once cooperatively start a program to develop new curricula so that Americans may become better acquainted with world affairs and the other cultures of mankind.

THE COMMITTEE ON EDUCATION AND TRAINING

Health

Unless minimum standards of health are achieved in the developing nations, our own well-being, even our survival, is in jeopardy. Our security is not something that we can provide entirely from within ourselves. Poverty, rising population rates, inadequate nutritional standards, and poor health are linked in their roles as threats to our security.

Along with such self-interest, ethics make it mandatory that an accelerated attack on disease and ill-health begin immediately.

The promotion of health is a distinctive activity, with its own methodology, history, and philosophy, but it is an activity that is closely allied to other policies. Health objectives are reasonably well-defined, but they are such as to require coordinated and associated programs in many other areas. Our goals should be to make this coordination of health with other factors more feasible and more productive.

Although we have looked at the state of the world's health largely in terms of the health professional's traditional preoccupations with disease and its control, it is important to stress that health is inextricably bound with such other factors as poverty, population, and nutrition.

Basic to the improvement of world health are the steps that must be taken to effect an overall rise in standards of living throughout the world. The increasing gap between the rich and the poor, the haves and the have-nots, must be halted, and narrowed. This implies a commitment to programs of economic development, family planning, and the provision of adequate food supplies.

Communicable diseases in general, and, to a lesser and more specific degree, some chronic diseases, still threaten peoples around the world unnecessarily, although known effective control measures are available. This threat, then, does not rest upon our lack of knowledge or our lack of mechanisms to bring this knowledge into play. Most nations in the world have created organizational structures for health affairs, and the attack on disease could begin in many places almost immediately, were it not for one fact: the lack of health and medical manpower. The structures for health administration exist, and are often elaborate; yet some stand nearly empty.

The building of a strong body of health workers in each country of the world is a necessary task. Health interests impinge on other societal needs. Health manpower is not to be found where basic educational efforts are weak or non-existent. But even where basic education is widespread, health workers are in short supply. In order to meet this need, it might be possible for the United States to assist in the establishment of regional training centers in Latin America, Africa, and Asia, through the use of financial resources and educational techniques. Such centers could be staffed by an international team of educators which would include Americans. The centers could be created through a consortium of countries, and financed by joint funds. As an experiment alone, such a scheme would test the usefulness of mass injections of assistance with a definite goal— the creation of health workers—in a way which has not often been tested. As more than experiment, such regional training centers would begin, within a short time, to produce health workers trained in meeting the problems most prevalent in their areas.

Consideration might also be given to an adaptation of the Peace Corps idea to health services, including direct medical care.

A demonstration of U.S. interest in the individual health problems of people of other nations would extend the benefits of the Peace Corps idea more fully into the human and "people-centered" field of health and medicine. Americans, too, would gain a better appreciation of the very real problems of the world's underprivileged majority. Similarly, no field is better than health in which to demonstrate our honest, sincere interests in individual human problems wherever they might exist.

With an increase in the supply of health workers, both indigenous and external, the attack on the communicable and some of the chronic diseases could be stepped up.

In order to strengthen the current efforts of the World Health Organization and other international organizations engaged in disease eradication programs, and to ensure that the full weight of U.S. resources is placed behind these efforts, a U.S. Disease Eradication Authority might be created by the President. Our commitments to the eradication of quarantinable diseases, especially the global eradication of malaria, smallpox, and cholera, are clear, and were restressed with the President's pledge to the WHO to assist fully in the smallpox eradication effort, and in his remarks on other occasions.

This Disease Eradication Authority could also be given the goal of eradication of syphilis, gonorrhea, tuberculosis, and poliomyelitis from the United States, and could use its resources and example to urge other nations to adopt the same goals. The Authority could also consider what other communicable diseases are currently amenable to eradication, and assure that the causative agents of these fully preventable diseases are kept under study with the objective of eventual eradication.

Research into the causes and cures of disease must continue to expand. Gaining more knowledge of health problems cannot be slighted. In this connection, the world center on adverse drug reactions, a mechanism to be established under WHO auspices, with the cooperation of the U.S. Food and Drug Administration, is a good start toward gaining new knowledge in this important area. It is conceivable that this system might serve as the model for the establishment, according to well-defined priorities, of similar systems for the monitoring of environmental contaminants such as pesticide residues, industrial chemicals and wastes, infectious agents, and so forth.

Research, research training, and the development of research tools are well-recognized and generally productive methods of attack upon disease, and there are many ways in which such projects can be realized: the recent decision of WHO to establish an International Agency for Research on Cancer, and the United States–

financed International Centers for Medical Research and Training (ICMRT), are but two examples that come readily to mind.

We make the following recommendations:

1. That the United States increase its commitment to programs of international economic and social development, with special attention given to programs for improvement of nutritional standards and control of population increases.
2. That the United States assign to the Public Health Service an expanded, more activist role in international health affairs.
3. That the United States enlarge its commitment to increasing the world's supply of medical manpower and facilities, including the establishment of regional health training centers in Latin America, Africa, and Asia, the establishment of an International Health Corps, and support of health and medical facility construction programs.
4. That the United States continue to support fully the global disease eradication efforts of the World Health Organization, and take steps toward the creation of a U.S. Disease Eradication Authority.
5. That the United States continue and expand its support of international health research, through the use of its own facilities, and the development of research facilities and potential abroad.
6. That the United States initiate a program of international health education, drawing upon the educational and technological resources of governmental and non-governmental agencies.
7. That the United States support and encourage participation in international health activities among non-governmental and private organizations.

THE COMMITTEE ON HEALTH

Labor

The AFL–CIO has estimated that approximately 25 per cent of its total budget is spent on international activities. Many of its affiliated unions also devote substantial amounts to overseas operations. The international trade union situation today requires that greater effort be made in the developing nations. The American trade union horizon must be expanded to provide firm and effective leadership in a changing world.

In projecting trade union plans and making recommendations in the trade union field, it is essential to bear in mind that wherever free institutions exist and democracy is practiced, there is rapid development and improvement of working conditions. It is only when democratic institutions are strengthened and developed continuously that real and lasting democratic nation building takes place. If this premise is accepted and desired, then it follows that free-trade unions, as democratic institutions, must be strengthened and developed in emerging countries. Free-trade unionism reaches to the very roots of a democratic society while simultaneously reaching and affecting all types of labor-based organizations and auxiliaries.

The prevailing policy of strengthening and developing democratic institutions should be encouraged and protected, not only in the United States, but throughout the world. One of the unfortunate inadequacies today is the lack of an adequate investigative and compliance mechanism for the various International Labor Organization Conventions and Organization of American States instruments ratified by the respective member nations.

It is truly deceitful for tyrannical governments such as Cuba, Czechoslovakia, Bulgaria, Haiti, Paraguay, the U.S.S.R. and Yugoslavia to say that their workers enjoy rights, guarantees, and liberty under the International Labor Organization Conventions, but there it is on record. There is no recourse or adequate mechanism to establish the truth of the situation or to enforce compliance by exposing forced labor camps and the miserable exploitation of workers outside the labor camps in these and in other countries with totalitarian governments.

As the importance of trade unions grows in the developing countries, greater demands are being made on the free-labor movement.

Great hopes are placed on the future constructive role of the International Confederation of Free Trade Unions, especially in view of its recent decision to clear and coordinate independent activities by its affiliates. Consequently, projected plans for qualifying and integrating experienced trade unionists in the broad spectrum of international affairs are being studied.

All of the efforts of the American Institute for Free Labor Development—education, social projects, and community services—are directed toward the development of democratic institutions within the labor field. The AIFLD also helps to provide stability in Latin America by combating conditions which foster Communist agitation and activity, both in urban centers and in rural areas. It also seeks to provide a wholesome atmosphere conducive to free enterprise. In other words, the AIFLD is pro-labor and pro-management—pro-labor since it fosters the development of free-trade unions and pro-management since it performs a service in the maintenance and preservation of economic systems which has proven beneficial to business, workers, and national economies.

Because of the danger involved in government ownership of the total means of production, the promotion of a rapprochement between labor and management is essential if free enterprise is to survive. Workers should be given the opportunity to know and understand our type of economic system and why American labor considers it more beneficial and better suited for the achievement of workers' needs and desires. Conversely, foreign management and governments must realize that free enterprise can only survive within the framework of a democratic and enlightened pluralistic society. This means a form of free enterprise stripped of all the inherent evils of the old nineteenth-century capitalism.

There is a great potential in an expanded joint effort between labor and management in international affairs. The American Institute for Free Labor Development has opened new avenues of labor-management cooperation, but it has only begun to scratch the surface. There are possibilities in the expansion and the establishment of action programs designed specifically for the promotion of free enterprise and the elimination of Communist infiltration throughout the free world. We propose bolstering good democratic trade unions with practical apprenticeship ("on-the-job") training programs and a good shop steward system that will eliminate small conflicts and grievances before they become big issues or are blown up by subversive elements and become a major threat to the stability of the national economy.

We also make the following additional recommendations:

1. That the U.S. Government review the Conventions of the International Labor Organization and ratify those in compliance with existing law. In particular, special attention should be given to the ratification of Convention No. 87 on Freedom of Association and Protection of the Right to Organize; Convention No. 98 on the Right to Organize and Collective Bargaining; and Convention No. 105 on Abolition of Forced Labor.
2. That the U.S. Government take steps to support and maintain the tripartite character of the International Labor Organization and to strengthen U.S. participation.

3. That the U.S. Government provide for official participation of trade union representatives in U.S. delegations to meetings of the UN, ECOSOC, UNESCO, and other UN organizations.

4. That the U.S. Government encourage and coordinate with the AFL-CIO the increased use of non-profit organizations to provide technical assistance in the labor field (union-to-union programs), especially in areas such as the Near East, South Asia, and Far East.

5. That the U.S. Government give higher priority and more recognition to manpower, skill training, and Labor Ministry development in its bilateral assistance program, in coordination with the labor programs undertaken by United Nations agencies and non-profit private groups with legitimate interests.

THE COMMITTEE ON LABOR

Research on the Development of International Institutions

Everyone understands the importance of research in this technicological era; that it is synonymous with better living, and that it carries the world forward to undreamed-of realms of material and scientific progress. However, it strangely does not occur to many that it is possible to utilize research for an analysis of problems relating to war and peace, for an understanding of the peoples of other lands, and for understanding how to deal with them.

There is an urgent need for the planned development and strengthened utilization of existing or additional institutions concerned with systematic investigation of the requirements of international cooperation and world peace. But how to utilize the competence of colleges and universities, institutes, and foundations is still unresolved; and how better to link research results and national policies is yet to be proposed.

We make the following recommendations:

1. That a Commission be established by the President, to be comprised of designated representatives from the Government sector and designated representatives from the private sector, including members from colleges, universities, research institutes, foundations, and the public.

2. That this Commission be provided with a qualified professional

staff and sufficient time and resources to make specific recommendations on how best to develop existing or additional institutions, to carry out the "assignment of the century"—international cooperation—through independent investigation, the marshalling of existing knowledge and the acquisition of new knowledge, and its application to national policy and the resolutional conflict.

THE COMMITTEE FOR RESEARCH ON THE
DEVELOPMENT OF INTERNATIONAL INSTITUTIONS

Social Welfare

International programs in social welfare are growing in numbers and scope as evidence mounts that all parties derive mutual benefits and as the importance of human and social factors in broad developmental programs gains increasing recognition.

The universality of basic human needs and aspirations and the determination of most of the world's governments to meet those needs afford a broad and significant area for international cooperation, singularly free from partisanship. The needs of the homeless, the hungry, and the isolated do not require translation.

The traditional concept, as well as the role, of social welfare is undergoing modification as a result, in part, of new knowledge gained through international exchange. While retaining its central concern for "man in his environment," social welfare is now deeply concerned with the human and social consequences of broad planning programs and with the prevention, along with the amelioration, of the social stresses which accompany change.

Present-day international social welfare activities are carried out by the United Nations, various regional intergovernmental organizations, and by international non-governmental agencies. Many governments and national voluntary organizations sponsor technical and cultural programs providing for intercountry cooperation in various phases of social welfare.

International programs of various kinds are now going forward in such areas of common concern as population control; urbanization; investment in children and youth; the aging; emergency welfare services for natural or man-made disasters; community development; family life; income insurance.

Training, recruitment, and utilization of skilled personnel represent a challenging and, as yet, unsolved problem. Despite substantial increases in the numbers and size of exchanges in this area, demand for skilled manpower exceeds supply.

We make the following recommendations:

1. That there be a clearly defined identity and elevated status for the United Nations Social Welfare Programs by means of the formation of a standing committee or similar instrumentality.
2. That the United States support the First International Conference of Ministers of Social Welfare proposed for 1968. The formation of a widely representative planning committee is recommended.
3. That the United States support the United Nations projected social planning research and training program as related to ongoing economic development projects. The United States is asked to initiate pilot studies in countries where there are appropriate U.S. development programs.
4. That the U.S. Government agencies administering technical assistance and exchange programs overseas assert a strong initiative in international social welfare by (a) promulgating a clear policy statement in support of social welfare as an essential element in social and economic development and assisting mission personnel to implement such policy; and (b) according priority status to social welfare in country, educational and cultural exchange, and Fulbright programs in a concerted effort to strengthen overseas resources and to enhance U.S. contributions to international social welfare.
5. That non-governmental, voluntary organizations give increased support and status to their international programs.
6. That United States–sponsored training programs be expanded and that the International Association of Schools of Social Work initiate studies designed to help close the manpower gap and to develop new strategies and materials for this purpose.
7. That (a) a new instrumentality, under the leadership of the Welfare Administration and the Agency for International Development, be created to foster and facilitate international social welfare research; (b) greater support be given to expanding the research and survey activities of the UN in New York and Geneva; and (c) present Welfare Administration–sponsored research programs be expanded through making available additional funds for this purpose.

8. That a review be undertaken of U.S. policy concerning the entire field of international refugees and migration.

9. That international programs be developed specifically focused upon the problems of the aging and that the United States assume leadership in establishing a permanent executive staff for the International Association of Gerontology.

10. That efforts be continued to develop universal treaties and conventions on human rights.

11. That there be at least one U.S. Social Welfare Attaché in every major region, with high priority being given to developing countries where they can be expected to make major contributions.

12. That the statutory basis for the international programs of the Welfare Administration be made comparable to the bases for major service programs in similar governmental units.

13. That qualified social welfare personnel assist (a) in the evaluation of data now being collected in South Vietnam on problems of homeless children and separated families and (b) in establishing child and family services directed toward reuniting families insofar as is possible.

THE COMMITTEE ON SOCIAL WELFARE

Transportation

International transportation today is beset with numerous problems that impede progress and hinder the efforts of nations to take advantage of the benefits which modern technologies offer. Some of these problems are created at the local level, others at the national level, and still others at the international level.

Reduction of Paperwork

In order to eliminate unnecessary or outmoded governmental formalities and requirements, and reduce to a minimum the paperwork involved in the international movement of goods and people, it is recommended that our national transportation policy support action to:

1. Subject all existing formalities and paperwork requirements to basic and intensive management science review to assess their value, need, and effectiveness.

2. Establish an adequately manned staff of specialists in an appropriate governmental department, authorized to develop improved intra-governmental paperwork procedures for trade and travel facilitation.
3. Institute continuing international negotiations as necessary to obtain review and coordinating action on existing paperwork requirements in other countries of the world.

Transportation Facility Development and Transportation Technology

It is recommended that:

1. Coordination of extensive programs for the improvement of port, terminal, and transportation facilities now in being or under active consideration by various U.S. Government agencies and/or industry organizations be continued and expedited.
2. These improvement projects be centralized under the support and coordination of the Department of Commerce, Office of the Under Secretary for Transportation, so that a maximization of efforts may be achieved.

Container Movement and Standardization

In order to promote further economies in international goods transport, it is recommended that the U.S. Government:

1. Proclaim as a national transportation policy objective the achievement of total intermodal integration in equipment, and coordination in systems and procedures, with special emphasis on containerized and unitized shipments.
2. Propose the establishment of an intergovernmental policy committee to coordinate the efforts of various agencies and industries involved in transportation for the purpose of eliminating all non-essential regulatory, procedural, and unreasonable economic barriers to expeditious through movement of containerized and unitized cargoes.
3. Appoint a permanent committee including Government and industry personnel for continuing and effective technical liaison on a national and international basis so as to achieve workable agreements on compatible intermodal equipment and the movement of containerized and unitized shipments.
4. Undertake an overall examination and scientific review of national and international transportation systems with the view of deter-

mining the changes required to bring about more effective inter-modal integration to further the demonstrated advantages of using containers in international trade.

International Transportation Training

In order to facilitate orderly development of essential training required for the future tasks in international transportation, it is recommended:

1. That the transportation policy of the United States be clearly enunciated so as to support international efforts toward better training of personnel engaged in international transportation at the technical, managerial, and operational levels.
2. That the United States explore the steps needed for expanding private international training practices and take necessary action to support expansion of such activities where practicable.
3. That an organized effort be made to intensify the present activities of educational institutions in the field of international transportation trade.

International Transportation Statistics

It is recommended that the U.S. Government sponsor within the United Nations a program to establish, as rapidly as possible, international standards for accurate and compatible, meaningful and timely transportation statistics and prescribe criteria for the collection and exchange of needed information.

International Traffic Safety

It is recommended that the President's Committee for Traffic Safety be authorized to sponsor an International Conference on Traffic Safety which will focus its attention on all matters of mutual benefit and concern and to further the full and free exchange of information and ideas.

International Travel and Tourism

It is recommended that:

1. The U.S. Government reaffirm freedom of two-way travel as a firm tenet of international policy.
2. The immigration laws be amended to permit waiver of visa requirements on a reciprocal basis.
3. The U.S. Government fully support continuing efforts to increase

the free movement of students and technical trainees between this and all other countries of the world.

Central Clearinghouse for Transportation Safety

It is recommended that there be established in an appropriate agency of the Government an Office of Transportation Aid to review requests for assistance and coordinate requests for all non-grant transportation assistance and activities.

World Transportation Center

It is recommended that the United States assist in the establishment of a World Transportation Center, within the framework of the United Nations, to pursue but not be limited to the following objectives:

1. The conduct of high-priority research and the promotion and support of such research elsewhere in universities, industry, and research institutions throughout the world;
2. The retrieval, dissemination, translation, and publication of transport research, experience, and other relevant information;
3. The assistance in the provision of advisory services to member countries;
4. The conduct of conference programs, including the preparation of advance materials, the mobilizing of talent in industry, government, and the universities, and the analysis and distribution of results.

THE COMMITTEE ON TRANSPORTATION

Women

In the United States and throughout the world, the pattern of women's lives is being re-cut by social changes. The twentieth century has witnessed more upheavals in their condition than any comparable period in the history of mankind.

Urgently needed changes in private practice and public attitude —improving health, nutrition, sanitation; controlling population growth; remedying the dislocations of family patterns caused by urbanization; bridging the gap of communication between metropolitan dwellers and rural villagers; coping with aspirations and frustrations of youth; creating responsive and responsible governments—can only occur if women consciously and constructively share in the making of effective decisions.

As wives and mothers, women continue to be the center of the home, and the foundation of family life. Maintenance of a modern home and preparation of today's generation of children for entry into tomorrow's society require new understanding and new skills. Urgent social problems demand increased participation by women in civic and political life. Economic development at the rate required to meet rising expectations necessitates more effective use of womanpower.

The power of rural women and women of the villages, who constitute the great majority in the developing nations, remains to be more fully asserted. In countries where women grow the crops, prepare the family food, and determine domestic health and sanitation practices, a nation's level of health and vigor may be crucially affected by their knowledge of nutrition, hygiene, and child care.

International cooperation enables women of all regions of the world, from various nations, backgrounds, and cultures, to move forward. Vehicles of their advance include the UN, the governmental structures of their respective states, private foundations, corporations and non-profit enterprises and the women's voluntary organizations whose specific experience in development of political, social, and economic participation by women is coupled with broad contacts in many countries.

We make the following recommendations:

1. That international conventions relating to women be ratified.
2. That fuller utilization of women be made in international offices and in particular that:

    (a) The United States support the appointment of qualified women to a wider range of planning and policy-making positions in the United Nations, specialized agencies, and other international secretariats.

    (b) The United States appoint qualified women to serve as attachés, regional and Women's Affairs officers in overseas embassies for international cooperation with women and voluntary organizations and that the changing role of women be emphasized in orientation courses.

    (c) The United States appoint qualified women in increasing numbers to delegations attending international meetings.

    (d) Voluntary organizations suggest qualified women to be appointed in the international field and that the United States support the principle of full participation of women at every level of international cooperation.

3. That the U.S. Government and voluntary organizations give increasing support to multilateral and bilateral governmental and privately supported programs designed to improve educational, political, economic, social, and legal status of women.

4. That the U.S. Government and voluntary organizations give increasing support to programs of international cooperation which strengthen family life, including social welfare, housing, and homemaker education, with consumer training.

5. That the U.S. Government and voluntary organizations give increasing support to regional, national, and local seminars to equip women for leadership in public life and non-governmental organizations.

6. That the U.S. Government and voluntary organizations support international cooperation programs to improve the vocational guidance, training, and retraining of women; to assure women equal access to training and job opportunity; equal pay for equal work and freedom from discrimination in employment on the basis of sex; to expand services essential to working women, particularly those with family responsibilities; and to develop standards with respect to conditions of work, applicable alike, insofar as feasible and appropriate, to men and women.

7. That the United States continue to assist other countries, upon request, in the establishment of Women's Bureaus and Status of Women Commissions.

8. That the U.S. Government and voluntary organizations support international cooperation programs to improve educational opportunities for women at all levels including training in foreign language; supply visual aids and interesting material and make available other information which will stimulate their full participation in community development and public life.

9. That the U.S. Government and voluntary organizations provide, when requested, educational information and technical assistance in family planning programs.

10. That U.S. foundations and voluntary organizations make more funds available to expand exchange of persons programs and to assure a greater number of women as exchangees and that particular attention be given to promoting international cooperation by the recognition of women of outstanding achievement.

11. That U.S. foundations and voluntary organizations assist, on re-

quest, rural women in the developing countries to participate more fully in village development through the establishment of adequate educational opportunities, and facilities for training in nutrition, family life, and community organization.

12. That the U.S. Government foundations and voluntary organizations make available to the UN funds-in-trust for particular projects in developing countries for the advancement of women and for the publication of studies and reports which are now unavailable because of lack of funds.

13. That U.S. foundations and voluntary organizations make available to the UN funds-in-trust for technical assistance to establish commissions to study the legal position of women in family law in developing countries and to help create public opinion which would support the elimination of outworn laws that deprive women of essential human dignity.

14. That the U.S. Government and voluntary organizations use all available channels (a) to promote understanding of the United Nations and its work to advance the position of women and (b) to help to create through the full use of mass media an area of acceptance of the full contribution of women to the building of a peaceful world.

THE COMMITTEE ON WOMEN

Youth Activities

In many parts of the world today young leaders are emerging amid the social pain and political turbulence of rapid modernization. In this country, too, youth are on the move, passionately anxious to put their decisive stamp on the tone, quality, and direction of our society. This offers a tremendous opportunity to build understanding between American youth and the youth of the rest of the world.

In the United States, organized youth programs have developed almost exclusively in the private sector. Individual commitment, voluntary service, and personal contact have been their hallmarks.

The dramatic increase in international contact and foreign study since World War II, and our growing commitment to foreign aid and exchange of persons, have led to the presence of over 80,000 foreign students on our campuses and 20,000 American students abroad. At the same time a large and complex matrix of international youth organizations has grown up. These developments, together with the rapid rise of young leaders to political power in newly independent countries, have impelled greater efforts, both private and governmental, toward international cooperation among youth.

The present situation offers a rare opportunity and a splendid challenge. Despite the significant progress made in recent years, the youth programs that exist in great profusion in the United States are not adequately financed or sufficiently coordinated. This lack of financial support and the accompanying lack of a consistent pattern of programming for youth dull imagination, stifle initiative, and prevent good projects from achieving their full potential. Moreover, youth themselves do not seem to be recognized as making a major positive contribution. They are too often looked upon as the subjects *for whom* things are done, rather than as principal actors.

We make the following recommendations:

1. That the excess capacity in our domestic and overseas carriers be used to provide low-cost domestic and international travel for qualified youth and students and that low-cost accommodations be developed and promoted for foreign and American youth through expansion of the youth hostel system in cities and national parks.

2. That the Federal Government establish a Special Office to stimulate, and provide part of the financial support for, a nationwide program of services to foreign students; and that the effort to establish a foreign student center in the District of Columbia be encouraged.

3. That U.S. political parties, trade unions, and farm organizations increase the exchange of their young leaders with similar organizations abroad.

4. That Government and private agencies seek qualified persons with firsthand overseas experience for use as speakers, resource persons, and lecturers in schools and community programs, and that lists of such persons be provided regularly by the Federal Government.

5. That the Federal Government, in conjunction with other governments and private agencies, encourage a program of bringing young people from abroad to serve and train in school and community projects in the United States.

6. That the Federal Government encourage and aid schools and community groups to develop more and better contacts with related groups abroad to exchange views, experiences, and materials by every means of communication.

7. That governmental and private agencies join in launching a nationwide campaign among American youth to learn a second language.

8. That sports, recreation, and physical education organizations sharply increase the exchange of coaches, athletes, and specialists in physical education, and expand international sports competitions among youth groups.

9. That the Federal Government, in conjunction with private and UN-related agencies, promote increased research into youth programs and behavior, and foster the exchange of findings and conclusions.

10. That the United States Youth Council, in conjunction with other appropriate organizations, compile a directory of youth-serving organizations engaged in international programs in the United States and publish it periodically.

11. That the President appoint a Presidential Committee on International Youth Affairs, drawn from government and private life, to stimulate action and promote coordination with respect to these recommendations, and that the Committee be provided with appropriate staff and budget.

THE COMMITTEE ON YOUTH ACTIVITIES

Appendix: The Committees and Government Consultants

AGRICULTURE AND FOOD

COMMITTEE MEMBERS

Hazel K. Stiebeling, Chairman
Nutrition Consultant

Clarence G. Adamy, Executive Vice President, National Association of Food Chains

John T. Caldwell, Chancellor, North Carolina State University

Herbert Cleaves, Senior Vice President, General Foods Corporation

John Eklund, Director of Education, National Farmers Union

Erik J. Erikson

Hugh D. Farley, Associate Secretary, Division of Overseas Ministries, National Council of Churches

Frank Goffio, Executive Director, CARE

Samuel Haber, Assistant Executive Secretary, American Jewish Joint Distribution Committee, Inc.

Clifford Hope, Consultant, Great Plains Wheat, Inc.

Leon Keyserling, Economist

A.N. McFarlane, Chairman of the Board, Corn Products Company

Joseph M. McGarry, Director of Public Relations, International

Minerals and Chemicals Corporation

Kenneth Naden, Executive Vice President, National Council of Farmer Cooperatives

Robert R. Nathan, President, Robert R. Nathan Associates, Inc.

Herschel Newsom, Master, National Grange

James J. O'Connor, Executive Director, Academy of Food Marketing, St. Joseph's College

Michael J. O'Connor, Executive Director, Super Market Institute

Paul B. Pearson, President, The Nutrition Foundation, Inc.

J.C. Staiger, President, Massey-Ferguson, Inc.

The Most Rev. Edward E. Swanstrom, Executive Director, National Catholic Relief Services

Mrs. Raphael Tourover

LeRoy Voris, Executive Secretary, Food and Nutrition Board, National Research Council, National Academy of Sciences

Walter F. Whittier, President, Hannaford Brothers

Francis R. Wilcox, Member, Central Bank of Cooperatives

Paul S. Willis, President, Grocery Manufacturers of America

371

GOVERNMENT CONSULTANTS

Mrs. Dorothy H. Jacobson, Assistant Secretary for International Affairs, U.S. Department of Agriculture

Irwin Hedges, Agricultural Trade Specialist, Office of the Special Representative for Trade Negotiations

J. Erven Long, Associate Assistant Administrator, Office of Technical Cooperation and Research, Agency for International Development, Department of State

James M. Quigley, Assistant Secretary, Department of Health, Education and Welfare

Arnold E. Schaefer, Executive Director, Office of International Research, National Institutes of Health, Department of Health, Education and Welfare

Leighton van Nort, Officer-in-Charge, International Economic Affairs, Office of International Economic and Social Affairs, Bureau of International Organization Affairs, Department of State

Herbert J. Waters, Assistant Administrator for Material Resources, Agency for International Development, Department of State

ARMS CONTROL AND DISARMAMENT

COMMITTEE MEMBERS

Dr. Jerome B. Wiesner, Chairman Dean, School of Science, Massachusetts Institute of Technology, former Special Assistant to the President for Science and Technology

Dr. Donald G. Brennan, Hudson Institute

Fredrick M. Eaton, of the New York Bar, former Representative of the U.S. at the Ten-Nation Disarmament Committee

Dr. Vernon Ferwerda, Assistant General Secretary, National Council of the Churches of Christ in the U.S.A.

John Fischer, Editor, *Harper's*

Roswell Gilpatric, of the New York Bar, former Under Secretary of Defense

Joseph J. Johnston, of the Montgomery, Ala., Bar

Dr. Carl Kaysen, Littauer Professor of Political Economy, Harvard University, former Dep. Special Assistant to the President for National Security Affairs

Dr. Robert Martin, Professor of Political Science, Howard University

John M. Mitchell, Executive Vice President, Aluminum Company of America

Dr. William V. O'Brien, Chairman, Institute of World Polity, Georgetown University

Mrs. Josephine Pomerance, civic leader, Cos Cob, Conn.

Rev. Richard Spillane, S.J., Director, Center for Peace Research, The Creighton University

Harold E. Stassen, of the Philadelphia Bar, former Special Assistant to the President and U.S. Representative to the Disarmament Subcommittee

COMMITTEE STAFF

Dr. Walter C. Clemens, Jr., Executive Officer, Assistant Professor of Political Science, Massachusetts Institute of Technology

GOVERNMENT CONSULTANTS

Jacob D. Beam, Assistant Director, Arms Control & Disarmament Agency

Arthur W. Barber, Deputy Assistant Secretary of Defense for International Security Affairs

Raymond L. Garthoff, Department of State

Dr. George Rathjens, Arms Control and Disarmament Agency

Jerome H. Spingarn, Arms Control and Disarmament Agency

Lawrence D. Weiler, Arms Control and Disarmament Agency

AVIATION

COMMITTEE MEMBERS

S.G. Tipton, Chairman
President, Air Transport Association of America

Russell Adams, Vice President, Pan American World Airways, Inc.

E. Thomas Burnard, Executive Vice President, Airport Operators Council

Karl G. Harr, Jr., President and General Manager, Aerospace Industries Association of America, Inc.

J.B. Hartranft, Jr., President, Aircraft Owners & Pilots Association

Hans Heymann, Research Staff Member, Economics Division, Rand Corporation

Frank N. Ikard, President, American Petroleum Institute

Jerome Lederer, Director, Guggenheim Aviation Safety Center

Robert J. Murphy, Vice President, Washington Representatives, Boeing Company

Wayne Parrish, President and Publisher, American Aviation Publications, Inc.

Welch Pogue, Attorney, Pogue & Neal

Charles H. Ruby, President, Air Lines Pilots Association, International

Robert J. Serling, Aviation Editor, United Press International

P.L. Siemiller, International President, International Association of Machinists and Aerospace Workers

GOVERNMENT CONSULTANTS

B. Paul Blaine, Jr., Air Transportation Coordinator, Department of Commerce

Alan S. Boyd, Under Secretary for Transportation, Department of Commerce

Robert P. Boyle, Deputy Assistant Administrator for International

Aviation Affairs, Federal Aviation Agency

Vincent F. Caputo, Director of Transportation and Warehousing Policy, Department of Defense

Miss Joan Coward, Special Assistant to Chairman, Civil Aeronautics Board

Allen R. Ferguson, Coordinator for Aviation, Department of State

Harold O. Frederick, Aviation Advisor, Agency for International Development

Mrs. Joan S. Gravatt, Foreign Affairs Officer, Office of Aviation, Department of State

Alfred Hand, International Affairs Officer, Federal Aviation Agency

William J. Hartigan, Assistant Postmaster General, Post Office Department

Frank E. Loy, Deputy Assistant Secretary, Bureau of Economic Affairs, Department of State

Hobart N. Luppi, Chief, Aviation Liaison Division, Department of State

William A. McGowan, Aerospace Technologist, National Aeronautics and Space Administration

M. Cecil Mackey, Director, Office of Transportation Policy Development, Department of Commerce

Clarence D. Martin, Jr., (Former) Under Secretary for Transportation, Department of Commerce

Charles S. Murphy, Chairman, Civil Aeronautics Board

Mrs. Frances Nolde, IGIA Liaison Officer, Office of Under Secretary for Transportation, Department of Commerce

Paul L. Sitton, Deputy Coordinator for Aviation, Department of State

Chester C. Spurgeon, International Planning Officer, Federal Aviation Agency

Marion H. Uhrich, Assistant Staff Director, Transportation, Plans and Programs Division, Department of Defense

BUSINESS AND INDUSTRY

COMMITTEE MEMBERS

I.M. Stewart, Chairman
Vice President, Union Carbide Corporation

Robert M. Brunson, Vice President, General Precision, Inc.

Jose de Cubas, President, Westinghouse Electric International

James H. Goss, Vice President, General Electric Company

W.P. Gullander, President, National Association of Manufacturers

Frank N. Ikard, President, American Petroleum Institute

Neil McElroy, Chairman of the Board, Procter and Gamble Company

John M. Mitchell, Executive Vice President, Aluminum Company of America

Robert C. Sprague, Chairman of

the Board, Sprague Electric Company

William G. Carter, Associate Assistant Administrator for Private Enterprise, Agency for International Development

GOVERNMENT CONSULTANTS

A.B. Trowbridge, Assistant Secretary, Domestic and International Business, Department of Commerce

Eugene P. Foley, Assistant Secretary of Commerce and Director of Economic Development, Department of Commerce (formerly Administrator, Small Business Administration)

J. Cordell Moore, Assistant Secretary for Mineral Resources, Department of Interior

Irwin Fine, Director, International Organizations Staff, Department of Commerce

Robert B. Dollison, International Organizations Staff, Department of Commerce

Merlyn Trued, Assistant Secretary for International Affairs, Department of the Treasury

Arthur Okun, Member, Council of Economic Advisers

Harry Weiss, Deputy Assistant Secretary for International Labor Affairs, Department of Labor

Allen V. Astin, Director, National Bureau of Standards

Edward J. Brenner, Commissioner, Patent Office

COMMUNICATIONS

COMMITTEE MEMBERS

Harold Geneen, Chairman Chairman of the Board and President, International Telephone and Telegraph Corporation

Palmer Hoyt, Editor, *Denver Post*

Frederick R. Kappel Chairman of

the Board, American Telephone and Telegraph Company

William B. Quarton, President, American Broadcasting Stations, Inc.

General David Sarnoff, Chairman of the Board, Radio Corporation of America

GOVERNMENT CONSULTANTS

Lee Loevinger, Commissioner, Federal Communications Commission

Paul F. Geren, Director, Office of Telecommunications and Maritime Affairs, Department of State

General Harold W. Grant, Direc-

tor, Telecommunications Policy, Department of Defense

Harry D. Yankey, Chief, Communications Division, Agency for International Development, Department of State

Edgar T. Martin, Engineering Manager, Voice of America, United States Information Agency

CULTURE AND INTELLECTUAL EXCHANGE

COMMITTEE MEMBERS

Norman Cousins, *Saturday Review* (Co-Chairman)

Luther H. Evans, Columbia University (Co-Chairman)

John F. White, National Educational Television (Co-Chairman)

Leslie Paffrath, The Johnson Foundation (Member at large)

Mrs. Emily Otis Barnes (Member at large)

David Hall, Composers Recordings Inc. (Rapporteur)

Robert B. Hudson, National Educational Television (Committee Coordinator)

SUBCOMMITTEES

Architecture
Vincent Scully (Chairman), Yale University

Business Organizations
H.F. Johnson (Chairman), S.C. Johnson & Son, Inc.
Richard O. Lang, S.C. Johnson & Son, Inc.

Ethnic Relations
Daniel Patrick Moynihan (Chairman), Wesleyan University

Foreign Students
Robert H. Thayer (Chairman), American Field Service
Furman Bridges, University of Maryland
James Davis, Institute of International Education
Hugh Jenkins, Foreign Service Student Council

International Travel
William D. Patterson (Chairman), *Saturday Review*
Robert Caverly, Hilton Hotels
John Everett, The New School for Social Research
Voit Gilmore, Southern Pines, N.C.

Walter Johnson, Interpublic
Milton Marks, Institute of Certified Travel Agents
Robert Mathews, American Express
Willis Player, Pan American World Airways
Daniel P. Reid, Trans World Airlines, Inc.
Warren Titus, P&O Orient Lines, Inc.

Libraries and Archives
Luther H. Evans (Chairman), Columbia University
Lester Asheim, American Library Association
Robert Bahmer, National Archives
Douglas W. Bryant, Harvard University Library
Jack Dalton, Columbia University
William S. Dix, Princeton University
Edward G. Freehafer, New York Public Library
John G. Lorenz, Library of Congress

Motion Pictures
Arthur Krim (Chairman), United Artists Corporation

Mrs. Anna Rosenberg Hoffman, New York, New York

Arnold Picker, United Artists Corporation

Music

Erich Leinsdorf (Chairman), Boston Symphony Orchestra

Miss Marian Anderson, Danbury, Connecticut

Van Cliburn, New York, New York

Seiji Ozawa, Toronto Symphony Orchestra

William Schuman, Lincoln Center for the Performing Arts

Newspapers and Periodicals

Herbert R. Mayes (Chairman), McCall Corporation

Barry Bingham, *Louisville Courier Journal*

Erwin D. Canham, *Christian Science Monitor*

Gardner Cowles, Cowles Magazines & Broadcasting

Palmer Hoyt, The *Denver Post*

Donald Layman, *Scholastic Magazine*

Painting, Sculpture, Crafts

Rene d'Harnoncourt, Museum of Modern Art

Roy Neuberger, American Federation of Arts

Mrs. Vanderbilt Webb, World Crafts Council

Publishing and Writing

James Laughlin (Chairman), *New Directions*

John Ciardi, *Saturday Review*

Alfred A. Knopf, Alfred A. Knopf, Inc.

James A. Michener, Pipersville, Pa.

Datus C. Smith, Franklin Book Programs

Radio and Television

John F. White (Chairman), National Educational Television

Technological Development

R. Buckminster Fuller (Chairman), Southern Illinois University

Charles Butcher, Butcher Polish Company

Edward T. Hall, Anthropologist

John McHale, World Resources Inventory

Theater and Dance

Milton Lyon (Chairman), Actors' Equity Foundation

Arthur Cantor, Producer

Hy Faine, American Guild of Musical Artists

Dr. Esther Jackson, New York Shakespeare Festival

Sidney Kingsley, Playwright

Mrs. Ruth Mayleas, International Theater Institute

Robert Rowe Paddock, United Scenic Artists

Robert Whitehead, Producer

Stanley Young, American National Theater and Academy

CONSULTANTS

Noel Brown, United Nations

Pearl Buck, Perkasie, Pa.

Mrs. W. Randolph Burgess, Washington, D.C.

Gibson Danes, Yale University

John Hope Franklin, University of Chicago

Kenneth Holland, Institute of International Education

Arthur Howe, Jr., American Field Service

Victor Christ Janer, Architect

Wilmer H. Kingsford, Centre d'Echanges Technologiques Internationaux

Sol Linowitz, Xerox Corporation

Mrs. Maurice Moore, Westport, Conn.

Bishop Reuben H. Mueller, National Council of the Churches of Christ

Mrs. Richard Persinger, Young Women's Christian Assoc.

Mrs. Dorothy Porter, Howard University

Dana Pratt, Association of American University Presses

William B. Quarton, American Broadcasting Stations, Inc.

John Reurs, Holland-America Line

Marshall Shulman, Russian Research Center, Harvard University

Shepard Stone, The Ford Foundation

Arthur Hays Sulzberger, *The New York Times*

Kenneth Thompson, The Rockefeller Foundation

Christopher Tunnard, Yale University

Government Consultants

Burnett Anderson, Deputy Director, Policy and Plans, U.S. Information Agency

Charles Frankel, Assistant Secretary of State for Educational, and Cultural Affairs

Eric Goldman, Special Consultant to the President

Daly C. Lavergne, Director, Office of International Training, Agency for International Development

Mrs. Katie Louchheim, Deputy Assistant Secretary of State for Community Advisory Services

Harry C. McPherson, Jr., Special Assistant to the President

L. Quincy Mumford, Librarian of Congress

Charles Nagel, Director, National Portrait Gallery, Smithsonian Institution

Roger Stevens, Special Assistant to the President on the Arts

Hugh B. Sutherland, Bureau of Educational and Cultural Affairs, Department of State

John Walker, Director, National Gallery of Art

Mrs. Margaret Hicks Williams, Bureau of Educational and Cultural Affairs, Department of State

Howard Woods, Associate Director, Program Development, U.S. Information Agency

DISASTER RELIEF

Committee Members

Gen. James F. Collins, Chairman

President, American National Red Cross

Ugo Carusi, Member, Advisory Committee on Foreign Aid

John Couric, Vice President, Public Relations, National Association of Broadcasters

A.I. Davies, Vice President in Charge of Operations, Sears Roebuck & Company

C.C. Duncan, Long Lines Division, American Telephone & Telegraph Company

Ramone S. Eaton, Vice President, American National Red Cross

Frank L. Goffio, Executive Director, CARE, Inc.

Dr. J. Eugene Haas, Director, Behavioral Sciences Laboratory, The Ohio State University

Mrs. William H. Hasebroock, President, General Federation of Women's Clubs

George W. Healy, Jr., Times-Picayune Publishing Co.

James MacCracken, Executive Director, Church World Service

Dept., National Council of Churches of Christ in the USA

The Right Reverend Monsignor, John F. McCarthy, Assistant Executive Director, Catholic Relief Services

Norman J. Philion, Vice President, International Air Transport Association

Robert M. Pierpont, Deputy National Director, Disaster Services, American National Red Cross

Dr. Austin Smith, President, Pharmaceutical Manufacturers Association

James A. Suffridge, Vice President, AFL-CIO

John W. Wilson, Vice President, Aluminum Company of America

Government Consultants

Dr. George W. Baker, Science Development Evaluation Group, Division of Institutional Programs, National Science Foundation

Robert A. Fordham, Office of International Affairs, Department of Health, Education and Welfare

Captain V.G. Holzapfel, USN, Foreign Disaster Relief Coordinator, Department of Defense

Michael W. Moynihan, Director, Information Staff, Agency for International Development

Stephen R. Tripp, Disaster Relief Coordinator, Office of Material Resources, Agency for International Development

Joseph F. Vaughan, Office of the Assistant, Secretary of State for Politico-Military Affairs

EDUCATION AND TRAINING

Committee Members

William G. Carr, Chairman Executive Secretary, National Education Association

John C. Baker

Emily Otis Barnes, United Nations

Association of the United States of America

Frank Bowles, The Ford Foundation

Erwin D. Canham, Editor-in-Chief, *Christian Science Monitor*

Mrs. Robert Carlson

Ben Cherrington, Regional Director, Institute of International Education

Rufus E. Clement, President, Atlanta University

Philip Davidson, President, University of Louisville

Ray Ehrensburger, Dean, University College, University of Maryland

Robert L. Fischelis, Dean, Morse College, Yale University

John H. Fischer, President, Teachers College

William W. Hagerty, President, Drexel Institute of Technology

William J. Haggerty, President, State University College

Francis N. Hamblin, Dean, School of Education, George Washington University

Edgar L. Harden, President, Northern Michigan University

David Henry, Director, Harvard International Office

Monsignor Frederick G. Hockwalt, Executive Director, National Catholic Educational Association

Arthur Howe, Jr., President, American Field Service

Eleanor Apt Kaplan, Information Officer, United States Committee for UNICEF

James M. Nabrit, Jr., President, Howard University

James A. Perkins, President, Cornell University

Alan Pifer, Vice President, Carnegie Corporation

Dorothy Porter, Howard University

Felix C. Robb, President, George Peabody College for Teachers

Mrs. Zelia Ruebhausem, Chairman, Women's Africa Committee

Cyril Sargent, School of Education, The City College of the City, University of New York

Herman B. Wells, Chancellor, Indiana University

Robert L. West, Associate Director, Rockefeller Foundation

Logan Wilson, Head, American Council on Education

Shephard Witman, Office of Cultural and Educational Exchange, University of Pittsburgh

GOVERNMENT CONSULTANTS

Francis Keppel, U.S. Commissioner of Education

Norman Auburn, Special Assistant for University Relations, Agency for International Development

Francis J. Colligan, Director, Policy Review and Coordination Staff, Department of State

Martin G. Cramer, Chief, Educational Projects Staff, Department of State

Ralph C.M. Flynt, Associate Commissioner for International Education, Office of Education

Elizabeth E. Hamer, Assistant Librarian, Library of Congress

Ernest M. Mannino, Director, Office of Overseas Schools, Department of State

Joseph L. Matthews, Director, Division of Extension and Training, Department of Agriculture

Russell S. Poor, Director, Division of Nuclear Education and Training, Atomic Energy Commission

Henry W. Riecken, Associate Director (Education), National Science Foundation

Jerold Roschwalb, Division of Education and Training, Smithsonian Institution

Aaron P. Seamster, Deputy Director of Educational Programs and Services, National Aeronautics and Space Administration

Paul L. Stanchfield, Research Analyst, Department of Labor

Hildegard Thompson, Chief, Branch of Education, Bureau of Indian Affairs, Department of Interior

George Henry, Chief, Cultural Operations Division, United States Information Agency

Stanley Wilcox, Office of the Associate Commissioner for International Education, Office of Education

Harris L. Wofford, Associate Director, Planning, Evaluation, and Research, Peace Corps

Ben M. Zeff, Deputy Director for Education Programs, Department of Defense

FINANCE AND MONETARY AFFAIRS

COMMITTEE MEMBERS

David M. Kennedy, Chairman Chairman of the Board, Continental Illinois National Bank and Trust Company

Eugene R. Black, Special Adviser to the President on Southeast Asia Economic and Social Development

Arthur H. Dean, Sullivan and Cromwell

Emile Despres, Research Center in Economic Growth, Stanford University

Frederick M. Eaton, Shearman and Sterling

Thomas S. Gates, Chairman of the Board, Morgan Guaranty Trust Company

Kenneth Hansen, Vice President, Syntex Corporation

Charles H. Percy, Chairman of the Board, Bell and Howell Company

Maxwell M. Raab, Attorney

Jesse W. Tapp, Director, Bank of America

J. Cameron Thomson, Retired Chairman, Northwest Bank Corporation

Frazar B. Wilde, Chairman of the Board, Connecticut General Life Insurance Company

Robert P. Mayo, Committee Coordinator. Vice President, Continental Illinois National Bank and Trust Company

GOVERNMENT CONSULTANTS

Merlyn N. Trued, Assistant Secretary of the Treasury for International Affairs

J. Dewey Daane, Board of Governors of the Federal Reserve System

William B. Dale, U.S. Executive Director, International Monetary Fund

Harold O. Folk, Associate Assistant Administrator for Finance Development, Agency for International Development

Ralph Hirschtritt, Deputy to the Assistant Secretary for International Finance and Economic Affairs, Treasury Department

Arthur M. Okun, Council of Economic Advisers

Anthony M. Solomon, Assistant Secretary of State for Economic Affairs

HEALTH

COMMITTEE MEMBERS

Dr. Leroy E. Burney, Chairman Vice President for Health Sciences Temple University Medical Center

Dr. Stanhope Bayne-Jones, formerly Dean of the Yale University School of Medicine, and President of the Joint Administrative Board of the New York Hospital-Cornell Medical Center

Dr. W. Montague Cobb, Head of the Department of Anatomy, Howard University

Dr. Dana L. Farnsworth, Professor of Hygiene and Director, University Health Services, Harvard University

Dr. Eli Ginzberg, Director, Conservation of Human Resources, Columbia University

Dr. Charles LeMaistre, Associate Dean and Professor of Internal Medicine, University of Texas, Southwestern Medical School

Dr. Walsh McDermott, Chairman, Department of Public Health, Cornell University

Robert R. Nathan, President, Robert R. Nathan Associates, Inc.

Walter P. Reuther, President, International Union, United Automobile, Aerospace and Agricultural Implement Workers of America

GOVERNMENT CONSULTANTS

Dr. Shirley Fisk, Deputy Assistant Secretary of Defense for Health and Medical Affairs, Department of Defense

Joseph LaRocca, Chief, Division of International Activities, Vocational Rehabilitation Administration, Department of Health, Education, and Welfare

Dr. Philip R. Lee, Assistant Secretary for Health and Medical Affairs, Department of Health, Education, and Welfare

F.E. McLaughlin, Assistant to Assistant Commissioner for Operations, Food and Drug Administration, Department of Health, Education, and Welfare

Mrs. Ruth Van Cleve, Director, Office of Territories, Department of Interior

Dr. James Watt, Director, Office of International Health, Public

Health Service, Department of Health, Education, and Welfare
Dr. Charles L. Williams, Jr., Chief, Office of International Research,

National Institutes of Health, Public Health Service, Department of Health, Education, and Welfare

HUMAN RIGHTS

COMMITTEE MEMBERS

Louis B. Sohn, Chairman
Bemis Professor of International Law, Law School of Harvard University

Leonard P. Aries, Vice President, National Conference of Christians and Jews

Roger N. Baldwin, Chairman, International League for the Rights of Man

Bruno V. Bitker, Attorney at Law; Chairman, (Wisconsin) Governor's Committee on the United Nations

Jacob Blaustein, Former Member U.S. Delegation to the UN General Assembly

Michael H. Cardozo, Executive Director, Association of American Law Schools

Rev. John J. Dougherty, President, Seton Hall University

Clarence Clyde Ferguson, Jr., Dean, Howard University, School of Law

Rev. Theodore M. Hesburgh, President, University of Notre Dame

Rabbi Philip Hiat, Director, Jewish Center for the United Nations

Sidney Liskofsky, Director, UN Division, American Jewish Committee

Mrs. Oswald B. Lord, Former U.S. Representative on the UN Commission on Human Rights

Alan M. Stroock, Attorney at Law; Member U.S. National Commission for UNESCO

Lyman M. Tondel, Jr., Attorney at Law

GOVERNMENT CONSULTANTS

Walter M. Kotschnig, Deputy Assistant Secretary for International Organization Affairs, Department of State

John E. Lawyer, Director, Office of International Organizations, Bureau of International Labor Affairs, Department of Labor

Leonard C. Meeker, Legal Adviser, Department of State

James M. Quigley, Assistant Secretary, Department of Health, Education and Welfare

Norbert A. Schlei, Assistant Attorney General, Department of Justice

William Taylor, Staff Director, U.S. Commission on Civil Rights

Franklin H. Williams, Ambassador to Ghana

Harris L. Wofford, Staff Assistant, Field Operations, Peace Corps

INTERNATIONAL LAW

COMMITTEE MEMBERS

Charles S. Rhyne, Chairman
President, World Peace Through
Law Center

Richard R. Baxter, Professor of
Law, Harvard Law School

Bruno V. Bitker, Chairman, Governor's Committee on United Nations, Wisconsin

Charles F. Brannan, Attorney, Denver, Colorado

Herbert W. Briggs, Professor of
Law, Cornell University

Michael H. Cardozo, Executive Director, Association of American
Law Schools

Abram Chayes, Former Legal Adviser, Department of State

Frederic R. Coudert, Jr., Attorney,
New York

Oscar Cox, Attorney, Washington,
D.C., formerly U.S. Assistant Solicitor General

Hardy Dillard, Dean, University of
Virginia School of Law

Robert F. Drinan, S.J., Dean, Boston College Law School

G. Homer Durham, President, Arizona State University

Albert A. Ehrenzweig, Professor of
Law, University of California
(Berkeley) School of Law

Samuel D. Estep, Professor of Law,
University of Michigan Law
School

John N. Hazard, Professor of Law,
Columbia University Law School

Bert E. Hopkins, Dean, University
of Connecticut School of Law

Sarah T. Hughes, U.S. District

Judge, Northern District of
Texas

Marion K. Kellogg, Professor of
Law, University of Virginia

Heinrich Kronstein, Director, Institute for International and Foreign Trade Law, Georgetown
University Law Center

Arthur Larson, Director, Rule of
Law Research Center, Duke University

Marjorie McKenzie Lawson, formerly Judge, Juvenile Court of
the District of Columbia

Peter James Liacouras, Professor of
Law, Temple University School
of Law

Richard B. Lillich, Director, International Legal Studies, Syracuse
University

John Lyons, Professor of Law,
George Washington Law School

Charles E. Martin, Past President,
American Society of International Law

Soia Mentschikoff, Professor of
Law, University of Chicago Law
School

H.C.L. Merillat, Executive Vice
President, American Society of
International Law

Newton N. Minow, Attorney, Chicago, Illinois, formerly Chairman, Federal Communications
Commission

Wallace N. McClure, formerly Assistant Legal Adviser, Department of State

Myres Smith McDougal, Professor
of Law, Yale Law School

James M. Nabrit, Jr., President, Howard University

Jess Nathan, Attorney, Washington, D.C.

Charles B. Nutting, Dean, George Washington Law School

Joseph A. Sinclitico, Jr., Dean, University of San Diego School of Law

Charles M. Spofford, Attorney, New York

Robert G. Storey, President, Southwestern Legal Foundation

E.D. Surrency, Professor of Law, Temple Law School

Leonard V.B. Sutton, Justice, Supreme Court of Colorado

Samuel D. Thurman, Dean, University of Utah College of Law

Kenneth Wang, Professor of Law, St. John's University School of Law

Robert R. Wilson, Professor of Law, Duke University

Quincy Wright, Professor of Law, University of Virginia

GOVERNMENT CONSULTANTS

Norbert A. Schlei, Assistant Attorney General, Office of Legal Counsel, Department of Justice

Leonard C. Meeker, Legal Adviser, Department of State

Lee Loevinger, Commissioner, Federal Communications Commission

Thomas L. Farmer, General Counsel, Agency for International Development

Fred B. Smith, Acting Counsel, Department of the Treasury

Leon Ulman, Second Assistant, Office of Legal Counsel, Department of Justice

LABOR

COMMITTEE MEMBERS

George M. Harrison, Chairman
Chief Executive Officer, Brotherhood of Railway Clerks

George Meany, President, American Federation of Labor and Congress of Industrial Organizations

Walter P. Reuther, President, International Union, United Automobile, Aerospace and Agricultural Implement Workers of America

Joseph A. Beirne, President, Communications Workers of America

GOVERNMENT CONSULTANTS

George L. P. Weaver, Assistant Secretary, International Affairs, U.S. Department of Labor

Stephen N. Shulman, General

Counsel, U.S. Department of Air Force

George P. Delaney, Special Assistant to the Secretary and Coordinator of International Labor Affairs, U.S. Department of State and Director, Office of Labor Affairs, Agency for International Development

Arnold Zempel, Deputy Coordina-

tor for International Affairs, U.S. Department of State

Edward C. Sylvester, Jr., Deputy Administrator, Bureau of International Labor Affairs, U.S. Department of Labor

MANPOWER

COMMITTEE MEMBERS

Professor Milton Katz (Chairman), Director, International Legal Studies, Law School of Harvard University

Dr. Eli Ginzberg, Professor of Economics, Graduate School of Business, Columbia University

Dr. Frederick Harbison, Director, Industrial Relations Section, Department of Economics, Princeton University

Mrs. Anna Rosenberg Hoffman, President, Anna M. Rosenberg Associates

GOVERNMENT CONSULTANTS

Dr. Henry David, Head, Office of Science Resources Planning, National Science Foundation

Dr. Joseph A. Cavanaugh, Chief, Mental Health Manpower Studies Program, National Institute of Mental Health

Miss Mary Robinson, Formerly Acting Director, Program Planning Division, U.S. Office of Education, Department of Health, Education and Welfare,

Currently Research Sociologist, Office of Economic Opportunity

Stanley Ruttenberg, Manpower Administrator, Department of Labor

Edward C. Sylvester, Formerly Deputy Administrator, Bureau of International Labor Affairs, Department of Labor, Currently Director, Office of Federal Contract Compliance, Department of Labor

METEOROLOGY

COMMITTEE MEMBERS

Thomas F. Malone, Chairman, The Travelers Insurance Companies

John C. Beckman, Beckman and Whitley, Inc.

Jacob A. Bjerknes, University of California

Jule G. Charney, Massachusetts Institute of Technology

Donald W. Douglas, Jr., Douglas Aircraft Co., Inc.

Robert G. Fleagle, University of Washington

Henry G. Houghton, Massachusetts Institute of Technology

Mack Kac, Rockefeller University

Joseph Kaplan, University of California

Robert Kay, Hughes Aircraft Corporation

William Kellogg, National Center for Atmospheric Research

Paul Klopsteg, Glenview, Illinois

Joseph B. Koepfli, California Institute of Technology

Edward J. Minser, Trans World Airlines

Emanuel R. Piore, IBM Corporation

Richard W. Porter, General Electric Corporation

Francis W. Reichelderfer, Retired Chief, U.S. Weather Bureau

Roger Revelle, Harvard University

Walter O. Roberts, National Center for Atmospheric Research

Ragnar Rollefson, University of Wisconsin

S. Fred Singer, University of Miami

Kenneth C. Spengler, American Meteorological Society

Athelstan F. Spilhaus, University of Minnesota

Verner E. Suomi, University of Wisconsin

Philip D. Thompson, National Center for Atmospheric Research

Merle A. Tuve, Carnegie Institute of Washington

GOVERNMENT CONSULTANTS

J. Herbert Hollomon, Assistant Secretary for Science and Technology, Department of Commerce

Harold Brown, Director of Defense Research and Engineering, Department of Defense

Hugh L. Dryden, Deputy Administrator, National Aeronautics and Space Administration

Leland J. Haworth, Director, National Science Foundation

Robert M. White, Administrator, Environmental Science Services Administration

NATURAL RESOURCES CONSERVATION AND DEVELOPMENT

COMMITTEE MEMBERS

Joseph L. Fisher, Chairman
President, Resources for the Future, Inc.

James Boyd, President and Director, Copper Range Company

Francis T. Christy, Jr., Research Associate, Resources for the Future, Inc.

Edward J. Cleary, Executive Director, Ohio River Valley Water Sanitation Commission

Harold J. Coolidge, Executive Director, National Research Council

Edward H. Graham, Consulting Ecologist

Luther Gulick, Chairman, Institute of Public Administration

Ralph W. Johnson, Professor of Law, University of Washington

Walter J. Levy, President, Walter J. Levy, Inc.

George O.G. Löf, Consulting Chemical Engineer

Frank Masland, Jr., Chairman of the Board, C.H. Masland and Sons, Inc.

Chandler Morse, Professor of Economics, Cornell University

Harry S. Mosebrook, Manager of

Public Affairs, Eastern Region, Weyerhaeuser Co.

John B. Oakes, Editor of Editorial Pages, *The New York Times*

Roger Revelle, Director, Center for Population Studies, Harvard University

Mrs. Robert J. Stuart, President, League of Women Voters

Russell E. Train, President, Conservation Foundation

Conrad Wirth, American Conservation Association

GOVERNMENT CONSULTANTS

John T. Barnhill, Public Health Service, Department of Health, Education and Welfare

Virgil L. Barr, Bureau of Mines, Department of the Interior

Charles Butler, Bureau of Commercial Fisheries, Department of the Interior

Henry P. Caulfield, Jr., Resources Program Staff, Department of the Interior

Byron C. Denny, Bureau of Land Management, Department of the Interior

Alfred L. Edwards, Rural Development and Conservation, Department of Agriculture

Howard H. Eckles, Office of the Science Adviser, Department of the Interior

C. Gordon Fredine, National Park Service, Department of the Interior

Gerard F. Horne, Bureau of Land Management, Department of the Interior

Wendell E. Johnson, Office of Chief of Engineers, Department of the Army

Samuel E. Jorgensen, Bureau of Sports Fisheries and Wildlife, Department of the Interior

David D. Keck, Division of Biological and Medical Sciences, National Science Foundation

Val G. Killin, Bureau of Reclamation, Department of the Interior

Douglas J. McFarlane, Office of Saline Water, Department of the Interior

Andrew L. Newman, Office of Information, Department of the Interior

John A. Reinemund, Geological Survey, Department of the Interior

George L. Schoechle, Geological Survey, Department of the Interior

James A. Slater, Resources Program Staff, Department of the Interior

John A. Swartout, Office of the General Manager, Atomic Energy Commission

William M. Terry, Fish and Wildlife Service, Department of the Interior

George E. Tomlinson, Bureau of

Power, Federal Power Commission

Leighton van Nort, Bureau of International Organization Affairs, Department of State

William W. Warner, Office of International Activities, Smithsonian Institution

Clifford H. Willson, Bureau for the Far East, Agency for International Development

PEACEFUL SETTLEMENT OF DISPUTES

COMMITTEE MEMBERS

James N. Hyde, Chairman
Counselor at Law

Donald Straus, President, American Arbitration Association

Kenneth Boulding, Professor of Economics, University of Michigan

GOVERNMENT CONSULTANTS

George Bunn, General Counsel, U.S. Arms Control and Disarmament Agency

Lawrence S. Finkelstein, Deputy Assistant Secretary of Defense

Elmore Jackson, Special Assistant to the Assistant Secretary of State for International Organization Affairs

Leonard C. Meeker, Legal Adviser, Department of State

Stephen M. Schwebel, Assistant Legal Adviser, Department of State

William E. Simkin, Director, Federal Mediation and Conciliation Service

PEACEFUL USES OF ATOMIC ENERGY

COMMITTEE MEMBERS

Dr. I.I. Rabi, Chairman
Professor of Physics, Columbia University

Alan F. Burch, Director of Safety, International Union of Operating Engineers, AFL-CIO

Dr. Melvin Calvin, Professor of Chemistry, University of California

W. Kenneth Davis, Vice President, Bechtel Corporation

Dr. Robert J. Hasterlik, Professor, Department of Medicine, University of Chicago

Dr. Alexander Hollaender, Director, Biology Division, Oak Ridge National Laboratory

John R. Menke, Member, Board of Directors, United Nuclear Corporation

Charles Robbins, Executive Manager and Secretary Atomic Industrial Forum

Dr. Philip Sporn, Chairman, System Division Committee, American Electric Power Service Corporation

William Webster, President, Yankee Atomic Electric Company

Dr. Walter H. Zinn, Director, Nuclear Division, Vice Presi-

dent, Combustion Engineering Corporation

Aston J. O'Donnell, Manager of Development, Bechtel Corporation (*Committee Coordinator*)

GOVERNMENT CONSULTANTS

John G. Palfrey, Commissioner, U.S. Atomic Energy Commission

John A. Hall, Assistant General Manager for International Activities, U.S. Atomic Energy Commission

Arthur W. Barber, Deputy Assistant Secretary, International Security Affairs, Department of Defense

Dr. Donald R. Chadwick, Chief, Division of Radiological Health, Department of Health, Education and Welfare

D.L. Crook, Manager, Nuclear Projects, Maritime Administration

Clyde C. Crosswhite, National Security Affairs Officer, Department of the Treasury

Morgan D. Dubrow, Office of

Assistant Secretary for Water and Power, Department of the Interior

L.M. Hale, Office of Engineering, Agency for International Development

Dr. R.W. Johnston, Executive Assistant to the Director, National Science Foundation

W.D. Maclay, Director, Research Program Development and Evaluation Staff, Department of Agriculture

Dr. Herbert Scoville, Jr., Assistant Director, Arms Control and Disarmament Agency

Ambassador Henry D. Smyth, U.S. Representative to the International Atomic Energy Agency

George C. Spiegel, Foreign Affairs Officer, U.S. Atomic Energy Commission

PEACEKEEPING OPERATIONS

COMMITTEE MEMBERS

Andrew W. Cordier, Chairman Dean of the Graduate School of International Affairs, Columbia University

Frank Altschul, Vice President and Secretary, Council on Foreign Relations

Donald G. Brennan, Former President, Hudson Institute

Clark Eichelberger, Vice President, United Nations Association of the United States of America

Ernest Gross, Curtis, Mallet-Prevost, Colt, and Mosel

Joseph E. Johnson, President, Carnegie Endowment for International Peace

Sol Linowitz, Chairman, Xerox Corporation

Francis O. Wilcox, Dean, School

of Advanced International Studies, Johns Hopkins University

Miss Ruth E. Russell, Coordinator (Rapporteur), The Brookings Institution

GOVERNMENT CONSULTANTS

David H. Popper, Deputy Assistant Secretary of State for International Organization Affairs

John T. McNaughton, Assistant Secretary of Defense for International Security Affairs

Arthur W. Barber, Deputy Assistant Secretary of Defense for International Security Affairs (Arms Control)

Jacob Beam, Assistant Director, U.S. Arms Control and Disarmament Agency

POPULATION

COMMITTEE MEMBERS

Richard N. Gardner, Chairman
Professor of Law and International Relations, Columbia University

Eugene R. Black, Former President, International Bank for Reconstruction and Development

Cass Canfield, Chairman, Executive Committee, Harper & Row

Dr. Leslie Corsa, Jr., Director, Center for Population Planning, University of Michigan

Gardner Cowles, Chairman of the Board and Editor-in-Chief, Cowles Magazines & Broadcasting Co.

GOVERNMENT CONSULTANTS

Dr. Leona Baumgartner, Special Adviser to the Administrator, Agency for International Development

Dr. Peter Bing, Office of Science

A.W. Dent, President, Dillard University

William H. Draper, Jr., Partner, Draper, Gaither and Anderson

Mrs. Albert D. Lasker, President, Albert and Mary Lasker Foundation

David E. Lilienthal, Chairman, Development and Resources Corporation

John D. Rockefeller, 3d, Chairman of the Board, Population Council

Mrs. Edith S. Sampson, Circuit Court of Cook County

George N. Shuster, Assistant to the President, University of Notre Dame

Dr. Aaron Stern, Psychoanalyst

and Technology, Executive Office of the President

Dr. Edward Dempsey, Acting Assistant Secretary, Department of Health, Education and Welfare

Dr. Bruce Jessup, Director, Population Reference and Research Branch, Agency for International Development

Dr. Philip Lee, Assistant Secretary for Health, Department of Health, Education and Welfare

Albert Moseman, Assistant Administrator for Technical Cooperation and Research, Agency for International Development

Robert Smith, Associate Assistant Administrator for Programs, Agency for International Development

Dr. Lewis Spellman, Council of Economic Advisers

Dr. Conrad Taeuber, Assistant Director, Bureau of the Census

Leighton Van Nort, Officer in Charge, International Economic Affairs, Bureau of International Organization Affairs, Department of State

Herbert Waters, Assistant Administrator for Material Resources, Agency for International Development

RESEARCH ON THE DEVELOPMENT OF INTERNATIONAL INSTITUTIONS

COMMITTEE MEMBERS

Joseph A. Amter, Esq., Chairman, President and Executive Director, Peace Research Organization Fund

Frank Altschul, Vice President and Secretary, Council on Foreign Relations

Harry S. Ashmore, Chairman, Executive Committee, Fund for the Republic

Roger N. Baldwin, Founder and International Affairs Advisor, American Civil Liberties Union

Mrs. Emily Otis Barnes, Cofounder, New Mexico chapter of UNA-USA

George A. Beebe, Director, Institute for International Order

Dr. Donald G. Brennan, Hudson Institute

Erwin D. Canham, Director, World Peace Foundation

Dr. Ben M. Cherrington, Director, Rocky Mountain Office, Institute of International Education

Dr. Rufus E. Clement, President, Atlanta University

Dr. Harold J. Coolidge, Director of Pacific Science Board, Office of the Foreign Secretary of the National Academy of Sciences-National Research Council

Most Rev. John J. Dougherty, President, Seton Hall University

Dr. Peter F. Drucker, Director, Council for International Progress in Management

Erik J. Eriksen

Dr. Luther H. Evans, Chairman, U.S. Committee for Refugees

Dana L. Farnsworth, M.D., Director, University Health Services, Harvard University

Irvin M. Frankel, Esq., President, American Society of Travel Agents

Ernest A. Gross, Esq., Curtis, Mallet-Prevost, Colt, and Mosle

Dr. William W. Hagerty, President, Drexel Institute of Technology

George M. Harrison, Vice-President, AFL-CIO

Dr. George W. Hoffman, Professor of Geography, University of Texas

Palmer Hoyt, Editor and Publisher, *Denver Post*

Dr. Eldon L. Johnson, President, Great Lakes Colleges Association

Dr. Joseph Kaplan, Professor of Physics, University of California

Dr. Arthur Larson, Director, Rule of Law Research Center and Professor of Law

Charles A. Le Maistre, M.D., Professor of Internal Medicine and Associate Dean, The University of Texas Southwestern Medical School

Forrest D. Murden, Jr., Member, Executive Committee, Board of Directors, UNA-USA

James G. Patton, President, National Farmers Union

Maxwell M. Rabb, President, U.S. Committee for Refugees

Irving Salomon, Chairman, Board of Directors, Royal Metal Manufacturing Co.

Donald A. Schmechel, Esq., Member, Board of Directors, UNA-USA

Mrs. James Schramm, Member, Executive Committee, Board of Directors, UNA-USA

Dr. Thomas K. Sherwood, Member, National Academy of Sciences and National Academy of Engineering

Dr. Joseph R. Smiley, President, University of Colorado

Dr. Mabel M. Smythe, Principal, New Lincoln School, New York

Dr. Frank Stanton, President, Columbia Broadcasting System

Governor Harold E. Stassen, Stassen, Kephart, Sarkis and Kostos

William P. Steven, Former Editor, *Houston Chronicle*

Jesse W. Tapp, Director, Bank of America

J. Cameron Thompson, Retired Chairman, Northwest Bank Corp.

SCIENCE AND TECHNOLOGY

COMMITTEE MEMBERS

Dr. Detlev W. Bronk, Co-Chairman, Rockefeller University

Dr. Harrison Brown, Co-Chairman, National Academy of Science

Dr. L.V. Berkner, Graduate Center of the Southwest

Dr. L.M. Gould, University of Arizona

Dr. Joseph Kaplan, University of California

Robert Kay, Hughes Aircraft Company

Dr. G.B. Kistiakowsky, Harvard University

Dr. Joseph B. Koepfli, California Institute of Technology

Dr. John Pierce, Bell Telephone Laboratories

Dr. Roger Revelle, Harvard University

Dr. Ragnar Rollefson, University of Wisconsin

Dr. Milner B. Schaefer, University of California

Dr. Abel Wolman, Johns Hopkins University

Dr. Hugh C. Wolfe, American Institute of Physics

GOVERNMENT CONSULTANTS

Dr. Arthur Roe, National Science Foundation

S.B. Bourgin, United States Information Agency

Howard Eckles, Department of Interior

Arnold Frutkin, National Aeronautics and Space Administration

Dr. G.E. Hilbert, Department of Agriculture

Robert A. Kevan, Department of Health, Education and Welfare

John Palfrey, United States Atomic Energy Commission

Herman Pollack, Department of State

Dr. Edward M. Reilly, Department of Defense

Dr. I.C. Schoonover, National Bureau of Standards

Dr. John D. Wilkes, Agency for International Development

Roland D. Paine, Jr., National Science Foundation

SOCIAL WELFARE

MEMBERS

Mrs. Joseph Willen, Chairman President, National Council of Jewish Women

Arthur J. Altmeyer, former Commissioner of Social Security

Harry S. Ashmore, Chairman, Executive Committee, Fund for the Republic

George A. Beebe, Director, Institute for International Order

Rosemary Cass, Attorney

Rudolf Danstedt, Director, National Association of Social Workers

James Dumpson, Associate Dean, Hunter College School of Social Work

James Fogarty, Executive Director, Community Council of Greater New York

Mrs. Michael Harris, Vice-Chairman, Committee on International Social Welfare, National Social Welfare Assembly

Margaret Hickey, Public Affairs Editor, *Ladies' Home Journal*

Jane Hoey, former Director, Bureau of Public Assistance, Social Security Administration

Moe Hoffman, Washington Representative, National Jewish Welfare Board

Katherine Kendall, Executive Director, Council of Social Work Education

York Langton, Vice President, Coast-to-Coast Stores

Gordon Manser, Associate Director, National Social Welfare Assembly

Mrs. John McCloy

George Rabinoff, Social Planning Consultant, Department of Social and Community Services, New York City Housing Authority

Irwin T. Sanders, Associate Director, Ford Foundation

Charles I. Schottland, Dean, Florence Heller Graduate School for Advanced Studies in Social Welfare, Brandeis University

Mrs. John Shepard, Vice President, International Affairs, American Red Cross

Dr. Herman Stein, Dean, School of Applied Social Sciences, Western Reserve University

Anna Lord Strauss, Trustee, Committee for Economic Development

Elizabeth Wickenden, Technical Consultant on Public Social Policy, National Social Welfare Assembly

Ruth M. Williams, Executive Secretary, U.S. Committee of the International Conference of Social Work

GOVERNMENT CONSULTANTS

Ellen Winston, U.S. Commissioner of Welfare, HEW

Mary E. Blake, Assistant to the Chief for Cooperative Planning, Children's Bureau, Welfare Administration, HEW

Lucy Brown, Chief, Community Development Division, Office of Institutional Development, Bureau for Africa, AID

Marjorie Farley, Research and Reports Specialist, International Office, Welfare Administration, HEW

Paul Fisher, Chief, International Social Security Branch, Division of Research and Statistics, Social Security Administration, HEW

John J. Hurley, Deputy Director, Bureau of Family Services, Welfare Administration, HEW

Joan E. Kain, Deputy Director, Voluntary Foreign Aid Service, Office of Material Resources, AID

Robert A. Kevan, Deputy Assistant Secretary for International Affairs, HEW

Alexander F. Kiefer, Deputy Director, Office of International Economic and Social Affairs, State

Dorothy Lally, Chief, International Office, Welfare Administration, HEW

Jeanette Stats, Consultant, HEW

Clark Tibbitts, Deputy Director, Office of Aging, Welfare Administration, HEW

Cecile M. Whalen, Chief International Training Programs, International Office, Welfare Administration, HEW

SPACE

COMMITTEE MEMBERS

Joseph V. Charyk, Chairman Communications Satellite Corporation, Chairman

Lloyd V. Berkner, Southwest Center for Advanced Studies

Karl Harr, Aerospace Industries Association

Robert Kay, Hughes Aircraft Company

W. Randolph Lovelace II, Lovelace Clinic

James S. McDonnell, McDonnell Aircraft Corporation

Hilliard Paige, General Electric Company

Courtland D. Perkins, Princeton University

GOVERNMENT CONSULTANTS

Arnold W. Frutkin, National Aeronautics and Space Administration

Robert F. Packard, Department of State

John G. Palfrey, Atomic Energy Commission

Julian W. Scheer, National Aeronautics and Space Administration

Albert Weinstein, Department of Defense

Robert W. White, Environmental Science Services Administration

John D. Wilkes, Agency for International Development

TECHNICAL COOPERATION AND INVESTMENT

COMMITTEE MEMBERS

Philip Klutznick, Chairman
·Chicago, Illinois

Oscar Cox, Washington, D.C.

David M. Kennedy, Continental Illinois National Bank & Trust Company, Chicago, Illinois

Forrest D. Murden, Jr., New York

Robert R. Nathan, Robert R. Nathan Associates, Inc., Washington, D.C.

Waldemar A. Nielsen, The African-American Institute, New York

Earl D. Osborn, Institute for International Order, New York

Frazar B. Wilde, Connecticut General Life Insurance, Hartford, Connecticut

Erwin Schuller, International Financial Advisor, New York

Andrew Rice, Rapporteur, Society for International Development, Washington, D.C.

GOVERNMENT CONSULTANTS

Bartlett Harvey, Deputy Assistant Administrator for Program, Agency for International Development

Robert S. Smith, Associate Assistant Administrator for Program, Agency for International Development

Edgar A. Comee, Information Staff,

Agency for International Development

Donald W. Hoagland, Assistant Administrator, Office of Development Finance and Private Enterprise, Agency for International Development

Howard S. Kresge, Director, Voluntary Foreign Aid Service, Agency for International Development

Ervin R. Marlin, Director, Office of International Organization Recruitment, Department of State

Kenneth G. Olson, Consultant, Agency for International Development

Frank W. Parker, Assistant Director for Research and Technology, Rural and Community Development Service, Office of Technical Cooperation and Research, Agency for International Development

David Richardson, Chief, UN Trade and Regional Division, Office of Program Coordination, Agency for International Development

William J. Stibravy, Director, Office of International Economic and Social Affairs, Department of State

Matthew Drosdoff, Administrator, International Agricultural Development Service, U.S. Department of Agriculture

Ralph Hirschtritt, Deputy to the Assistant Secretary for International Financial and Economic Affairs, Department of the Treasury

James A. Moore, Assistant Administrator, Office of International Housing, Housing and Home Finance Agency

E.D. Trowbridge, Assistant Secretary for Domestic and International Business, Department of Commerce

Robert L. Oshins, Director, Office of International Investment, Bureau of International Commerce, Department of Commerce

Edward C. Sylvester, Jr., Deputy Administrator, Bureau of International Labor Affairs, Department of Labor

Juan DeZengotita, Acting Far East Specialist, Bureau of International Labor Affairs, Department of Labor

Robert A. Fordham, Special Assistant for Aid Relations, Office of International Affairs, Department of Health, Education, and Welfare

Warren Wiggins, Deputy Director, The Peace Corps

TRADE

COMMITTEE MEMBERS

Stacy May, Chairman

General Lucius D. Clay, Senior Partner, Lehman Brothers

John S. Dickey, President, Dartmouth College

Edward Gudeman, Partner, Lehman Brothers

Harry W. Knight, Vice President, Booz, Allen & Hamilton, Inc.

Herschel Newsom, National Master, National Grange

Mrs. Ruth Phillips, Past President, League of Women Voters of the United States

Walter P. Reuther, President, International Union, UAW

Marlin E. Sandlin, Chairman, Pan American Sulphur Company, Inc.

Ralph I. Straus, Director, R.H. Macy & Company, Inc.

Charles P. Taft, Taft & Lavercombe

John W. Hight, Rapporteur, Executive Director, Committee for a National Trade Policy

David J. Steinberg, Consultant, Director of Program, Foundation for Int'l. Trade Research

GOVERNMENT CONSULTANTS

William M. Roth, Deputy Special Representative for Trade Negotiations

A.B. Trowbridge, Assistant Secretary of Commerce for Domestic and International Business

Dorothy H. Jacobson, Assistant Secretary of Agriculture for International Affairs

Harold F. Linder, President, Export-Import Bank of Washington

Merlyn N. Trued, Assistant Secretary of the Treasury for International Affairs

Joseph A. Greenwald, Deputy Assistant Secretary for International Trade Policy, Department of State

Charles D. Hyson, Special Assistant to the Assistant Administrator for Material Resources, Agency for International Development

David C. Williams, Special Assistant to the Secretary of Commerce

Robert McNeill, Deputy Assistant Secretary for Trade Policy, Department of Commerce

Ralph Hirschtritt, Deputy to the Assistant Secretary of the Treasury for International Financial and Economic Affairs

Bernard Norwood, Chairman, Trade Staff Committee, Office of the Special Representative for Trade Negotiations

Julius Katz, Director, Office of International Trade, Department of State

A.R. DeFelice, Assistant Administrator, Foreign Agricultural Service, Department of Agriculture

Lawrence A. Fox, Director, Bureau of International Commerce, Department of Commerce

Selma G. Kallis, Adviser, Office of International Trade, Department of State

Robert C. Patterson, Business Liaison Office, Export-Import Bank of Washington

TRANSPORTATION

COMMITTEE MEMBERS

William B. Johnson, Chairman President, REA Express, Inc.

Dr. George P. Baker, Dean of the Graduate School of Business Administration, Harvard University

Charles H. Beard, General Traffic Manager, Union Carbide Corporation

D.W. Brosnan, President, Southern Railway System

Russell I. Brown, President, Insurance Institute for Highway Safety

Walter F. Carey, President, Automobile Carriers-Dealers Transit Incorporated

E.J. Davis, Director of Traffic, Caterpillar Tractor Company

William S. Foulis, President's Committee on Traffic Safety

Roger H. Gilman, Director, Port Development Dept., Port of New York Authority

William R. Hearst, Jr., President's Committee on Traffic Safety

Romuald P. Holubowicz, Grace Line, Inc.

William M. Keller, Vice President, Research, Assn. of American Railroads

George Killion, President, American President Lines

George E. Leighty, President, Transportation-Communication Employees Union

James G. Lyne, *Railway Age*

Rex Manion, Vice President, Operations & Maintenance, Assn. of American Railroads

J. O. Mattson, President, Automotive Safety Foundation

Wilfred J. McNeil, President, Grace Line Inc.

Frank L. Merwin, Vice President, American Smelting & Refining Company

Major-Gen. I. Sewell Moriss, USA (Ret.), Assistant Vice President, Assn. of American Railroads

Wilfred Owen, Brookings Institution

William D. Patterson, *Saturday Review*

James Pinkney, Vice President, American Trucking Assn., Inc.

Howard Pyle, President, National Safety Council

Joseph C. Scheleen, *Traffic World*

Jay Sheppard, Pan American World Airways, Inc.

A. J. Shields, Director of Traffic, AMETALCO, Inc.

James N. Sites, Assistant Vice President Public Relations, Assn. of American Railroads

Stuart G. Tipton, President, Air Transport Assn.

James A. Warren, REA Express, Inc.

William G. White, President, Consolidated Freightways

Frederic B. Whitman, President, Western Pacific Railroad Company

Ernest W. Williams, Jr.

J. Handley Wright, Vice President, Assn. of American Railroads

Douglas Wynn, Attorney

Dr. Paul V. Joliet, Chief, Accident Prevention Division, U.S. Public Health Service

Lawson B. Knott, Jr., Administrator, General Services Administration

Howard J. Marsden, Chief, Division of Ports, Maritime Administration

John T. McNaughton, Asst. Secretary for International Security Affairs, Department of Defense

Dr. Robinson Newcomb, Deputy Director for Transportation, Department of State

Maitland S. Pennington, Special Assistant to the Maritime Administrator, Maritime Administration

Gerald W. Russell, Associate Director of International Affairs & Relations, Federal Maritime Commission

Anthony M. Solomon, Asst. Secretary of State for Economic Affairs, Department of State

B.E. Stillwell, Director, Office of Proceedings, Interstate Commerce Commission

Marion Uhrich, Assistant Staff Director, Department of Defense

Dino S. Villa, Chief, Division of Foreign Trade, Bureau of Census

Charles A. Webb, Chairman, Interstate Commerce Commission

Rex M. Whitton, Federal Highway Administrator, Bureau of Public Roads

Thomas H. Wilkenson, Army Director of Safety, Office of the Deputy Chief of Staff for Personnel

Miss Mary Proctor, International Liaison Assistant, Maritime Administration

GOVERNMENT CONSULTANTS

Lowell K. Bridwell, Deputy Under Secretary for Transportation, Department of Commerce

Frederick E. Batrus, Deputy Assistant Postmaster General, Post Office Department

Evelyn T. Beaumont, U.S. Travel Service, Department of Commerce

David E. Bell, Administrator, Agency for International Development

Charles I. Bevins, Assistant Legal Advisor for Treaty Affairs, Department of State

Robert T. Boyle, Deputy Assistant Administrator for International Aviation Affairs, Federal Aviation Agency

Vincent F. Caputo, Director for Transportation & Warehouse Policy, Department of Defense

James A. Cowling, Deputy Asst. Commissioner for Transportation, General Services Administration

Paul F. Geren, Director, Office of Maritime Affairs, Department of State

Angelo F. Ghiglione, Deputy Director for Operations, Office of Engineering & Operations Bureau of Public Roads

Thomas J. Gorman, Jr., Deputy Commissioner, Bureau of Customs

Rear Admiral John Harllee, Chairman, Federal Maritime Commission

William J. Hartigan, Assistant Postmaster General, Post Office Department

Edward W. Hassell, Assistant to the Deputy Under Secretary for Transportation, Department of Commerce

John L. Hoen, Assistant for Cargo Promotion, Maritime Administration

John Hudgins, Asst. to the Director of the Foreign Agriculture Service, Department of Agriculture

Dorothy H. Jacobson, Assistant Secretary, Department of Agriculture

Nicholas Johnson, Maritime Administrator, Maritime Administration

URBAN DEVELOPMENT

COMMITTEE MEMBERS

Raymond D. Nasher, Chairman President, Nasher Properties, Dallas, Texas

Charles Abrams, Professor, Columbia University

Oscar A. de Lima, President, Roger Smith Hotel Corporation

George Duggar, Director, Urban Affairs Program, Graduate School of Public and International Affairs, University of Pittsburgh

Patrick Healy, Executive Director, National League of Cities

Ralph Lazarus, President, Federated Department Stores, Inc.

Stanley Marcus, President, Neiman-Marcus

Margaret Mead, American Museum of Natural History

Harvey S. Perloff, Director, Regional and Urban Planning Studies, Resources for the Future

Raphael D. Silver, President, Keller-Silver Corporation

Herman W. Steinkraus, United Nations Association of the U.S.A.

Lawrence A. Wien, Partner, Wien, Lane and Klein

Frazar B. Wilde, Chairman of the Board, Connecticut General Life Insurance Company

COMMITTEE COORDINATOR:

Shelby Southard, Cooperative League of the U.S.A.

GOVERNMENT CONSULTANTS

Robert C. Weaver, Administrator, Housing and Home Finance Agency

John E. Horne, Chairman, Federal Home Loan Bank Board

James A. Moore, Housing and Home Finance Agency

Bartlett Harvey, Agency for International Development

Simon Trevas, Federal Home Loan Bank Board

Osborne T. Boyd, Agency for International Development

Stanley E. Smigel, Housing and Home Finance Agency

WOMEN

COMMITTEE MEMBERS

Mrs. Esther W. Hymer, Chairman, International Relations Department, American Baptist Convention

Mrs. India Edwards, Vice Chairman, Civic Leader and former Editor

Miss Genevieve Blatt, Penn. State Official

Mrs. Mildred Boone, National Council of Negro Women

Dr. Rosemary Cass, Attorney at Law

Miss E. Christenson, Bureau of Research, National Board YWCA

Mrs. Martha Cogan, Civic Leader and Lecturer

Mrs. Helen G. Douglas, Lecturer and former Congresswoman

Mrs. Bess Furman, Newswoman and Author

Mrs. Charles Gambrell, National Board YWCA

Mrs. Olive Goldman, Former UN Commission on the Status of Women

Mrs. R. Goldenberg, National Council of Jewish Women

Mrs. Lorena Hahn, Former UN Commission on the Status of Women

Mrs. Althea Hottel, President, I.F.W.U.

Judge Sarah T. Hughes, U.S. District Judge, Texas

Dr. Guion Johnson, African Affairs, University of North Carolina

Mrs. Ribert Kintner, Civic Leader

Dr. Flemmie Kittrell, Professor of Home Economics, Howard University

Mrs. Joseph McCarthy, N.C.C.W., California

Miss Frieda Miller, Former Director of Women's Bureau

Mrs. Dale Miller, Co-chairman of 1964 Inaugural Committee

Mrs. Maurice T. Moore, National Board YWCA

Mrs. Esther Murray, COPE–AFL–CIO–E. Area

Dr. Anne Pannell, President of Sweet Briar College

Mrs. Fred Patterson, U.C.W. Georgia

Mrs. L. Richardson Preyer, North Carolina Conference for Social Service

Mrs. Martha Ragland, President, Tennessee Council on Human Relations

Mrs. Louis Robbins, President, National Council of Women, USA

Mrs. Dollie L. Robinson, Director of Voluntary Hospital Campaign, BSEIU

Mrs. Laurence Rockefeller, Chairman of International Division YWCA

Miss Lisa Sergio, Writer, Lecturer and World Traveler

Mrs. Murray Silverstone, Civic Leader

Dr. Dorothy Stratton, UN Rep., I.F.U.W.

Mrs. Arthur Zepf, National Council of Catholic Women

GOVERNMENT CONSULTANTS

Dr. Margaret C. Browne, Director, Division of Home Economics, Federal Extension Service

Miss Evelyn Harrison, Deputy Director, Bureau of Programs and Standards, Civil Service Commission

Mrs. Mary N. Hilton, Deputy Director, Women's Bureau, U.S. Department of Labor

Mrs. Frances H. Howard, Liaison Officer, MR/VSA, AID

Mrs. Dorothy Jacobson, Assistant Secretary of Agriculture for International Affairs, Department of Agriculture

Mrs. Mary Dublin Keyserling, Director, Women's Bureau, U.S. Department of Labor

Mrs. Carl Marcy, Women's Activities Advisor, USIA

Mrs. Elizabeth Stoffregen May, Director, Export-Import Bank

Mrs. Marie C. McGuire, Commissioner, Public Housing Administration

Mrs. Rachel C. Nason, Human Rights Officer, Office of Economic and Social Affairs, Department of State

Mrs. Esther Peterson, Special Assistant to the President for Consumer Affairs, Chairman of President's Committee on Consumer Interests, and Assistant Secretary of Labor

Mrs. Katherine Pringle, Women's Activities Advisor, Department of State

Mrs. Gladys A. Tillett, U.S. Representative, UN Commission on the Status of Women

Mrs. Irene Walker, Procedures and Directives Division, Office of Management Planning, AID

Dr. Ellen Winston, Commissioner of Welfare Administration, Department of Health, Education and Welfare

Staff Advisors:

Miss Mary M. Cannon, Chief, International Division, Women's Bureau, U.S. Department of Labor

Mrs. Alice A. Morrison, Chief, Division of Legislation and Standards, Women's Bureau, U.S. Department of Labor

YOUTH ACTIVITIES

COMMITTEE MEMBERS

Rev. James H. Robinson, Chairman Operation Crossroads Africa, Inc.

Gordon Boyce, President, Experiment in International Living

Rev. Theodore Braun, Peace Corps Liaison, National Council of Churches

Howard Cook, President, International House

Frank Cosgrove, Executive Director, American Youth Hostels

Clarence R. Decker, Vice President, Fairleigh Dickinson University

Joseph Fallon, President, U.S. Youth Council

Hugh M. Jenkins, Director, Foreign Student Service Council

William Kahn, Executive Director, Jewish Community Center Associations

Rev. Raymond Kelly, Pax Romana Secretariat for North America

Mrs. Ann Catherine Menninger, Kansas Representative for UNICEF

Mrs. Richard B. Persinger, UN Observer for National YWCA

Frederick A. Ricci, Youth Division, Democratic National Committee

Steven Robins, U.S. National Students Association

Miss Lisa Sergio

Mrs. Eleanor Schnurr

Mrs. Margaret E. Sims, President, Jack & Jill, Inc.

Dr. Mabel Smythe, Principal, New Lincoln School

GOVERNMENT CONSULTANTS

Department of Health, Education, and Welfare

Dr. Helen K. Mackintosh, Associate Director, Administrative-Instructional Support Branch, Office of Education

Milton Lehman, Bureau of Information, Office of Education

Miss Mary Blake, Executive Secretary, Interdepartmental Committee on Children and Youth, Children's Bureau

Miss Roberta Church, Vocational Rehabilitation Administration

Lincoln Daniels, Children's Bureau

Aaron Goldstein, Bureau of Family Services

Joseph Kessler, Social Security Administration

Department of State

Curtis Barker, AID

Martin McLaughlin, Special Assistant to Assistant Secretary for Educational and Cultural Affairs

Department of Agriculture

Joseph McAuliffe, Federal Extension Service

Department of Defense

Col. James Kisgen, Management Affairs, Manpower

Department of Labor

Mrs. Jane C. Perry, Bureau of Labor Standards

Library of Congress

Miss Virginia Haviland, Head, Children's Book Section

Peace Corps

David Schimmel, Executive Officer, Office of Planning, Evaluation and Research

United States Courts

Merrill Smith, Assistant Chief of Probation, Supreme Court Building

United States Information Agency

Blake Robinson, Student and Youth Advisor

About the Author

Richard N. Gardner was born in New York City in 1927. A graduate of Harvard College and the Yale Law School, he holds a Doctor of Philosophy degree in economics from Oxford University, where he studied as a Rhodes Scholar. Mr. Gardner served from 1961 to 1965 as Deputy Assistant Secretary of State for International Organization Affairs. In this assignment he played a leading role in developing programs of international cooperation, not only in peacekeeping and disarmament but in aid and trade, and served as U.S. delegate at many UN meetings. He received the Arthur S. Fleming Award for 1963 as one of the ten outstanding young men in the Federal Government. Author of two widely praised books on world affairs, *Sterling-Dollar Diplomacy* and *In Pursuit of World Order*, he is now Professor of Law and International Relations at Columbia University.